Dance and Ritual Play in Greek Religion

Ancient Society and History

Dance and

STEVEN H. LONSDALE

Ritual Play in Greek Religion

The Johns Hopkins University Press
Baltimore and London

© 1993 The Johns Hopkins University Press
All rights reserved
Printed in the United States of America
on acid-free paper

The Johns Hopkins University Press
2715 North Charles Street
Baltimore, Maryland 21218-4319
The Johns Hopkins Press Ltd., London

Library of Congress Cataloging-in-Publication Data

Lonsdale, Steven, 1952–
Dance and ritual play in Greek religion / Steven H. Lonsdale.
        p.   cm. — (Ancient society and history)
    Includes bibliographical references and indexes.

    1. Dancing—Religious aspects.   2. Dancing—Greece—History.
3. Play—Religious aspects.   4. Play—Greece—History.   5. Rites and
ceremonies—Greece.   6. Dancing—Greece—Anthropological aspects.
7. Greece—Religion.   I. Title.   II. Series.
BL788.L66   1993
306.4'84—dc20   93-2787

A catalog record for this book is available
from the British Library.

To Lincoln Kirstein

and in memory of Joseph Duell, First Dancer

"At the sacrifices I led the revel for the god who shouts 'Euai!' in the mystic rites of initiation at the triennial festival."
—Inscription from Amastris in the Pontus, dated to 155 C.E., from the tomb of one Aemilianus, an athlete who competed successfully in the satyr-dance

Contents

Contents

List of Figures

Preface

[The early Arcadians,] desirous of softening and taming the harsh-
ness and stubbornness of nature, . . . habituated the people, men
and women alike, to festivals and sacrifices and choral dances of
young girls and young boys.
—Polybius 4.21.3–4

As Polybius's words suggest, from earliest times dancing in a group
was a vital concomitant of religious worship in a festival setting and
one that led to the acculturation of the participants. Despite the
widely recognized importance of the role of dance and related phenomena in Greek cults and festivals, we still lack a critical study in
English of the function of dance.[1] Lillian Lawler's useful survey of
dance from prehistoric to Hellenistic times treats ritual dances in a
summary fashion, relying extensively in this and in other areas on
such Hellenistic writers as Lucian and Pollux, who observed Greek
dance at one remove as it had evolved under the influence of Ro-
man pantomime.[2]

The purpose of the present work is to situate the fragmentary
evidence for dance in the cults and festivals of Greece in the archaic
and classical periods (c. 750–323 B.C.E.) in an appropriate context
so as to relate the subject to contemporary Greek social and religious institutions. What do the overlapping roles of dance as an
act of divine adoration and as an expression of human festivity reveal about the place of religion in Greek society? This book investigates the implications of this and related questions by examining
dance as a social mechanism and as a form of ritual behavior. This

Figure 1 (a). Bearded male directing a chorus of women.

study is based first on literary texts, broadly defined, and second on archaeological sources, especially representations of dancing in vase painting. Occasionally I supplement the archaic and classical evidence with material from other periods and provide a context for the fragmentary ancient sources with theories and approaches taken by comparative anthropology. Because of the disparate nature of the sources for dance in ancient Greece, my approach combines the methodology of contextualization that seeks to bring historical and literary texts in touch with iconographic and epigraphic sources, and anthropological criticism that assumes that these texts and images, broadly interpreted, reflect and contribute to the understanding of the complexities of social behavior.

In a work that relies in part on an anthropological approach, I have made extensive critical use of books 2 and 7 of Plato's *Laws* where dance, music, and various practices relating to religious festivals are discussed in the context of *paideia,* or what might be called socialization. The use of Plato's *Laws* as a theoretical guide for investigating musical phenomena may be felt by some to require some justification. Although the *Laws* has been seen as an idiosyncratic philosophical work,[3] when it comes to matters of religion and social custom the final Platonic dialogue has long been recognized as a valuable source relevant to the reality as well as the theorizing of classical Greece. It is, in the view of one of the leading scholars of Greek religion, "the most comprehensive literary account of the Greek polis we have, including its religion."[4] Despite its usefulness as a source, the limitations of the *Laws* must also be recognized. It must be kept in mind that the *Laws* is a philosophical, not a historical source. Because Plato's observations are shaped by his political agenda it is necessary to distinguish between fact and theory and not fall into the state of confusion that prompts the main speaker of the dialogue to explain to his interlocutor, "I was only saying what I want to see happen in the arts, but perhaps I used expressions that made you think I was referring to facts."[5]

Dance permeated many areas of Greek society, including weddings and banquets, harvest celebrations, status transition rites, drama, and civic worship. The phenomenon was so widespread that no single work can adequately consider dance in all its richness from all points of view, literary, iconographic, and historical. This book is concerned principally with dance as a group activity in the context of the cults and festivals of Greece in the archaic and classical periods. Spectacular dances by *hetairai* for guests at banquets, dramatic dances in the theater of Dionysus, acrobatic dances, and the like, will be left aside. The decision to exclude dramatic dances from this study may at first strike some as a serious omission, since the mention of the Greek chorus most readily brings to mind the dances of the Greek theater.[6] But as a discussion of the sources in the Introduction makes clear, in the fifth century ritual choruses diverge from dramatic choruses whose very identity was altered and transformed into a collective character with the help of masks and costumes.

This work falls into two parts. The first provides a theoretical framework for dance grounded in Plato's *Laws* and in divine prototypes of dance in Greek art and literature. How did the Greeks themselves regard the nature and function of dance in society? With this theoretical understanding various human realizations of dance in the body politic will be examined in the second part. The Introduction surveys the literary and artistic sources and outlines the contribution of comparative anthropology. The first chapter provides a survey of the nature and theoretical underpinnings of dance and play from the classical perspective of Plato's *Laws*. To what extent did Platonic categories and theories anticipate modern anthropological approaches to the cultural categories of dance and play? Chapter 2 presents a myth of origin for orderly dancing current in Plato's fourth-century Athens and illustrates that the perceived origins of dance in religious festivals and paideia are also found in literary portraits of divine and human festivity in the *Homeric Hymn to Apollo* and elsewhere.

In chapter 3 an opposite, disorderly tendency in dance conducing to *communitas* is explored against the backdrop of divine prototypes of Dionysian dance in art and literature. Chapter 4 investigates the meeting of the divine and human on the dancing ground (*choros*) in the polis and takes the Anthesteria festival at Athens, the oldest of the festivals of Dionysus in that city, as a representative example of civic festivity involving the body politic as well as special groups. From general considerations of dance in the polis we turn to examine the role of dance in four phases of social and biological development. Chapter 5 examines the contribution of dancing with weapons in training boys to be men on the battlefield, especially in relation to the Athenian ephebeia. In chapter 6 female status transition rites leading to marriage are considered. Because the evidence for the role of dancing in female status transition is fragmentary and dispersed, discussion of this phenomenon will center on two examples, the Arkteia at Brauron and other cults of Artemis in Attica, and evidence from the text of the first "Maiden Song" of Alcman. Chapter 7 examines the evidence for dance and the dancing ground in bringing together young citizens in courtship and wedding rituals. Chapter 8 looks at the dynamics of ritual mourning in a group, both as a discrete phenomenon and as it interacts with other forms of ritual play discussed in the three preceding chapters. Chapter 9 investigates dance and related phenomena in the cults of Pan in the fourth century as an expression of private, as opposed to civic, worship.

The abbreviations used in citing ancient authors and works are generally those found in *The Oxford Classical Dictionary* or in H. G. Liddell, R. Scott, and H. Stuart Jones, eds., *A Greek-English Lexicon* (hereafter cited as LSJ).

All ancient dates are B.C.E. unless otherwise indicated.

Where desirable I have used translations from Andrew Barker, *Greek Musical Writings*, vol. 1, because they are attuned to the musical nuances in the texts; Barker's translations are indicated in the notes by the citation from the Greek source, followed by the author's last name and page number. Unless otherwise noted the remaining translations are mine.

Ever since completing *Animals and the Origins of Dance*, a comparative study of origin myths for dance based in the folklore and mythology of traditional societies, I had wanted to focus on the Greek evidence for dance and related phenomena. The opportunity to do so came about as a result of the 1988 NEH Summer Seminar "Society and Religion in Ancient Greece" at Stanford University directed by Michael Jameson, whose guidance and interest in this project have provided unfailing inspiration. The results of my effort would not have been possible without the work of many scholars, but I mention five in particular: Walter Burkert, whose panoramic and penetrating vision of Greek religion provides a context for understanding its constituent elements; Claude Calame, who opened up the study of musical culture by applying an anthropological approach to a textual study of Alcman; John Herington, who demonstrated to what extent archaic and classical Greece was a song culture; William Mullen, who illuminates the integral position of male choruses in the Greek polis; and Gregory Nagy, whose recent work on choral lyric challenges us to rethink the relationship of epic to lyric poetry, especially in the context of performance.

The research for this book was undertaken while I was a Junior Fellow at the Center for Hellenic Studies in Washington, D.C., under circumstances made ideal by the director Zeph Stewart and Diana Childers Stewart. During that year I received additional support from a Fellowship from the National Endowment for the Humanities. The final version of the manuscript was prepared while a Fellow at the National Humanities Center in North Carolina; my fellowship there was supported in part by a grant from The Jessie Ball duPont Religious, Charitable, and Educational Fund. I want to thank the Director of the National Humanities Center, W. R. Connor, for sharing his important work on Athenian festivals. While writing the manuscript I had the valuable experience of presenting aspects of my research at the Sorbonne and the Centre Louis Gernet in Paris; I am grateful to my hosts, Pierre Vidal-Naquet, Pauline Schmitt-Pantel, Stella Georgoudi, and John Scheid. It is a pleasure to thank Davidson College and Robert C. Williams, Vice President for Academic Affairs, for granting me generous leave to take advantage of these opportunities.

It remains for me to thank colleagues who were unusually generous in discussing substantive points or reading portions of the manuscript, especially Susan Ackerman, Geneviève Hoffmann, and Kenneth Reckford, as well as the anonymous readers for the Johns Hopkins University Press, Elizabeth Belfiore, Edwin Brown, Walter Burkert, Anne Pippin Burnett, Claude Calame, Anne Carson, Graeme Clarke, Patricia Kenig Curd, Grant Dawson, Patricia Easterling, Eyjólfur Kjalar Emilsson, Christopher Faraone, Michael Flower, Dirk French, Françoise Frontisi-Ducroux, Robert Garland, Maud Gleason, Jack Goody, Richard Green, Eric Handley, Richard Janko, Peter Krentz, Mary Lefkowitz, François Lissarrague, Irad Malkin, Gregory Nagy, Gloria Ferrari Pinney, Richard Seaford, Charles Segal, Alan Shapiro, Rebecca Sinos, Paul Spencer, Michael Toumazou, Jean-Pierre Vernant, Alexandra Goulaki Voutira, Emmanuel Voutiras, Robert Wallace, and Jack Winkler.

For help in the preparation of the indexes I am indebted to Elizabeth Jackson. For assistance in obtaining photographs I am most grateful to Irène Aghion, Cabinet des Médailles, Bibliothèque Nationale, Paris; Virginia R. Anderson-Stojanovic, Wilson College; Nancy Bookides, American School of Classical Studies Corinth Excavations; Stefano De Caro, Soprintendente, Soprintendenza Archeologica delle Province di Napoli e Caserta; Jan Diamant, American School of Classical Studies Agora Excavations; Lilly Kahil, Université de Fribourg; François Lissarrague, Centre Nationale de Recherche Scientifique, Paris; Jeanne H. Lonsdale; Gertrud Platz, Antikenmuseum Berlin; Margot Schmidt, Antikenmuseum Basel und Sammlung Ludwig; Erika Simon, Martin von Wagner-Museum der Universität Würzburg; Cornelius C. Vermeule III, Museum of Fine Arts, Boston; and Russell Workman.

Finally, I would like to express special thanks to Eric Halpern, editor-in-chief of the Johns Hopkins University Press, and the staff of the Press for their courtesy and attention in preparing the manuscript.

Figure 1 (b). The chorus, continued.

Dance and Ritual Play in Greek Religion

Figure 2. An *aulos* player; boy leaping before a chorus of six dancers.

Introduction: Problems and Sources

Rhythmically repeated movement, directed to no end and
performed together as a group, is, as it were, ritual crystallized
in its purest form.
—Walter Burkert, *Greek Religion*, 102

Much of ancient Greek culture is lost without an understanding of religious festivals and games. Among the elements that made for a successful and satisfying celebration were dances, processions, and other types of structured movement that circumscribed the central act of sacrifice. Depending on the occasion and the presiding divinities, ritual actions communicated various religious and social messages while conveying emotions that ranged from the solemn to the hilarious. To worship often implied engaging in collective rites regulated by playful behavior. Among the most enduring and versatile forms of worshipful playfulness in a group were hymns and choral dances. Dances in particular could be of a playful nature, as one of the verbs for dance in ancient Greek (*paizō*), with its ambiguous meanings "to dance" and "to play," indicates. To dance is in a sense to become once again a child, as suggested by the derivation of *paizō* from *pais* (child). To play meant to represent the "other" mimetically in dance dramas. It also meant to compete formally in order to win the attention and favor of the god. The urge to play was harnessed in contests. The agonistic nature of dance, which became institutionalized in music and dance competitions, is attested in the earliest surviving alphabetic inscription on a prize jug from the potter's quarter in Athens that was destined for the most lithe and playful dancer.[1] Such dance contests often served the dual purposes of training the young and honoring the divinity. A Corinthian aryballos (Fig. 2) found in the excavations of the archaic temple of Apollo at Corinth represents what was presumably the winning chorus in a dance competition. It bears an inscription indicating that the vase was dedicated to its youthful chorus leader, Pyrrhias, who is depicted leaping before the chorus (*prochoreuomenos*) of six other dancers to the strains of a musician playing the *aulos*.[2] The prize vase in all likelihood was commissioned as a votive offering to commemorate a successful choral contest.

Has antiquity bequeathed adequate words and images to understand such an evanescent phenomenon as Greek dance? In a famous passage on the cosmic dance Plato has the astronomer Timaeus from the Italian town of Locri describe how the divine craftsman created the stars and set them in motion. Then, referring to the divine motion of the planets, Timaeus mentions earth, which he calls the first and eldest of gods in the heavens. "To put into words the choral dances (*choreias*) of these same gods," that is, to tell of "the juxtapositions, retrogradations, and progressions or their orbits, or to say which of these gods meet in conjunction and which in opposition, and to specify at what times which ones eclipse one another, disappearing and appearing again . . . to tell all this without recourse to visual models would be labor in vain."[3] In a similar vein, it must be conceded that we will never be able to describe ancient Greek dance as it was performed in the archaic and classical periods. As with the performance of Greek drama, we can only make informed guesses about how dances were staged. We cannot recreate with assurance a single step of choreography: there was no ancient system of dance notation. No treatise on the dance exists from the classical period, such as Lucian or Athenaeus later wrote. While written and artistic evidence for dance, when correctly interpreted, can provide important information about the configuration, personnel, context, and social and religious dynamics of dance, sequential steps and the very movement are irretrievably lost. Despite glimpses afforded by the incomplete visual record, we probably have less of an idea about what dance looked like than how Greek music sounded. Whereas we can read literary texts and view works of art, when it comes to the dance we are deprived of experiencing, even vicariously, what was undoubtedly one of the most aesthetically pleasing and emotionally satisfying aspects of Greek culture. Attempts to describe the dances of the Greeks, then, would seem as futile as Timaeus's efforts to articulate the movements of the stars and planets—the so-called cosmic dance—without a celestial globe or planetarium.

The unsuccessful search for a visual model has led to the mistaken inference that since dance cannot be visualized, its significance cannot be apprehended. Once we go beyond the urge to reconstruct the visual aspect, however, and consider dance as a collective phenomenon in Greek religion and society, the boundary between ancient Greek dances and the modern interpreter is not impenetrable. We do in fact have various means to construct paradigms for dance and to recover a wide range of meanings that dancing had for the ancient Greeks. There are three principal sources: written, archaeological, and anthropological. The written sources can be divided between literary sources (early Greek hexameter poetry, choral lyric, Athenian drama, fifth- and fourth-century orators, and historical and philosophical writers) and inscriptions relating to cults and festivals. Archaeological sources for dance consist mainly in representations in vase painting and other media. We must accept, however, the fragmentary nature of the evidence, and recognize the inherent limitations of our sources. Given the incomplete picture offered by the ancient testimony it is all the more essential to understand how to situate our findings in an intelligible context, for neither the poets, artists, or organizers of festivals have left anything that may be construed as an ethnographic record of the dance. Unlike the modern anthropologist who can observe and record firsthand the song and dance culture of a society, we are always looking at the phenomenon as it was presented selectively and allusively. But we should perhaps not regret the loss too deeply. Even in modern anthropological studies of cultures whose steps can be recorded and analyzed, the form and structure of dance are not always central to its interpretation, nor are these necessarily the most compelling aspects.[4]

The Use of Written Sources

The mention of Greek dance most readily brings to mind the choral dances of the Greek theater. But as Webster's *The Greek Chorus* illustrates, the phenomenon of choral dancing in the classical Athenian theater is but one manifestation of choreographic movement by a group. Bands of singers and dancers performed paeans, so-called maiden songs, hyporchemes, and many other genres first described by Homer, Hesiod, and in the Homeric Hymns, and known by example from the surviving texts of choral poetry, including perhaps epinicia, or victory odes, the largest and best known body of choral lyrics to survive. It has generally been assumed that these poetic celebrations of victors in athletic (and musical) contests were performed by a chorus of singers and dancers, possibly with the poet or his delegate as leader. Although inconclusive, the ancient evidence argues in favor of choral performance, and I am inclined to believe that a wealthy aristocratic patron in Thessaly or Sicily, when offered the choice of celebrating victory by a chorus or by a solo singer, would opt for the former. But the evidence leading to such an assumption has recently been debated afresh, and some have forcefully argued for a solo performance by the poet.[5] Upon careful reflection, it does not seem that there is indeed sufficient evidence to make a conclusive case for either choral *or* solo performance of victory odes, and that whatever position one takes is necessarily a theoretical one. There is room to allow that epinicians could be performed by choruses, but that they were always or typically performed in that way lacks textual support. Other performance configurations are plausible. For instance, Pindar or his delegate may have performed alone, while ancillary to his performance (not necessarily at the same time), a less formal choral group known as the *kōmos* could have performed a choral offering complementary to social and religious ideals embodied in Pindar's words. Even if it could be conclusively shown that Pindar's odes were intended for choral performance, the surviving text does not

justify detailed analysis of the nature or the dynamics of performance. As attempts to visualize the shape and movement of the
odes in a performance context demonstrate, such analysis is sub-
jective and speculative.[6]

Looking beyond the performance of epinicians, independent evidence confirms the impression that many other types of poetry
classified as "choral" by the ancients were executed by groups of
dancers and singers. Several signs point to Stesichorean poetry, for
example, being choral, beginning with the very name Stesichoros,
meaning "setting up choruses," in reference to that poet's putative
function as choreographer as well as composer of music and lyrics.
Performance of his poetry took place in a public forum as shared
experiences of the community.[7] The poet can refer to his production as the "public performances of the Charites" (*Charitōn
dāmōmata*) in reference to that graceful society of gods who provide
a divine prototype of communal dancing.[8]

Certain texts of choral poetry preserve self-referential, prescrip-
tive language for movement, costume, and the manipulation of cult
paraphernalia, as found in the maiden songs of Alcman, a poet of
Lydian origin who lived in Sparta where he flourished in the middle of the seventh century before Sparta became proverbially Spartan. His poems in part retell divine and heroic legends that serve as
paradigms for mortal behavior; in this respect they are not unlike
other genres of Greek poetry beginning with Homer. But they are
unique among the surviving examples of choral lyric in the degree
and intimacy of detail they provide about the female singers and
dancers who narrated the myths. In the course of rehearsing divine
and heroic legends, the chorus would shift from the timeless mythical past to relay immediate details of their own choral performance. Descriptions of the appearance and behavior of the chorus
are best known from the two substantial fragments of maiden
songs, but can be found in other types of poems by Alcman. The
dramatization of the chorus as a character through self-referential
language affords glimpses of the composition and dynamics of the
chorus, its outward movements and inner emotions. From the
shorter of the two maiden songs we learn the number and names of
the chorus leader and chorus members.[9] There are ten followers, all

noted for their beauty. They wear purple garments, headbands imported from Lydia, and gold jewelry in the form of snakes. But none is so beautiful or sings as perfectly as Hagesichora, the leader of the chorus. The emotional life of the *thiasos* (troupe) comes to life as we hear of rivalry among the members of the chorus for the attention or approval of Hagesichora and expressions of fear about the perfectibility of their performance, which appears to be a contest with another eleven-member choir, even if their adversary is only a projection of an ideal choir against which they measure themselves. Portions of the other surviving maiden song of Alcman focus on the singing and movements of the chorus. One passage mentions a gathering place where "I [for the unison voice of the chorus] shall toss my yellow hair . . . my delicate feet."[10] Another fragment tells of the leader of the choirs, Astymeloisa, of her aloofness, as she moves fleetly on slender feet like a shooting star or the wing of a bird.[11] In the poems of Alcman we also gain a clear idea of the role of the poet, who, in addition to composing the music and lyrics, had the task of rehearsing and producing the choral performance. The poet himself would sometimes take part in his production. In an extraordinary autobiographical fragment we hear of the poet's infirmity in old age when, no longer able to join in with the whirling of dancing girls in his chorus, they physically elevate him.[12]

The congruence of ritual choruses and dramatic choruses at first glance seems obvious. Drama and mimetic dancing share many similarities, especially their emphasis on portraying the "other."[13] Indeed, the evolution of dramatic choruses from those of choral lyric has been established by, among others, Gregory Nagy, who has argued that dramatic choruses in festivals such as the City Dionysia evolved from a pattern of differentiation between *chorēgos*, actor, and chorus members not unlike that reconstructed for nondramatic, civic choruses.[14] The dramatic texts reflect the deeply felt influence of the ritual chorus on Athenian drama, in tragedy, comedy, and satyr-play alike; the impression is left in frequent references to choruses and choral genres, in the form, tone, and nature of many choral passages, and the very presence of the chorus on stage. Yet, despite the prominence of the dramatic chorus and its supposed mimetic and choreographic modes of performance, it develops on its own in the fifth century as a separate entity conditioned by scenic conventions and the requirements of the plot. In writing for the chorus, dramatists such as Aeschylus and Sophocles, who were themselves renowned dancers and choreographers, nevertheless created fictional acts for fictional persons. Are we justified in taking references to ritual in general in Greek drama and relating them to everyday ritual observances? Unlike ritual, which is embedded into daily life, "ritual" dancing on the stage is not integral to the dramatic action. Thus whenever a chorus acts as a dancing body it does so in an artificially created ritual context and must invoke words such as *choros* ("choral dance") and various hymnic genres that evoke the ritual setting.

The divergence of ritual and dramatic choruses emerges in three principal ways: dramatic conventions, considerations of space, and considerations of time. The dramatic convention that transformed the ritual chorus into a dramatic chorus was the ever-present mask. With this contrivance, the chorus was able to assume a different character. When added to costume, it was possible for the male performers to take on female roles, or those of aged citizens or other marginalized groups. Members of a civic chorus, by contrast, present themselves in their own person. A ritual chorus also performs in a civic space. Whereas the Theater of Dionysus was a public space, the dramatic action typically took place in Thebes, Troy, and other areas outside of Athens. The action of tragedies occurred in the distant past, whereas civic choruses performed in the here and now. Perhaps the most striking disjunction between choral and dramatic choruses is the transition from the choral function of worshipping the divinity to a narrative function. The chorus moreover loses its self-referential quality and assumes a descriptive role. In short, the disassociation of the ritual chorus from the dramatic chorus was encouraged by costume and mask, temporal and local illusions.

Despite the differences between ritual and dramatic choruses, it would be a mistake to overlook crucial evidence provided by drama. As has been noted for the study of choral hymns, anyone seriously interested in these areas must grapple with the intersection of cultic and theatrical forms of expression.[15] Certain works, such as the *Bacchae* and *Cyclops* of Euripides, where a ritual context is clearly indicated, are rich in their implications for festival dances. The comedies of Aristophanes, especially *Frogs, Clouds, Plutus, Wasps,* and *Lysistrata,* illuminate phenomena such as the dynamics of epiphany or the socializing role of dance in contexts such as the symposium. And yet a circumspect use of dramatic texts as sources for ritual dance is called for.

Perhaps the most valuable and underused ancient written source for dance is Plato's *Laws*. Plato's observations on the subject not only provide a wealth of information, but distinguish what is significant about dance, situate it in an appropriate context, and allow us to forge links with modern theoretical views on dance and ritual play. Books 2 and 7 are virtually an ancient anthropology of dance. Unlike Aristotle, who gives us received opinions about *mousikē*, the Greeks' word for song and dance culture, Plato's is the last voice to speak to us directly and with authority about musical, and especially, choral traditions. As a conservative, Plato had a somewhat nostalgic view of the role of civic choruses. He had an exact knowledge of choral practices in Attica and elsewhere in Greece prior to the fourth century and is forthcoming about them. He seems to have been especially well informed about persisting choral traditions at Sparta, whose unchanging values Plato holds up as a standard.

In spite of its usefulness as a source, the limitations of the *Laws* must also be recognized. The *Laws* is a philosophical, not a historical source. Plato's theories, however, are not without basis in fact: social theory is grounded in the reality of Athenian (and sometimes Spartan) society. The picture of musical culture drawn in the *Laws* is complete and accurate insofar as it concerns the polis. Plato's conservative tastes in matters musical and his focus on musical forms that pertain to the polis lead him, for example, to pass over discussion of Bacchic dances.[16] But he acknowledges their importance in the *Laws* by reporting views on the origins of manic dancing current in his day; in the *Phaedrus* and elsewhere he discusses the benefits of ecstatic dancing.[17] Plato, in short, does not offer a complete and definitive perspective of a Greek musical and choreographic phenomena, but rather a useful way of how to look at the function of dance as a collective act of worship and play in a community in its widest social and religious contexts. His theoretical model, far from being idiosyncratic, uses many of the same categories and theoretical positions as modern anthropological studies interested in the social functions of dance.

The Use of Artistic Sources

Artistic representations are an important, if difficult, form of evidence for dance. They can reveal aspects of dance not touched on by written sources, and amplify the written testimony. For example, without visual documents of young Athenian girls dancing the so-called pyrrhic or weapon dance, the epigraphic and literary evidence from the classical period would lead one to suppose that the manipulation of shield and spear in dance was a choral competition and paramilitary exercise reserved for males, and performed by women only as entertainment at the banquet. However, among the approximately sixty representations of weapon dances in Attic vase painting of the fifth century, nearly half depict female pyrrhicists, some in cultic contexts not otherwise attested in the contemporary written sources.[18] To take another example: whereas Plato excludes Bacchic dances from his discussion of choruses in the *Laws* on the grounds that they are of no concern to the polis, drinking cups, wine mixing bowls, and the like are often decorated with images reflecting their function in the symposium where informal dancing in a group surrounds the principal activity of imbibing after the meal.

The body of material evidence for dancing in ancient Greece beginning in the Geometric period is large. Geometric and archaic representations of dance in sculpture and especially painted pottery are attested from Attica, Argos, Boeotia, Eretria, Laconia, Corinth, the Cyclades, and from Clazomenae and Miletus among other places in Asia Minor. In the classical period by far the largest group of artistic representations are vases from Attic workshops, although choral dancing continues to engage artists and sculptors throughout Greece. Portrayals of dance appear in various media, such as terra cotta and bronze votive figurines, gems, and especially painted pottery. Choruses are one of the most common scenes in early Greek art, and dances of various sorts continue to be popular through the classical period.[19] The frequency of dance scenes in ceramic art can be explained by the intrinsic charm of the theme and also by the special relationship of potters to dancers and celebrants in festivals in general. It was potters who were commissioned to make the votive offerings and prizes awarded to the best dancers in festival competitions. Moreover, certain products of their trade, such as wine-mixing bowls, were often the focus of ritual dances, and in a self-referential manner ceramic vessels are sometimes included in representations of wine rituals dominated by dancing activity.

There are two basic iconographic criteria for identifying human movement as dance, as opposed to random movement. The linkage of figures in a row by arms held by the hand or at the wrist invariably indicates a choral dance. This is the vase painter's version of the epic formula *cheir epi karpōi* ("hand on wrist") used to describe choruses.[20] The impression of dancing may also be confirmed by the presence of a musician or instrument elsewhere in the scene. The instrumentalist plays the *aulos* (the distinctive wind instrument with twin tubes), or occasionally a stringed or percussive instrument; the dancer may hold a pair of *krotala* (clappers) or cymbals, or a drum or tambourine. And yet, just as the music accompanying the dancers is inaudible, so the essential sequences of movement that make up the dance are lost to the viewer. When we look at a representation of a dance, we see the dancers frozen in a single moment; nor is it possible to line up poses side by side and recreate the choreography. The artist is not showing us a photographic likeness of a dance but rather an allusion to what he has seen and been able to capture within the confines of the space and format. It was sometimes possible, however, for the artist to represent the basic configuration of a dance, as on a lekythos in Brussels, one of several vases depicting a ritual taking place around the mask of Dionysus. In the midst of a group of four women holding *krotala* in their hands is a pillar decked out with the mask of the god. As seen in the schematic drawing (Fig. 3), all of the women, even those whose feet indicate that they are moving away from the pillar, turn their gaze toward

Figure 3. Four women dancing around pillar affixed with mask of Dionysus.

the visage of the god as they circulate about the central pole in a dance.[21] Moreover, the body of the vase is cylindrical and the painter has exploited the shape to suggest the round form of the dance.[22]

As such examples show, vases do not portray so much the dance itself, as the context. But one must be careful about assuming a clear context.[23] Unlike a literary description such as that of Apollo's musical interlude on Olympus in his *Homeric Hymn* where the mythological context is clear, we cannot always be sure of the setting of an artistic representation of dance. Are we, for example, looking at a representation of a foundation legend for a festival dance, or at the artist's version of an actual performance? In a depiction of dancing nymphs are we being shown a chorus of girls dressed up as nymphs or an artistic rendering of nymphs of the mythical realm? Many dance performances were themselves representations, and it is often impossible to distinguish for certain between fiction and real performance. The problem of how artists conveyed dance representations is similar to that encountered in artistic renderings of subjects treated in Athenian drama. Was the artist showing us the myth that forms the core of the play, or was he illustrating actors playing out the myth with costume, masks, props? In the case of representations of dramatic themes it is generally agreed that, except on rare occasions, the artist bypassed the

11

reality of performance and gave us his version of the story. And so it would seem for representations of dancing.

In dealing with the artistic material, distinctions between mythological and nonmythological dances are not helpful or valid, any more than is a division between religious and secular. In fact, the willful confusion of the "imaginary" and "real" worlds may be precisely the point the painter wants to emphasize. The overlapping of fantasy and reality can be seen in a frieze on an archaic dinos in the Louvre.[24] The frieze running around the ceramic goblet represents the Return of Hephaestus to Olympus, a favorite theme of vase painters (discussed in chapter 3). The divine smith's progress is interrupted by Dionysus and his band of dancing satyrs, who initiate him into the mysteries of wine. In the midst of these mythological figures are human actors whose gestures clearly link them with the dancing satyrs and merge the worlds of revelers divine and mortal.

An example from Corinthian pottery may illustrate the possibilities and limitations encountered when interpreting a visual source. A pyxis in Berlin (Fig. 4) depicts, among other figures, the enigmatic "padded" or fat-belly dancers.[25] These comic figures appear with great frequency in the seventh and sixth centuries on vessels of many types, especially drinking cups. In a significant number of examples wine vessels such as drinking horns are held in the hands or danced around. Anatomically the dancers are distinguished by large bellies and buttocks, and they characteristically slap their rumps with one hand. In Corinthian pottery, fat-belly dancers coincide with representations of episodes from epic poetry. On a Corinthian skyphos in the Louvre dated 580, for example, Heracles and Iolaus combat the Lernean Hydra on one side, while on the other side so-called padded dancers grouped in pairs and slapping their buttocks dance around a wine krater.[26] They are given such names as Kōmos (Revel), Paichnios (Playful), Loxias (Crooked), Lodrios (Bent Backward). Does the juxtaposition of epic and ritual scenes on such vases give us a context for the performance of serious epic narratives in the midst of playful celebrations?

Unfortunately we have no such suggestive context for the Berlin pyxis, but there are clear hints of a festival in progress. The body of the pyxis is divided into three zones, with a decorative frieze consisting of widely placed flames and close vertical lines that frame the figured scene on the belly. The decorative motif is repeated on the lid and knob. The focal point of the middle, figured band is a wine krater on a stand. Above it hangs a circular disk, representing a drinking cup. A bearded male figure dressed like the fat-belly dancers elsewhere in the scene fills a jug with wine, to offer a drink to the file of nine men lining up before the krater. The apparatus for storing, mixing, pouring, and drinking the fruit of the vine identifies the scene as a wine ritual. Already intoxicated by the liquid are the padded dancers to the left of the wine server. Their movement can be securely identified as dance by the presence of an *aulos* player. To the left of the padded dancers is a third group of six women; the last two women carry wreaths. Their gesture of holding hands identifies their activity as dance as well.

Are we being shown three separate scenes, or a single, unified scene? What makes it likely that the three groups are to be related to the same festival are the conjunctive figures between the groups and the direction in which these figures have been placed. Thus behind the pairs of antithetically placed dancers is a single dancer facing the line of six female dancers. The single dancer not only faces them but stretches out his right hand, as if to invite the women to join him. In a similar way the last of the six dancers farthest from the single male dancer is distinguished by holding a wreath and by her orientation away from her group and toward the band of older men. One cannot assume that what is portrayed on the vase is a single, simultaneous action; but it is hard to avoid the inference that the activities are coordinate within the same occasion.

But what is the context for the occasion? A festival, no doubt, but is it a real or an imaginary one, a contemporary event or one taking place in the past? Has the painter represented fanciful, mythical figures like satyrs, or a cultic group, or a combination of real and imaginary types? Are the dancers with exaggerated bellies and buttocks wearing costumes and masks? We have no certain answers to these questions. At most we can speculate that the distinctive but enigmatic "fat-belly" dancers usually known in isolated contexts in vases from Corinth and other parts of Greece here are placed in the intelligible context of a women's festival, perhaps in honor of Aph-

Figure 4. Ritual around wine vessel.

14

15

rodite, and that the message conveyed by the interlinking figures, whether they are real or imaginary, cultic or dramatic, is that the communal activities of dancing and drinking unite the participants into a single act that has religious and social meaning to them.[27] But this leaves many questions unanswered. Are we to see in the unsightly bodies and buttock-slapping gestures of the inebriated fat-belly dancers an inverted display of the moral values and traditions encoded in the "undignified" dancing suggested by the names on the Louvre skyphos? Do we have in these clownish figures a parallel to the custom of the Spartans who had the disenfranchised Helots dance drunkenly before Spartan cadets to illustrate the excesses of alcohol, or merely an appropriately lively response to the god contained in the wine?[28]

Modern Interpretive Sources

Modern historians and contemporary studies in anthropology have shown the importance of patterns of behavior and collective activities among social groups who define themselves in part by the type of actions they regularly engage in. This approach has been popular in the last two decades among ancient historians interested in the relationship between activities such as hunting, sacrifice and the communal feast, and athletic training in the Greek polis. Studies on the social and religious dimensions of the polis recognize the close interdependence between such activities and the groups that reaffirm their unity by practicing them, while stressing the role of the polis in creating and developing these social institutions. As a contribution to a recent volume on the Greek city in the archaic and classic periods demonstrates, such an approach avoids the tendency fostered by antiquarian methods to see communal activities as disconnected fragments of daily life.[29] It also cautions against erecting a false or misleading hierarchy that places a group's festival practices in a position subordinate to political activities such as public debates, military organization, and other institutional mechanisms. The practices of exchanging gifts, songs, and speeches, and the experiences of sharing in sacrifices and banquets, of belonging to a group of ephebes or hoplites, of taking part in choruses, games, and the *kōmos*, or of participating in assemblies have an equal value and form a continuum of behavior, the constituent parts of which are not definable as either being social *or* political, religious *or* profane. Such distinctions are arbitrary when applied to communal practices, especially in the archaic city-state which recognizes a religious dimension for all collective practices. The religious element is especially pronounced in choral activities that express the purpose of renewing solidarity among the group by sharing the experience with the divine followers (*thiasos*) on which the earthly activities are modeled.

Dances formally sanctioned by the polis coexisted alongside expressions of ritual conviviality among self-selected groups of citizens. Throughout Greece there existed voluntary societies composed of persons who organized themselves permanently for the pursuit of common ends—the tending of a cult or sanctuary, the promotion of music and drama, commerce, or professional interests. Even for those guilds with secular interests, religious observances and rites played a significant role and allowed individuals to express devotion to deities or heroes not recognized by the state religion. Despite their large number and prevalence the activities of guilds are rarely mentioned in the literary sources; they are known to us through glimpses in inscriptions, mainly from Attica. *Koinon* ("common"), the generic Greek word for an association, defines the essential quality of such groups, the reciprocal sharing of what is held in common among the members. Among the key groups with cultic concerns was the *thiasos*. In this context *thiasos* designated a cultic association of persons who, as followers of a god such as Dionysus, expressed their devotion by dancing and singing. Groups of the followers of Dionysus—maenads, satyrs, and *thyiades*—had not only a theatrical embodiment but are historically attested. The Greeks believed that these *thiasoi* were a reflection of their divine prototypes, and their imitation meant the use of costume, accoutrements, and appropriate ritual movement to carry out the illusion.

As a collective activity membership in a chorus belongs to what have been called "rituals of conviviality" that involved "the consecration of the wine; its sharing, distribution, and consumption; the exchange of speeches; songs, games, the *kōmos*, and dancing."[30] It is in the context of such practices shared under the eyes of the gods that the ties necessary for social cohesion in the city are reinforced. As an instrument of paideia, ritual dancing, in which the customs and gestures of the group are encoded, implied the acquisition of moral virtues and a sense of civic responsibility, of mature allegiance to the community, an espousal of its traditions and values. A valuable text for showing how collective activities consolidate the feeling of belonging to the city is the speech that Xenophon invents for Cleocritus in the context of civil war. "Fellow citizens, why do you drive us out of the city? Why do you want to kill us? We have never done any harm to you. In fact we have shared with you in the most solemn rites, in sacrifices, and in the most splendid festivals; we have joined in choral dances with you, gone to school with you, and been comrades in arms, braving together with you the dangers of land and sea in defense of our common safety and freedom."[31]

Comparative anthropology helps to coordinate dance with sacrifice and other forms of collective ritual behavior. Moreover its methodology is consistent with current approaches in the study of ancient Greek religion, which see religion as a cultural phenomenon, a product of various types of social intercourse. The use of anthropological insights to illuminate classical antiquity is not, of course, new. The French scholar of Greek religion, Henri Jeanmaire, employed such an approach in 1939 in examining the role of dancing in Spartan initiation structures in the light of contemporary parallels in initiation and masquerade societies in traditional Africa.[32] But this bicultural approach is problematic because of its arbitrariness. The tendency to separate and seclude members of a community at certain ages is universal and should theoretically be studied in all possible cultures. Without being able to prove historical connections, similarities between cultural phenomena in two societies may be attributed to chance or to the fact that human nature in its general outlines is similar.

Until recently, ethnographic studies that considered dancing in individual groups or societies traditionally reported the results at the level of description or from the point of view of the participants, without analyzing the larger social function and context of choreographic phenomena. There had been undue emphasis on revealing the inner experience of the dancer and on defining the category of dance, as if it were a self-contained, discrete thing. In the past decade, however, studies in the anthropology of dance have sought to situate dance in a much broader context, for example in relation to possession and other ecstatic states, and to examine the social codes and institutional mechanisms that shape patterned movement of various kinds. The positive results of this approach for understanding the social and religious dimensions of dance have been shown in *Society and the Dance*, in which seven anthropologists drawing from groups in Africa, Southeast Asia, Melanesia, and Oceania look beyond the experience of the performer to ask what dance reveals about ritual behavior and society at large.[33] The collection makes three major contributions. First, it shows that in a given society dance and related activities can best be understood by situating them in their broadest and most appropriate cultural context. Second, it demonstrates how "dance" resists attempts at definition in terms of Western categories and conceptions and may be productively considered alongside other forms of ritual movement. Third, it reveals that, despite the protean forms dance assumes and the different functions it acquires from culture to culture, a finite number of recurrent themes emerges from among published studies on dance complexes.[34] These themes or theories can be succinctly stated as follows. Dance is a kind of safety valve (the cathartic theory). Dance is an organ of social control for transmitting sentiments (the homeostatic theory). Interaction within the dance maintains sentiments (a variation on the homeostatic theory). Dance collectively leads to an emotional climax (the theory of self-generation). Dance contains an element of competition (theories of boundary display). Dance is a form of ritual drama that temporarily reverses or inverts the everyday social order (Victor Turner's theory of *communitas* and antistructure). Finally, dance is a metaphorical language with an underlying structure that communicates patterns of behavior not consciously perceived by the members of a culture.

The relevance of several of these themes to Greek dance is obvious. The element of competition, for example, attested in the earliest alphabetic inscription on the prize jug from the Kerameikos, is writ large in the agonistic context for dithyrambic and other choral competitions at Athens. The exhilarating pitch of excitement that ecstatic dance generates among its participants is well known from Euripides' *Bacchae*. Plato's legislation for musical activity in the *Laws* indicates the power of choral song and dance as an organ of social control for the transmission and maintenance of sentiments among citizens. In fact, a careful reading of the *Laws* reveals that Plato defined and conceived of the dance in the Platonic polis in terms remarkably consistent with modern anthropological positions. Plato's insistence on the verbal and nonverbal aspects of *choreia* and the lack of distinction he makes between dances, processions, and playful activity in general argues for the need to relax the definition of dance in ancient Greece. As we will see in chapter 1, his emphasis on the overlap between dance and play also points to the religious life of the polis with its emphasis on paideia in musical forms as the most appropriate context in which to consider the dance.

One

Dance and Play in Plato's *Laws*: Anticipating an Anthropological Paradigm

> Singing and choral dancing used to be the musical education of
> early Greece. They had lost this function in the new intellec-
> tualized world, and survived (particularly in Athens) only as
> highly elaborate forms of art. But as soon as Plato set about dis-
> covering how to mould the ethos in early youth, he felt there was
> nothing in contemporary education to replace them. So in the
> *Laws* he declared that the ancient Greek round dance should be
> revived and made one of the fundamental elements in education.
> —Werner Jaeger, *Paideia*, 3:228

Plato's Laws: Dance and Play in Moral Education

We must spend our whole lives 'playing' at certain games—sacrifice, singing, and dancing—so as to win the gods' favor, protect ourselves from our enemies, and conquer them in battle."[1] So Plato summarizes the chief ritual duties of pious citizens and the benefits derived from dance and ritual play in the *Laws*, a vital contemporary source for ancient Greek dance and music. Indeed the word *nomos* (law, custom) in the Greek title of the work (*Nomoi*) also has a musical meaning (melody), and Plato puns on the legal and musical senses of the word on several occasions in reference to the so-called kitharodic *nomos*, a genre associated early on with Terpander and Dorian Sparta, whose conservative musical

21

Figure 5. Satyrs dancing in a ring on the *polos* of a goddess.

traditions served as models for Plato's own polis.[2] As the political *nomos* is the basis of social order, so the musical *nomos* is the underpinning of choral dancing that conduces to ethical order in the body politic. The *Laws* in fact represents the only sustained and comprehensive treatment of dance as a social and religious phenomenon to survive from the classical period. In it Plato not only accounts for the origins and nature of dance but classifies choreographic types, discusses their role in moral education, describes in the greatest detail civic choruses, and regulates the participation of the citizenry in this vital form of worshipful play. Plato's comments provide a solid basis for exploring in greater detail the nature of Greek dance, indicate how to define dance, and how to situate it in the context of *paideia,* a word meaning "education" but based, like the verb *paizō* (to dance and play) on the word for child, *pais.* In short, Plato furnishes the link that makes it possible to place ancient Greek dance within a coherent anthropological framework while preserving the cultural categories that shaped it.

The *Laws* is Plato's last work. Left unfinished in 348, a year before the philosopher's death at age eighty-two, this dialogue in twelve books works out in practical detail for the legislator what is left to the discretion of the philosopher-king in the *Republic* concerning the administration of the polis. The dialogue takes place on Crete between three elderly men, an anonymous Athenian, a Spartan named Megillus, and Cleinias the Cretan. The Athenian (representing Plato's point of view) dominates and orchestrates the conversation, which concerns the formulation of laws for a virgin tract of land on the island of Crete. The island, renowned for its dancers as early as Homer, was rich in choreographic associations. We are to imagine the dialogue in progress as the three interlocutors stroll from Knossos (famed in antiquity for the dancing ground that Daedalus built for Ariadne) to the sacred cave on Mt. Ida where, according to legend, the band of Couretes danced with weapons to protect the infant Zeus.[3] They pause along the way to take shade, and it is on these occasions that we hear what Plato (continuing his musical metaphor) calls preludes (*prooimia*) to the formulation of actual laws (*nomoi*), with the ambiguous meanings of musical pieces/laws.

The particular preludes and pieces of interest to us concern education (paideia) in the broadest sense of the word. As the chapter epigram from Werner Jaeger's classic three-volume work, *Paideia*, suggests, music and dancer were *the* form of education in archaic Greece; they amounted to a virtual language for communicating the tribal traditions. The Pythagoreans considered the art of *mousikē* as a gift of the gods and made it the cornerstone of all moral education. In Plato's scheme music and dance were the first and fundamental steps of education; these forms of training constituted, as it were, the *unwritten* laws. They were crucial because they allowed the child to become habituated to virtue (*aretē*) before reason had formed. The overall goal of education, to like and dislike the right things, was achieved through the agency of pain and pleasure. In this regard dance and music were of special utility to the lawmaker, since they were pleasurable activities. It was a matter of harnessing the natural delight of the young in things musical and turning it to good ends in a process of social habituation that the French sociologist Bourdieu calls by its Latin root *habitus*.[4]

The discussion of *choreia* as paideia in the *Laws* springs from consideration of another pleasurable agent in moral education in Plato's scheme, namely the consumption of wine in moderate quantities at drinking parties. Wine, music, and dance were key elements in the Greek institution of the symposium, where the young were tested for skill in poetic memorization, and where improvisation in song and dance under the influence of alcohol was encouraged. The prelude on dance and music in book 2 of the *Laws* is a theoretical consideration of what comes from the perfectly balanced mix of wine and *mousikē* at the ideal symposium, which here is a metaphor of the Platonic polis.

Plato's insistence on music and dance in moral education in the *Laws* is one of the ways in which his views differ most strikingly from Socrates of the early dialogues, for whom knowledge of the good was sufficient to attain virtue. But Plato, who was acutely aware of the effect of music and dance on the irrational, believed that gymnastic and musical training, as well as philosophical investigations, contributed to civic virtue "because rhythm and harmony penetrate most easily into the soul and influence it most strongly, bringing with it decorum and making those who are correctly trained well-behaved."[5] Without proper training, music could exercise a dangerous influence on the soul: laxness in these areas, he felt, led to degeneration in the political sphere.[6] A person who does not know how to dance is called *achoreutos*, by which Plato means "uneducated," in short, not a citizen.[7] That person would be fundamentally excluded from the ideal polis because of lack of socialization.

In the second book of the *Laws* Plato, speaking through the Athenian, outlines the organization and administration of choruses and establishes criteria for judging their performances. The citizens of the polis are divided into three choruses according to age and the divinities assigned to each. The first, the Muses' chorus, is composed of children of an unspecified age. The second consists of males under thirty and is sacred to Apollo. To the third chorus belong citizens between thirty and sixty; this chorus of older men is consecrated to Dionysus. The Muses, Apollo, and Dionysus are none other than the three divine patrons mentioned as having been given to mortals as "partners in the dance" in a passage on the origins of festival dancing.[8] It is the third, Dionysiac chorus that is called the "noblest element" in the polis because of the maturity and discerning experience of its members. They are the guardians of education. This chorus is deemed noblest, moreover, because it establishes an ideal for the chorus of young men to emulate, just as the intermediate chorus of Apollo by offering its paean encourages the youngest chorus.[9] The administration of choruses falls to the elder males. The sixty-year-old choristers of Dionysus, for example, who are particularly sensitive to rhythm and harmony, are designated to select the songs to be performed. The elders who are no longer able to dance with their former agility organize choral competitions for the younger members of the polis; in watching them they derive pleasure and are in a sense rejuvenated.[10] The pleasure so derived is one among many criteria for judging the excellence of dances. In addition to the intrinsic grace (*charis*) of the performance, two criteria for choral performance emerge: its correctness (*orthotēs*) in relation to its ideal model and its beneficial effect (*opheleia*).[11]

In book 7 of the *Laws* Plato situates dancing (*orchēsis*) between gymnastic training and music proper and classifies civic dances. Among the repertory of dances for all citizens he distinguishes broadly between dances of the serious (*to semnon*) and the common (*to phaulon*) type.[12] The former are representations (*mimēmata*) of graceful bodies in order to produce an effect of grandeur, while the latter imitate the movements of ungainly bodies to show them in an unfavorable light. Dances of the common type imply the dramatic choral dances of comedy and satyr-play, the *kordax* and the *sikinnis*. The serious dances fall into two subdivisions, dances of war (*pyrrhichē*) and dances of peace (*eirenikē*). The warlike class consists of weapon dances to honor Athena and train soldiers for hoplite warfare. Peaceful dances are expressions of joy and thanksgiving performed by citizens "who enjoy prosperity and who pursue moderate pleasures."[13] In the dialogue, the Athenian distinguishes two kinds of peaceful dance, those expressive of acute pleasure, and those communicating a deeper, more permanent pleasure. By the first type Plato has in mind dances of thanksgiving offered by the community to Apollo for release from plague and war, or to observe occasions of success or victory. The chorus of women in Euripides' *Electra*, for example, upon learning of Orestes' victory exhort the protagonist to "dance—leaping lightly with joy like a bounding fawn," while the chorus will themselves perform a choral dance and raise the cry of joy with the sound of the *aulos*.[14]

In describing the two subdivisions of serious dances the Athenian states that he is following the classification and nomenclature established by traditional and longstanding usage.[15] The Athenian praises the unnamed sage who, for example, invented the generic term that describes pacific dances, *emmeleia*, related to the adjective *emmelēs*. It means to be literally "in tune," and implies that the emotions of the performer are in concord with the gestures and words expressing the dance. Although Plato does not name particular dances classed among *emmeleia*, they included, on the one hand, the dramatic dances of the tragic chorus, and on the other the wide range of civic dances performed in combination with the proper musical accompaniments at sacrificial feasts and other religious holidays. Foremost among these were hymns, especially the paean, which was a regular feature of feasts of Apollo. The degree of choreographic movement in conjunction with hymns varied. We know from a late source (drawing in all likelihood on Plato's contemporary, the musicologist Aristoxenus) that hymns were sometimes danced, sometimes not.[16] Another danced hymn implied by this class is the dithyramb in honor of Dionysus.[17] It originated at Corinth in the sixth century and developed in the fifth century into a choral competition among the *phylai* (tribes) of Attica at festivals not only for Dionysus but for Apollo and other gods as well. Yet another type of choral song perhaps implied by *emmeleia* are *enkōmia*—not the odes in praise of athletic victors known from Pindar and Bacchylides, but the choral songs in praise of gods and heroes such as those that the Delian Maidens performed for Apollo, Artemis, and Leto, as well as for "famous men and women of former times."[18]

Bacchic dances (see chapter 3) constitute a separate class. These are representations of figures drunk on wine whom the performers call nymphs, Pans, silens, and satyrs. The Athenian does not actually condemn such imitations of the inebriated *thiasos* of Dionysus; rather he leaves them to one side since they are of no direct concern to the legislator.[19] He apparently has in mind possession dances and other long-established rites in mystery religions rather than theatrical representations as known from satyr-plays, for, as we have seen, dramatic dances, even of a comic nature, were of civic concern.

Plato enjoins participation in choral activity on the entire citizenry—men, women, and children from six onward. Involvement in choral performance either as a participant or as a spectator is one of the signal ways by which a citizen can reaffirm membership in the community, and the participation of the entire body politic guarantees the transmission and reinforcing of sentiments throughout the polis. The noncitizen, however, is excluded from experiencing the pleasures and moral benefits of *choreia* sanctioned by the state. Conversely, citizens shall be prevented from performing certain types of tunes and dances that have a corrupting influence. For example, comic dances of the trivial class in which performers imitate the actions of unsightly bodies and enact unseemly behavior should actually be seen by citizens, in order that they may learn by contrast what is serious and avoid doing or saying anything ludicrous. But it is slaves and hired foreigners who should perform these negative examples of conduct.[20] In making this recommendation Plato seems to be following a practice employed by the Spartans, who, according to Plutarch, forced the Helots to perform humiliating dances in a drunken state before the beardless Spartan initiates so as to exhibit the ridiculous consequences of excessive alcohol.[21]

Girls are to be included in all forms of dance training. Although Plato was conservative in many areas, in matters of educational equality between the sexes he was, to his contemporaries, shockingly revolutionary, and to our eyes, "modern." Laws concerning physical education (*gymnastikē*), the Athenian asserts, "will apply just as much to females as to males. The girls must undergo training in precisely the same way [as the boys], and I make my law without any qualification about making horse-riding or athletics being suitable activities for males but not for females."[22] It is well known that the Spartans required physical training for girls as well as for boys, but they stopped short of making girls undertake military service. In Plato's city-state, however, girls will not be trained like boys up to a certain point and then left with no civic responsibilities when they grow up. If there were an emergency involving warfare, the Athenian argues, untrained women would not be able to use bows and arrows to defend the state and their children; nor would they be able to take up shield and spear in imitation of the war goddess so as to terrify the enemy.[23] This is a reference to Plato's earlier discussion about the need for both boys and girls to learn weapon dances such as Athena executed.[24] In recommending the weapon dance for girls as well as for boys Plato was not, in fact, flying in the face of conventional practice. We know from fifth-century vase paintings that girls as well as boys performed weapon dances, although it is difficult to specify the context and purpose of pyrrhic dances for girls.[25]

In ancient Greece, both boys and girls were trained to dance, but they did not ordinarily dance together: from independent sources it is known that Greek dances tended to be gender-specific (as indeed they are in many parts of Greece today). In the *Laws* Plato reflects the normal distinction between male and female dances.[26] The lawmaker says, for example, that boys and girls will both learn dancing and gymnastics, but boys will be assigned dancing masters (*orchēstai*), and the girls dancing mistresses (*orchēstrides*).[27] The Athenian stresses that regulations about female performances must be based on the natural difference between the sexes.[28] Rhythms and modes (which are imposed by the words of a song) must be appropriate to the characteristics of each sex, "for the Muses would never make so gross an error as to compose words suitable for men, and then give the melody a coloring proper to women."[29] Dances are no more interchangeable between the sexes than are the tunes. Plato's recommendation of different songs for men and women is based on a belief in natural differences of temperament between the sexes; certain modes of music impart certain types of ethical behavior. Characteristic of the male are magnificence (*megaloprepeia*) and courage (*andreia*), while decorum and moderation are feminine traits. Boys and girls, however, come together in the dance at appropriate times such as courtship; but when they do, each gender group is expected to display the temperamental qualities appropriate to its training.[30]

The Nature of Greek Dance

The *Laws* serves as a reliable point of departure for understanding three chief characteristics of Greek dance: its combination of verbal and nonverbal aspects, its mimetic dimension, and the peculiarly playful nature of this most serious form of ritual communication. *Choreia*, the term Plato consistently uses for choral activity in the polis, represents, as we have seen, the combined activities of singing *and* dancing. Plato explains that the essential links between the two activities are rhythm (*rhythmos*) and movement (*kinēsis*). Just as there is vocal movement when the voice rises or falls according to the tune (*melos*) it sings, so there is bodily movement when the body moves according to the gestures and postures it enacts rhythmically.[31] In choral performance the voice and the body must be in perfect concord. The harmony of voice and body represented by

29

choreia is thus an idealized and stylized form of ordinary verbal and nonverbal communication. This phenomenon is revealingly commented upon in the passage on the anthropological origins of dance.[32] Plato observes that everyone who is using his voice, either in speaking or singing, is quite unable to keep the body still. He then goes on to say that the representation of spoken things through gestures is the source of the art of dancing: "This is the origin of dancing: the gestures that express what one is saying."[33] From the context it can be inferred that the propensity to complement verbal expression with body language in ancient Greece was elevated to an art form corresponding to Plato's term *choreia*. This in turn became a standard of ideal behavior in the Platonic polis. It was in this sense a restricted linguistic code with social meaning. Only those who were educated knew how to use it and by using it demonstrated socialization.

The mixture of the verbal and nonverbal are two elements of what was understood by the Greek word *mousikē*, which consisted almost indivisibly of music (both instrumental and sung), poetry, and rhythmic movement. The use of significant gestures in dancing is evident from the earliest artistic representations of choral groups depicted with arms upraised or hands linked in the Geometric period. Gestures continued to exert an enormous influence in the dramatic and oratorical arts. The importance of hand gestures in particular in ancient Greece is confirmed by the term *cheironomia*, an elaborate and complex system of gesticulations. The term is a compound derived from the Greek word for hand and the same root found in *nomos* (law/melody). It is a sort of musical sign language akin to the Indian *mudras*. In Hellenistic times *cheironomia* came to be associated with the art of pantomime where a story could be told by gestures alone. Lucian, in his treatise on the dance, relates that Demetrius the Cynic, after seeing a mime dance the story of Ares and Aphrodite, exclaimed, "I hear, my man, the story you are acting, I don't only see it; for you seem to me to be speaking with your hands."[34] But the verb *cheironomeō* is attested already in Herodotus, and from a passage in Xenophon's *Symposium* it can be inferred that "dancing with the hands" was a common practice in the fourth century B.C.E.[35]

A second major characteristic of *choreia* is its imitative (*mimētikē*) nature, which is closely related to its verbal and nonverbal dimensions. Imitation could be effected both by voice or by gesture: one thinks of Helen's perfidious simulation of the voices of the wives of the warriors inside the Trojan Horse, the shape-shifting of Proteus, whom Lucian called a "dancer, an imitative person" (*mimētikos anthrōpos*), or the enthralling talent of the Delian Maidens to imitate the voices and rhythms of all peoples.[36] Choreographic *schēmata*, for which the proverbially inventive fifth-century tragedian Phrynichus was renowned, imitated activities from everyday life such as rowing, threshing, pounding the anvil, spinning, and weaving. Plato, who acknowledges the capacity of dance to represent things and qualities, alludes to the innate and acquired mimetic abilities of performers. "Performances given by choruses are representations (*mimēmata*) of character and deal with the most varied kinds of actions and situations. The individual performers depend for their rendering on a mixture of trained habit and imitative power."[37]

In the works of Plato the concept of *mimēsis* has many and varied meanings. But in a musical context *mimēsis* does not so much imply the attempt to recreate the outward appearance of a thing as it does to represent different kinds of character (*tropos*), both good and bad. The mimetic capacity inherent in choric activity thus has the power to reinforce moral education, as well as to corrupt. In the *Laws* the Athenian argues that the mimetic component of *choreia* can and ought to be used to reinforce paideia, since in the course of a person's life educational discipline, which teaches a person to distinguish between good and bad, pleasure and pain, grows slack and weakens.[38] Choral activity, he maintains, can reverse this tendency toward moral degeneration. At this point in the argument the Athenian introduces the first of two accounts of the origins of dance (examined in greater detail in the next two chapters) whereby the gods, in pity for the tendency of the human race to grow slack, ordained feasts and granted them Apollo, the Muses, and Dionysus as their companions and partners in the dance so that they may set right their modes of discipline.

On the other hand, by imitating or even taking pleasure in the wrong things, such as one finds represented in gestures and tunes not sanctioned by the gods, a person undermines the moral purpose of festival dances.[39] Knowing how to distinguish between good and bad postures and tunes in choral performance is therefore confirmation of an educated person. A well-educated person performs well and what he performs must be good, because imitation of the opposite will lead to moral turpitude. A person correctly trained in *choreia* will take pleasure in good gestures and tunes. If a person does not do this and takes pleasure in a performance that is bad (even though it may appear pleasant to the viewer) he can weaken his moral goodness.[40] The potential for imitative dances to corrupt leads Plato to call for regulations about musical education that will restrict the form of rhythm and tunes which may be taught to citizens. He holds up as a standard the laws of Egypt which forbid any innovations in the musical and choreographic traditions. Some of the tunes, he says, have been preserved since time immemorial and are reported to be the compositions of the god Isis. The Egyptian parallel suggests that what is good to imitate has a divine origin. It is introduced to suggest that tampering with Greek ritual dances not only undermines their original intent, which is to reinforce moral education, but is a sacred offense.

The concept of *mimēsis* as a linguistic category does not, of course, originate with Plato. It is first mentioned in the passage on the mimetic abilities of the Delian Maidens in the *Homeric Hymn to Apollo*.[41] In *Die Mimēsis in der Antike*, a study of *mimēsis* and etymologically related words, Hermann Koller suggests that before Plato the term referred exclusively to the capacity of music and dancing to represent dramatically the appearance, behavior, and utterances of humans and animals in song and dance.[42] Plato marks the shift from *mimēsis* as "representation" to a more abstract concept of "likeness or imitation," often with an ethical component. *Mimēsis* in the restricted representational sense is essential to ritual play as an "as if" activity. Ritual proceeds as if there were no real distinction between the object represented and the purveyors of the illusion. The participants in archaic rituals, with or without the help of masks and costume, behave as if they were the "other"—as if they were gods or animals. The playful deception that envelopes their activity must in an important sense be perceived as reality by their audience, both imaginary (divine) and human, otherwise the desired fictional quality enveloping the performance is somehow incomplete. In the Platonic city *mimēsis* is played out in the three choruses: the choir of the Muses has as its model the choir of Apollo, which in turn relies on the choir of Dionysus for its prototype. But as the names Plato gives the choirs imply, each is essentially a *mimēsis* of its divine prototypes: Apollo, the Muses, and Dionysus.

The imitative qualities of dance lead to the third and perhaps most dynamic characteristic of dance stressed by Plato: its pleasure-giving and playful quality, as found in the imitative play to which children naturally turn as a form of expression. Dance, along with song, Plato says, originates in the leaping and wailing of infants. But when these unrestrained tendencies of the young are subjugated to rigorous training, singing and dancing become the highest form of human play. Yet we are all children in ritual worship, the philosopher seems to suggest. In a passage on the playful character of human beings, Plato calls the human animal the puppet or plaything (*paignion*) of the god.[43] The ability to be playful is, in his view, the best part of human character since it leads to appropriate forms of worship. Every man and woman ought to pass through life in accordance with this character, playing at the noblest of pastimes.[44] Plato emphasizes the pleasurable and playful aspects of dance in etymological puns. The gods invented the word *choros* because of the "cheer" (*chara*) in it. By situating *choreia* in the context of moral education the philosopher is also able to make a punning relationship between *paideia* and *paidia* (play), both linguistically related to the verb *paizō* (to dance/play).[45]

What is the relationship of dance to play in Plato's view of education (*paideia*)? Beneath the social edifice built by *choreia* is an elaborate substructure of play (*paidia*), that is, the formal and informal games of children.[46] The social importance of play is suggested in personifications of Paidia in Athenian art, as on a pyxis in New York (Fig. 6).[47] The legislator prescribes that children between three and six years play at games which they invent on their own, that is to say, spontaneous play (*autophuēs*).[48] A program of organized games is then to be imposed on children six years and older. Plato is ex-

Figure 6. Paidia (play personified) balancing a stick.

tremely conservative about the structured play of children. The Athenian, speaking as usual for Plato, complains that in all societies there is an ignorance about the effect that innovations have on children's games. Legislators who permit innovations do not realize that children introducing changes in their games will grow up in a manner different from their fathers. They will pursue another mode of life and will demand new institutions and new laws. Undesirable changes in the moral fabric will result. Children therefore should play the same games as their parents played and under the same conditions.[49] This homeostatic model for games assures that the laws of society remain intact. Like collective dancing, Platonic games are an organ of social control. Indeed the discussion of children's games in the *Laws* leads the Athenian back to the subject of *choreia*. As with games, so melodies underlying dances must not alter. To violate choral hymns (*nomoi*) destined for the gods by altering them in effect constitutes a transgression of the laws (*nomoi*).[50]

Plato derives the origin of play (*paidia*)—and consequently *paideia*—from the natural tendency of young creatures to leap, making a third play on words by using the verb *pedaō* for leaping: since rhythm is awakened by melody, the union of the forces (melody and rhythm), Plato says, gave birth to *choreia* and *paidia*.[51] In short, Plato considers dance to be play. *Choreia* is play and *paideia* par excellence.

Plato's characterization of dance as a form of playful imitation for serious religious and moral ends indicates the appropriate setting in which to examine ritual dance in ancient Greece. Dancing in Plato's state functions as a highly pleasurable form of communal worship, but the contexts in which it is discussed are social and political. *Choreia* is equivalent to moral education (*paideia*), which falls under the control of the state. The activity of dancing is therefore a cultural form of play, which along with singing and sacrificing, is specifically a form of ritual activity that should concern a citizen. Although the ability to dance and sing originally derives from the impulse of the unformed human being to leap about and wail uncontrollably, *choreia*, the realization of the innate impulse, is the most highly structured form of moral and religious behavior controlled by elaborate mechanisms. There is a productive interaction between the crude natural impulse toward disorderly sounds and movement and the social and political organs that transform sensibility to rhythm and harmony into civic choruses. Plato accounts for this productive interaction by the intermingling of *paideia* (education) and *paidia* (play). For Plato *paideia* implies the right mixture of rational and antirational elements. The legislator must, in short, regulate the proper combination of the fiery tendency to make wailing sounds and leaping motions and the orderly perception of harmony and rhythm to produce music and dance. Although *choreia* as *paideia* is directed toward the young, it is not restricted to them. Dancing and singing achieve such a central status in the Platonic polis because a citizen can and should play before the gods throughout his life.

Play, like dance, is a notoriously difficult term to define, and some scholars have been content to classify it as a paradox.[52] Others have thought that play should be defined in relation to games, making a distinction between informal play (*jeu*) and more formal games (*jeux*). The distinction between play and contest is emphasized by verbal determinants in several languages, including Sanskrit, Chinese, and Greek.[53] Greek contrasts *paidia*, which denotes childish, innocent play, with *agōn*, which implies a structured game limited by rules. The opposition between joyful, innocent, and childlike play and a structured game (often a contest for power) is also reflected in Greek words for dance, *paizō* and *choreuō*.[54] In the *Odyssey* the place for dancing (*choros*) is synonymous with the place for contest (*agōn*) at the court of the Phaeaceans, and the dancing contests staged for Odysseus constitute the most important event.[55] In the Panathenaea and other civic festivals called *agōnes* at Athens in the classical period, the choral competitions were central. The agonistic nature and context for ancient Greek dances is accommodated by the anthropological paradigm which holds that dance in general has a competitive element.

The larger social and religious context for play and contest alike is the communal gathering. This assembly of people that provides the setting for the play sphere is designated by various terms, including *agōn*, whose root "ag-" (bring together) sometimes gives it the neutral meaning of an assembly. *Agōn* is both the contest itself, as in the phrase *mousikoi agōnes* (musical contests), and the larger festival context for such competitive events. The festival on Delos in the *Homeric Hymn to Apollo* examined in the next chapter included contests (*agōnes*) of boxing, singing, and dancing.[56] In the private sphere, play and contests of various kinds take place at weddings (*gamoi*), the symposium, informal gatherings (*synodoi*),[57] and even funerals.

The playful and mimetic elements of Greek *mousikē* can be related to the agonistic context by coordinating them with sacrifice, the other activity at which Plato says a citizen must play throughout life. Sacrifice is itself an *agōn*, the culmination of a ritualized hunt in which the human animal shows itself superior to the animal victim, even though it may represent in symbolic terms the god. According to a so-called social Darwinian view of the function of agonistic play articulated by Karl Groos in two works from the turn of the century, *The Play of Animals* and *The Play of Man*, competition within and among species (natural selection) has a critical role in the process of evolution.[58] More recently, the mathematician René Thom examined the succession of forms in nature and offered a different approach to the evolutionary process anticipated by the pre-Socratics: "The dynamical situations governing the evolution of natural phenomena are basically the same as those governing the evolution of man and societies." Thom developed a concept of play as a biological phenomenon related to the struggle among "attractors" (his term for "predator" and "prey"). The principal need of an animal is food, and feeding implies predation of another living thing. According to Thom, the predator identifies with its prey until the critical moment when it recognizes the prey as distinct and becomes itself again. The ability to simulate the prey enables the predator to create fictitious objects of predation. This simulative capacity leads Thom to call the nervous system of the higher animals an "organ of alienation" that permits them to become the "other." In adult human play the motivation may be an aesthetic sense governed by a set of rules "in which the player . . . tries to form the most attractive and effective moves" to attain the goal.[59]

In human ritual activities such as hunting and sacrifice the participants may take on the appearance of prey or predator by use of mask, costume, ritual movement, or other symbolic identification. The tendency of the human predator to identify with its victim carries over into the ritualized hunt implied by sacrifice in the ancient Mediterranean where the close link between human and animal is reflected in the widespread mythical motif of the substitute of an animal for a human victim and vice versa. Ritual dance behavior is ancillary to the need for spiritual union through sacrificial and wine rituals and other symbolic forms in which the imitative element in dance permits the participants to become the "other." The need for divine succor experienced communally as a feast is a requirement as strong as that for material sustenance. Plato acknowledges the priority and interdependence of such aesthetic forms in spiritual life when he names sacrificing, singing, and dancing as the activities to which a Greek must continuously turn attention.

Plato's Laws: *Toward an Anthropological Paradigm*

Plato's insistence on treating ritual dance in the *Laws* in its broadest political and social setting anticipates modern anthropological paradigms for understanding the interaction of dance and society, beginning with the homeostatic theory that dance is an organ of social control ideal for transmitting and maintaining sentiments. The fact that Plato gives the place of honor to *choreia* in his program for education, going so far as to equate *choreia* with paideia, anticipates the commonplace in the anthropological literature that dance is used to communicate social codes, especially to the young. The prevalence of manuals of dance such as Thoineau Arbeau's *Orchesographie* (1588) in the early modern period bears eloquent testimony to the belief in the power of the minuet and other dances to teach comportment and moral virtues.[60] Dance is an instrument of socialization, and in the hands of the older members of the group it can be used as an organ of social control of its members, particularly the adolescent population. In ancient Greece socialization through dance was especially salient among girls approaching the age of marriage. No single ritual is implied, but rather a sequence of preparatory dances in the context of cults of Artemis that led up to the nuptial ceremony where dancing again was prominent. John Blacking's valuable study of the initiation cycle of the Venda girls of southern Africa shows that over a period as long as four years girls are taught by ritual specialists a series of dances that prepare them for marriage and motherhood. The initiation school culminates in a collective dance called the *domba*, metaphorically described by the Venda as "a huge drawing of breath of the whole countryside."[61] Paul Spencer, the editor of the volume in which Blacking's essay appears, comments on the relationship between the girls and the controlling group: "They are not in the grip of the elders and alienated from power, but through the power of music and dance they become aware of the transformation within themselves as they pass from girlhood to the adult world."[62]

In the Platonic city, dance is a mechanism of social control, with the third Dionysiac choir made up of elders as the arbiters of the codes to be transmitted through *choreia*.[63] Although Plato expresses his distaste for innovation in musical practices, nowhere does he advocate a repressive or tyrannical exercise of power over the young. The three choruses exist to reinforce one another, like the Spartan choruses of old men, young men, and boys who, according to Plutarch, would sing responsively to one another before performing.[64] The elders in Plato's polis are portrayed as willing to yield gracefully the things of youth in exchange for the pleasures of watching the dances of the young, the mere sight of which infuses them with energy and pleasure. "While our young ones are ready to join in dancing and singing themselves, we old men deem the proper thing is to pass the time watching them. We delight in their play and holiday-making. Our former agility is deserting us, and as we yearn for it we take delight in arranging competitions for those who can best arouse in us the memory of our youth."[65] *Choreia* in Plato's paradigm is equated with *paidia* and paideia, but as a socializing process it does not stop with the young. Its benefits continue throughout the life of a citizen, either through direct participation or by viewing the pleasure-giving performances of the younger group under the control of the elders who stage dance competitions and other physical displays for mutual pleasure and edification. By giving *choreia* such a place of honor in his polis Plato acknowledges that, as with sacrifice, the combined activities of singing and dancing are uniquely suited for defining, expressing, and sustaining the fragile relations between worshipper and divinity where verbal expressions on their own might fall short or be considered unsubtle. It is important to recognize, however, that while Plato clearly favors a homeostatic model whereby musical activity is used to transmit and reinforce favorable sentiments among the body politic in an orderly way, he does not deny the widespread existence of ecstatic dances or the cathartic effects of dance, as we will see in a later chapter.

If Plato accords a high position to *choreia* in moral education in the polis, he gives an equally prominent place to play as the activity to which *choreia* is joined, as it were, at the hip. The benefit of play is illuminated by a comparative example from a nomadic group of East Africa. In his study of the role of dance as form of play among the Samburu of that region, Paul Spencer has suggested that the genesis of *communitas* may be attributed to the play of childhood as much as to ritual and dance, "beyond the authoritarian structure of the family and of the culture it represents. . . . In this way one can reconcile the apparent contradiction that the Samburu regard dance as play and yet give it pride of place in so many of their rituals and endow it with the sanctity of collective representation."[66] In calling *choreia* a form of play Plato sets up a continuum between the unstructured activity of infants (leaping and wailing) and the disciplined choral music and dance of the well-trained chorus of citizens. The process of education through *choreia* implies a progression from the informal and crude play of children to the type of activity appropriate for a citizen and pleasing to the gods. But the two types of play, childish and adult, are not divided by an inseparable gulf. Moreover, there is something salutary in the ability of the citizenry at large to share in play in a festival setting. The transition from civic structure to antistructure, the progression from inhibition toward play, can be seen as one of the essential mechanisms for the development of *communitas*. Dance, which has the power to order, also has a disruptive force contributing to a positive breakdown in the social order by conducing its participants to communal diversion.

Plato's theoretical discussion of *choreia* challenges us to rethink so basic a question as how dance may be appropriately defined in its particular cultural context. One of the chief obstacles to understanding ritual dance in ancient Greece, or any society alien to ours, derives from the cultural assumptions that we bring to bear on the category of dance. The Greek word for collective ritual dancing, *choros*, underlines the inadequacies of defining in our own terms the activity that we call dance. *Choros* means, in addition to the choreographic activity, the group that performs it and the locus of performance, implying an indissoluble bond among the participants, the ritual act, and the sacred space. The very idea of dance as a form of religious expression is foreign to modern sensibilities. We tend to think of dance as a nonverbal form of recreation or a spectacular display, often performed by couples. Greek dance, on the other hand, typically combined singing and bodily movement. It was enacted among groups of the same gender and social status who mimetically represented things or qualities embodied by divine or heroic prototypes. Rarely were dances performed by couples, or even mixed groups of males and females. The dual nature of *choreia*, with its components of singing as well as dancing, its emphasis on imitation, and its playful essence make it stand apart from what springs to mind when we use the word "dance." Many of the rhythmic activities which we would hardly consider as dancing were deemed such by the ancient Greeks. In the *Laws* choral activity is not differentiated from gymnastic contests, and there is no real division between dances and processions. Plato calls military training contests *choreia*, and processions of children in honor of the gods are synonymous with dancing.[67]

The lack of clear distinction between dance and procession and other forms of ritual movement encourages us to broaden the definition of Greek dance to consider rhythmic movement as another form of communal behavior cognate with the acts of sacrifice and drinking wine. As a category of ritual play, dancing must be regarded as operating within the particular context of festivals and gatherings. Although dance incorporates movements from the day-to-day world, it assumes a divine model and thus functions according to rules that are fundamentally different from those that interpret behavior outside of this context.

An anthropological parallel may serve to illustrate the differences (and similarities) of interpreting dance phenomena in a society where dance can be directly observed, and in ancient Greece where our evidence is indirect. Alfred Gell, who has studied the ritual dances among the Umeda of Papua New Guinea, shows that the "ceremonial walking" of the musicians who parade around the dancing ground as they play their wooden trumpets during the *ida* ceremony (consisting of a sequence of masked dancers) emphasizes and exaggerates elements of normal walking among the populace.[68] The ceremonial walking is what Gell calls a "hypostatisation" of the normal walk and as such it is already a dance. The particular gait of the Umeda is characterized by an exaggerated knee bend that can be related to environment and technology (the lack of roads and footwear, on the one hand, and the many obstructions to locomotion that pose potential injury to the unshod foot, on the other). The exaggerated knee bend minimizes injuries to the foot by distributing as evenly as possible the weight of the body on the largest surface of the foot. In everyday locomotion, then, there is already a thin line between a deliberately graceful walk that evokes the dance without becoming it. Yet, as Gell explains,

> it also remains true that there is a gap, a threshold however impalpable, that is crossed when the body begins to dance, rather than simply move. This gap is less a matter of movement per se than of meaning, for what distinguishes dance movements from nondance movements is the fact that they have dance meanings attached to them. But here is a paradox, fundamental to the whole question of dance, because what source can these dance meanings possibly have except the patterned contrasts, the intentional clues, embodied in everyday, nondance movement? Dance seems to separate itself from nondance by its atypicality, its nonnormal, nonmundane character, but dance acquires its meanings by referring us back always to the world of mundane actions, to what these performers would be doing, were they doing anything but dance.

As Gell observes, dance meanings originate "through a process whereby elements . . . of nondance motor patterns are seized upon . . . and set within a particular context. The logic of dance is, in this respect, highly akin to the logic of play; the message 'this is dance' is a metamessage, one that sets the subsequent communicative transaction in its correct logical context."[69]

The evidence from ancient Greece does not allow us to perceive the interaction of dance and everyday, nondance movements, but that there was such an interplay can be inferred from its mimetic properties. What was recognized as dance among the Greeks was also patterned on everyday human locomotion no less than among the Umeda. However, among the Greeks the pattern was not thought to be "nonmundane, nondance" actions, but rather supernatural, extraordinary movement implying a divine standard. According to the logic of play (to continue the parallel with Gell's example) the metamessage of Greek dance is to be understood in the context of festival play in relation to the prototypes of dance which the human performers used as models. Behind Plato's philosophical theory of dance as a *mimēsis* of good and bad *tropoi* lies a more fundamental divine and cosmic model for dance to which we turn in the next two chapters. Comparative anthropology offers numerous parallels among groups seeking through dance and song to reenact the origins of their universe or to reorder the cosmos after disruption caused by crisis in the social or biological realm. The metaphorical nature of the dance medium in which the message was expressed has unique affinities with the allusive qualities of the poetic, mythological, and artistic media that preserve the divine prototypes of dance and to which we fortunately have access.

Dance and ritual play in ancient Greece, in summary, can be most productively studied first by recognizing several Platonic categories based on the nature, function, and organization of dance, and second, by situating it in the context of socialization, cultural play, and contest (paideia, *paidia, agōn*). This approach is far more likely to yield results than one that attempts to define dance in Western terms and analyze it accordingly. In addition to the overarching contextual category of paideia/*agōn*, the categories for choral activity that emerge from a consideration of Plato's writings on dance concern competing trends within a musical tradition (conservative-innovative), the nature of bodily movement (orderly-disorderly, i.e., *emmeleia-plēmmeleia*), moral qualities (decent-disreputable), mental states (pleasure-pain), physical states (sober-drunken), aesthetic criteria (beautiful-ugly), mode of communication (verbal-nonverbal expression), performance dynamics (audience-performer), political context (civic-Bacchic), age (young-old), civic status (citizen-noncitizen), spiritual status (immortal-mortal), and gender considerations (male-female).

In subsequent chapters we will have occasion to build on and refine these categories and correlate them with others suggested by different types of sources. Of course, the elements of any one category are not mutually exclusive but variable and in many cases form a continuum. Dance by nature erodes or crosses boundaries, sometimes reversing the structuring elements to arrive at a new order. The fluidity of the various continuums is a function of the fundamental fact that there is no clear boundary between *choreia*— song and dance—and nonsong and nondance, and between the gods and mortals who performed the dances, as we shall now see in investigating divine prototypes of dance.

43

Two

Origins and Divine Prototypes: Dance as an Ordering Force

In the groups of Nymphs and Charites, in the bands of Kouretes,
and even in the case of the dance-loving satyrs, divine archetype
and human reality are often virtually inseparable, except that what
for man is the short-lived blossom of youth attains permanence in
the mythical-divine archetype.
—Walter Burkert, *Greek Religion*, 103

Demiurge and Legislator: The Cosmic Dance and
the Dance of the Body Politic

As we turn from the context and nature of dance and ritual play to look at how the Greeks perceived their origins, it is noteworthy that explanations of the function and significance of rituals and festivals in general are rare in classical sources. Possibly it was felt that since the meanings were so varied for the different groups participating in them, it was undesirable to specify any one interpretation. The most common rationale offered for festivity was that it provided relief from daily labor, a holiday. It was also a commonplace that the anthropomorphic Greek divinities and certain societies of gods regularly engaged in festivity and that human festivity was modeled on divine prototypes. This belief, which has a special religious meaning for choral ritual, with its emphasis on *mimēsis*, is conveyed by archetypes of dance and festivity in poetry. Plato mirrors and elaborates on these prototypes in the *Laws*. He provides two explanations for the origins of dance. In the first, which is developed in this chapter, dance is viewed as a gift of Apollo and the Muses, and secondarily of Dionysus in a restricted sense. According to the first view, dance conduces to order in the soul and the body politic. The second explanation, taken up in chapter 3, focuses on the Dionysiac origins of manic dance resulting from the madness induced in Dionysus by Hera. Outwardly the second explanation, which sees dance as a disruptive force, would seem to be opposing and contradictory to the first. But whereas the character and immediate effects of orderly and disorderly dancing are different, the end result of both is similar. Although it was Plato who articulated these myths of origin, the philosopher makes clear that they are drawn on beliefs current in his day. Indeed similar explanations of the origin and meaning of festivity in general can be recovered from the sources in the archaic period, including the *Homeric Hymn to Apollo*, which forms the nucleus of this chapter.

In Plato's *Timaeus*, as in several other passages of Greek literature beginning with the classical period, the planets and other heavenly bodies are said to revolve around a common center in a cosmic dance.[1] Plato's account of how the divine craftsman was able to coax order from chaos and so choreograph the primitive stuff constituting the universe is complex and remains cryptic in certain respects. But as a recent interpretation of a crucial passage in the *Timaeus* has shown, a rich analogy exists between the demiurge who sets in order the heavenly bodies and the legislator in the *Laws* who regulates the body politic through music and dance. Analysis of the means by which each director brings things under control provides mutually illuminating insights consistent with Greek beliefs in the process of bringing *kosmos* to something disorderly.[2]

Plato maintained that the ordering of the world, like the organization of the political sphere, depended not on force but on persuasion.[3] In its chaotic, unformed state the universe consisted of unequal forces randomly jerking about in a state of disequilibrium. To explain how order was teased from this primitive, undisciplined mass without resorting to violent constraints, Plato compares the process of separating out the primitive stuff making up the universe to the action of a sieve winnowing grain. When the grain is shaken and sifted the heavy particles go one way, while the light granules are carried in another direction and settle there. In the same way the shaking and tossing of the primitive universe separated what is unalike in the primitive stuff from what is similar. From this action the elements of the universe were divided into separate regions before its ordering ever occurred. In other words, Plato suggests that there is already a predisposition within primitive disorder to bring forth a sense of order. When the marshaling process begins, it relies on being able to persuade an existing embryonic order to emerge from chaos.

The orchestration of the primeval universe through persuasion is remarkably similar to the formation of a balanced and orderly soul through rhythm and harmony in two related passages in Plato's *Laws* on kinetic disorders in animate beings. In the first of these passages all young animals are said to be chaotic by nature.[4] Unable to keep their voices or bodies still, they leap about aimlessly and wail involuntarily. The human child alone can attain order from this chaotic state because it is the nature of humankind (*anthrōpou physis*) to develop a sense of order in body and voice. Human beings have the ability to distinguish—much like the winnowing fan in Plato's comparison in the *Timaeus*—rhythm and harmony from kinetic and harmonic commotion. The habit of acting in accord with rhythm and harmony, moreover, can be trained by persuasion rather than by force because a sense of pleasure accompanies the musical predisposition. As in the primitive universe, a propensity toward order already exists within the disorderly soul. Thus when the process of education begins, music, pleasure, and reason conspire to bring about order and balance within the soul. Although the soul continues throughout life to be composed of conflicting strains of passion and of reason, when properly performed song and dance can maintain a harmony between the constituent parts. Orderly dancing in particular displays the ability to harmonize the opposing strains. The intrinsic order in dance and music explains in part why in Plato's educational scheme rhythm and harmony, the two elements of *choreia*, assume, along with philosophical pursuit of virtue, such a central role in the formation of character.

In a second, related passage on the human propensity to perceive rhythm and harmony and the educational function of these elements, the Athenian, representing Plato's general view, accounts for the divine origin of *choreia* and the pleasure that conduces to musical training.

> In the course of a lifetime the effects of education wear off and in many respects disappear completely. The gods, however, took pity on the mortal race born to suffering and gave it periodic religious festivals as relief from their labors. They gave us the Muses and Apollo their leader and Dionysus as companions in the feast. And they granted as well the refreshment produced by these festivals with the help of the gods in order that by associating with them we might be set right.[5]

The tale of the divine origins of education prompts the Athenian to consider whether the theory about the natural and unique human ability to perceive rhythm and harmony (which he says is widespread in his day) is true or not. He then formulates the theory just summarized, characterizing all young beings as disorderly but singling out the uniquely human ability to perceive order and disorder in rhythm and movement. Reverting to the thread of the divine narrative he says: "As we said, the gods were given to us as partners in the dance (*synchoreutai*) and have granted us the pleasurable perception (*aisthēsin meth' hēdonēs*) of rhythm and harmony. Thanks to this perception they animate us and lead us in the dance as they join us one to another in songs and dances; and because of the charm inherent in the activity they invented the word 'chorus.'"[6] At this point the Athenian concludes that education (paideia) through music and dance (*choreia*) has a divine origin in Apollo and the Muses. But whereas his interest lies in accounting for the divine origins of dance, music, and festivity in general, the widespread theory seems to follow the reasoning espoused by other philosophers who were interested in explaining the natural (as opposed to mythological) causes and origins of various phenomena. The theory appears, for example, substantially the same in Aristotle's *Politics,* and has antecedents in poetry.[7] The Athenian seems to take the natural explanation and weave it into his own mythological account. He grafts onto the natural sensibility to rhythm and harmony the element of pleasure inherent in the dance. This delight, he says, is not natural but divine in origin. The gods who are given to mortals as partners in the dance (*synchoreutai*) not only made them sensitive to music and dance but gave them the ability to enjoy their artistic sensibilities. This god-given delight is the crux of the argument. Just as the propensity to order in the embryonic universe makes it possible for the demiurge to set in motion the heavenly bodies, so pleasure in musical activity simplifies the legislator's task of social orchestration through *choreia* leading to the formation of desirable character in the body politic. This ethical training leads in turn to social harmony and stability.

Plato's linking of the divine origins of *choreia* as an ordering force in society to the spontaneous attachment of human beings to rhythm and harmony fits into a larger pattern of Greek thought. In a fragment of Pindar it is said that when Zeus once asked the gods if anything was missing, they demanded gods who would put in order all affairs by words and by the musical arts.[8] Indeed, the belief in *choreia* as a means for persuading order out of chaos led dance to become a metaphor of peace, stability, and social harmony throughout classical and Christian antiquity.

Divine Prototypes of Dance: An Overview

As we examine modern theoretical models for analyzing dance we can also reconstruct from the ancient evidence the archetypes on which the Greeks themselves based their dances. Despite the random and fragmentary nature of the literary evidence for dance outside the *Laws*, a consistent portrayal of prototypes of human festivity in the dances of the Olympians and various societies of quasi-divine beings emerges from Greek poetry of the archaic and classical period. Virtually all of the Olympian gods are portrayed dancing in literature, even Zeus. A fragment of the *Titanomachy*, a lost poem of the Epic Cycle, asserts that Zeus, "the father of gods and men," danced in the middle of his choir.[9] It seemed natural to extend the paternal role of Zeus contained in his epithet to the office of *chorēgos* presiding over his Olympian choristers. The existence of choral dances of the Olympians and other societies of gods assured that communal harmony and stability reigned before mortal communities ever came into being. The idea of a divine precedent for musical activity in human society is thus a mythological analogue to the philosophical belief in a preexisting, embryonic order in the cosmos and in the microcosm of the human soul.

Choral dance and related forms of festivity typify the blessed existence of various marginal societies to which heroes and other privileged mortals are occasionally privy. When Theseus dives into the sea and visits the house of Amphitrite and Poseidon he finds the Nereids engaged in choral dancing. Bacchylides has us glimpse through the hero's awe-struck eyes the splendid activity of the sea-nymphs: "From their shining limbs a flame like fire glowed and about their locks their headbands woven with gold spun while in their hearts they took pleasure in the dance on their supple feet."[10] The nymphs in the *Hymn to Aphrodite* are said to be neither precisely like gods nor like mortals but to exist somewhere betwixt and between. They live a very long time and dine on ambrosial food, and dance in the beautiful dancing place (*choros*) with the immortals.[11] The Hyperboreans, as described by Pindar, closely resemble the golden race of men in Hesiod's *Works and Days*. When Perseus tours their realm at the ends of the world he finds that their customs consist of sacrificing hecatombs of asses to Apollo, feasting, and dancing: "Everywhere are dances of young women, and the sounds of the lyre and of the *aulos* swirl about in circles; and binding their hair with bay-leaves of gold they revel contentedly. Illness and baneful old age do not mingle with this blessed race. Free from toil and war they dwell apart from the archly just wrath of Nemesis."[12] During Odysseus's sojourn to the otherworldly land of the Phaeaceans, a people renowned for their seafaring, running, dancing, and festivity in general, the hero is treated to entertainment by the famed dancers, the Betarmones.[13] In all of these groups of blessed people, the Nereids and nymphs, the Hyperboreans and the Phaeaceans, dance is a source of delight as well as a symbol of the social order and harmony that mortals can urge upon their own

communities by emulating dance and other festive activities poet-
ically conjured up in paradigms of privileged existence.

Dance has a primordial existence and plays an ordering role in
the consolidation of the Olympian dynasty. The fragment from the
Titanomachy mentioned earlier suggests that when Zeus celebrated
his victory over the Titans with choral dancing, his central position
as *chorēgos* symbolized control and authority. The myth that specifically accounts for the origins of human dancing concerns the birth
of Zeus, which heralded a new hierarchy among the gods. Upon
giving birth to Zeus, Rhea, in order to protect her infant from the
devouring jaws of Cronos, substituted a stone in swaddling cloths.
She hid Zeus in a cave on Crete where the Couretes (who are sometimes interchanged in the ancient sources with the Corybantes)
danced in armor around the infant.[14] Lucian retells the story most
fully in the Hellenistic treatise *On the Dance*. In the beginning, he
recounts, Rhea, delighted by the art of dancing, ordered the Corybantes and the Couretes on Crete to dance. She benefited greatly
from teaching the Couretes, who danced around Zeus and so protected him from the maw of Cronos. The story appears in a passage
on the origins of dance in which Lucian says that the art is as old as
Eros, one of three primeval forces issuing from Chaos and responsible for the generation of the cosmos in Hesiod's *Theogony*.[15]
Dance, he avers, is primordial, and as proof he offers the choral
dance (*choreia*) of the stars and planets, which coexist in rhythmic
agreement and harmony. This celestial concord is linked to the advent of peaceful coexistence in the first communities. Although the
mythical explanation for the origin of human dancing appears explicitly in late sources, the belief in the seminal role of Rhea and of
the Corybantes and Couretes in introducing human dancing can
already be inferred as early as the classical period.[16]

In Hesiod the "dance-loving" Couretes, like their siblings the
nymphs and satyrs,[17] were followers of gods, and hence models of
human worshippers. Their activities in general prefigured human
social concerns and organization. They were the first to dance collectively, to practice animal husbandry and beekeeping, and to
conduct other social and cultic activities that paved the way for
communal life. In their cultic embodiment the Couretes were cele-

brated as upholders of the civilizing institutions that made flourish the fields, flocks, and citizens. By protecting Zeus at his birth with dancing the Couretes put an end to the cycle of violent succession of fathers by sons. The stability in the divine community in turn fostered balance among human groups. In the mythological as in the philosophical tradition dance became a metaphor for social as well as cosmic order.

Prototype and Paradigm in the Homeric Hymn to Apollo

As we investigate in greater detail divine prototypes in poetry and how they were played out in human festival celebrations, we may begin by visiting, with Apollo, a festival of Zeus on Olympus and a festival in Apollo's honor on sea-girt Delos. As Callimachus recalls in his *Hymn* to the island, the birthplace of Apollo and Artemis formed the central point—the *chorēgos*, so to speak—around which the other islands in the Cyclades were positioned, as if in a chorus.[18] It was to Delos that communities from near and far sent choruses of their best young singers and dancers to display to Apollo and his twin *kourotrophos* beauty and energy in an ensemble. On Delos, as in many parts of the Greek world, choral hymns and dance were the ideal medium to celebrate divine birth and epiphany and became, by cultural consent, the organ through which to encourage and enjoy contests in the pursuit of child-rearing and spiritual renewal.

At Delos the principal religious, cultural, and even dramatic dimensions of the institution known as the Greek chorus intersect. A pair of descriptions of festivity in the *Homeric Hymn to Apollo* allow us to examine a segment of choral performance conjectured to have been performed at 522 (even if the *Hymn* is of earlier and unitary composition) at a moment when the tragic chorus is beginning to be differentiated from the actor in Attica.[19] They describe a festival of Zeus on Olympus and a festival for Apollo on Delos—one divine and eternal, the other mortal and anchored to a time and a place. The two festival descriptions form a sequence, the first presenting, among other things, the crisis of mortal exclusion from divine festivity, the second offering a solution to that crisis in choral performance: the *Hymn to Apollo* contains a sort of myth of origin for *choreia* and festivity in general echoed in Plato's *Laws*.

Like other hexameter hymns attributed in antiquity to Homer, Apollo's sixth-century *Hymn* invokes and praises the divinity, as it celebrates key events in his life, including a series of epiphanies beginning with Apollo's birth on Delos and continuing with the young god's appearance at an earthly festival in his honor, his entry into Olympus, and finally his arrival at Delphi, the site of his main cult. Although the exact date and circumstances of composition of the *Hymn to Apollo* are unclear, it is aetiological in tone and may have been inspired by a festival on Delos in the last quarter of the sixth century in which choral and rhapsodic contests took place. But the *Hymn* is not to be read as a sacred text. Like the festival setting for which it was composed, it is playful and exuberant in tone and contains light-hearted elements that from our point of view are inconsistent with the piety we might expect in a hymn of praise. A translator of the *Homeric Hymns* has written in his introduction, "We must be careful not to project our own ideas of religious propriety onto those of the ancient Greeks, whose gods laughed and danced, whereas ours do not."[20]

Homēguris *on Olympus*   The description of Olympian festivity in the *Hymn to Apollo* is the most extensive prototype of choral performance we possess.[21] The passage, which is quoted here in full, celebrates the transition of the youthful god with his stringed lyre from the earthly realm of Pytho (Delphi) to Olympus, where the gods are enjoying a festive gathering (*homēguris*).

> The radiant son of Leto goes to rocky Pytho playing his hollow lyre and wearing fragrant garments befitting a god. Plucked by a golden plectrum, his lyre (*phorminx*) sends forth a sharp sound provoking desire. From there he goes swift as thought to Olympus to the house of Zeus to join the gathering (*homēguris*) with the other gods. All of a sudden the immortals turn their attention to the lyre (*kithara*) and song. The Muses all take up the strain from one another with beautiful voice as they sing hymns about the divine gifts enjoyed by the gods and the suffering of mortals, such as they endure living under the immortal gods witless and without resource, unable to find a charm against death

or a defense against old age. Meanwhile, the Charites with their well-plaited hair, and the blissful Horai, along with Harmonia, Hebe, and Zeus's daughter Aphrodite dance, holding each other's hands at the wrist. Among them sings and dances one who is neither short nor shameful, but truly tall to look at and admirable in form, Artemis of the scattering arrows and twin of Apollo. And in their midst Ares and keen-sighted Hermes dance playfully. But it is Phoebus Apollo who plucks the lyre, stepping high and beautifully, while around him a radiance emanates from the gleaming of his feet and his well-spun glistening chiton. Leto with golden hair and Zeus the Counselor take great pleasure in their hearts as they see their child dancing among the immortal gods.[22]

The passage indicates how a divine musical performance was organized and highlights various qualities inherent in the dance that contribute to the basic order and pleasure of the activity. The entire proceedings involve as many as twenty-one dancers and singers, following Hesiod's enumeration of nine Muses, three Charites (Graces), and three Horai (Hours).[23] The nine singing Muses are balanced by the nine dancing divinities in Artemis's choir. It is unlikely that the poet thinks of all participants performing together at all times. Rather we are to imagine first a procession, led by the musician, with the Muses and Artemis and her choir in train. Then comes a sequence of events beginning with songs by the Muses divided into two groups. Next follows the choral dance. The dances of Ares and Hermes are somehow coordinate with the group dance, either as interludes or as capricious challenges to the symmetry and order implied by the ring dance; judging from parallel passages in Homer that mention pairs of tumblers (*kubistētēre*), their movements are acrobatic.[24] Finally the troupe, with Apollo in the lead, present themselves to Leto and Zeus, their divine audience, for their approval.

The chief ordering force of the performance is Apollo, the musician. The sudden appearance of the exuberant young god makes the entire troupe of Olympians, even Ares, immediately fall into place: among the gods as well exists a predisposition to orderly movement. The gods' instinctive response to rhythm and harmony (which Plato says distinguishes human children from the young of other creatures) is underlined by the use of the verb *paizō* for the movement of the male deities, Apollo, Hermes, and Ares. With the dual meanings "to dance" and "to play," it emphasizes the innocent, refreshing, and playful nature of the activity that easily persuades others to join in.

The Muses are the first to heed the god's call. They sing antiphonal hymns about the privileges of immortals and the sufferings of mortals. The other deities react by choral dancing: the Charites and Horai join hands with Harmonia (Harmony), Hebe (Youth), and Aphrodite in a ring dance, with Artemis as leader of their chorus. Ares and Hermes complement the formal choral dance with informal solos or duos. Apollo, who takes charge of the whole affair, performs a kind of high-stepping dance, a strutting movement which is perhaps captured in a black-figure olpe (Fig. 7).[25] The divine choral performance has an audience in Zeus and Leto, who look on with parental pride at their offspring taking charge in ways pleasing to them. The organization of the performers and spectators is clearly delineated, and among the participants there is a division of labor: Apollo and the Muses, Artemis and her choir, Hermes and Ares.

The lyre, Apollo's chief attribute along with the bow, as much as the god's rhythmic movement, compels the gods to respond. Song and dance emanate from the immortal instrument, which provides not only the melody but the rhythmic impulse. It too is an ordering force. Pindar calls the *phorminx* a joint possession of Apollo and the Muses. When its strings begin to vibrate, the choral leader, the singers, and the dance-step (*basis*) all "listen."[26] So the Olympian and lesser gods fall into place behind Apollo's lyre. Remarkably, the verb for "listening" (*peithomai*) in the Pindaric parallel means literally "to be persuaded." As in the Platonic models for the ordering of the universe and the soul, persuasion, not force, is required to set in motion the choreographic process. In the present passage the irresistible sound of Apollo's lyre stirs up the singing of the Muses and animates the choral dancing and singing of the groups of Artemis and her band. Greek choral performances were woven from the strands of music, song, and dance; but as on Olympus the arrangement is not indiscriminate: there is an implied hierarchy, with instrumental music preeminent, then singing, then dancing.

Figure 7. A musician strutting like Apollo, *hypsi bibas*, with stringed instrument.

The lyre is a quasi-divine being with its own myth of origin. The story of the invention and manufacture of the tortoise-shell lyre is told in the *Hymn to Hermes*, in which the mischievous god, still an infant, engages in his first deceitful act when he finds a tortoise on the threshold of the cave where he was born. Immediately he sees a use for his toy (*athurma*) which he duplicitously addresses, "Greetings, companion of the feast, pleasing in nature, beating out the rhythm in the dance."[27] Hermes slays the unwitting tortoise, boils and hollows out its shell, attaches strings, and eventually presents the resulting lyre to Apollo, telling him to bring it from now on to the feast, the dance, and the revel.[28] The invocation to the tortoise, which Hermes proleptically calls "companion in the dance" and a "plaything" (*athurma*) accentuates the importance of the lyre in providing the rhythmic and harmonic impulse in musical performances. Relying on his precocious wit Hermes puns on the meanings of *athurma*, which can signify either a toy or a song; the related verb *athurō* is used in Plato's *Laws* to mean "dance."[29] The ironic forms of address to the tortoise are reminders of the pleasing and playful nature of rhythm and harmony that draws the god to master and transmit them at an early age.

In Greek theogonic myth the Muses represent a primordial ordering power. In Hesiod's *Theogony* the genealogical account of the gods does not begin with an account of the generation of the gods from Chaos, but, in accordance with conventional hymn structure, with the Muses, the nine daughters born to Mnemosyne and Zeus. The lengthy invocation to the Muses celebrates them as the divine source of all poetic and musical inspiration. Whereas the Muses' activity in the *Hymn to Apollo* seems to be restricted to singing, in Hesiod's description they are portrayed as both singers and dancers. Dance is their characteristic mode of locomotion in their native haunts. On Mt. Helicon where they have their homes they dance around the spring and altar of Zeus, and at the highest point they establish their dancing grounds.[30] On the highest peak of snowy Mt. Olympus too they have their dancing places.[31] When they shuttle from their mountainous haunts to their father in heavenly Olympus they sing, and a lovely sound rises up beneath their delicate pattering feet.[32]

Let us begin our song with the Heliconian Muses,
Who dwell on the great and sacred mount of Helicon,
And dance with delicate feet around
The purple fountain and around the altar of mighty Zeus;
And when they have washed their soft skin in Permessus
Or in the Horse's Spring or in Olmeius they perform
On Helicon's sacred summit choral dances,
Both lovely and delightful, with swift motions of their feet.[33]

The Muses attach themselves to Apollo, who is their chorus leader (*chorēgos*). The idea of a male god directing a female chorus is very old. An early prototype for a male divinity leading files of dancers appears in a Mycenaean ring found in the Athenian agora.[34] But Apollo also derives inspiration from the Muses and is in a sense subordinate to them. In the *Homeric Hymn to Hermes* Apollo says, "I too am a follower (*opēdos*) of the Olympian Muses, who cherish the dance and the bright path of singing, the bloom of song and dance (*molpē*), and the lovely resonance of *auloi*."[35] The prominent position of the Muses in the *Theogony* suggests their primacy as animators and arrangers of the cosmic order. They are the source of all creative inspiration for recreating the divine and heroic past through songs and dances. The theme of their songs in Apollo's *Hymn*—the privilege of the gods and sufferings of mortals—is a reminder of both the gulf between gods and mortals and the poetic means for bridging the gap: music and dance are ways of remembering the gods, but also of forgetting human cares.

Still another ordering force in the musical performance is Artemis, who serves as leader of the ring dance. Artemis is the twin of Apollo, and Hesiod mentions their birth and common attribute, the bow, in the catalogue of Zeus's wives and offspring.[36] Hunting, the goddess's characteristic activity, is closely coordinate with dancing. In the *Homeric Hymn to Artemis*, upon returning from the hunt the goddess unstrings her bow and goes to Apollo's house at Delphi and there orders the dances of the Muses and Charites. "But when Artemis who rains arrows, the goddess who is on the lookout for wild beasts, has taken her pleasure [in the hunt] and delighted her mind, she unloosens her quiver and comes to the great house of her beloved brother Phoebus Apollo, to the rich district of

Delphi to order the lovely choral dancing of the Muses and Charites."[37] In Apollo's *Hymn* the criteria for leading the choral dance are physical beauty and stature. The leader must not be ugly but rather beautiful and shapely, not short but tall and conspicuous so that she can be easily distinguished from the other members of the chorus.

The Charites and goddesses named along with Artemis in Apollo's *Hymn* define ideal qualities inherent in the choral dances of young women: grace (*charis*), beauty and erotic charm (Aphrodite), youthfulness (Hebe), and rhythmic harmony (Harmonia)—qualities that bring order and pleasure to the dance and its audience. The pleasing and ordering forces of rhythm and harmony converge in the Greek word *kosmos*, which means on the one hand "order," and "ornament" or "decoration," on the other. In the first sense *kosmos* can imply the ordering of tunes and of dance steps. The word for harmony (*harmonia*) is derived from the root of the verb *harmozō*, to "fit" or "join together." It is used to describe the activity of the carpenter when he binds together wood, metal, and other material objects to make, for instance, a lyre. The technical ability of the joiner is a necessary talent of those who make songs and dances by uniting voices, joining bodies, and linking steps. The verbal root for fitting together (*ar-*) appears in the Delian passage in the verb *sunarariskō* used to describe the way the Deliades (Delian Maidens) carefully craft their song.[38] But Harmonia also implies a corporeal unity. Typically, as in the *Hymn* the dancers form a ring by holding each other's hands at the wrist, as they place their feet on the earth in rhythmically marked steps: the verb *harmozō* is used of joining feet to the earth.[39] The corporate body so formed by hands conjoined reproduces on a microcosmic scale the *harmonia* that Pythagoras in his mathematical studies found in the majestic movements of the cosmos, and outwardly reflects the *harmonia* that Plato in the *Phaedo* believed reigned in the well-regulated soul.[40]

In the second sense *kosmos* refers to aesthetically pleasing objects, often worn by women and produced through technical skills such as dyeing and weaving. The cosmetic and ornamental aspects of choral performance suggested by coordinated steps and by the use of costume, wreaths, and other accoutrements of the dance are personified by other members of Artemis's choir. There are two groups of dancers in the choir led by Artemis, the fair-haired Charites, and the joy-giving Horai. Both groups are examples of female societies of gods who gravitate toward a major fertility divinity such as Artemis or Aphrodite. As members of the divine chorus they are models to human worshippers. The epithets of the Charites and Horai, respectively "fair-haired" and "joy-giving," underline the cosmetic and pleasurable components of dance. They are concerned with making a pleasing arrangement through singing, dancing, and personal adornment. In the *Cypria* the Charites are attendants of Aphrodite.[41] The goddess and her attendants weave crowns of flowers which they wear during choral performances; this salient feature earns the nymphs, Charites, and Aphrodite the epithet "with radiant head-dress" (*liparokrēdemnoi*).[42] Along with the Horai the Charites make for the goddess colorful garments dyed in spring flowers. The dyeing process also imparts a perfumed scent to her attire, much like the fragrant garments of Apollo. Personal adornment is a concomitant and prelude to the dance. When Athena wants to beautify Penelope so that she will appear irresistible like a goddess, she cleanses her with ambrosia, "such as Aphrodite uses when she joins the lovely dance of the Charites."[43]

The Charites, the name for the group of three goddesses, is the plural of *charis*, meaning favor, charm, or outward grace. Hesiod gives their names as Thaleia (Festivity), Aglaia (Splendor), and Euphrosyne (Mirth) in a catalogue of children born to Eurynome, the third wife of Zeus.[44] Their epithet is "fair-cheeked." Because they share many concerns in common with the Muses, especially music and dance, they are closely associated with them and are said to have their homes near the Muses.[45] Indeed the Muses and Charites have overlapping names: one of the Muses is Thalia. Pindar's ode to the Charites, which invokes the goddesses by the names given in Hesiod, celebrates their indispensable role in promoting divine and mortal festivity through song and dance. "Not even the gods regulate dances and feasts without the sacred Charites. For they are dispensers of all works in heaven, and situate their thrones by Pythian

Apollo with the golden bow."[46] The Horai in the *Theogony* are also three in number.[47] They are the daughters of Zeus and his second wife, Themis (Customary Law), and like their mother they personify civic order: Eunomia (Proper Apportionment), Dike (Justice), and Eirene (Peace). They protect the agricultural efforts of humankind. They too have a cosmetic function, as their epithets— *kallikomoi* ("with beautiful hair") and *polyanthemoi* ("with many flowers," i.e., woven into the hair as a fillet)—recall.[48]

Like the other gods mentioned in Apollo's hymn, the Charites and Horai were not merely poetic fabrications but were worshipped in cult for their promotion of natural growth and reproduction. The Athenians originally venerated two Horai, Thallo (Flowering) and Karpo (Crop). Their names stress their association with agricultural festivals, and their protection of all things young, including the adolescent citizenry. The meaning of the Charites, however, goes beyond general fecundity to include the creation of beauty in the technical arts and in human activities like dancing. It is therefore appropriate to express thanks through ritual dancing for the happiness that results from the renewed blessing from the Charites, and the idea of pleasure derived from this essential reciprocity is contained in the word *charis*. Although they were worshipped in Attica, the Peloponnese, and in Asia Minor, their most famous cult was at Minyan Orchomenos in Boeotia, and the Charitesia festival there included musical contests and dancing through the night.[49]

The presence of Youth (Hebe) in the passage, like the use of the verb *paizō* for the playful movement of the male gods, accentuates the rejuvenating force of the dance in contrast with old age and death mentioned in the song of the Muses. The activity of dance and constant festivity among such blessed groups is just such an antidote; by practicing the musical arts mortals may enjoy them, but only in temporary and illusory ways. And so there is a tendency to identify the dancer, especially the most youthful ones, with natural growth, as emphasized by the crowns, branches, and flowers carried by dancers in rows in archaic art.[50] In the sixth-century *Hymn to Gaia* we hear of the young girls who "with gladdened hearts in flower-bearing dances skip and play over soft flowers of the field."[51]

The effect of all the ordering and cosmetic forces of the musical performance on the spectators is one of *terpsis* ("joy"), and it is felt at the very core of the divine parents. Zeus and Leto "take great delight in their hearts upon seeing their son dancing." Despite the emphasis in the passage on the instrumental music of Apollo, the participle *eisoroōntes* ("looking on intently") suggests that the parents' pleasure derives principally from the visual impact of the choreographic spectacle.[52] Plato, in the *Laws*, we may recall, spoke of the rejuvenating effects dance had on the older members watching the younger ones dance.[53] The *terp-* root in the verb for taking delight in this passage is related to the Sanskrit *trpnoti*, "to take one's fill." It is used in similar contexts to imply the satisfaction of an appetite for momentary or habitual pleasures such as sleep, and the things associated with merriment, including food, wine, dance, and song, and in particular the lyre whose sharp sound provokes desire. At the end of the first book of the *Iliad* after the quarrel on Olympus the gods feast all day long, "nor did the breast of any one of them go wanting for a fair share of the feast, nor of the exquisite *phorminx* of Apollo, nor of the Muses who sing antiphonally with beautiful voice."[54] The pleasure (*terpsis*) furnished by the Muses and earthly musicians gives rise to names and epithets such as Terpiades for the father of one of the bards in the *Odyssey* and Terpander ("Giving Pleasure to Man"), a quasi-historical Spartan poet of the seventh century.[55] Indeed, it is in the active sense of "giving pleasure" that the *terp-* root is combined with the word for dance, *choros*, to form the name of the Muse of the dance, Terpsichore. She already is designated as one of the nine Muses in Hesiod's *Theogony*, which, as we have seen, opens with a passage describing how the Muses give delight in their dances.[56] The complementary meanings of giving and taking pleasure in the dance are echoed in Plato and again demonstrate that dance is not simply a mutually satisfying activity for the performer and spectator alike; it is virtually a craving that needs to be satisfied throughout one's life either by participation or by viewing. It is upon this assumption that the literary topos of a divinity taking delight in his own festival dances is grounded.

Panēgyris *on Delos*   In his *Hymn* we also hear of Apollo visiting his rites on Delos in a companion description of festivity occurring some twenty lines earlier in the poem. This is a celebration of the god by mortals, but the pleasure taken in the spectacle is shared by god and worshipper alike. In this short passage the *terp-* root occurs no less than four times.

> But it is in Delos, Phoebus, that you most delight (*epiterpeai*) in your heart. There the Ionians with trailing chitons gather with their children and noble wives. Whenever they stage a contest they take pleasure (*terpousin*) in remembering you through boxing, dancing, and singing. Whoever might chance upon the scene when the Ionians are gathered would say that they will be immortal and ageless forever. For he would see the grace of them all, and would take joy (*terpsaito*) in his heart looking upon the men and the women with their beautiful waistbands, swift ships, and considerable possessions. In addition there is a great wonder whose glory will never fade: the Deliades, the servants of the Far-Shooter. When they have praised first Apollo with a hymn, then Leto and then Artemis of the shedding arrows, they sing a hymn of praise for the men and women of old, and they enchant the tribes of men. They know how to imitate the voices and gestures of all men. A spectator would say that he himself were singing, so skillful is their beautiful song. But come, may Apollo, and Artemis with him, be gracious, and farewell to all of you maidens. And afterward remember me, whenever one of the earthly mortals suffering hardship might come as a foreigner and ask, "O maidens, which man in your opinion is the sweetest of the poets to come here, and in whom do you take the greatest pleasure (*terpesthe*)?" All of you reply on my behalf, "A blind man, he lives in rocky Chios where forever after the poets are best."[57]

The Delian description opens with a claim concerning Apollo's preference for Delos, where the Ionians, along with their wives and children, gather to commemorate the god with contests in boxing, dancing, and singing. The narrator remarks that an observer would voice pleasure upon witnessing the spiritual transformation enjoyed by the Ionians when they assemble with their possessions.

The description moves from the general gathering to the hand-picked choral band of Deliades, the renowned followers of Apollo. They praise first Apollo in a hymn, then Leto and Artemis. Their divine hymn gives way to a hymn about heroes and heroines. As a kind of finale they imitate voices and reproduce rhythms with hand-clappers (*krotala*).[58] A singer bids farewell to the Deliades, but before leaving he instructs them what to say whenever a wandering stranger comes and asks who the sweetest singer is. He in turn promises to broadcast the fame of the Deliades in his travels. A lebes gamikos, a wedding vessel, found on Delos shows such a group of young girls dancing to the accompaniment of a male musician (Fig. 8).[59]

Just as the chief function of the hymn is to remember the god, so the competitive events of boxing, dancing, and singing are means of commemorating Apollo at his festival. The human pleasure taken in these tokens of adoration is also acknowledged. The act of remembering Apollo is a source of mutual joy to the divinity as well as to the Ionian participants and the imaginary mortal witness. The name for the type of festival in this passage, a *panēgyris*, literally means a "coming together of all," and was used to describe any public assembly, especially a festive one in honor of a nonlocal deity, such as Apollo. It was a festival that transcended the boundaries of local cult beliefs, as it acknowledged ties of common worship. The festival at Delos drew on participants from the surrounding islands, and from both shores of the Aegean, especially the areas around Athens and the fringes of Asia Minor near Miletus. All attending, except for a small minority of local inhabitants from Delos itself, had to undergo a voyage by sea lasting several hours. This mode of transportation on the sometimes rough and always unpredictable Aegean required seaworthy vessels, referred to as the "swift" ships that transported the Ionians along with many material possessions, including dedications to Apollo, splendid textiles for the ceremonial robes, and wares for trade. The festival held a commercial as well as a spiritual reward for the participants. In addition to providing ships, religious paraphernalia, and commodities, those sponsoring a trip would have been required to furnish food and other supplies for men, women, and children. The length of

Figure 8. Young girls (the Deliades or Muses?) dancing, accompanied by male musician (Apollo?) (*second from left*).

the gathering on Delos is not specified, although a festival requiring such elaborate preparations was not over in a day.

For corroboration of certain details sketched out in the hymn we are fortunate to have a passage in Thucydides on the ritual purification of Delos in 417 and the revival in 426/5 of the ancient Ionian festival known as the Delia.[60] The Athenians' establishment of this new festival prompted Thucydides to deduce from the *Hymn to Apollo* the existence of a previous festival on Delos, and indeed choral hymns may have been celebrated on the island as early as the eighth century.[61] The passage demonstrates the continuity, with modifications, of festivals involving choral and other productions at holy places:

> In ancient times as well there had been a great gathering on Delos of the Ionians and the neighboring islanders; they would attend the festival with their wives and children, just as the Ionians now attend the Ephesian festival. Athletic and musical contests were held there, and various cities mounted choral dances. Homer, above all, makes clear that this was so, in the following verses, which are from his hymn to Apollo. [Thucydides then quotes *Hymn to Apollo* 146–50.] And in the following verses, which are from the same hymn, Homer makes plain that there was an *agōn* in music to which people came to compete. After celebrating the chorus of Delian women, he ended his praise with these verses, in which he actually mentioned himself. [He quotes *Hymn to Apollo* 165–72.] Such is Homer's testimony that in ancient times also there was a great gathering and festival on Delos. At a later time the islanders and the Athenians continued to send choruses and sacrifices; but the contests and the majority of the rites were abandoned, probably as a result

of the island's misfortunes, until now, when the Athenians revived the games. To them they added horse races, which had not been held before.[62]

From Thucydides' account it is clear that the earlier pan-Ionian festival was an event of enormous magnitude, drawing thousands of islanders and mainlanders. The *archon basileus* at Athens appointed *chorēgoi* for the choruses and a leader of the pilgrimage (*architheōros*) who commanded the thirty-oared ship that transported the young men.[63] No other *panēgyris* at the time could come close to rivaling the Delian festival in splendor and intensity. Singing and dancing played a central role in allowing the participants to worship their god while calling attention to their god-given talents.

Paradigm and Prototype: Delian and Olympian Festivity   The description of the Ionian festival for Apollo on Delos in his *Hymn* has been called a paradigm of all such festivals.[64] If the description of the Delian festival is paradigmatic, the description of Zeus's *homēguris* on Olympus is a prototype of all choral performance; taken together with the Delian description, which interacts with it on several planes—linguistic, thematic, and structural—the composite portrait reveals a number of combinations of choral performance, as well as the principal religious and cultural concerns underlying choruses in the archaic period.[65] In analyzing the performance dynamics encoded in the two festival descriptions, it is useful to point out that the passages form a kind of ring framed by the appearance of the divine musician and the departure of the mortal singer.

Within each description there is a progression from generalized festivity to musical, and specifically choral, performance. The progression from the general to the specific can be coordinated with the differentiation of elements constituting the musical celebration. In the Olympian festival, Apollo, representing the male singer and instrumentalist, is distinguished from the female chorus of singers, the Muses. They are at once separate and dependent on the musician for composition and instrumental accompaniment.

At one remove from Apollo and the Muses is the chorus with its own internal leader, Artemis. As *chorēgos*, Apollo's twin exercises immediate authority over the *choreutai* made up of Aphrodite and the societies of gods. The chorus as a whole is differentiated by its members' collective activity of dancing.[66] They are positioned in the classic ring dance, for which hexameter poetry and archaic art each have their own formulas to express the essential gesture of solidarity in the dance by linking hands at the wrist, *cheir epi karpōi*. The prominence of Artemis as the focus of choral activity is consistent with what we know of the Deliades' ritual function of hymning, in addition to Apollo, Artemis, as mentioned in the Delian description, and alluded to, for example, in Euripides' *Hecuba*.[67]

The Delian festival consists of a throng of human spectators whose very act of gathering is related linguistically to the assembling of choruses who are ideal representatives of the larger, undifferentiated group.[68] The competing choral groups become further differentiated in the agonistic context in which they perform. The act of gathering and the collective but competitive activities that ensue lead to an extraordinary outcome: the Ionians become—or so an ideal observer would say—immortal and ageless forever. By assembling, as the Olympians do at Zeus's *homēguris*, and also by segregating themselves in choral groups after the divine model, they become temporarily godlike.

The insistence on the reception of the spectacle by an audience encourages an interpretation of the passages on the level of performance. The Olympian and Delian descriptions focus on the visual act of watching the spectacle by introducing into the text various internal observers: Zeus and Leto in the Olympian passage, Apollo and a hypothetical witness in the Delian passage. Each time the act of seeing is mentioned, it is complemented with a description of the pleasurable effect of the spectacle on the innermost emotions of the observer.[69] The centerpiece of the Delian spectacle, the Deliades, is called a great wonder (*mega thauma*).[70]

The pleasurable aesthetic experience attributed to the divine and ideal observers draws heightened attention to the organization and hierarchy of performers. The differentiation of singer-composer and choral band at the level of spectacle is underlined in the Olympian description by Apollo's musical instrument, his acrobatic gait, his splendid garments. A similar differentiation obtains for *chorēgos* and chorus members in Artemis's choir. As *chorēgos* Artemis is distinguished by physical criteria. She is taller than the chorus members by a head, and striking in beauty. The special function of the one who is so distinguished as *chorēgos* is expressed in a parallel passage in the *Odyssey* where Nausicaa's preeminence while at play with her servants is compared in a simile to Artemis's greater stature and beauty among her nymphs at the chase. As leader of the ball game and dancing song (*molpē*) Nausicaa has the privilege of leading off: *archeto molpēs*.[71] The prerogative of the lead female in performance is found in the *Iliad* in the choral laments for Hector led by Andromache and Hecabe, who possess this authority over the female chorus, despite the competing presence of male bards.[72]

The formal, hand-linked dancing of Artemis and her chorus is contrasted with the informal, perhaps solo, dancing of Ares and Hermes, described by the verb *paizō*. Hermes' presence in a choreographic context is perhaps a variation on the theme of the visual delight taken in dancing found in the theme of the abduction of the young girl from the dancing ground of Artemis by the god (analyzed in chapter 7). In *Iliad* 16, where the theme is first attested, when Hermes espies Polymele lovely in the dance, he scrutinizes Artemis's devotee with his eyes. In the *Hymn to Apollo* Hermes' epithet is *euskopos*: keen-sighted.[73]

While the Muses' choir has a certain autonomy (as does Artemis's choir and the soloists), the Muses are also dependent on the instrumental accompaniment of Apollo. The phrase "but it is Phoebus Apollo who plucks the lyre" insists that, despite the independence of the other performers, nothing could stand on its own without the authority and inspiration of Apollo's kithara.[74] In actual choral performance the singer's composition might be accompanied by the *aulos*, as in tragedy.[75]

The emphasis on the visual component of the spectacle also draws attention to the criteria used to discern excellence in an agonistic context at the Delian festival. The pleasure in viewing presupposes a critical judgment concerning composition and performance. Which performance most faithfully conforms to the divine model, and which most successfully makes the human audience feel immortal and ageless? The Ionians, like other groups who organized festival contests, presumably appointed officials to judge those poetic and choral efforts that were the most agreeable to the divinity, as well as to the spectators. The process of judging, like the choral performance itself, takes place at two levels, divine and human; the divine pleasure is shared by and reflected in the glow of the human spectators. This mutual pleasure is expressed in the Delian passage by the word *charis*.[76]

One criterion for judging the excellence of a performance is indicated by the choice of epithet for that hypothetical person who seeks the "sweetest" of singers. That ideal judge is *talapeiros*, "one who has much experience of suffering."[77] Though the quest is specifically to determine the sweetest *singer*, the implicit criterion can be applied to judging performance in general. Ideally, a performance should console and compensate for mortal suffering by providing, through music and dance, a temporary antidote to death and a defense against old age. The process of judging the outcome of the choral *agōn* by discerning which group best charms the divinity—and thereby attaches divine attributes of immortality and agelessness to the human worshippers—marks the happy resolution of the crisis of estrangement between mortal and worshipper that every festival seeks to avert.

Choral Performance as Metaphor of Olympian Worship

When seen in its larger festival context, to what extent is choral performance a reflex of Olympian religion? The hierarchy of Olympus is expressed, among other ways, by the musical metaphor of the youthful Apollo, representing Zeus, as leader and animator of the gods. Yet Apollo's authority is dependent upon the cooperation of choral groups, both singers and dancers; while they represent the voice and body of the god, they have their own internal leaders and thus enjoy autonomy. The Muses mirror and merge with Apollo in performance and yet are differentiated from and independent of him.

This choral metaphor of Olympian worship is played out in choral performance as an act of adoration through the interaction of the composer and chorus, or of the *chorēgos* and chorus members.

Since the chorus is an ideal representation of the members of the community, the dynamic between leader and bands of followers in performance embodies the larger experience of the worshippers, who are fundamentally distinct from Apollo and the other Olympians, and still participate vicariously as followers through their choral delegates.

Yet despite the similarities in the *Hymn to Apollo* between prototype and paradigm noted earlier, a striking difference between the Olympian gathering and its Delian counterpart emerges. Whereas divine and mortal intermingle in the festival to the extent that the participants assume the divine epithets "immortal" and "ageless," mortals are naturally excluded from the Olympian gathering. The gulf between the privileged existence of the Olympians and the sufferings of mortals is emphasized by the twin subjects of the Muses' hymns: the unending gifts enjoyed by the gods and the sufferings of humans. These mortals, unable to find an antidote to death or even old age, are the inverse of the godlike Ionians in the full swing of the festival. This pathetic state of things—the condition of the human race after the Golden Age when gods and mortals no longer danced together at the same festivals—is taken up and transformed by Plato into the origins of paideia in the *Laws* examined earlier. The collusion of mortal and god in festival dancing is expressed by the compound *syn-choreutai*—"fellow chorus members"—attributed to the gods. This expression is symptomatic of the symbiotic relationship of worshipper and divinity in the festival.

That temporary rapprochement, however, is not automatically won. There is a potential crisis in a permanent division between human and divine. This is a concern to gods as well as humans, for the divinity is dependent on the worshipper, represented by the choral band.

The gifts belonging to the gods by birth include activities such as continual dancing and singing. According to religious belief, the gods are dependent on mortals for gifts of another sort—not simply sacrificial offerings, but the accompanying poetic and choral presentations that give body and shape to their existence—that render visible the invisible. Through choral worship the gods are dramatized, brought to life. The human performers fashion and hold up the mirror of performance like a mask before the divinity. God and worshipper are involved in a symbiotic process of creation. Though the human performance is a *mimēsis* of its divine prototype, without it, the divine would in a sense cease to exist. The interdependence of prototype and human manifestation is acted out in every festival performance.

The relationship between divinity and adorants is a metaphor of the evolving relationship between the epic bard and choral performers. The poet's apostrophe to the Deliades implies that, since the maidens excel in mimetic representation, they surpass the dramatic capabilities of the solo singer. They can do everything the singer can do, and more. They can complement vocal performance by amplifying the rhythmic patterns of poetry with the hands (*cheironomia*) and body (*orchēsis*). Their greater dramatic technique allows them to imitate the dialects and the gestures of people from all over Greece, whereas the wandering bard speaks everywhere in his own dialect. The choral performance presents a challenge to the solo rhapsode because it is more artful, brimming with illusion; it has the power to enthrall: *thelgein*.[78] Without the varied performances of the choral band, the poet and his tradition are threatened with extinction; the singer is dependent on the choral performance of the Deliades to broadcast his voice and fame in his absence.[79] The Deliades, for their part, depend on the epic tradition for their themes; they rely on the singer for scripts and dance-steps, as well as for spreading their renown abroad. Singer and chorus are engaged in a sort of reciprocal *do ut des* relationship.

The literary topos of the god visiting his rites is the prototype of the itinerant bard. The singer enjoys a certain mobility not possessed by choruses. He can praise Apollo throughout Greece with the portable version of the *Hymn*.[80] Although a fragment by the Corinthian poet Eumelus indicates that choruses were sent to the island as early as the eighth century, they were dispatched by their communities for specific competitions.[81] The Deliades, by contrast, were a more localized phenomenon, perhaps available to be commissioned by cities who would send their choirmaster to train them.

Prototypes of Choreia *as* Paideia

The religious dynamics of choral performance in the *Hymn to Apollo* can be correlated with the cultural pretext of the festival. In the Olympian description the presentation of a youthful musician to Zeus and Leto for their approval indicates that one of the pretexts the poet had in mind was child-rearing through *mousikē*, widely attested for the festivals of Apollo and Artemis on Delos and elsewhere.[82] Just as the young were sometimes required to perform choral rites to Apollo, so the adolescent god in the prototype is made to undergo a musical review before the gods. Indeed there may be some allusion to a kourotrophic aspect in the mention of the Ionians attending the Delian festival with their children (*paidessi*).[83] In the Olympian passage a strong distinction is made in general between the older and the younger gods, especially Apollo, but also Artemis, and notably Hebe. Apollo's parents, Zeus and Leto, witness their offspring playing and dancing (*paizonta*).[84]

The ambiguous meanings of the verb *paizō* recall Plato's theoretical discussion in the *Laws* on the continuity between the informal play (*paidia*) of very young children and the organized games of older children that take on musical and choreographic forms, such as the weapon dance. The Olympian passage of the *Hymn* clearly delineates how the components of choral performance—instrumental music, poetry, song, and choral dancing—function together as ordering forces to forge what might be called Eunomia, sibling of the dance-loving Horai. The choral interlude on Olympus is also a prototype of the civic order fostered by music and dance.

The division of Olympians into youthful performers and mature spectators must be related back to the theme of the visual pleasure taken in dance. In Plato's polis the elders who are no longer able to dance with their former agility organize choral competitions for the younger members of the polis; in watching them they derive pleasure and are rejuvenated.[85] This reciprocity is implicit in the *Hymn*: the visual delight of the spectators, expressed no less than five times through the *terp-* root, is related linguistically to the nourishment (*trophē*) instilled in the young through musical performance.[86]

The emphasis on choral dancing for young girls in particular is alluded to in the description of Artemis's chorus, where the Charites, Hebe, and other chorus members embody qualities deemed desirable for marriageable girls to acquire through choral rites. The equivalent form of choreographic training for adolescent boys was the weapon dance. The presence of Ares can perhaps best be explained as an allusion to this widespread form of paramilitary training which is attested in the cults of Apollo and Artemis.

Young boys and girls come together in choruses on the dancing ground, an acceptable place to see and be seen in courtship rites. Such a ritual is portrayed in the final vignette of the Shield of Achilles describing a mixed dance composed of males in ceremonial armor and females wearing golden diadems. The ancient scholia on this Homeric passage saw an allusion to the dances of Theseus and the seven youths and maidens, which Plato in the *Phaedo* construed as the *aition* (origin myth) for the Delian festival.[87] Indeed there is much in the *aition* for the Delian festival to suggest that the sending of adolescent choruses in tandem with first-fruit offerings was related to the culmination of kourotrophy in suitable marriages and eventual births. Herodotus first recounts the story of how the daughters of Boreas, escorted by five young men, were entrusted with the sacred offerings to Apollo on Delos.[88] The Hyperborean girls did not return but died on the island. Thereafter the boys and girls of Delos dedicated a lock of hair at the Hyperborean girls' tomb before marrying. Herodotus gives no context for the dedication, but a passage in Euripides' *Hippolytus* indicates that the offering of hair by girls to Hippolytus before marriage takes place in the context of a choral performance.[89]

One of the daughters of Boreas mentioned by Herodotus is named Hyperoche. The very meaning of the name, "preeminence," corresponds precisely to the physical criterion by which Artemis is distinguished as *chorēgos* in the choral prototype. Perhaps we should see in Hyperoche the *chorēgos*, detached from the circular choir and leading, as it were, the procession from the land of the Hyperboreans to the island. The particular significance of the first-fruit offerings in the *aition* for the Delian festival lies in their place of origin: the earthly paradise where the Hyperboreans live. The privileged existence of these quasi-divine people is typified by their ring dances and their exotic sacrifices to Apollo.[90] Unlike the ordinary mortals hymned by the Muses in the Olympian description, the Hyperboreans have a shield against disease and old age. As intermediaries between gods and men the Hyperboreans are the embodiment of the divine qualities possessed by the Ionians in the midst of their festival.

The Delian *aition* is instructive about beliefs in the life-renewing force of choruses and the use of floriculture in expressing a wish for biological continuity and social harmony. The grafting of first growth and youthful dancing is found elsewhere in literature and in art of the early archaic period, where male and female choruses are represented with plant offerings in their hands. In Odysseus's flattering words to Nausicaa, the hero remarks on the pleasure her parents must experience when seeing her, a young slip—*thalos*—entering into the dance in anticipation of her marriage.[91] Dancing not only renews ties of worship but promotes social links as well. The use of choruses to effect the union of adolescent males and females and so stabilize the community at large can be seen as a variation on the festival theme of uniting mortal and immortal. The willful confusion of mythical prototype and human choir is seen in the closing lines of a dithyramb by Bacchylides where the chorus of Theseus blends with the chorus of Ceans for whom Bacchylides wrote the dithyramb, according to a recent interpretation, for performance on Delos at a moment prior to initiation into matrimony.[92]

Conclusions

The frequent appearance of divine prototypes of dance in literary genres (and its virtual absence in artistic representations, at least for the Olympian gods) can be explained by the belief that in a festival context choral performances were human manifestations of divine models. In a sense, the divine archetypes lent them authority and conferred a sense of immortality on performer and spectator alike, as is reflected in the divine epithets for the singer, and in our Delian passage, for the Ionians watching the festival proceedings.[93]

The close interaction of prototype and paradigm in the Olympian and Delian festival descriptions makes them a kind of doublet.[94] Although both the Olympian and Delian descriptions of festivity are based on elements of human festivals, neither can be taken as an accurate mirror of an actual choral performance. Like any poetic description they are to an extent idealizations shot through with fantasy. What emerges rather is a composite portrait that reflects in broad outlines the performative and religious dynamics of a generic festival in honor of a major deity such as Apollo and the religious goal of dance as a vehicle for invoking the divinity. As an ordering force dance aligns and realigns choruses mortal and immortal. The choral performance on Olympus implies several categories relating to age and gender and performative dynamics such as performer and audience, verbal and nonverbal, solo and choral performance. These categories recall those established by Plato and like his are useful for analyzing dance events in a larger, anthropological context. It is possible to see in the Olympian and Delian passages a sort of myth of origin for human dance and song that provides a solution to the crisis that divides divine and human existence. The solution is a compromise, since the experience of sharing privileged gifts with the gods is vicarious and temporary. Yet it is also illusory and based on the distinctly human ability to represent mimetically through *ludus* human and divine themes.

The play of festival choruses develops in two directions. Such play provides a pretext for paideia in the context of an *agōn*; it also has the potential to embody dramatic illusion as it weaves the narrative thread into the fabric of vocal and rhythmic representation. In the same way that tragedy is a melting pot for various types of choral genres, so the *Hymn to Apollo* alludes to choral types: hymns with divine and heroic subjects; various songs or dances concerned with paideia, including maiden songs, weapon dances, and perhaps courtship dances; in addition one hears of the paean which Apollo teaches the Delphic priesthood toward the end of the poem.[95]

The ritual function of the chorus was closely tied to technique and excellence in performance. Worshipping the divinity successfully meant staging choruses that would attract and hold attention by creating a pleasuring sense of order, or *kosmos*. Alcaeus in his *Hymn to Apollo* indicates that when the Delphians wished to bring Apollo back from visiting the Hyperboreans, they composed a paean and brought together a chorus of youths.[96] The *Homeric Hymn to Apollo* insists that in choral productions a great deal of pleasure was taken in the spectacle itself. Attention is drawn to the technique of *mimēsis*, of creating illusions and staging effects for the pleasure of divine and mortal spectator alike.

Three

Further Divine Prototypes:
Dance as a Disruptive Force

Dance, in combination with wine and other manifestations of divinity in Dionysus's cult, can be considered as a leveling activity in which all must ineluctably participate as a condition of humanity, in short, as a mechanism leading to *communitas*. Evidence for the power of dance to invert and at times subvert the normal order will be analyzed in four areas, beginning with a second origin myth for dance in Plato's *Laws* in which Dionysus, crazed by Hera, gives wine-induced manic dancing to mortals. Next we will consider the triumph of another of Hera's victims, the lowly Hephaestus, who can be seen as a prototype of festivals of reversal. We then turn to examine how Dionysus's cult hymn, the dithyramb, displays aspects of the topsy-turvy world. Finally, we briefly examine dancing and other liminal qualities of the members of Dionysus's *thiasos* and argue that the same kinds of liminal behavior are embodied by initiates in status transition rites that challenge and temporarily disrupt the social structure.

A Second Origin Myth for Dance

Plato reserved a separate category for Bacchic dancing, which involved the imitation of nymphs (maenads), Pans, satyrs, and silens in the context of purifications and initiations. These dances are of no concern to the lawmaker because they do not pertain to the city (*ou politikon*).[1] Bacchic dances do, however, belong to the wider spectrum of religious and social experience in Greece, as Plato recognizes when he acknowledges that explanations of the origins of dance and its role in achieving order in the soul and in the community were not unanimous in the fourth century. In a passage in the *Laws* Plato reports a rival account of the genesis of dancing in a myth about the madness of Dionysus. It is called a *phēmē*, a divine utterance with religious sanction, as opposed to the earlier, quasi-scientific *logos*. According to this popular tale (it is alluded to at the beginning of Euripides' *Cyclops*) dancing originated in a punishment that Dionysus devised for mortals in revenge for having been robbed of his wits by his stepmother Hera.[2] "There is a traditional tale that Dionysus's stepmother Hera deprived him of reason in his soul, and that he gains revenge by inflicting on us all manner of mad dancing; for this very reason he made a present of wine."[3] Whereas dance is seen by the *logos* as a beneficent and pleasurable means for correcting and refreshing the behavior of citizens, the divine *phēmē* for the Dionysiac origins of music and dance traces the source of human dance to the violence of divine nemesis. The punishment takes on a form similar to Dionysus's own altered state: he goads mortals to Bacchic frenzies and all "mad" (*manikē*) dancing. In order to produce the requisite madness in mortals, Dionysus gives them wine.[4]

This traditional explanation arises from the widespread custom of dances in honor of Dionysus involving wine rituals in which the god's presence was made manifest by wine and the inspiration of the *aulos*. Like wine, the sounds of the instrument induce involuntary movement of an uncontrollable nature. Said to have its origins in the ecstatic cults of Phrygia, the *aulos* was banned from the polis by Plato in the *Republic*, while Aristotle in the *Politics* would not permit the use of this amoral instrument in education.[5] In Euripides' *Bacchae* the invention of the *aulos*, along with the ox-hide drum, is traced to the Cretan caves where Zeus was born amidst violence and deceit. In the same caves the Corybantes discovered the drum, and mixing the beat with the sounds of the Phrygian *aulos*, gave it to Rhea the Mother Goddess. "From the Mother Goddess the maddened (*mainomenoi*) satyrs acquired it and attached it to the biennial dances in which Dionysus delights."[6]

Whereas wailing and leaping in the Platonic *logos* indicate a special human sensitivity to rhythm and harmony that can be tamed by *choreia*, in the ecstatic realm wine and the *aulos* would actually seem to conspire with Bacchic dancing to compel harmonic and kinetic disorder. Apollo and Muses are given to mortals to correct their training, to make them whole; Dionysus, on the other hand, according to the popular myth, is given, it appears, to unhinge them through manic dancing. But depending on how the gift is received by the worshipper, *mania* may be beneficial or destructive. Beneficial *mania* is a divine form of wisdom (*sōphrosynē*) given to those who accept it willingly, that is, those who are persuaded. For those who submit, Dionysus maintains the manic dancer within the twin poles of chaos and order. Conversely, those who refuse to be persuaded are punished by destructive *mania* taking the form of frenzied, uncontrollable motion. Those resisting the god's impulse are unleashed and collide with the destructive forces of *mania* that lead to frenzied dancing and wandering. In a striking example from Dionysiac myth the daughters of Proetus disdain Dionysus's rites by failing to join the other women of Argos in dancing. For their refusal to become part of the throng they are driven to manic dancing, endless wandering, and eventually the slaying of their own children.[7] Paradoxically, the daughters of Proetus are finally cured of their madness by the seer Melampus through violent dances. The homeopathic method of healing is important, since it follows the model indicated in the myth of the Dionysiac origins of dance: when Dionysus wished to avenge himself for his crazed state he stimulated mortals to manic dancing.

Mania can be used to cure internal commotion. Plato says that mothers and nursemaids know this homeopathic cure by motion, kinesetherapy. When a mother wants to put a wakeful child to sleep, far from keeping her still, she takes care to move her about, rocking the child constantly in her arms, not silently, but humming a kind of tune. The cure consists of movement to the rhythms of dance and song: "The mother makes her child 'pipe down' just as

surely as the music of the pipes bewitches the frenzied Bacchic rev-
eller."[8] In this passage on the proper handling of infants Plato ad-
duces as evidence the Corybantic ritual, which treats frenzied
pathological states (characterized in the first instance by an involuntary craze to dance) through dancing accompanied by the
sounds of the *aulos*. "The result is very satisfying. Whereas the children are lulled to sleep, the frenzied Bacchants, by being made to
dance to the *aulos* with the gods whom they venerate auspiciously
with sacrifices, are possessed of sound mind instead of their manic
state."[9] According to the homeopathic model, the inner turmoil of
the soul is cured by activity imposed from without. Both are forms
of *mania*. But whereas the inner *mania* is considered harmful, the
outer *mania* is thought to be salutary because it restores a state of
inward calm and repose.[10]

The catharsis implied by the use of external agitation to quell or
purge internal disorder in the *Laws* is often compared with Aristotle's views of catharsis in the *Politics*, and in turn his theory of tragic
catharsis in the *Poetics*.[11] Elsewhere in the *Laws* Plato provides a
different theory of catharsis consistent with the earlier view that
persuasion, not force, is effective for achieving order in the soul
and in the community.[12] According to this theory catharsis begins
with increased disorder: chaos must first be deliberately produced
for purposes of establishing a better, more lasting order.[13] Plato develops this controversial theory in direct response to the folk origin
of dance in the Hera-induced madness of Dionysus and the use of
wine. This mythological explanation is precisely the type of tale
Plato abjured because it represented the gods in an unfavorable
light. The Athenian spokesman for Plato in the dialogue in fact
counters the negative views reflected in the traditional tale and offers a totally different interpretation. Whereas wine in the myth is a
violent punishment used to drive people insane, according to
Plato's interpretation it is to be used as a gentle form of persuasion:
wine is truly a *pharmakon* in the double Greek sense of a poison and
a drug. Like *mania* and dance, wine can be harmful or beneficent.

Plato's endorsement of wine follows the traditional view of its
liberating effects, first attested in a passage in the *Odyssey*, in which
the liquid is said to compel even a thoughtful man to sing, dance,

laugh, and speak freely.[14] Referring to the earlier *logos*, Plato argues that the tendency to frenzied motion is in fact already present in the young child, whose fiery soul promotes leaping and wailing from which develops the art of *choreia*. The young, for their part, do not require any such stimulant as wine. The souls of the older members of the polis, however, tend to grow cold and dry, and these older citizens experience embarrassment about performing. Wine, which is seen as a fiery liquid, is an antidote to the excessive coldness and dryness brought on by old age. When administered as a drug (*pharmakon*) it enhances emotions, weakens reason, and endows adults with the disposition of children. By drinking it the elderly may renew their youth and lose their inhibitions to sing and dance. The use of wine to facilitate a return to a childish state conducive to singing and dancing is complemented by the etymology of the Greek word for playful dancing, *paizō*, which is derived from the word for child (*pais*). Wine in proper measure, like playful dancing, can reproduce the original state of disorder in the soul characterized by leaping and wailing. By creating disorder a better and more permanent order can be won.

The medicinal use of wine is well known in the medical corpus, and Plato's own view on the beneficial effects of wine as a stimulant in the service of paideia is indebted to ancient medical theory.[15] For some types of illness drugs must be administered to weaken the body temporarily in order to create conditions that will restore it to permanent health. An analogy for the cure of the human body exists in the festival use of wine and musical activity to restore the body politic. What Plato recommends for the reordering of the soul by wine, song, and dance occurs in festivals of Dionysus, such as the Anthesteria which involved singing and dancing, the consumption of wine, and other activities leading to the temporary disruption of the social order with the goal of restoring an improved and more lasting order.[16] The capacity of festivity to stir up disorder that settles into a more satisfying and permanent pattern relies on the assumption that there is a preexisting, embryonic order in the cosmos, the community, and in the soul of the unformed child. This view of the potential of festivity to invert, reverse, and thus stabilize the larger structure in which festivity functions has been documented in numerous studies of carnival and other potentially subversive rituals that, far from being disruptive or revolutionary, have as an end securing a more stable social order.

Dionysus on the Move

What prototypes of festivity do Dionysus and his worshipping throng provide, and how does ritual movement operate in his realm? In myth and cult Dionysus is the god of epiphany, a divinity constantly on the move, presenting himself in animal shapes and human form. The god of epiphany is also present in the particular—in wine, in the siffle of the *aulos*, in the mask, in the dances of the maenads, and in his cult hymn, the dithyramb. The divine shape-shifter is portrayed as *chorēgos* and dancer in poetry, and with great frequency in art, especially on vessels used for storing, mixing, and drinking the god's wine. In the final choral ode of Sophocles' *Antigone*, Dionysus is invoked as the *chorēgos* of the fiery stars, as overseer (*episkopos*) of the nocturnal cries of his worshippers, the frenzied Thyiads who celebrate him in all-night revels.[17] In a fragment from Euripides' *Hypsipyle*, Dionysus, carrying a thyrsus and animal skin, dances with the maidens at Delphi.[18] The god leads, even drives on, his worshippers to ecstatic expression. Male and female, young and old alike respond to his call, as indeed they must. Cadmus and Teiresias, though old and decrepit, join in with the god's rites at Thebes, and the daughters of Proetus refuse his call to their peril.

In archaic and classical vase painting the god dances alone or with others. A red-figure pelike in London shows a bearded Dionysus dressed in a chiton covered by an ependytes and himation; holding the two halves of a kid he dances before an altar to the sound of the *aulos* played by a satyr.[19] On the François vase Dionysus dances with the Horai in the midst of the wedding procession of Peleus and Thetis. Yet though the god may be caught up in the excited movement of his *thiasos* (Fig. 11b),[20] it is usually his followers, the satyrs and maenads, that dance, while Dionysus serves as a stationary *chorēgos*. The god remains the still point in the dance, to borrow a phrase from T. S. Eliot.[21]

Although genres of choral performance such as the dithyramb found their way into the cults of both Apollo and Dionysus, the mythological personnel, the religious dynamics, and musical instruments found in Dionysiac cult are distinct, as are the underlying assumptions about the pleasurable and ordering aspects of music and dance. Dionysus presents a competing prototype of dance, another model of social and religious experience. These differences explain why, in Plato's origin myth for *choreia*, Dionysus, who is vital to his polis, is introduced as a sort of afterthought to Apollo and the Muses, and why, as we saw, Plato feels it necessary to report a rival account for the origin of dance.[22]

Apollo's Olympian dance and its constituent elements work to structure the universe, to arrange all things in a hierarchy; the fixed order and structure on Olympus is reflected and played out in human society. The pattern achieved by the ordering forces of music and dance on Olympus, however, leads to inequalities on all planes: among the Olympians, between gods and mortals, and in human communities. Hephaestus, the lame god who is servile to the physically perfect Olympians, is excluded from their choir. Despite the merging of divine and human worlds attained during moments of festivity, the gap between gods and mortals is wide and seemingly irreversible; and the noncitizen is barred from taking part in civic dances.

Dance, however, is a great leveler, drawing into its midst people of all ages, classes, and professions. Hence in the Middle Ages the devastating effects of plagues on the population—rich and poor, doctor and bishop alike—found compelling expression in the literary and artistic theme of the Dance of Death. Dance is a marginal activity removed from everyday life, allowing its participants to step outside of themselves. It transports them from the ennui of day-to-day existence and permits them to associate with higher spiritual forces. The equalizing and ecstatic effects of dance can be seen as a metaphor of *communitas*. This anthropological concept, first developed by Victor Turner and since applied and reinterpreted in numerous studies, assumes that, despite the inequalities of class, power, and property ownership determined according to arbitrarily imposed social and political structures, a more fundamental human bond unites all members of society into a single group, a *communitas*.[23] The suspension, and in certain cases reversal, of the temporal order typically emerges at times of disruption in the normal routine, when cosmic crisis threatens to impinge upon the world order, or when the social and political structure is shaken up by changes in status through adolescent initiations, weddings, or death. Yet neither structure nor the antistructure exposed by *communitas* is self-sufficient. The competing forces of each interact to choreograph and give meaning to the human pageant.

Notions of *communitas* and the reversal of temporal order appear in the Greek world in several contexts, but with some consistency in the setting of Dionysus and his cult. They are manifest in several areas: Aristophanic comedy (where Dionysus appears as a character), in the larger framework in which Dionysian drama appears, in protodramatic genres such as the dithyramb where dance played a significant role, and in literary and artistic representations of festivity. In these Dionysian models dance can be seen to unhinge social and political structures, revealing gaps and inequalities. At the same time it closes up the seams, rewarding all who are persuaded by the god with the type of religious experience viscerally felt through dance and related means.

The Return of Hephaestus to Olympus as Festival of Reversal

Dionysus, who disrupts and reverses the civic structure through his demands that he be worshipped by all, in particular insists on the loyal following of women, requiring them to leave their homes, husbands, and children to participate in mountain dancing (*oreibasia*). He subverts the institution of marriage and the biological role of motherhood. To be a maenad implies a denial of the *oikos*. Those who resist the call must deny their identity in extreme ways by destroying the very children they bear; they lose control of bodily movements and mental functions, wandering ceaselessly. Hera, the goddess of weddings and motherhood, is therefore the natural adversary of Dionysus. Yet though she watches over motherhood she is not herself a mother except on one occasion when, without sire, she gives birth to Hephaestus, whose ugly appearance causes her such shame that she hurls the infant from Olympian heights, maiming him for life.[24]

Like Dionysus who suffered Hera's madness, Hephaestus endured Hera's insult but in the end triumphed with the help of the god of wine. The story of the lame smith's eventual revenge on his mother was well known throughout Greece.[25] Relying on an invisible contrivance Hephaestus managed to enchain Hera in her throne. Unable to escape she called on the gods for help. Ares attempted to remove her by force without success, and so all the gods tried but failed. Finally Dionysus resorted to a more powerful force: he persuaded Hephaestus with wine and merriment and brought him to Olympus so that with his special skill he could free Hera.

The story of the return of Hephaestus to Olympus was represented in vase painting in many parts of Greece. The scene appears first in Corinthian art around 590 and then enters the Attic vase painters' repertoire between 570 and 560, notably on the François vase; in Attica it remained one of the most popular subjects for the next two centuries.[26] Typically the lame smith is shown carrying a drinking vessel and mounted on a mule in a procession led by Dionysus or a satyr and accompanied by an *aulētēs* and the ubiquitous dancing satyrs and maenads. On a Corinthian amphoriskos in Athens, for example, Hephaestus is seated on a donkey led by a satyr engaged in spirited movement; the lame legs of the smith are shown with back-turned feet, like the claws of a crab.[27]

An especially fine Attic black-figure representation of the return of Hephaestus appears on a wide band running around one side of the belly of a column crater in New York (Fig. 9). The bearded smith, astride a mule, holds a drinking horn in one hand and reins in the animal with the other, as if to keep it under control in the midst of such exuberant activity. The mounted god is escorted by Dionysus, satyrs, and maenads. The wine god and his *thiasos* are portrayed in attitudes of playful release with arms flung above the head, bent knee, and the foot at times raised slightly above the ground line. Among the entourage trudges one servile satyr weighed down by a wineskin on the back; in his outstretched hand

Figure 9. The return of Hephaestus to Olympus, escorted by Dionysus, satyrs, and maenads.

he carries a cluster of grapes. His gesture and pose is mirrored by that of Dionysus, antithetically placed beyond the mule, and holding a snake that links the god formally with the curvaceous tails of the satyrs and the sinuous movements of the dancers' bodies. Hephaestus's status as a rider is a sign of privilege but also a reminder of the god's lameness. All about him his escorts, the satyrs and maenads, perform ecstatic dances; the centermost satyr gazes head-on at the viewer.

What is the significance of Hephaestus as the central figure in this and related scenes of festivity? Hephaestus is a paradoxical divinity. In some respects he is inferior to the other Olympians, and yet he exercises special powers over them, as the myth of Hera's confinement so clearly illustrates. Hephaestus, the divine smith lame in both legs, and therefore ugly and imperfect, is an outsider on Olympus. Hephaestus's physical imperfections lead the other gods to ridicule him and treat him like a slave. Hephaestus is the only god who is imagined as working on Olympus. He labors not only as an artisan creating pleasing statues and fantastic robots but as a menial, a cup-bearer for Zeus and the other Olympians.[28] As master of the forge, however, Hephaestus alone has technical knowledge of fire. Though lame, the demiurge has the unique ability to control the mobility of objects and, as in the case of Hera, the other gods. Hephaestus is an animator but also constrains. He is to be associated with divine smiths from the ancient Near East, such as Kothar-wa-Hasis, the craftsman god worshipped at Ugarit, who makes magical weapons and builds palaces for the other gods. Remarkably, the people of Ugarit believed that this god originated from Crete, where the Greeks looked for the origins of their dance rituals. It is on Crete that evidence for bronze percussion instruments, including the sistrum and cymbals has been found. These products of the forge are attested from the third millennium in the ancient Near East, and suggest earthly guilds of smiths throughout the eastern Mediterranean. In traditional societies with knowledge of the art of metallurgy the smith is often also dancer and sorcerer.[29]

Hephaestus's paradoxical nature manifests itself especially in terms of movement. It is sometimes said that the only Olympian god who does not dance is Hephaestus. But the lame god in fact enjoys extraordinary movement—backward and forward, sideways, up and down.[30] In the epic formula describing how, despite his lameness, Hephaestus maneuvers about deftly on his skinny legs,[31] the verb for speedy motion (*rōomai*) also means to dance, and is used, for example, of the nymphs of Mt. Sipylos dancing with the river god Acheloös.[32] In the *Iliad* he is married to Charis, one of the Charites.[33] Notably, Hephaestus also makes representations of dances and dancing places. The most elaborate creation of Hephaestus we hear about is the Shield of Achilles. On it are three vignettes involving dance: a wedding procession and dance, a vintage dance, and an exquisite description of the dances of boys and girls.[34] This last dance is compared to the dancing floor made for Ariadne by the Athenian craftsman Daedalus whose traditional association with Hephaestus is well known.[35] Related to Hephaestus's ability to please by animation is his talent for dissolving conflict, and it is in both capacities that Hephaestus is finally cajoled by Dionysus to liberate Hera.

Hephaestus alone of the gods knows how to defuse a tense situation. To avert the quarrel of the gods on Olympus at the end of the first book of the *Iliad* he placates the gods with words of entreaty, and ample servings of wine.[36] Moreover, he is a comic figure, and the mere sight of him limping about in inimitable fashion moves them to laughter.[37] Hephaestus's capacity to restrict and liberate movements and his related ability to deflect tense situations through merriment make him a sort of *éminence grise,* a virtual choreographer of festivity.[38]

As Hephaestus is a paradoxical figure, so is the interpretation of the return of the smith to Olympus. On the one hand the appearance of Hephaestus belongs to the common situation of the epiphany of a god that occasions festivity; here the roles of Hephaestus and Dionysus, the god best known for his epiphanies, are reversed. On the other hand, Hephaestus is a prototype of human festivals of reversal arising at times of crisis. Hephaestus's ability to resolve Hera's predicament can be understood in the context of festivals for the goddess of weddings. As Burkert observes, "Whenever we learn any details about Hera festivals we discover that it is never simply a joyful wedding feast, but a deep crisis in which the established order breaks down."[39] In the background of the Return of Hephaestus the enchaining of the wife of Zeus causes a disruption in the Olympian order which the smith alone has the technical means to resolve. The gods, reduced to an anxious state, can survive only by involvement and cooperation with the lowliest of the Olympians. But Hephaestus's knowledge cannot be applied without Dionysus's arts of persuasion: wine, music, and dancing.

Once again we see, as in the cosmic paradigm for dance, the theme of order won from persuasion, not force. The move from crisis and disorder to order through the intermediary of wine, music, and dance in the story of Hera and Hephaestus is a metaphor for the dynamics of festivity. Hephaestus's marginal status on Olympus brings him in closer league with mortals who, like the divine smith, attempt to placate the gods by drink offerings, music, and dance. With these gifts they avert crises in the social and civic order while temporarily experiencing, like Hephaestus, the life of Olympian festivity. Hephaestus is thus a model of the human worshipper, and Dionysus the initiator.[40]

The myth of the maiming and return of Hephaestus belongs, broadly speaking, to the topsy-turvy world of reversals celebrating the triumph of the oppressed. As a marginal figure on Olympus Hephaestus is normally excluded from participating as an equal on Olympus. In the story of the Return of Hephaestus, however, the smith's situation is reversed. Hephaestus is elevated on a mule, given wine, and treated to music and dancing. The slave is treated like his masters and given the best place at the banquet. The implied distinction between work and leisure obtains in the *symposion* where the privileged guests recline on benches while they are served wine and entertained by slaves who often dance.[41] Indeed, on an amphora formerly in the Castellani collection, Hephaestus, holding a drinking vessel as if to have it filled, actually reclines on the back of a donkey led by a dancing satyr.[42] The once-exiled Hephaestus symbolizes the early race of mortals now distinct from the gods but still allowed to participate in their activities on festival occasions. They do so by performing actions pleasing to the gods, such as making and dedicating statues, pouring libations, establishing festive dances, and staging contests. In return for these offerings that require technical skills and physical stamina Hephaestus and worshipper alike are rewarded. In the *Iliad* the granting of Charis as wife to Hephaestus as a compensation for his misery is echoed in the *Laws* by Plato, who said that the gods gave mortals festivals as a relaxation from their labors and granted the gods to be copartners in the dance.[43] The myth of the Return of Hephaestus is a paradigm of festivals of reversal in the social order in archaic and classical Greece, elements of which can be glimpsed in festivals such as the Athenian Anthesteria examined in the next chapter.

Early Dithyramb and the Topsy-turvy World

Evidence for dance as a disruptive force emerges in the early life of the dithyramb, the cult hymn of Dionysus. The word "dithyramb," like paean, denotes both the god and the choral song and dance in his honor and once again provides evidence for the perception among the Greeks that musical performance was of divine origin and character. The history of the dithyramb, the most widespread genre of choral lyric in the worship of Dionysus, is very old and begins on the island of Paros with Archilochus.[44] Born on Paros in 680, Archilochus composed a famous poem in which he recklessly boasts, "I know how to lead (*exarxai*) the fair song of lord Dionysus, the dithyramb, when my wits are lightning-struck (*synkeraunō-theis*) by wine."[45] These verses reveal that originally the dithyramb is an improvised celebration by a band of revelers led by an *exarchōn*, the functional equivalent of the *chorēgos*. As such the poet does not merely sing the words but teaches a chorus song and dance movements. The poem indicates that the drinking of wine, an important aspect of worship in the cult of Dionysus, was integral to the performance. "There's no dithyramb when you drink water," quipped the comic poet Epicharmus.[46] The inspiration for composing a suitable dithyramb came, in short, only to the poet who had experienced the god through the liquid medium that made the poet *theios* (godly). The wine-induced state of ecstasy allowed the revelers to experience at one remove the madness inflicted on Dionysus by Hera that led the god, according to the popular myth, to invent frenzied dancing.[47] The components of music, wine, and revelry are suggestively gathered together on a fragment of an Attic red-figure wine vessel in Copenhagen.[48] On it a variant of the name Dithyramb (*Dithyramphos*) is inscribed next to a satyr holding a lyre and leading a procession of revelers.[49]

A late source records that the dance of the dithyramb was called the *tyrbasia*, related to Latin *turba* and our adjective "turbid."[50] Whatever the exact nature of the dance was, the word tells us that dithyrambic movement did not amount to a solemn and orderly dance, but rather something bordering on riotous horseplay retaining the characteristics of revelry implied by Archilochus's improvisatory dithyramb. Pindar, who considered himself an innovator in this genre, suggests in his dithyramb for the Thebans that in contrast to his fast-paced poem those of his immediate predecessors crept along (*herpē*) in tempo.[51] From this comment it can be inferred that, in Pindar's opinion, the ecstatic dance element had been lost or excessively suppressed and was therefore inappropriate for the spirit of Dionysiac worship.

The dithyramb is perhaps the object of attack by Pindar's contemporary, Pratinas of Phlius. One of the early Athenian tragedians, Pratinas, expressed anger about the excessive emphasis on the *aulos* and on frenzied dancing in a poem of disputed genre.[52] The poem invokes Dionysus as "Dithyrambus" and perhaps was performed by a chorus of men dressed as satyrs.[53] It is not unlikely that Pratinas composed his attack in the wake of reforms introduced by Lasus of Hermione, the musician famous for expanding the technical capabilities of the *aulētēs* and responsible for introducing the dithyramb on a regular basis to the festivals of Athens in the late sixth century. If not itself a dithyramb or a parody on dithyrambic style, Pratinas's poem is an important source for understanding the variable relationship between poetry, instrumental music, and dance in Dionysiac ritual.[54]

> What is this hubbub? What are these dances? What loud-clattering arrogance has come upon the Dionysian altar? Mine, mine is Bromios [Dionysus]: it is I who must cry aloud, I who must make a clatter as I run across the mountains with the Naiads, uttering like a swan a dapple-feathered melody. It is song that the Muse made queen. Let the *aulos* dance after it, since it is a servant: it should be content to be commander only in the revel and the fist-fights of young drunks quarrelling at the door. Batter the one that has a mottled toad's breath! Burn that spittle-wasting reed with its deep-chattering mouth and its step that wrecks tune and rhythm, a menial whose body is formed with a drill. Look and see! This is the tossing of right hand and foot that is yours, dithyramb-triumphing, ivy-wreathed lord! Listen to my Dorian dance and song.[55]

Pratinas's chief complaint is not the presence of dancing in a song in Dionysus's honor but of the preeminence of *aulos* playing over the poetry.[56] The chorus in performances of the dithyrambic type, he seems to say, sings in accompaniment to the *aulos*, thus violating the hierarchy of song over woodwind music established, according to Pratinas, by the Muse. What Pratinas seems to object to is the lack of restraint in the accompaniment that leads to an imbalance between the constituent elements making up choral performance. Not only is the *aulos* overbearing, but the dance-steps it inspires is inappropriate for worship around the altar (*thymelē*) of the god which stood in the orchestra of the theater. Raucous behavior and unruly movements are better suited, he implies, for the antics of the mythological followers of Dionysus in the mountains. The poem ends with the chorus defiantly describing how it would position the hand and foot when invoking Dionysus by his epithet "dithyrambus." Clearly the *aulos* has become not so much an ordering force as a tyrant; there is a lack of harmony in the elements of *choreia*, the chorus seems to say.

As in Pratinas's poem, the subjects of dithyrambs included aspects of Dionysus's life (especially his birth) and worship, as well as other divine and heroic legends.[57] Thus the reference to lightning in the Archilochus fragment may, as has recently been argued, allude to the first birth of Dionysus that resulted when the pregnant Semele, who desired to see Zeus, the father of her child, in all his glory, was visited by him in the fatal form of lightning.[58] In Archilochus's poem the verb to be lightning-struck (*synkeraunōtheis*) by wine seems to suggest that in the act of improvising his dithyramb the poet sympathetically experiences through wine the equivalent of Semele's lightning-induced death. The liquid makes the poet, as we would say, dead-drunk, the appropriate state in which to deliver his poetic creation about Dionysus's birth, perhaps the most common theme of the literary dithyramb.

The successful poet in the dithyrambic contest received as a prize a bull, as indicated by the Pindaric epithet "ox-driving" dithyramb.[59] The poet Simonides boasts having won during his lifetime a total of fifty-six bulls, one for each time he trained and led a chorus of men to dithyrambic victory and himself earned the right to "step upon the bright chariot of Victory."[60] The epigram containing this boast was composed in 477/6 in the eightieth year of the poet's life, to be inscribed beneath the tripod awarded to the victorious tribe. The large number of prizes suggests that a poet proficient in dithyrambic composition might compete frequently in contests not only in Athens but in other parts of Greece as well.

Dithyrambic performance took place around an altar and was circular in configuration. "Circular choruses" (*kyklioi choroi*) was a synonym for the dithyramb and later came to distinguish the characteristic round shape of this type of chorus from the tetragonal form of tragic choruses.[61] In a Pindaric passage on the invention of the dithyramb at Corinth, the epithet "ox-driving" indicates that the sacrificial victim was escorted from the field to the altar that may have doubled as stage for the drama of sacrifice and as focal point for the choral performance.[62] This culmination of linear movement in a circular activity follows the pattern of circumambulation rituals that are typically coordinate with sacrifice in the eastern Mediterranean.[63] The workaday agricultural task of driving and herding cattle, contained in the Greek word *boēlasiē*, would take on a playful meaning in the procession. The reluctant bull which was to become the center of the sacrificial and perhaps musical drama, was probably given prominence at the head of the procession. There were various ways of sweetening the progress of the intractable animal—by displaying colorful garments, fragrant flowers, and possibly the use of desensitizing drugs. These, mixed with the sounds and movements of the escorting *thiasos*, had a confusing and intimidating effect on the beast. When wrapped in the festive envelope of the *pompē* the bull, now fractious, now tame, became willy-nilly a playful partner in the procession to Dionysus's altar.

The fiction of playfully involving the beast in the procession would extend to making the god who is incarnate in the beast witness his cult hymn. Pindar, in a fragment of a dithyramb for the Thebans, may allude to this when he says that Bromios (an epithet for Dionysus) is "enchanted by the dancing herds of wild beasts."[64] Dionysian mythology makes it clear that the god could easily assume the shape of a bull.[65] In a Dionysiac festival where transformation and reversal are the rules of the game, the sacrificial victim was perhaps given the viewing place of honor at the spectacle. The bull, which is in reality an animal to be brutally slain, is treated in a jocose vein as if it were the judge of the contest for which it is in fact offered as prize. Such a fiction accomplishes three religious goals. First, it ensures the presence of a divine witness. Second, the special treatment accorded the animal by enveloping it in music, song, and dance, sanitizes the victim and compensates for the slaughter. Third, it allows for reciprocity between the divine and animal victim, and the poetic victor.

The god also appears in the person of the poet, who thereby enjoys a quasi-divine status. Archilochus in antiquity was closely associated with Dionysus.[66] An inscription of the third century indicates that an oracle of Apollo had decreed that two altars should be erected in the hero shrine for Archilochus on Paros, one for the Muses, Apollo, and Mnemosyne, the other for Dionysus, the nymphs, and the Horai.[67] The divine status accorded the dithyrambic poet is also told in the story of the Lesbian poet Arion, the most distinguished musician during the rule of Periander (625–585) at Corinth. According to Herodotus, Arion first composed the dithyramb and trained choruses to perform it in Corinth.[68] Herodotus, who is not ignorant of Archilochus, probably means that Arion was the first to develop the dithyramb heretofore conceived as an informal song and dance in honor of Dionysus into a literary form, since he is said to have rehearsed (*didaxanta*) the chorus and to have given titles to individual dithyrambic compositions.[69]

After providing the bare facts about Arion as a choral poet, Herodotus modulates into an entertaining account about an episode from the life of the quasi-historical musician. This fragment of biographical fiction relates how Arion left his adopted home of Corinth for a tour of Sicily and southern Italy. Upon his return he escaped the murderous plot of Corinthian sailors and was miraculously rescued by a dolphin and carried to Taenarum on the southern tip of the Peloponnesus, whence he returned to the court of Periander.[70] The motive for Arion's trip west had been financial, and the poet in fact had earned a great deal of money from singing. But the Corinthian crew he hired proved to be untrustworthy, and once at sea they hatched a plot to rob Arion of his money and throw him overboard. The poet divined the stratagem and offered them his money but asked them to spare his life. The sailors, unwilling to accept this offer, told Arion that he must either kill himself or jump overboard immediately. Arion then plotted a counterstratagem by volunteering to sing a song and then kill himself. The sailors, lured by the prospect of hearing a fine concert by the world's most renowned singer, eagerly assembled in the middle of the ship. Meanwhile in the stern of the ship Arion, dressed in his singer's robes, and holding his lyre, played and sang a spirited melody of very high pitch (*nomon orthion*). Then, instead of killing himself, Arion jumped into the sea. While the ship continued its voyage to Corinth, a dolphin rescued Arion and carried him to the southern tip of the Peloponnesus. The poet, still in his singing costume, made his way overland to Corinth. When he arrived he told his story to Periander. The tyrant did not readily accept Arion's fantastic tale, but kept it in mind to ask the sailors upon their return if they had anything to tell about the poet. When questioned, they claimed that they left him safe in Italy. At that very moment Arion, still dressed in his ceremonial robes, appeared suddenly, causing the sailors to be panic-stricken. Their lie was detected and further denial was useless.

The tale about Arion portrays him as a solo performer. But this highly condensed narrative is appended to the claim that Arion formalized the dithyramb as a choral performance. Arion is specifically said to have rehearsed (*didaxanta*) the chorus. As we saw in the Delian paradigm in the *Hymn to Apollo* the itinerant bard may function both as a soloist and in relation to a chorus. Is it not possible that we have in the tale of Arion's travels a sort of foundation myth for the dithyramb that alludes to the eventual performance at Corinth of a choral genre in which the poet is the surrogate of Dionysus?[71]

To answer this question we may look at the *Homeric Hymn to Dionysus*, which tells of an *agōn* between the god and a group of pirates who escape in the form of dolphins. Dionysus's *Hymn* opens with a group of Tyrsenian pirates in a ship sighting the god, dressed in a purple robe, on the shore. They attempted to kidnap the god, whom they mistook for the son of a wealthy king. On board the ship they bound him in shackles from which the god miraculously escaped. The pirates took this as a sign that their victim was a god and were afraid to touch him. But the captain of the ship, refusing to believe in his divinity, hurled taunts at the god, whereupon strange things began to happen. Wine flowed through the ship. The mast of the ship became entwined in ivy and bloomed with flowers. The sailors, more frightened than before, begged the helmsman to turn to shore. At this point the god himself transformed into a lion and then a bear. All the sailors rushed to the stern, and, struck with amazement, crowded around the captain, whom Dionysus, in the shape of a lion, seized. The terrified sailors then leapt into the sea and were themselves transformed into dolphins. But Dionysus took pity on the helmsman, and identifying himself as the god, pardoned him.

In broad outlines and in certain striking details the two narratives share similarities. In the *Hymn* the god initially stands in an agonistic relationship to the Tyrsenian pirates, just as Arion, the ritual substitute of the god, is the would-be victim of the Corinthian sailors. In the *Hymn* we find the common motif of the reluctant worshipper who is persuaded by the sudden appearance of the god. In the Herodotean narrative, the sailors fail to respect the sanctity of the poet who is the representative of the god; when Arion suddenly appears at Periander's court their false claim that Arion is in Italy is exposed and further denial is useless. In both passages the dolphin appears as a vehicle of salvation. In the Herodotean tale Arion is rescued by a dolphin when he jumps overboard, while in the *Hymn* the pirates are saved by actually being transformed into dolphins when they dive into the sea. Before relating these tales to choral performance, we may adduce another passage in which a god, this time in the shape of a dolphin, confronts a group of sailors. In the *Hymn to Apollo* the god, transformed as a dolphin, leaps aboard a ship of Cretan sailors and commandeers the vessel to Delphi. Once at Delphi Apollo teaches the Cretan sailors the choral paean.

In all of these stories the marine imagery functions as a metaphor for the worship of the divinity, which, as we have seen in analyzing the *Hymn to Apollo*, is acted out in choral performance. There is an analogy of the choral leader and the chorus members in the helmsman, who guides the ship, and the crew.[72] In the *Hymn to*

Apollo the god in the guise of a dolphin usurps the role of the helmsman, and in his leading function becomes the *chorēgos* of the paean at Delphi.[73] In the *Hymn to Dionysus* the god asserts his command over the helmsman by appearing in animal shapes, while the pirates become, as it were, a dolphin chorus. In the tale of Arion, the directive role of the poet who is rescued by a dolphin is anticipated by the report that he is said to have taught choruses the dithyramb at Corinth. Retroactively, he shifts from being a solo performer to being a choral leader.

Like the Delian paradigm in the *Hymn to Apollo*, the *Hymn to Dionysus* seems to comment indirectly on choral modes of performance. In a similar way the Herodotean narrative, while portraying Arion as a solo singer, is presented in the context of the foundation of a choral genre. We see here the pattern of the itinerant bard detached from the choral band, only to reappear as a choral teacher.

Certain features of Dionysus's cult and the parallel use of cultic vocabulary in the Herodotean narrative and the *Hymn to Apollo* emphasize the fact that Arion is a representative of the god and suggest how this ritual role was played out in dithyrambic performance. In the *Hymn to Dionysus* when the god is first sighted by the Tyrsenian sailors, his would-be kidnappers, Dionysus wears a conspicuous robe. Arion's quasi-divine status is emphasized by his singer's robe which makes him inviolable. Arion's special status is also confirmed by the favorable and timely apparition of the dolphin, a quasi-divine creature associated with the worship of Dionysus and other gods. In his mysterious movements Arion also resembles the god. Like Dionysus, the god of epiphanies and disappearances, Arion suddenly disappears by diving overboard. The verb used to describe his leap, as well as that of the pirates in the guise of dolphins, is *pedaō*, used of Bacchic dancing in Euripides' *Bacchae* and elsewhere.[74] Arion then reappears twice, once at Taenarum on the back of the dolphin and later at the court of Periander. When he surprises the sailors at the Corinthian court, cultic vocabulary describing the appearance of a god is used (*epiphanēnai*, cf. epiphany).[75] The mobility implied by this divine epiphany is to be contrasted with the paralysis of the sailors. The thunderstruck reaction of the sailors is described by a verb for striking (*ekplēssō*) used in ritual possession rites.[76] The same word (*ekplēgentes*, from *ekplēssō*, to strike) is used in the *Hymn to Dionysus*.[77] A use of the verb to strike (*plēssō*) in a musical metaphor in Plotinus suggests that when the parts making up providence (*pronoia*) are struck, some parts will respond vocally, while "others will receive the blow (*plēgenta*) in silence and make the movements that follow on it."[78] The musical imagery alludes to the impact that musical accompaniment has on choral performers, some of whom sing, others of whom dance and gesture. In Herodotus the sailors react to the poet as if he were a terrifying apparition. The startling appearance of Arion and the response of the sailors may allusively reproduce the climactic moment in the dithyramb when the god, impersonated by the *chorēgos*, presents himself as the "other" to the chorus members, representing Dionysus's worshippers.

Like wine, the vehicle to the ecstatic state, the playful dolphin is a metaphor for divine transformation. The crucial importance of Arion's association with the dolphin is made clear from the first sentence of the story as told in Herodotus. In the midst of reporting the facts of Arion's origins and his invention of the dithyramb, he introduces the kernel of the story, namely that Arion rode on a dolphin's back to Taenarum. Then in the final sentence of the story Herodotus reports the existence of a bronze figurine of a man riding on a dolphin allegedly presented by Arion at the temple of Poseidon at Taenarum. Narratives about a man being rescued and transported by a dolphin were common in antiquity and based on eyewitness reports of such phenomena in the Mediterranean. Stories of this type found their way into various myths, especially those concerned with colonization.[79] Here the story type seems to be adapted to Arion as founder of a musical tradition.

The image of men riding on the back of dolphins is, like the *carrus navalis* (for which the ship in this story may be a metaphor), another *impossibilium* from the topsy-turvy world. The image is frequently represented in Attic vase paintings: a group of helmeted men ride dolphins as if they were horses.[80] The presence of an *aulētēs* on four examples indicates that the riders are clearly members of a comic chorus.[81]

But why the dolphin? The dolphin itself belongs to the literary topos of the world turned upside down: in one of Archilochus's poems the dolphin exchanges habitats with land beasts.[82] Since antiquity the dolphin has been known as a playful creature. It is not afraid of human beings but sports with their ships at sea. As it alternately leads and follows vessels it makes great leaps, to the delight and amazement of the crews and passengers. The dolphin came to be portrayed by ancient Greek poets and artists as a music-loving (*philomousos*) creature that, like the gods, imaginatively participated in the spirit of human festivity. The epithet "music-loving" occurs in a hymn which Arion supposedly wrote as a thank-offering to Poseidon for his rescue from the sea.[83] In vase painting the creature is shown playing the *aulos*, and the choreographic dimension of the playful mammal is conveyed by the verb *pedaō*, which is used elsewhere to describe the leaping of human beings in Bacchic dances.[84] Plato uses the same verb in the passage in the *Laws* on the relationship between dancing (expressed as a leaping movement) and the origin of play (*paidia*).[85] It suggests that under the influence of Dionysus movement could transform a man into a beast.

The mimetic nature of Greek dance and the projection of dance-like movements onto the dolphin make it extremely likely that the playful creature was the subject of imitative dances. This possibility is consistent with the choral context for dolphins ridden by men in the artistic sources. The performance of imitative dances of dolphins and other creatures associated with Dionysiac metamorphosis in dithyrambs puts into a new light the phrase in Pindar's dithyramb to the Thebans, "Dionysus is enchanted by the dancing herds of wild beasts."[86] Choreographic portrayals of animals that, like the dolphin, move in groups may well have been one of the variations undertaken by choruses performing dithyrambs in honor of Dionysus.

Dolphins were also associated with Apollo and Poseidon. Aelian quotes a hymn that Arion supposedly wrote as a thank-offering to Poseidon for his rescue from the sea. It could not have been written during the time of Periander, but may have been composed toward the end of the fifth century when reforms in dithyrambs gave increased prominence to the musician who sang a solo while the chorus only danced.[87] This is the impression conveyed by the hymn, which after an invocation to Poseidon describes how beasts dance in a circle, moving lightly with nimble leaps of their feet. It names apes with scraggly necks, swift-running puppies, and music-loving dolphins.[88] The anthropomorphic language suggests that a human chorus dressed as animals was intended or at least visualized by the poet. According to Aelian the hymn was inscribed on a statue (presumably on the statue base) dedicated by Arion to Poseidon at Cape Taenarum. This is presumably a reference to the bronze figurine mentioned by Herodotus. Indeed Pausanias saw a statue at Taenarum.[89] Although it is doubtful that such a statue existed in the time of Periander, it is not unreasonable to think that one existed for Herodotus to see. Whatever the authorship and circumstances of the composition, the portion of the text cited earlier supports the impression conveyed by the Arion story in Herodotus that dolphin dances in honor of a god such as Poseidon or Dionysus were considered an appropriate form of worship and were part of the repertoire of cyclical dances whose organization was attributed to Arion.[90] A dolphin dance by a chorus of men impersonating the music-loving and leaping animal may indeed have included one or more chorus members carrying the musician (representing Arion) on their backs in commemoration of his rescue by a dolphin.[91]

The Dancing Satyr and Maenad as Prototype of Communitas

Among the divine followers of Dionysus, dancing is the characteristic activity of the satyr as well as the maenad with whom the goat-man is often paired in artistic representations. In Turner's model, dancing, with its unusual physical properties and marked rhythms, is an extraordinary activity that leads to the breakdown of everyday rhythms and structures. In ancient Greece one of the chief structural barriers experienced by all mortals was exclusion from the divine experience of the Olympians. Another boundary that separated mortals in Greece, as in all traditional societies, was gender. Gender distinctions were defined and reinforced by the different collective activities that males and females typically engaged in (for example, hunting versus wool working). The evidence for mixed

Figure 10 (a). Four women, including Mainas with tambourine, around effigy of Dionysus.

dancing, especially among couples, in Greece is scanty. In the mythical realm, however, satyrs and maenads violate the boundaries of mortality and gender, and the medium through which they do so is choreographic.[92] The merging of genders in representations of satyrs and maenads is symptomatic of the blurring of boundaries achieved by dance. As they dance the satyr and maenad bond, representing a *communitas* united by Dionysus.

That dancing is conceived as the quintessential activity of the Dionysiac *thiasos* is confirmed by vase inscriptions. Several examples of satyrs named "Little Dancer" (Chorillos) exist; maenads

Figure 10 (b). Four women, including Choreia with tambourine, in ritual play.

named Choro (a derivative of *choros*) are attested three times.[93] Choreia appears as a maenad name on a well-known red-figure stamnos in Naples (Fig. 10).[94] Choreia is also attested as the name of a historical maenad in Dionysus's cult.[95] The appearance of Choreia both as a vase inscription and as a historically attested maenad raises the issue of the historicity of maenads in the classical period and the related question of satyrs in artistic and literary portrayals. As Albert Henrichs has shown in a sober study of the evidence for ritual maenadism, although the phenomenon is widely attested in Hellenistic cities there is no unambiguous evidence for maenadism in Greece before 350.[96] The only Attic vessels that portray maenads involved in ritual are the so-called Lenaia vases, such as the Naples stamnos. On it we see Choreia playing the tambourine while three other maenads, one named Thaleia (Festivity), dance. On the other side of the vase another maenad appropriately named Mainas plays the tambourine before a mask of the bearded Dionysus affixed to a post hung with a garment; a table in front supports two stamnoi from which a maenad ladles wine from a stamnos into a cup.[97] Although such vases have been assigned to a mid-January Dionysiac festival by some and to the March Anthesteria by others, it is altogether unclear in such scenes if we are being shown maenads of myth or cult.[98]

The situation is even more ambiguous for artistic and literary portrayals of satyrs. Do portrayals present mythological satyrs or men dressed as satyrs? In all probability dancers masked and clothed as satyrs and silens with long *phalloi* strapped to their waists appeared at festivals in many parts of Greece in the archaic and classical periods. The mingling of animal and human features in the face of the satyr with its shaggy beard, pointed ears, and pug nose should point to a masking phenomenon in which the wearer's identity was disguised and merged with the various shapes of the god of epiphany. But except for satyr-choruses, which are securely attested in Athenian dramas, and a few isolated artistic examples such as the Pronomos vase portraying the cast of a satyr-play, there is no compelling contextual evidence to decide the question.

But even if we could conclusively say that all ambiguous representations of satyrs and maenads were "mythical" they would still be valuable documents for understanding Dionysus's worship. As Henrichs has shown, the Greeks regarded the ritual maenadism (and the same could be said of satyr masking) as an imitation of mythical maenadism.[99] But the inability to establish a context in artistic portrayals makes the category of mythical versus cult representation problematic and ultimately misleading. The fact that the evidence does not allow us to distinguish satyrs and maenads of myth from those of cult is not to be treated with despair; the very ambiguity of the evidence is significant. The message being conveyed is that by enacting the role of the satyr or maenad, by merging with the divine prototype, the boundaries between the divine and mortal *thiasos* are dissolved.

The relaxation of boundaries between the divine and mortal *thiasos* are implicit on two iconographically related panel-amphoras by Amasis, one in Würzburg, the other in Basel, belonging to a group of vases by the Amasis Painter of the same shape depicting aspects of Dionysus and his followers.[100] All can be dated to the second half of the sixth century. When examined side by side, the examples in Würzburg and Basel show how divine archetype and human reality merge under the influence of dance and wine. One side of each vase represents Dionysus with his *thiasos* dancing, while the other side depicts a wine-making scene—a workaday image of agricultural production complemented by a scene expressing the joy taken in the labor. On the Würzburg amphora the revelers are all satyrs; on the Basel amphora the dancers on one side are the mythological maenad and satyr, whereas on the other side the dancers all have a human appearance. On the Würzburg amphora the process of making wine is shown from beginning to end (Fig. 11a). The satyr on the right picks grapes from the vine; the satyr to the left treads grapes in a basket to which another satyr adds whole bunches; a vessel beneath the basket collects the liquid. The satyr to the left of the scene pours wine into a storage vessel. The satyrs are engaged in labor, but their movements are frisky and rhythmically coordinated by the satyr playing the *aulos*. As on the Basel amphora, the boundaries of work and ritual play are dissolved by the presence of music and dancing in both scenes.

The musical activity in the main scene of the Würzburg amphora is mirrored in the frieze above in which enraptured satyrs and maenads approach Dionysus holding drinking horns. The satyrs and maenads continue their dance in the frieze on the opposite side, and this serves to unify the vintage scene with the scene of Dionysus and satyrs (Fig. 11b). A satyr again plays the *aulos*. The god is shown holding a branch of the vine in one hand and in the other a kantharos, into which a satyr, looking quizzically at the viewer, squirts wine from an askos. To their right a pair of satyrs holds drinking horns. The quartet dances responsively to the strains of the *aulētēs*.

Figure 11 (a). Satyrs making wine and music.

Figure 11 (b). Satyrs reveling with Dionysus, and with maenads (frieze, above).

On the Basel amphora satyrs are again shown making wine to the strains of an *aulos* played by a satyr. Dionysus, holding a kantharos, faces a dancing satyr and maenad (Fig. 12a). On the opposite side two additional couples dance with Dionysus in their midst; but the anatomically human males have taken the place of the satyrs (Fig. 12b). Whereas the Würzburg amphora represents a world of pure fantasy, there is a blurring of the mythological and "human worship" of Dionysus on the Basel amphora. A comparison of the couple dancers on the Basel amphora with a dancing maenad and satyr participating in the wine-making scene reveals an ambiguity. The female dancers on both sides are iconographically identical. They wear the same long-flowing garment, the same earring and headdress, and are portrayed in similar attitudes with one arm upraised. The partners of the maenads on each side are markedly different: a bearded satyr sporting a horse tail in the vintage scene, as opposed to an unbearded youth in the other. The women have an ambiguous status, hovering between the human and the divine. That ambiguity is resolved on the opposite side when the female is partnered by a satyr: she becomes a maenad, her other self. It is as if the human worshippers on one side of the vase are transported from the everyday world to the mythological realm of the divine *thiasos* on the other. The Amasis Painter seems to be suggesting that wine induces the ecstatic state that dissolves differences between god and mortal as divine prototype and human reality harmonize.

Turner has written that "structural custom, once broken, reveals two human traits. One is liberated intellect . . . ; the other is bodily energy, represented by animal disguises and gestures."[101] These traits are possessed in abundance by liminal entities, represented by neophytes in many traditional societies. They may go about disguised, wear only a strip of clothing, or even go naked. In their behavior they are usually passive and submissive, obedient to their instructors and accepting arbitrary punishment without complaint. The affinities of initiates with satyrs are obvious. The satyrs present a very different model from the Couretes who are mentioned together with the race of satyrs and the nymphs in a fragment of Hesiod. "The divine mountain nymphs came into being and the race of good-for-nothing satyrs, unfit for work, and the god-like Couretes, the play-loving dancers."[102] Unlike the communally organized Couretes, who practice activities that foreshadow civilized life among mortals, the satyrs are asocial. They live apart, often engaged in useless activities, as their epithets in the Hesiodic fragment emphasize.[103] Permanently drunk on wine and forever leaping about, they embody madness in their movements. In Pindar their epithets are "furious" (*zamenēs*) and "pounding the earth" (*choroitupos*).[104] Anarchic, irresponsible creatures, they are exempt from codes of structured behavior, answering only to Papposilenos or Dionysus. The liminal behavior of maenads of myth and cult, though less pronounced, begins with their segregation into all female groups outside the *oikos*. They conduct their rites in the mountains. In their move from the domestic to the natural world they clothe themselves in skins, taking on the typically male behavior of warriors and hunters.

The historical evidence for dressing up as maenads and satyrs for initiation into the Dionysiac mysteries in the Hellenistic period is ample. Richard Seaford has argued that traces of initiatory practices among male and female adolescents (*Pubertätsweihen*) are already visible in the early dithyramb and satyr-play of the classical period. This type of initiation, Seaford points out, differs from tribal initiation rites because those inducted are not being brought into the larger adult community but into a secret society where they perform an essentially religious function. As such they are socially marginalized.[105] Seaford's argument gains indirect support from the passage in the *Laws* in which Plato reserves a separate category for Bacchic dancing, which involved the imitation of nymphs (maenads), Pans, satyrs, and silens in the context of purifications and initiations. These dances are of no concern to the lawmaker because they do not pertain to the city.[106] The satyr and maenad are in a sense prototypes of all initiates, including those undergoing status transition rites when the breakdown in the social structure is occasioned by the implosion of liminal groups of all types. As we will see in chapters 5 through 8, the same kinds of liminal behavior exhibited by satyrs and maenads in the divine prototype are experienced in all types of initiation, including puberty rites, status transitions, and induction into the mysteries.

Figure 12 (a). Satyr and maenad (*right*) reveling in the presence of Dionysus and satyrs making wine.

Figure 12 (b). Male and female couples revel about Dionysus.

Conclusions

The existence of two distinct explanations for the origins and function of dance, one in violent constraint, the other in persuasion, corresponds with views since articulated by anthropologists interested in the role of dance in society. According to a functionalist approach, orderly social existence depends on the transmission and maintenance of desirable sentiments within members of a group; in Plato's model this means teaching appropriate cultural codes to the young in dance from an early age and revitalizing these sentiments periodically among the adult population through festival dances. According to another anthropological interpretation, certain types of ritual dances constitute a cumulative process building up to a climax that transports and transforms the community into something other. It would be arbitrary and mistaken to insist that dances in ancient Greece fell neatly into one or the other category. Neither structure nor *communitas* stands on its own. The homeostatic and generative models do not exclude one other. Both models, as we have seen, have a cathartic effect on the participants, and the possibility of achieving their common goals depends on the interaction of the two mechanisms for arriving at some semblance of order.

Four

Divine Prototypes and
Their Human Realizations

Chorus [addressing Athena]. To you is given the honor of unceasing sacrifices, and the day of the waning moon is not forgotten, when the young men sing and the music of dancers is heard. And on the windy hill the joyful cries of maidens ring out to the nightlong beating of their feet.
—Euripides, *Heraclidae* 777–83 (trans. A. Barker, 77)

As we have seen in examining divine prototypes of dance and festivity, a lack of clear distinction between divine and mortal is part of a playful fiction recognized by philosophers, poets, and artists that gods and humans interact in divinely sanctioned assemblies taking place under the eyes of the gods. The belief was vital in archaic Greece when the chorus represented a principal means of bringing about intervention in human affairs. The fiction was achieved in part through the dramatic nature of the cult dance that involved the impersonation of the god and the enactment of divine or heroic myth in a designated sacred space in cults and at civic celebrations such as the Panathenaea, alluded to in the chapter epigraph, the principal festival of the Athenians that had its beginnings in the dancing and singing of the young.

The intersection of divine prototypes and human realizations of dance can be appreciated by recalling the shared festival context in which choral performance took place and the range of meanings attached to *heortē*, the word in Greek for a festival that is a joyful

Figure 13. Female dancers linked by hands on the body of a female divinity (?).

112

religious experience.[1] For mortals as for gods, dances were one of several collective activities occurring at their playful gatherings. Like Plato, Aristotle situates festivals in the context of play (*paidia*) and associates them with laughter; in early times, he says, sacrifices and festival gatherings (*synodoi*) occurred after harvest, when people had the greatest leisure.[2] The chorus of initiates in Aristophanes' *Frogs* enjoys a permanent state of festivity, a *heortē* where they play and dance (*paisai te kai choreusai*).[3] Thucydides emphasizes *heortē* as a social mechanism of human festivity: a time of release, of respite from labors, a period of leisure and inactivity corresponding to our notion of a holiday.[4] But the meaning of human play is lost without the divine audience to which it is directed. In the lyric poets, Herodotus, and in Aristophanes *heortē* means a celebration in honor of a god. Herodotus calls, for example, the Attic Brauronia of Artemis a *heortē*, and Aristophanes employs the term for the well-known Athenian Anthesteria festival of Dionysus examined in this chapter.[5] Plato, as we have seen, combines the divine and social meanings. For him play is a serious religious activity. The religious focus of Greek festivals was reflected in the common practice of designating a festival by a term that described the principal rite through which the god was honored and around which the festival was organized, be it a sacrifice (*thysia* or *ta hiera*), a contest (*agōn*), a procession (*pompē*), or a choral performance (*choros*).[6]

The belief in the divine origins of choral dancing indicated by prototypes in art and literature is evident in assumptions about divine sanctions for choruses in civic oracles and religious decrees. In Demosthenes' speech against Meidias, the defendant after whom the work is named, stands accused of physically attacking the orator during a dithyrambic performance for which Demosthenes was serving as chorus producer (*chorēgos*). The orator, in order to drive home the impiety of the affront, reminds the jury that oracular decrees, in addition to civic regulations governing festivals, sanction choral dances. "You know very well that you produce all of these choral dances and hymns for the god not only according to decrees concerning the Dionysia but in accordance with the oracles both at Delphi and Dodona in which you will find it ordained for the city to set up choral dances according to ancestral custom and to make the streets steam with sacrifice and to wear garlands."[7] He then asks the jury to read the oracle: "I proclaim to you, sons of Erechtheus, as many as live in Pandion's city and who regulate festivals according to ancestral custom; remember Bacchus and along the broad (*euruchoros*, literally "with broad dancing places") streets all together give thanks to Bromios for the gifts of the season and cover your heads with garlands."[8] At this point the hexameter verses of the oracle end and a call for prayers to Zeus, Heracles, Apollo, Leto, and Artemis begins. Then follows a directive to set up dances, bowls of wine, and wear garlands. A similar oracle from Dodona decrees that all citizens and slaves wear garlands and observe one day of rest on a day of public sacrifice when dances and wine bowls are set up.[9]

There is no reason to doubt that the oracles quoted by Demosthenes are genuine. Although the orator cites only two, he says that many other oracles addressed to Athens exist. Though none survives from Attica, an inscription from the end of the fourth century from Eretria preserves a decree relating to a festival of Dionysus in which all the inhabitants were required to carry crowns, sing hymns, and offer dances.[10] "[It is decreed] that all Eretrians and inhabitants must wear an ivy crown in the procession of Dionysus and that the citizens take the wreaths [from the public building] . . . and that they dedicate choruses . . . and dispatch wine." The oracular sanctions and the decree from Eretria are similar enough in details to allow the inference that the wearing of wreaths and offering of wine and dances were standard practices to ensure and honor the divine presence.

The Dancing Ground: A Sacred Circle in the Polis

The interpenetration of the divine and human in the dance is apparent in the term *choros* and the related verb *choreuō*, "to dance a choral or round dance." *Choros* and its derivatives are regularly used of the choreographic activity of divinities such as Dionysus, Apollo, or Artemis in divine prototypes of dance; when used in human contexts they refer to the specific type of collective dances usually performed in a ring in cults and festivals. Whereas the generic word for dance in ancient Greek, *orcheomai*, serves for all types of dances, cultic, dramatic, and spectacular, the verb *choreuō* has a restricted meaning.[11] Pindar limits the use of the word *choros* to divine groups, such as Apollo and the Muses. In his victory odes the group of mortals celebrating the athlete, on the other hand, are never referred to as a *choros*, but rather as a *kōmos*, a band of revelers.[12] It was apparently inappropriate to refer to the celebrants as a *choros* since the honoree was a mortal victor. In fifth-century Athens the choral dance is called "holy" (*hiera*), while the participants are referred to as "sacred" (*hosios*).[13]

Note that the noun *choros* means at once the dancing ground, the activity, and the group performing it, which underscores the interdependence of the dancers and the place where they display their communal behavior. Since the exact nature of the word *choros* itself is vague, its etymology is uncertain.[14] All attempts, ancient and modern, to explain its derivation are hypothetical.[15] The most promising etymologies, however, proceed on the assumption that the essential meaning of *choros* is spatial, that it means either a wide, open space, or else a defined or limited area.[16] The word *choros* in early Greek hexameter poetry most often designates the locus where dancing takes place, for example the famous dancing ground of Odysseus's hosts, the Phaeaceans.[17] Significantly, the same word serves for both divine and mortal dancing grounds. The Muses have dancing grounds next to their splendid houses on Olympus, and on Mt. Helicon too they establish their dancing places.[18] The dance floors of the nymphs are hidden away in caves,[19] while Eos had hers on the island of Aeaea where Helius rises.[20] Dancing arenas were consecrated to various divinities such as Artemis. They served as meeting places for mortals and gods, "partners in the dance."[21] It was from a dancing ground sacred to Artemis that Hermes abducted the young girl Polymele, "beautiful in the dance."[22]

The concept of an area specifically designated for dancing seems to have been Minoan in origin. Although Minoan Crete was very different from the later Greek culture, echoes of the Minoan *choros* in Greek literature suggest that the idea of a quasi-sacred dancing ground had a lingering influence.[23] Minoan frescoes and glyptic art indicate that in the Bronze Age dances on Crete took place in settings of natural beauty, in and around caves, and in the vicinity of trees, altars, and other sacred objects conducive to the epiphany of a divinity. The power of the dance to attract a celestial presence to a dancing ground through prayer and gesture is depicted on the famous Isopata ring and on a gold signet ring from Knossos, which is the *locus classicus* for the "descending divinity" type.[24] The setting for the scene on the gem from Isopata (Fig. 14) is a field of lilies. Four female figures, some with their hands upraised in a gesture of greeting, seem to be engaged in a circular dance, while in the distance far above the ground line a much smaller female form hovers into view. This diminutive figure is generally taken to be the goddess descending through the air in response to an invocational dance.

It is in Knossos that three circular platforms were recently discovered in excavations of Minoan remains in the vicinity of the Stratigraphical Museum. The excavator interprets the stone structures as dancing platforms (or in the case of the smaller two, as stages for musicians) on the basis of their shape and construction, and by associated finds.[25] The largest of the three platforms is three meters in diameter and constructed of four courses of limestone ashlar rising to a height of approximately one meter. The area inside was filled with stone packing which provided a stable surface. The level area was reached by a stepped approach above which there was no construction. Engravings on gems found in the vicinity of the platforms depict women dancing and performing other ritual actions. The strongest evidence for identifying the platforms as dancing places is comparative. The circular shape of the raised areas recalls contemporary models of ring dancers from Kamelari and Palaikastro (Fig. 15).[26] Perhaps an architectural structure akin to the supposed dancing platforms at Knossos[27] lies in the background of Daedalus's famous *choros* for Ariadne mentioned in the Homeric description of the final vignette on the Shield of Achilles.[28]

The chief attribute of a dancing place is its openness, and a city, by virtue of having a *choros*, possesses this quality in general: Ariadne's dancing floor was made in "broad Knossos."[29] This

Figure 14. Epiphany of a Minoan goddess (*upper left*) before dancing adorants.

characteristic breadth is contained in the Homeric epithet *euruch-oros* ("with wide dancing floor").[30] It belongs to the large category of epic epithets for places in which man-made (as opposed to natural) features of the polis, such as streets, gates, walls, towers, and other signs of wealth, are singled out. Nine cities are accorded the epithet in the *Iliad* and *Odyssey*. Eight of them are located in Greece: four in northern Greece and four in the Peloponnesus and the neighboring island of Ithaca.[31] The ninth, Hypereia, is mythological, but significantly it is the former home of the Phaeaceans, who are known for seafaring, running, dancing, and festivity in general.[32] The related epithet *kallichoros* ("with beautiful dancing ground") is used of Panopeus, a city in Phocis where Pausanias says that the Thyiads stopped to dance on their way from Athens to Parnassus to celebrate a festival of Dionysus.[33]

Despite their sacred nature, dancing grounds were typically located in civic space, in the agora. The dancing floor of the Phaeaceans is situated in the agora, an area consecrated to Poseidon.[34]

Figure 15. Female ring dancers and a lyre player.

The agora in archaic Greece was a versatile, and to a certain extent, undifferentiated space—the locus for dance, various cults, political assemblies, and judicial proceedings. The first vignette on the Shield of Achilles, a description of the wedding dances at an unspecified place in the City at Peace, naturally gives way to the judicial process in the agora where the elders sat on polished stones in the "sacred circle" (*hierōi eni kuklōi*).[35] Aristophanes calls the place where cult dances for Demeter were performed the sacred circle (*hieros kyklos*).[36] Pausanias says that the Spartans called their agora the Choros,[37] because one of the principal civic activities for which it was suited was dancing. In Athens the area in the agora designated for dancing was called the *orchēstra*, at least in the fourth century when the word is first attested in Plato's *Apology*.[38] It was for performance in the agora, in the vicinity of the Altar of the Twelve Gods, that Pindar's dithyramb for the Athenians was written.[39] This *orchēstra* in the market place is not to be confused with the space in the Theater of Dionysus used for theatrical dancing.

However, even the *orchēstra* in the theater retained its sacred nature. In its center stood the sacrificial altar (*thymelē*), and the image of Dionysus Eleuthereus was brought nearby so that the god might enjoy the spectacles on festival days. A limestone relief decorated with dancing satyrs and maenads (which perhaps belonged to the mid-sixth-century temple of Dionysus in his precinct on the south slope of the Acropolis) recalls the original and enduring function of the *orchēstra* as a place for music and dancing.[40] It was in the *orchēstra* of the Theater of Dionysus that dithyrambic contests were held. On such occasions the theater was pared down to its irreducible nucleus, the sacred circle that, when activated by music, dance, and sacrifice, paid tribute to Dionysus as god of the civic foyer.[41]

A dancing ground, then, was a symbol of wealth, prestige, stability, and peaceful coexistence within the body politic. The existence of a permanent *choros* set a city apart from lesser cities. Whereas the dancing grounds of divinities were thought to have been located in natural settings, mortal dance floors typically were found in the polis, or, as in the case of the sanctuary of Artemis Orthia, in sanctuaries, often a short distance from the city. Given the potential influence of choral dances and hymns over the powers of the divinity, a *choros* implied an active and dynamic relation between polis and patron deity. A *choros* was a sign of divine favor and yet could become a target for divine displeasure. In Bacchylides 5, when Artemis wishes to express her anger at Oeneus for failing to sacrifice the first fruits of the harvest, she unleashes a boar on the dancing places at Calydon.[42] Perhaps here we are to imagine one of the threshing floors of circular shape adjacent to the fields in the Greek countryside that doubled as dancing arenas in antiquity, as in fact they do in parts of Greece today.[43]

Within the polis the dancing ground was fixed in the agora, and the terms *choros* and later *orchēstra* served equally to designate the area where dancing, often of a competitive nature, took place. The *choros* and *orchēstra* were not synonymous with the agora, but were the most important part of it, as the Spartan designation of Choros for its agora indicates. To judge from a passage in the *Odyssey* the administration of the dancing place fell to specially selected members of the community.[44] Yet despite the location of dances in the agora and organization by chosen officials, ultimate control over the sacred circle was attributed to the civic divinity in whose territory the dancing ground stood and to whom the dances were consecrated.

In its second sense *choros* refers to actual dances, that is, to the activity itself. In the fourth-century inscription from Eretria mentioned earlier it is decreed that in celebration of a civic festival for Dionysus the citizens are to stage dances (*choroi*) in the broad streets. Choral offerings to the god are so integral to certain celebrations that the word *choros* in the plural stands *pars pro toto* for the festival.[45] The activity of dance can be meaningfully related to its locus by observing that, as in the anthropological paradigm, one of the primary functions of dance is to establish a sense of place, to control a boundary by putting the feet in contact with the earth and circumscribing an area with a chain of human bodies. The specific connection between "territorial" concerns and the earth that serves as the primitive dancing floor is patent in romance languages which derive the word for earth from Latin *terra*, for example, in the French *terre/territoire*. The territorial function of dance must in turn be related to the religious dynamics of choral dancing, one of the chief religious goals of choral dance being to attract the favor of the patron deity. By dancing around an altar or effigy of the god in a sacred *temenos* it was possible to renew the divine sanction of that territory and so sustain the link with the force at its center. Ritual movement to this end is similar to circumambulation rituals in south India and other parts of the world where by encircling a mountain, a *temenos*, or other boundary, a divinity in myth or a group of worshippers acting on its behalf can reaffirm claims on sacred territory. The idea of reviving the claim is contained in the Latin phrase *instauro choros*, to "renew dances." In bringing about divine intervention in human affairs a vital concern was to focus attention on the space designated as the *choros* by activating it through ritual movement.

In its third sense *choros* refers to the group of participants who sang in unison and danced as a corporate body. A *choros* was a discrete body, an ideal representation of a group or community. A chorus implies a leader, the poet-musician, or one of its members, known as the *archēchoros* or *chorēgos* (chorus leader), a term which in classical Athens came to designate a wealthy citizen like Demosthenes who produced a chorus as a liturgical duty.[46] The act of leading a chorus shared obvious analogies with other spheres of life. Xenophon, speaking through Socrates, commented on the similarity between the military,[47] political, and choral functions of leading, respectively, an army, a city, and a chorus.[48] The emphasis on leading a group inherent in the relationship between *chorēgos* and *choros* may have drawn on the indelible image throughout the Mediterranean of the herdsman guiding his flocks.

Intermingling Divine and Human Play at an Athenian Festival: The Anthesteria

Plato's prescription in the *Laws* for the reordering of the soul by wine, song, and dance under divine supervision is played out in Athenian festivals such as the Anthesteria in March, which centered around the consumption of the new wine by the entire populace, including masters and slaves, adults and children. The oldest of the festivals of Dionysus at Athens, the Anthesteria involved drinking contests, singing and dancing, a sacred marriage, and other activities that led to the temporary disturbance of social structures with the goal of restoring an improved and more lasting order. Unlike most Athenian festivals which are known from sparse and extremely fragmentary sources, the Anthesteria is one about which we are fairly well informed from local historians, the so-called Atthidographers, from allusions in Attic comedy, and, according to certain scholars, from a ceramic type, the so-called *choes* pitchers.[49] The available evidence enables us to see the sequence of this three-day festival, with its shifts in moods from the somber to the hilarious. The Anthesteria embraced, among other elements, a sort of All Souls Day and a children's festival.

This is not the place to explore in detail topographical, calendrical, and other types of issues raised by a reconstruction of the Anthesteria. Our particular interests here are twofold. First, we will examine the evidence for dancing in the festival in general and suggest how musical activity and other types of ritual play establish temporal and spatial boundaries that define and propel the various stages of the festival. Second, the Anthesteria offers a context for analyzing an informal children's transition rite. On the second day of the festival, the Choes, when the new wine was consumed, the newest members of the body politic were, if only as spectators or reluctant participants, exposed to tests of wine consumption, which may have been modeled on the symposium. In their first brush with *paidia* as paideia, the iconography of the *choes* suggests that they imitated adult play, whose ritual significance Plato stressed in the *Laws*. On the third day the swinging rite for children, the Aiora, took place, in propitiation for the suicide by hanging of Erigone, the daughter of Icarius who first introduced wine into Attica. Analysis of the Choes and Aiora for children within the Anthesteria permits us to appreciate how age-status transition rites (in this case of the very young) are situated in a larger agricultural, religious, and social context. The Anthesteria allows us to appreciate how on the one hand dance and related play functioned for the polis, and on the other for special groups within it. In subsequent chapters we will be concerned with dance in rites of passage beginning with adolescence and concluding with the roles of dance and lamentation at the time of death. But it is important to recognize from the outset that most civic festivals like the Anthesteria addressed the collective concerns of the polis and its constituent groups—the living and the dead, mortals and immortals, children and adults, slaves and masters—who by being in touch with their liminal selves on such occasions were brought into contact with one another.

The Anthesteria was of such importance that it gave its name to the month Anthesterion, a calendrical designation found not only in Athens but in many parts of the Ionian world. In a passage on Athens before the *synoikismos* by Theseus, Thucydides states that the city had originally consisted of the Acropolis and what was at its southern base. As proof he points out that the sanctuaries of the gods are either on the Acropolis or, in the case of those outside, situated toward this portion of the city. He mentions the archaic sanctuaries of Olympian Zeus, the Pythion, and those of Gaia and of Dionysus of the Marshes. He goes on to say that there in the marshes the "most ancient festivals in honor of Dionysus were established, which took place on the twelfth day in the month of Anthesterion, as is the custom even today among the Ionians of Athenian origin."[50] Thucydides' assertion that the festival predates the consolidation of Athens by Theseus establishes that the festival and the name of the month existed before Ionian attempts to colonize Asia Minor in the eighth century; indeed it was possibly celebrated as early as the Late Bronze Age.[51] Although details of the Anthesteria are known only for Athens, the pan-Ionian festival is attested in Euboea, Asia Minor, and the Ionic colonies. It is thus, like the Thargelia, pan-Ionic, and one of the oldest festivals of Dionysus.

The name of the festival and the month Anthesterion is generally derived from the Greek word for flower, *anthos*. The festival occurred in spring, when the flowers came into blossom and when the wine from the fall harvest was opened, according to ritual prescription, for the first time. The importance of flowers for the festival is reflected in the garlands worn by the participants, especially the very youngest. The Anthesteria was in large measure a festival that celebrated new growth and transformation: the juice of the vine into a potent drink, the bud to the blossom, and Athenian infants into the newest members of the community. Wine, in collusion with various forms of a ritual movement, succeeded in marking the new rhythms of life.

The main outlines of the festival are well known.[52] Its three parts, Pithoigia ("Opening of Wine Storage Jars"), Choes ("Pitchers"), and Chytroi ("Cooking Pots"), are named after the ritual vessels connected with the opening and drinking of the wine, and with the pot for preparing a meal of seed. The first two days accordingly centered around the broaching and consumption of the wine from the fall harvest. The procedure for drinking wine was different from drinking parties where wine was dispensed from a communal mixing bowl. Each participant brought a personal jug (*chous*) in which wine was mixed with water. It was important, moreover, that everyone begin drinking from the vessel at the same moment signaled by a blast on the *salpinx*.[53] Contrary to normal practice, everyone drank in silence. The first to drain the *chous* was crowned with a wreath and received a wineskin made from a goat. These curious habits were explained in reference to Orestes' visit to Athens after killing his mother. Not wanting to refuse hospitality to the murderer, but equally reluctant to incur pollution by incorporating Orestes into a communal feast, the inhabitants of Athens offered him a separate table. In following this custom themselves the Athenians paradoxically shared in his blood guilt, as symbolized by the consumption of wine produced by the violent trampling of the vine.[54] In contrast to this august ceremony were tumultuous revels in the sanctuary of Dionysus in the Marshes, communal feasts for master and slave alike, and private banquets, such as that described in Aristophanes' *Acharnians* where a man, reminding his guests to bring their own pitchers, invites them to a table prepared with cushions, wreaths, myrrh, seeds, prostitutes, cakes, and beautiful dancing girls.[55] From this temporary breakdown of commensuality emerged a communal feast on a greater scale for adults and children, slaves and masters, which reaffirmed the shared purposes and solidarity of the entire community.

On the third day of the festival the mood again turned solemn. The pots of porridge were set out for Hermes of the Underworld, but left untouched, just as the survivors of the great flood of Deucalion had done on behalf of those who died. On this day the souls of the deceased returned. As a safeguard against the pollution emanating from the ghosts the celebrants chewed buckthorn and rubbed the doors of their houses with pitch, then banished the dead souls with shouts at the end of the festival. The festival thus had a distinct beginning, emphasized by the opening of the wine casks, and an end, marked by sending off the spirits of the dead with the formula "To the doors, Kares, it is no longer Anthesteria."[56]

Two sources most clearly attest the inclusion of dancing, formal and informal, at the Anthesteria. A second-century C.E. papyrus commentary on Thucydides 2.15 discussing the topography and sequence of the festival states that "in the Marshes [the Athenians] held festivals celebrated with choral dances" (*limnaioi de chorostadas ēgon heortas*).[57] The earlier appearance of the same phrase in the third century (in a fragment from Callimachus's *Hecale*) indicates that the tradition of choral dancing at the Anthesteria was a well known and archaic feature of the festival.[58] The epithet *chorostades* (literally "setting up dances") suggests officially organized choral rites of the kind indicated in the decree at Eretria for a Dionysian festival with garlands and dances. To what extent the dances were dramatic in content is uncertain. Presumably there were performances of the disorderly *silēnoi* retelling annually the story of their god Dionysus.[59] A red-figure bell-krater of the late fifth century with a representation of an *aulētēs* and a dithyrambic chorus ranged about a matlike object covered with ivy led K. Friis Johansen plausibly to identify the setting as the Anthesteria. But the performance of the dithyramb at the festival remains speculative.[60]

The existence of formal dances for Dionysus does not exclude playful capers by the celebrants of the festival at large. We have evidence of the informal dances in celebration of the broaching and drinking of the new wine from a reliable classical source. Phanodemus, a fourth-century Atthidographer interested in Attic cults and myths, remarks on the first day of the Anthesteria (Pithoigia): "Near the temple of Dionysus in the marshes the Athenians mix the sweet new wine which they bring from their wine-jars for the god, and then drink it themselves. For this reason Dionysus was called the god of the Marsh, because the sweet wine was mixed with water and drunk then for the first time. . . . Delighted with the mixture, the people celebrated Dionysus in songs, dancing (*choreuontes*) and calling upon him with the names Rich in Flowers, Dithyrambos, the Frenzied One, the Roarer."[61] Though Dionysus was called by many names, at the moment of the festival described by Phanodemus, the god appropriately made his epiphany in the wine. Here we notice the frequent conjunction of wine and divine epiphany, on the one hand, and the appropriate human response to that particular appearance in dancing, singing, and percussive music, on the other. The nature of the dancing is effectively described by the god's epithets which were shouted in a state of inebriated abandon: it was raucous and frenzied. The expression of the license and liberation set off by the outpouring of wine were accommodated for, as in other carnivalesque festivals, by loud music, shouting, and unstructured dancing. These are no choral dances organized for the god.

A great deal of informal dancing and play at the Anthesteria occurred which cannot be specified, including perhaps "devil dancing" with masks when the spirits of the dead wandered.[62] The scholion on Aristophanes' *Acharnians* 1000 mentions for the Anthesteria a kind of dancing contest in which the competitors vied to remain upright the longest on a greased wineskin, the gift awarded in the drinking contest.[63] Although the scholiast is possibly confusing this competition with the leaping feat known as *askoliasmos* attested in the Lesser Dionysia, this is the type of informal test of balance in an inebriated state under adverse circumstances that would have complemented the formal drinking match at the outset of the Anthesteria.

From the first choral ode in Aristophanes' *Frogs* we obtain a good idea of the atmosphere of the *kōmos* in the sanctuary of Dionysus in the Marshes on the eve of the Chytroi:

> Brekekekex koax koax,
> Brekekekex koax koax,
> marsh-dwellers, offspring
>   of fresh waters,
> raise our cry of praise to the pipes,
> raise articulate song
>   (koax koax)—
> the shout of joy we've roused for Zeus's
> son Dionysus in the Marshes (en *Limnais*),
> every time that hangover revel (*kraipalokōmos*)
> passes through our precinct on
> the holy Eve of the Pots (*Chytroi*).[64]

The passage and its scholia have been used as evidence for the processional revel through the precinct of Dionysus of the Marshes on the evening of the second day of the festival. This event ushered in the third phase, the Chytroi (Pots). The likelihood that the choral ode of the *Frogs* reveals paradramatic aspects of the festival is enhanced by the literary and musical subject of Aristophanes' play.

The *Frogs* culminates in a contest between Aeschylus and Euripides in which all aspects of dramaturgy are criticized, including the use of meters and rhythms, especially in choral passages. There is moreover an emphasis throughout the play on *choroi*, especially in the choral passages of the Mystai later in the play.[65] At the moment before the frogs begin to sing, Dionysus is struggling to row the boat of Charon on the Acherousian lake that joins up with the Underworld. He complains to Charon that, not being a seaman, he cannot possibly row. But Charon encourages him, telling him that as soon as he dips the oar into the water he will hear wonderful music. The "music" is, of course, the croaking of the frogs, magically transformed, in Charon's words, into "swan-music." When Dionysus hears the music he automatically responds as if he were a rower on a trireme: "Call out the time, then." An Athenian audience would have readily recognized the reference to a current practice in use on oared ships. Rowers on a Greek trireme had a boatswain (*keleustēs*, cf. *katakeleue*) who called the strokes and a piper (*triēraulēs*) who kept time.[66] The rower's song became a type of working song; Athenaeus mentions the *keleustēs*, "the one who keeps time for the rowers."[67]

But the passage may also refer to another naval image and the festival practice of *aischrologia* (ritual jests). Charon's boat in which Dionysus rides would also recall for an Athenian audience the magic ship in which Dionysus arrives by sea from abroad for his festivals, including the Anthesteria, according to some scholars.[68] This vehicle of epiphany was a popular subject with Athenian vase painters. It is shown as an *impossibilium*, a dolphin or a ship on wheels, combining the conveyances of land and sea. As Nilsson has pointed out, a ship with wheels is not the type of subject an artist would represent without having a living model.[69] In it sits Dionysus, sometimes with an *aulētēs* accompanying his progress. In its festival incarnation the *carrus navalis* bore an actor or cult statue representing Dionysus. It was followed by wagons from which the people shouted jests (*aischrologia*).[70] As it made its way to its destination it was perhaps thronged about by revelers who would taunt the lord of the festival, giving rise to the same type of tension between the privileged *chorēgos* and followers as between Dionysus and the frogs.

What do the frogs symbolize in the context of a festival? The frogs live in the Limnaion, the sanctuary of Dionysus "in the Marshes." The exact location of this sanctuary is unknown, but Thucydides suggests in the passage discussed earlier that it was in an area on the southern and southwest slope of the Acropolis. It was incorporated at the time of the play in the same city walls as the Acropolis that defined the earliest city. On the day of the Choes all other sanctuaries elsewhere in Athens were closed, and conversely it was only on the second day of the Anthesteria that the Dionysian precinct in the marshes was opened for the revel in the god's honor. It was thus a liminal area spatially and temporally distinct from all others. In Aristophanes' play the amphibian inhabitants of the marsh are ambiguous figures par excellence. They are not only said to live near the marshes but appear as denizens around the shore of the infernal lake that leads to the Underworld.[71] The liminal status of the frogs is accentuated by their being amphibious creatures, equally at home on land and in the water. They thus represent through a literary image the revelers and spirits from the Underworld, the living and the dead, who are permitted to converge in the sanctuary of Dionysus on the day of the Choes.

Aristophanes further expresses the ambiguous nature of the frogs, that "song-loving race" (*philōidon genos*), in musical terms. They are characterized in an *impossibilium* as "swan-frogs" (*batrachōn kuknōn thaumasta*). The swan is a bird sacred to Apollo known for its beautiful song, but only at time of death.[72] As the frogs themselves say, they are the favorite of Apollo with his *phorminx*, also of the Muses who play the lyre, and of Pan who plays games on his reed pipe. The emphasis on musical instruments is tied to the haunts of the frogs, the marshes where the reeds (*kalamoi*) for Pan's pipe (*syrinx*) and another type of reed (*donax*) used in the construction of the lyre, are grown. They sing hymns accompanied by the *aulos* and a choral song to be danced. The frogs naturally embody the two main elements of *choreia*, vocal harmony and rhythmic movement, in their own brand of singing—croaking, the very opposite of what passed for music—and extraordinarily versatile movement. They are avid leapers on land and skilled swimmers in the pond. They are a comic prototype of choral activity, but nonetheless hard to match. The many self-references to the musical and choral attributes of the topsy-turvy band of frogs in their choral ode suggest that the musical forces of Dionysus of the Marshes, whose creature they are, as well as of Apollo, the Muses, and Pan, are summoned on festival occasions. The magical powers of dance, in tandem with the spirit of the god unleashed in the wine, are the vehicles that allow the human counterparts to the frog revelers to make the internal transition to a mental and spiritual state consistent with the specially circumscribed locus in the marshes where the playful activities transpire. Although nothing in the choral ode of the *Frogs* is meant to be a description of specific events at the Anthesteria (any more than a vase painter furnishes a tableau of a festival dance), as a literary image the frogs provide as good an indication as any of the role of dance and music (formal and informal) and wine in putting the community in touch with its playful self.

The second day of Anthesteria served to mark the transition between infancy and childhood. That the Anthesteria was a status transition rite for the very young can be inferred from a second-century Attic decree that names marriage, birth, Choes, and *ephēbeia* as the transitions in the life of a young Athenian.[73] In this preadolescent rite, as in others, ritual movement in the form of trials of coordination played a crucial role. Even at birth, the first rite of passage, a kind of circumambulation ritual called the *amphidromia*, was performed. It was a rite of aggregation for the newborn occurring on the fifth day after birth. Friends and family circumambulated the foyer of the house with the child to incorporate the newest member into the household, establishing a link between the infant and the hearth, the focal point of the house.[74]

For very young children as well the Anthesteria was a rite of aggregation. When they were no longer infants they were presented to the phratry (family clan) as a way of symbolizing their admission to the religious community. On this occasion children were perhaps given their first taste of wine and crowned with garlands in keeping with the name and agricultural significance of the festival. The only literary evidence that gives details of the Anthesteria as a children's festival is found in a second-century C.E. dialogue by Philostratus.[75] He mentions that at Athens during the month of

Anthesterion when children reached their third birthday they were crowned with flowers and that bowls of wine were set up and sacrifices made. Vase paintings indicate that the child (usually male, but in some cases female) undergoing the Choes rite for the first time was presented, as the literary sources claim, with a leafy crown, a miniature version of the *chous* pitcher, and a table to put it on. These last details are known from the iconography of the miniature *choes* pitchers, which have been found in some abundance in Attic graves of the fifth and fourth century. They were given to the children by the parents, as an inscription on a *chous* in Baltimore, from the father to one Akryptos, indicates.[76] Not all were made for children's graves; some were used during lifetime and thought to be important enough reminders of this early milestone in life to be included as a grave gift for their mature adult owners.[77]

Interpretation of the iconography of the *choes* as it pertains to children is difficult, since some of the representations are found both on the pitchers of regular size and the miniature version given to children; moreover some scenes are clearly fantastical, with satyrs and maenads and fabulous animals. But the most persistent iconographic elements in the *choes* given to children, the miniature tables and juglets, can be related aetiologically to the communal guilt incurred by drinking wine in the wake of Orestes' matricide, and socially to the cultural emphasis on correct behavior at the symposium. The drinking party, we may recall, is the context in which Plato discusses the educational role of dance in the *Laws*. Book 2 is motivated by a concern to demonstrate how properly run drinking parties, far from being frivolous pursuits, actually safeguard education because they instill a sense of appropriate behavior and moderation in drinking. The subject of drinking parties leads Plato to consider singing and dancing, which along with conversation and the consumption of wine, occupy the participants at a symposium. The ability to think on one's feet, to sing, and to dance while partaking in wine is a proof of a youth's readiness to be included in adult company.

On the *choes* we find children engaged in athletic and musical contests (playing the lyre or dancing) and informal play of all kinds, in accordance with the agonistic spirit of the *Choes* ritual itself which culminated in a drinking contest.[78] For the young the *chous* commemorated the very first steps in this gradual process. Seen against the backdrop of the Platonic myth for the origins of dancing in the wailing and leaping of infants, and viewed through the iconography of the *choes*, the Anthesteria provided an occasion for children to be urged, perhaps by taunting and other forms of intimidation, to exhibit the human propensity toward rhythm and harmony for the first time in a larger, communal setting.

Without arguing that any of the scenes on the miniature *choes* commemorate the actual events in which the young owners participated, it is possible to point to assumptions and common themes in the representations of children's ritual play consistent with the view that norms of education are defined in the first instance in terms of *choreia*.[79] First, the actions of the children are mimetic. The children are portrayed imitating the ritual play of adolescents and adults. Thus we see a small boy wearing a helmet and holding a spear performing a weapon dance, a training and qualification rite for ephebes examined in the next chapter (Fig. 16).[80] He performs before a *chous*, his eventual reward. On another *chous* an *aulētēs* and tympanist, holding out their instruments toward a candidate, goad a mere toddler to attain some semblance of choral activity (Fig. 17).[81]

In other representations the artist, in keeping with the license of the festival, seems to be portraying horseplay, the inverse of desirable behavior. Are we to infer that the preponderantly male celebrants represented on the *choes* were induced to engage in the ritual play of the adult community by going through the motions of encountering the riotous god of wine embodied in the pint-sized vessels? On a *chous* in Berlin a child is given the name Kōmos (revel).[82] On another we see a tiny child performing a hand-stand before a cup from which he makes ready to drink.[83] In a scene from the topsy-turvy world a satyr-child holding a thyrsus in one hand and a *chous* in the other dances not on the ground, but on the back of another satyr who crawls, in the manner of an infant, on all fours.[84] On a *chous* in Copenhagen an inebriated boy in a *kōmos* group seems to let his lyre slip.[85] Even Dionysus, taking as it were the role of the youthful celebrant, is portrayed as drunken past the point of

Figure 16. Boy wearing helmet and holding spear performing a weapon dance before a *chous*.

being able to keep his balance. On a large *chous* in Athens, Dionysus, supported as he tries to walk along, looks painfully at the viewer, while before him a female *aulētēs* puts her instrument back into her case: there is not likely to be any dancing here.[86]

A related form of ritual movement that specifically involved children was the Aiora. On the last day of the Anthesteria very young girls, still crowned in the leafy fillets, were placed on swings sus-

Figure 17. An *aulos* player and tympanist urging a child toward *choreia*.

pended from trees and gently rocked back and forth.[87] The somber aetiology of this rite forms the sequel of a myth of the origin of wine referred to in the previous chapter. When Erigone, the daughter of Icarius, could not find her father, she mounted a desperate search led by her dog Maira, until she found her father's bloody body hurled down a well.[88] A second version makes Erigone the daughter of Aegisthus and Clytemnestra, and thus the stepsister of Orestes.[89] She hangs herself upon Orestes' acquittal. Although the second version would seem to fit more neatly with the *aition* (myth of origin) that accounts for separate *choes* for all in the story of Orestes' visit to Athens, in broad outlines the two versions are similar: both share the display of grief over the violent death of a parent. Details from each are useful for connecting the possible significance of the rite with the perceived origins.

The relationship between the suicidal hanging and the energetic motion of swinging that perpetuates the rhythms of life (swinging in many cultures is, like leaping dances, thought to enhance natural growth) is not at all obvious.[90] Why is the rite of swinging explained as a propitiation for the death of Erigone? The second (Orestes) version of the story goes on to say that the Athenian maidens, according to a curse uttered by the dying girl, followed Erigone's example and hung themselves, an epidemic that continued until an oracle of Apollo decreed that they must atone for her death by establishing a rite in which, seated on a board suspended by ropes, they would be swung by the wind.[91] There are two telling motifs of ritual behavior discernible in the background of the *aitia*. First, we may recognize that Erigone's suicide by hanging, provoked in the first version by the discovery of her father's corpse, is a form of ritual lamentation. In ancient Greece it was the female kin who tended and lamented the deceased through cries and violent gestures of annihilation directed toward their own bodies. Here, the mourning response of the daughter is carried to its extreme. The well in the story has a special significance, moreover, as a locus for lamentation for family members in myths in Greece and the Near East. Demeter sits at a well and mourns the loss of Core.[92] When Isis, who is looking for the body of Osiris, comes to Byblos, she sits at a spring in dejection and tears.[93] Like Erigone, whose other name is Aletris, "Wanderer," Demeter and Isis wander in their searches until they come to the well, where they express their grief.

The death of Erigone in response to her own father's death has been explained by Burkert as a sacrifice occasioned by the violence done to the father.[94] But in both Erigone stories it is noteworthy that the daughter is the focus. There is a song mentioned in several ancient sources called the Aletris, "The Wanderer," after the other name of Erigone. Athenaeus says that the Wanderer's song was sung in memory of Erigone at the Aiora. He then cites a passage from Aristotle in which the women at the Aiora sing the Aletris for the poet Theodorus who met a violent death.[95] It is no coincidence that the next song mentioned in Athenaeus's catalogue of songs is the Reaper's song, called Lityerses. Lityerses is one of several mythological figures in the eastern Mediterranean such as Linus, Adonis, and Egyptian Maneros,[96] all beautiful youths cut down in the prime of life in violent ways. In cult they were associated with the ripening and harvesting of the fruit and flowers, and especially in the case of Linus, with the vine. Their names were used as refrains or as the titles of songs of lamentation that, in part, mourn the spirit of the harvested vine or crops. The mention of the Aletris and the Lityerses together suggests that the song named after Erigone in her moment of grief was a song of mourning. But in harvest festivals, as in the Anthesteria festival itself, mourning and hilarity may closely follow one another. In the biblical tradition the congruence emerges when the joy of the vintage festival is replaced by mourning.[97] The women, who typically perform lamentation rituals in ancient Israel as in Greece, sing and dance at the vintage festival.[98] A similar conjunction of jubilation and lamentation is found in the singing of the Linus song at the vintage harvest. In one of the festival vignettes on the Shield of Achilles in the *Iliad* young boys and girls dance and sing joyously while in their midst a boy playing the *phorminx* sings the normally plaintive Linus song.[99]

The lament of Erigone for Icarius must be connected to the father's role as the inventor of wine. In the background of the *aition* for the Aiora, Icarius is murdered because his neighbors think that he has deliberately poisoned them with wine. But we can see in this violent death, in which Icarius's blood is mixed with wine, an expression of horror at the violence done to the sacrificial victim in which Dionysus is incarnate—the grape trampled, squashed, and squeezed to produce the liquid. The production of wine can be accomplished by dancing to the tune of the *aulētēs*, as seen in the previous chapter in the renderings of the vintage dance by the Amasis Painter. The image of the trampling of the vine in the vat to the accompaniment of music and dance in the harvest festival is echoed in a perverted form in the *aition* by the swinging of Erigone and the subsequent lamentation of the maiden in the Wanderer's song. Paradoxically, what was once a site of violence or lamentation becomes the place to reaffirm life through dances and ritual movement. It is in this light that Erigone, "the one born early" (and who dies tragically young like Linus and Lityerses), is symbolically reborn in the Aiora. In the most innocent of rituals the child swinging in the refreshing breezes of spring, in seeming defiance of gravity and the forces of the earth whence come the dead, purifies and counteracts the lingering impurities on the last day of the festival.[100]

In contradistinction to the Choes ritual, which seems to focus on introducing young boys to public wine drinking, the Aiora appears to address the ritual concerns of young girls. The segregation by gender of rituals is what one would expect in Dionysus's worship and is in fact provided for in the mythic prototypes: Orestes' killing of his mother is the model for male separation from the family (represented by the mother), while Erigone's myth stresses the separation of the young girl from the father. Ritually the divide between genders is emphasized by separate activities: wine drinking for boys, swinging for girls.

In classical vase painting the swinging of a young girl by a satyr is known from an often-reproduced skyphos by the Penelope Painter in Berlin, but examples closer to the Anthesteria can be seen on the larger *choes* pitchers.[101] On a *chous* in Athens a bearded male, perhaps the father, sets a child wreathed in flowers on a swing suspended from ropes entwined with garlands. Two females, perhaps the mother and an older sister, look on.[102] In the foreground stands a ritual vessel. The artist has placed this vessel in relation to the swing in such a way as to show that when set in motion the occupant of the swing will sway back and forth over what is presumably a *thymiatērion* or censer.[103] The fumes from the vessel would purify the child in a kind of baptism ceremony in which the youth is bathed by the wind. But the purifying process is interactive. At the same time the refreshing breezes stirred up by the florid swing and its crowned passenger breathe fresh air into the family and community at large.

Five

Preparations for Manhood: Zeus, Athena, and the Weapon Dance

One might properly designate the warlike category of dancing the
pyrrhic. It represents defensive postures against all kinds of blows
and shots by turning the head aside and ducking and leaping upward or crouching; and it also aims to represent the opposite
kinds of movements leading to active postures of offence when
shooting with bows or javelins, or delivering blows of any kind.
—Plato, *Laws* 815a

Dance is as old as warfare, and from earliest times
mutual influence between the two spheres of activity has been exercised. There are many types of
weapon dances the world over, and the reasons they
have been performed are almost as varied as the
dances themselves: physical and psychological preparation for war,
gymnastic training and athletic competition, celebration of victory
and thanksgiving, funerary display, initiation rite, apotropaic noise
magic, and fertility charm. Many of these same ideas can be detected in the Greek weapon dance, but here we will concentrate on
its significance as a passage dance for adolescent males.[1] In the *Laws*
the "pyrrhic" (the term used in this chapter, after Plato, as a generic
term for the weapon dance) represents the warlike class of dance
par excellence. His account of this quintessentially mimetic military dance with its offensive and defensive gestures, its crouching
and leaping, is the most detailed description of a dance to survive
from a classical source.[2] We have in fact more evidence for the pyr-

rhic than any other dance performed in the classical period, attesting its vital role in military training and the worship of war divinities.

Throughout the Greek world the decisive transition from childhood to manhood was effected through military training and service. The components of military preparation were many and complex, but as a famous Homeric passage indicates, paramilitary exercises of a musical nature constituted a critical means of training a soldier as early as the archaic period. In the seventh book of the *Iliad* Hector boasts of his practical knowledge in the art of warfare acquired through rigorous training. He knows how to maneuver his shield, to charge into the fray, and to fight in serried ranks. To express this last qualification he uses a choral metaphor: "I know how to 'tread my measures' for Ares in the hateful battle." The word he uses is *melpesthai* from *molpē*, "choral song and dance."[3] It is an allusion to military dances and processions, often to the rousing accompaniment of the *aulos* and lyrics intoned by a poet. Tyrtaeus of Sparta and other poets of the archaic period wrote elegiac poems with lyrics that incited the fighting spirit and exhorted soldiers to military excellence on the battlefield. Tyrtaeus's description of the clash of hoplite ranks suggests how diligent physical training proved useful for members of a phalanx in outmaneuvering, in "outdancing" their opponents. "Let each man going hand to hand close in on the foe with his long spear or sword. Let him set foot to foot, press shield to shield, crest to crest; jostling helmet on helmet, breast on breast, let him fight his man, clutching the hilt of the sword or the long spear."[4]

The technical difficulties of manipulating a heavy shield and spear, the standard equipment of the hoplite soldier, were accommodated in weapon dances. The stamina, agility, and ensemble required to execute the dance in a group made it an excellent training exercise for soldiers in hoplite warfare. Despite the practical import of the pyrrhic for training hoplite warriors, dancing in arms had social and religious meanings that can be accounted for by the ritual character of warfare in ancient Greece.[5] To Socrates was attributed the statement "Whosoever honor the gods best with dances are best at war."[6] At Athens, for instance, the dance was performed in choral competitions in honor of the war goddess during her principal festival. For the adolescent or ephebic warrior at Athens the pyrrhic was a passage rite with social and spiritual meanings connected with receiving from the state armor that was regarded as sacred.

It is possible to appreciate the interaction of the metaphorical meanings and the practical reality of the pyrrhic by examining the rich body of myths of origin or *aitia* for weapon dances, as well as the significance of weapons, the distinguishing accoutrements of this dance, in theogonic myth. Since the weapon dance is preparatory to actual combat it is important to consider its relation to fighting tactics. But rather than examine its affinities with the hoplite phalanx (with which a pyrrhic chorus is incontestably linked) it is more productive to consider the weapon dance in relation to the small band of fighters in an ambush (*lochos*), who engage in a furtive type of warfare associated with Sparta. In fact, in Plato's description there is nothing to suggest the tactics of hoplite warfare, but rather those of the light-armed archers and slingers (*psiloi*). The word *lochos*, like *choros*, is a versatile noun referring at once to the ambushers, their covert activity, and the place of ambush. Like *choros* it refers to a group with a leader, a *lochagos*, just as a *choros* has a *chorēgos*. Related to English "lie," the word *lochos* implies the prostrate position of the warriors in the ambush before rising up and attacking. In the *Iliad*, for example, when Paris issues forth from the ambush where he has been hiding he "leaps up" (*ek lochou ampēdēse*).[7] Leaping motion, in coordination with crouching, are the essential movements of the pyrrhic, as Plato makes clear in his description of the defensive and offensive postures of the dance. As a passage dance it was performed by ephebes who were organized in their second year in units under the leadership of a *lochagos*. In this chapter we will investigate the dual identity of the pyrrhic that oscillates between the treachery and disorder associated, on the one hand, with the Spartan institution for adolescent military formation (*krypteia*), and the positive virtues of order and group cooperation implied by the hoplite force, on the other.[8]

Historical Evidence

The Greek weapon dance is attested in Greek art as early as the eighth century.[9] Historically Crete and Sparta were responsible for the dissemination of the war dance, best known in an Athenian context as the "pyrrhic." Dances in arms, however, existed in virtually all Greek city-states and were known by such names as the *telesias*, the *orsitēs*, the *epikrēdios*, and the *prylis*.[10] In Crete the popularity of the weapon dance was due to one Thaletas, who toward the end of the seventh century composed songs and strains for the *aulos* to accompany the pyrrhic.[11] At Sparta dancing with weapons was required of children from age five onward as a training maneuver before engaging in actual military combat.[12] At Athens the dance was performed in the palaestra, where wrestling was practiced, and in choral competitions.

The adjective pyrrhic (*pyrrhichē*), for which the substantive for "dance" (*orchēsis*) is understood when referring to the weapon dance, is first attested in Euripides' account of Neoptolemos's last stand in *Andromache* (c. 425). The messenger in the play refers to Neoptolemos's deft manipulation of weaponry to defend himself singlehandedly against the ambush (*lochos*)[13] of the Delphians as a treacherous war dance (*deinas pyrrhichas*) involving a prodigious leap.[14] In this passage Euripides had in mind a solo dance. Aristophanes, on the other hand, was referring to a choral dance in an allusion to the pyrrhic in 423. An effete youth who comes under attack by the character Right in a debate about traditional *paideia* in the *Clouds* spoils the ensemble of the group of pyrrhicists dancing for the war goddess in the Panathenaea because he is too weak to keep his heavy round shield outstretched at a right angle to his chest. Instead, he holds it limply at waist-level and thus, with typical Aristophanic humor, offends Athena and prevents Right from scrutinizing all the boys' genitals: the pyrrhic was normally danced in the nude.[15]

These two nearly contemporary passages supply several salient facts about the pyrrhic in the classical period: its military and acrobatic nature, its defensive function, its stealthy character, and its connection with the war goddess. The pyrrhic was either a solo or a choral dance. It was a training and qualification rite for young boys, hence the appropriateness of Neoptolemos ("Young Warrior") executing pyrrhiclike movements. Pyrrhicists performed nude and were normally equipped with a shield and an offensive weapon, or at least imitated with hand movements the manipulation of a spear, sword, or javelin.[16] In dancing for Athena, the founder of the dance according to one *aition*, a pyrrhicist essentially donned the panoply which the warrior goddess wore from the moment of her birth from the head of Zeus.[17]

A considerably more detailed view of the weapon dance emerges in the sixth book of Xenophon's *Anabasis*.[18] Six weapon dances were performed by the Greeks under Xenophon's command at a reception for the Paphlagonian ambassadors who were sent to the Greek camp to assure them safe passage through their country. The first weapon dance was a mock duel so realistic that the Paphlagonian guests were stunned when one of the two Thracian dancers was overcome by his "enemy." The second dance was the Karpaia or "Crop Dance." It involved a skirmish between a bandit and a farmer who defended himself while sowing and driving his oxen. The title of the dance and its rural setting indicate that the concern to protect and defend oneself extended to defending the livestock and fields, and we receive independent confirmation of the civic and agricultural meanings of the dance in the *Hymn of the Couretes* examined later.

Xenophon next describes how a Mysian came forward with a light shield in each hand and danced two separate solo dances, one a mock combat, the other the Persian dance, in which he clashed the shields together in time to the *aulos*. The second of the two Mysian dances attests the percussive and musical aspects of weapon dances.[19] The next dance was choral. A chorus composed of an unspecified number of Mantineians and other Arcadians in ceremonial armor formed a line, moving to the rhythm used for war dances. Then they "sang the paean and danced as is done in processions to the gods."[20] Finally, the Mysian who performed earlier arranged for an encore when he saw how impressed the Paphlagonians were with the spectacle. "He obtained the permission of one of the Arcadians who owned a dancing girl (*orchēstris*) and brought her in, after he had got her the best dress he could and given her a light shield. She then danced the pyrrhic dance with great agility, and there was a lot of applause."

Xenophon organizes the six weapon dances according to whether they were mimetic or nonmimetic. Thus the first three, the Thracian duet, the Crop Dance, and the first of the Mysian's two solo dances, represent mock battles; the final female solo dance is also mimetic. The remaining two have a nonmimetic character. The shield-clashing Persian dance is a spectacular feat, while the choral dance performed to the paean demonstrates the ritual use of dance and procession under arms, presumably as an offering of thanksgiving. Xenophon's account makes clear that the pyrrhic was a pan-Hellenic, even international type of dance. He corroborates the impression offered by Athenian drama that the dance was both solo and choral, and that one of the types of weapon dance popular in the fourth century was the military training exercise Plato describes in this chapter's epigraph. Xenophon's account, however, tells us what we did not know before, namely that women performed it, at least in Arcadia, the part of Greece known to be the most conservative in its religious customs.

The richness of Xenophon's description of weapon dances at a banquet can be complemented by epigraphical, oratorical, and iconographic evidence indicating the social importance of the pyrrhic and its wide range of performative contexts. The oldest extant inscription referring to the pyrrhic is a partial list of prizes awarded for contests at the Panathenaea from the first half of the fourth century.[21] Under prizes for team events there are three separate entries for pyrrhicists: one for boys, one for the "beardless" (*ageneioi*) ones, and one for men. Each winning chorus is to be awarded an ox worth 100 drachmas which was probably sacrificed to Athena.[22]

Staging a pyrrhic chorus was an expensive form of public liturgy for a wealthy citizen chosen as producer (*chorēgos*), although it cost approximately one-quarter the amount necessary for underwriting a tragic chorus. The anonymous defendant in Lysias 21 states that he paid 800 drachmas for a chorus of pyrrhicists in the Great Panathenaea in 410/9.[23] (A skilled laborer in the late fifth century earned about 1 drachma a day.) Later he spent 700 drachmas for a chorus of beardless pyrrhicists in the Lesser Panathenaea of 403/2.[24]

A victorious pyrrhic chorus was a form of liturgical service worthy of artistic commemoration, as seen on three Athenian marble reliefs from the second half of the fourth century. The first of the three reliefs (320s), the so-called Atarbos base, shows eight pyrrhicists executing the dance in two rows of four to the right of their *chorēgos*, who wears a cloak. The pyrrhicists are nude and hold round hoplite shields (Fig. 18). An inscription states that Atarbos dedicated the monument, for which festival or festivals we do not know.[25] A nearly contemporary relief (c. 346) represents three figures from the choir of pyrrhicists at the Panathenaea. They are represented in a festive moment after their victory. One of the pyrrhicists stands triumphantly on the shoulder of another, who is escorted by his fellow chorus members, only one of whom survives.[26] On the third relief, dedicated by Xenokles c. 323, a single pyrrhicist survives on one side, while on the other side of the relief

Figure 18. Four pyrrhic dancers; to their left the *chorēgos* wearing cloak.

are visible the plumes from the helmets of two pyrrhicists.[27] A *chorēgos* himself could receive distinctions for his liturgical duty on behalf of pyrrhicists. A decree from the deme of Halai Araphenides records the honors paid to one Philoxenos for honorably carrying out his service as *chorēgos* for a group of pyrrhicists who had danced in the deme in honor of Artemis, perhaps at the Tauropolia. He was given a gold crown, and the dispensers at the feast were instructed to pay him for his services.[28]

Classical vase painting is a vital source for our knowledge of the pyrrhic in the fifth century. Although the pyrrhic in some form antedates the institution of the Great Panathenaea in 566/5, our literary and epigraphic evidence, apart from brief allusions to the pyrrhic in Aristophanes and Euripides, dates from the fourth century. The large sample of weapon dances (over fifty examples survive) also gives evidence for contexts of pyrrhic performance nowhere else attested. Surprisingly, the most widely represented group of weapon dancers extant is female. They are depicted performing publicly at banquets,[29] in private in the *gynaikeia*, and possibly in the cults of Artemis and Bendis.[30] In addition, satyrs, and once even a small child, are seen performing under arms. The pyrrhic is also attested in funerary cult on two Attic vases. Although they were made for export to Etruria, a funerary context for the pyrrhic is contained in an *aition* reported by Aristotle that connects the armed dance with the funeral of Patroclus.[31]

Depictions of the solo male training dance to which Plato refers are extremely common. In such depictions the dancers perform nude to the accompaniment of an *aulētēs* (Fig. 19).[32] Pyrrhic training dances are a motif freely used in certain workshops around 490–80 for decorating black-figure lekythoi destined for holding oil. They belong to the category of scenes of the palaestra, which were especially frequent on this vase type.[33] The likelihood that the various armed figures are engaged in an actual dance and not some other military maneuver or random movement is confirmed by the presence of an *aulos* player or a judge with forked stick in the vast majority of the scenes, and also by the repeated postures of defense and attack that can be reduced to two basic schemes considered later.[34]

Figure 19. A male pyrrhicist and *aulos* player.

Clearly the pyrrhic was performed in several contexts, both sacred and secular, public and private. The performance contexts can be discerned by iconographic conventions. For example a garment draped over a special chair (*diphros*) indicates the *palaestra*.[35] On a pyxis in Naples (Fig. 20) a female pyrrhicist is shown performing before an altar which stands in front of the entrance to a temple; inside is a cult statue of Artemis holding a bow. The altar, temple, and cult statue suggest a dance in the cult of Artemis, al-

Figure 20. Two views of a female pyrrhicist dancing in the vicinity of a cult statue of Artemis.

though the possibility of a representation of a scene from a play or a parody of male activity cannot be ruled out.[36]

Both male and female pyrrhicists perform with a shield in the left hand, an attack weapon in the right, a helmet of the Corinthian or Attic types, and sometimes greaves.[37] The shield is either of the round hoplite type, or the lighter *peltē* referred to in Xenophon's description. Sometimes the dancer carries a sword (*machaira*) instead of a spear.[38] It has been argued that whereas the shield is constant in the weapon dance, the offensive weapon may vary, as Plato's description indicates. Indeed, sometimes no actual offensive weapon is carried, in which case the dancer mimetically represented the deployment of such a weapon, thus giving greater flexibility to demonstrate the ability to manipulate all offensive weapons—bow, arrow, javelin, spear, or sword—through hand gestures (*cheironomia*).[39] A dancer wearing a cloak could even simulate a shield by wrapping a portion of the garment around the left arm.[40]

Analysis of the orientation and attitude of the figures reveals two typical schemes, corresponding with the offensive and defensive maneuvers of a warrior as described by Plato.[41] In the offensive pose the dancing figure appears to be rushing to attack. The body is inclined forward, the head is tilted downward; the shield is held out straight, while the spear is carried horizontally at waist level. The running speed of the figure is indicated by the position of the legs. The forward leg is straight, whereas the hind leg is bent at the knee. In the defensive pose, the head of the dancer is turned sharply backward. In the majority of the depictions the dancer is shown rushing toward the right, while the head is turned back to the left. As he covers his rear side with an alert gaze, he protects his front with the shield, which is tilted upward away from the chest. The spear is held horizontally at waist level. Again the forward leg is nearly straight, whereas the back leg is bent at the knee with the heel raised in the air. The defensive posture with back-turned head is the more frequently portrayed attitude.[42]

The iconographic evidence in general complements and confirms the impression conveyed by literary descriptions that as a type, the Greek weapon dance was subject to many variations, and that its performance was appropriate to several contexts. An icono-graphic study, however, provides intriguing information not evi-dent in literary or epigraphic sources about the contexts for femi-nine pyrrhic dances in the classical period. When we see a young Athenian girl skillfully executing the pyrrhic to the tune of the *aulētēs* in the *gynaikeia*, are we being shown an actual practice or a parody of a society that has a female war goddess but no civic, much less military roles for its female citizens? Both possibilities have been argued.[43] But we must leave aside the fascinating ques-tion of females dancing with weapons, which lies ultimately in the domain of iconographic studies.

In summary, there are two basic schemes in the pyrrhic based on the defensive and offensive attitudes and gestures of the dance so clearly delineated by Plato. As the absence of spear in the Mysian's dance shows, the offensive and defensive aspects of the weapon dance can be selectively emphasized. The armorial accoutrements of the weapon dance, the military audience of the banquet dances described by Xenophon, and the mock combat portrayed in the Thracian dance underline the obviously military character of weapon dances. On the other hand, one of the characters in the "Crop Dance" is a ploughman. Even though the dance involves a duel, its setting is agricultural. Clearly the meaning of the pyrrhic dance goes beyond the military realm, as indicated by the pyrrhic aetiologies to which we now turn.

The Birth of Zeus and the Birth of Athena: Pyrrhic Aetiologies

In antiquity legends tied to the origins of the word *pyrrhichē* and to the dance itself proliferated.[44] Aristotle, as we have seen, derives the name of the dance from the fact that Achilles allegedly first per-formed the pyrrhic around the pyre (*pyr*) of Patroclus.[45] Similar etymologizing led to its attribution to one Pyrrhichos or to Neop-tolemos, who was also known by the name Pyrrhos.[46] Local leg-ends ascribed its origins to war gods or heroes: the Couretes on Crete; the Dioscouroi at Sparta, and Athena at Athens.[47] The war-rior goddess was said to have performed the weapon dance to cele-brate her victory over the Titans or Giants, or according to other versions, when she emerged fully armed at birth from the head of Zeus. In an article on the figure of Athena on Panathenaic prize amphoras, G. Pinney suggests that Athena's victory dance in triumph over the death of the Giant Asterios is the *aition* for the Panathenaea and that the goddess's celebratory dance in turn becomes the *aition* of pyrrhic competitions at the festival in her honor.[48] Plato derives the epithet "Pallas" from the verb "to leap" (*pallesthai*), which he says describes the characteristic leaping motion of the dance.[49] Athena, he states, is the divine prototype of weapon dancers and gave sanction to armed dancing.[50] In another prevalent *aition* the weapon dance was connected with the Couretes shielding Zeus or Artemis from harm at their births.[51] Clearly Plato's war dance had several nonwar aetiologies, with birth as an equally prominent motif.

In none of the *aitia* do the divine or heroic pyrrhicists confront an actual adversary.[52] Athena's dance is either an epiphany or a triumphal display. Neoptolemos dances exultantly after defeating Eurypylus,[53] or in an alternate version mentioned by Hesychius, as a scare tactic upon leaping from the Trojan Horse.[54] The Couretes dance around Zeus or Leto when she is in labor. Finally, Achilles performs the dance around a pyre. The written and visual evidence for the historical weapon dance is also marked by an absence of opponents.[55] Where adversaries do appear, it is in the mock battles staged for purposes of entertainment at the banquet in Xenophon's account. The lack of opponent in the mythological weapon dance corroborates the impression that, whereas mock duels are attested in spectacular entertainments, the emphasis in the historical weapon dance was on the display of military potential.

The exhibition of military prowess in the weapon dance corresponds with the triumphant appearance of a divinity or hero in myth. In Greek the sudden appearance of a god or a warrior can be described by the same word, *epiphaneia* (epiphany).[56] The overlapping military and religious connotations of the word *epiphaneia* are attested in numerous historical accounts of the appearance of tutelary deities prior to or during battles.[57] The triumphant or intimidating appearance of the military figure, heroic or divine, presupposes a place from which to emerge, that is, a place of hiding. The idea of hiding can be expressed by the linguistic category of *lochos*, which means either a place of hiding or the act of ambush. The dual motifs of hiding and emerging figure prominently in the legend of the sudden appearance of Athena dancing the pyrrhic as she issues forth from the head of Zeus (divine epiphany) where she has lain hidden. In a similar way Neoptolemos/Pyrrhos leaps from the cavity within the Trojan Horse (*lochos*) and surprises the Trojans with a pyrrhic display (military epiphany). In all of these *aitia* the idea of birth figures prominently; the relationship between hiding and emerging at birth, so obvious in the biological process, is contained in the word for *lochos*.

The word *lochos* in fact has a gynecological significance in addition to its military significance: it means "childbirth."[58] The ambiguous meanings can be recovered in several contexts. The ideas of a birth, hiding, and sudden appearance of armed dancing warriors are explicit in the legend of the birth of Zeus. A composite picture of his divine birth and the ritual dance it occasioned can be reconstructed from the *Theogony* and the *Bacchae*. Hesiod tells how when Rhea was about to give birth to Zeus, Gaia helped her to plot a deceitful stratagem (*mētin*).[59] After giving birth she secreted (*krupsen*)[60] Zeus to a cave on Crete where Earth received him (*lochos* as place of hiding/childbirth). The first choral ode of the *Bacchae* states that the cave of the Couretes actually gave birth to Zeus, and that the Cretan Couretes, here called the Corybantes, invented the ox-hide drum, which they placed, along with the *aulos*, in Rhea's hands for use in the Bacchic rites.[61] From her the satyrs obtained the drum for Dionysus's festival. This aetiology, which in the context of Euripides' play accounts for the origins of Dionysus's orgiastic rites, also contains the foundation legend for the percussive dance of the Couretes: the ox-hide drum is an elaboration of the shield which could be used to percussive ends, as one of the weapon dances in Xenophon's account shows. In other versions the clanging of the spear against the shield was said to drown out the cries of the infant Zeus.[62]

The ideas of hiding, birth, and emergence are more narrowly focused on the single figure of Athena in literary and artistic portrayals of the birth of the goddess. The earliest written evidence for the belief that Athena was born dancing from the head of Zeus comes from the Hellenistic period. A late second- or third-century C.E. oracle of Apollo at Miletus begins "Concerning a priestess of Athena have you come to hear the divine inspired voice—[Athena] who split the head of her very wise father and leaping among the immortals danced a martial rhythm [*einoplion*] whence she obtained as her lot to preside over . . . citadels."[63] Lucian, in a contemporary (second century C.E.) dialogue between Hephaestus and Zeus, has the smith exclaim upon cleaving the god's skull with his axe that he was breeding in his brain a big girl, "and she's leaping up and down in a war dance, shaking her shield and poising her spear."[64] Artistic representations of the birth of Athena in the sixth and fifth centuries and references to Athena's weapon dance in fifth-century drama, however, strongly suggest that there was already a widespread tradition in the archaic period that Athena was dancing as she emerged fully armed from the head of Zeus.

The iconography of the birth of Athena may be very old, perhaps dating back to Mycenaean times.[65] In the historical period, examples are first seen around 600. On a shield-band from Olympia dated 580/70 Hephaestus's left hand is raised in amazement at the birth of Athena from the head of the enthroned Zeus.[66] The presence of the demiurge in this and other scenes of the Birth of Athena should be construed with his role as animator and *éminence grise* of choreographic marvels such as occur on the Shield of Achilles. The unusual birth is also assisted by Eileithyia, whose hands are outstretched in wonder. Beyond these gestures there is no explicit reference to dance in the shield-band from Olympia, but beginning in the archaic period and continuing into the classical, Attic representations of the birth of Athena in vase painting show more than the upper torso of the goddess; significantly, one of her feet is depicted. On a tripod kothon by the C Painter, dated 570, the Eileithyiai, Hephaestus, Poseidon, and Hera all react to the birth of Athena with the upraised arm gesture.[67] The clothed goddess is fully in view except for her right foot; the left foot is raised in a vigorous leap as she prepares to hurl her spear.

A particularly lively representation of the leaping birth of Athena occurs on a black-figure vase in Basel from the middle of the sixth century (Fig. 21).[68] The goddess emerges with spear and shield from the head of Zeus, seated in his throne and holding in his hand his weapon, the lightning bolt, while Hera and other divinities look on. The same spirited leap can be seen a century later on a pelike, the name vase of the Painter of the Birth of Athena (c. 475–50).[69] The representations of Athena show the foot of the goddess, not merely her bust, perhaps because by the sixth century an allusion to the pyrrhic dance as known from the Panathenaea is legible. The likelihood is enhanced by comparing the figure of Athena on the name vase with the armed figure of a child performing the pyrrhic on the miniature *chous* seen in the previous chapter (Fig. 16).[70] In both cases the body inclines forward; the head is tilted downward; the spear is held horizontally at waist level, as so often seen in representations of male pyrrhicists. The position of the right leg, which is bent at the knee on the *chous*, is remarkably similar to that on the pelike. The occasional presence of Apollo assisting with his lyre encourages the interpretation that portrayals of the birth of Athena carry allusions to dance;[71] on the obverse of a black-figure amphora in the Louvre depicting the birth of Athena, a chorus of four kitharodes parades with high steps, which has led to the suggestion that the birth of Athena may have been the subject of a hyporcheme.[72] Finally, the pyrrhicist's standard armor, a spear and round shield, is the same as that of Athena.

The Weapon in Theogonic Myth

The distinguishing feature of the weapon dance are, of course, the military accoutrements carried by the dancer. In order to understand further the significance of dancing with weapons at the births of Zeus and Athena, we may examine the double-edged role of the weapon in Greek theogonic myth, where the ideas of hiding and emerging with a weapon take on ambiguous meanings. Hesiod in the *Theogony* tells how Ouranos would not permit any of the children born in union with Gaia (Earth) to see the light of day. Feeling constrained, Gaia devised a stratagem. She created a new type of hard metal called adamant, fashioned from it a great sickle, and displayed it to her children, calling upon them to assist her in

Figure 21. The leaping birth of Athena from the head of Zeus.

avenging the wickedness of their father. When Cronos volunteered to assist Gaia, she hid him (*krupsasa*) in an ambush (*lochos*),[73] placing in his hands the sickle. Cronos then reached out from his hiding place to castrate Ouranos with the instrument, thus enabling Gaia to give birth. The deceitful use of the sickle, an agricultural implement, is underlined by the word for trick (*dolos*).[74]

> She hid him in an ambush (*lochos*) and put the jagged-toothed sickle into his hands, revealing to him all her deceit. So when great Ouranos, bringing on night and desiring her love, lay about Gaia, stretching everywhere over her, then his son from the hiding place (*locheos*) stretched out his left hand, and with his right hand grabbed the long, jagged-toothed sickle, and swiftly cut off his own father's genitals. He threw them backward so that they went behind him, nor did they fall in vain from his hand. As many drops of blood as were scattered fell upon Gaia, who, when the seasons circled round, produced the mighty

153

Erinyes, and the great strong giants resplendent in armor and holding long spears in their hands, as well as the nymphs whom they call Meliae all over the boundless earth.[75]

Here again we see the ambiguous significance of the *lochos* as a place of birth and as an ambush, a hidden place from which Cronos emerges with his weapon to carry out what amounts to a military offensive against his father. Cronos's weapon has a destructive aspect, but in keeping with the setting of the ambush in Gaia's womb it also has a procreative end. The blood from the genitals of Ouranos gives birth to the Erinyes, the nymphs, and the giants, who, like Athena at her birth, are born with a spear and other arms. The military ambush against Ouranos, though destructive to him, ensures the continuity of his line.

We hear again of weapons hidden in the recesses of earth (Gaia) in connection with the motif of giving weapons, on this occasion to Zeus. Like Zeus, who was hidden in (or, according to some accounts, born from) a cave, his weapons—the thunderbolt, lightning, and thunder—were released by the Cyclopes from a cavity in earth, where previously they lay hidden (*prin de pelōrē Gaia kekeuthei*);[76] the Cyclopes give him the weapons as a reward for freeing them and the other brothers of Cronos. It is after Zeus's first show of strength that he is awarded his weapons.

The manner in which Zeus deploys his weaponry in the narrative of Dionysus's birth as told in the *Bacchae* is similar to Cronos's use of the sickle in the *Theogony*—strikingly so, because it is expressed again by the ambiguous meaning of *lochos* as ambush and childbirth. In order to punish Semele but rescue the divine child she is carrying, Zeus appears with his weapon, the thunderbolt, to induce "forced labor" (*lochiais anankaisi*),[77] whereupon he hides the child "in secret recesses of birth" (*lochiois d' autika nin dexato thalamais*)[78] from which Dionysus is eventually born. The word *lochos* is used for the male womb, that is, Zeus's thigh to which Dionysus is transferred.

The weapon in theogonic myth thus has a dual function. It functions as a destructive stratagem (*dolos*) and as a charm to ensure release or birth from a hidden area. The double-edged nature of

Zeus's thunderbolt is especially clear in Dionysus's birth narrative. The force of the divine weapon kills the mortal mother, while achieving the eventual birth of the divine infant. Like certain gods, divine weapons are themselves, as we have seen, concealed in treacherous cavities. The Cyclopes release Zeus's weapons from earth and award them to him; Gaia fashions a sickle and gives it to Cronos in a *lochos*. The images of hidden weapons and divinity are condensed in the birth of Athena as portrayed in art. Here the divinity is not actually distinguished from the weapon. The goddess emerges already encased in protective panoply. The weapon is virtually synonymous with its divine owner. The synonymity of weapon and divinity was fatally clear to Semele who ardently desired for Zeus to appear to her in his full glory—in the event, as a bolt of lightning.

The ambiguity of Athena's identity as weapon goddess is emphasized by her inverted birth (from a male womb) and complemented by her dual (androgynous) sexuality. Similarly, Zeus removes the threat of overpowering offspring that were to be born to Metis by assuming the male and female roles, expressed again by the concept of the *lochos*.[79] By hiding Athena within him he carries out a deceitful ambush, a typically male activity; but the hiding also leads to childbirth, the female biological function. Athena's birth successfully averts the threat that Metis poses to Zeus. The birth is both part of a deceitful action (*lochos*), at the same time that it is literally the birth of Zeus's child. Moreover, when Zeus gives birth to an armed Athena he also in effect gives her weapons. The story of the birth of Athena thus shares in common with the narratives of Cronos and Zeus the motifs of hidden weapons and the giving of weapons. The interconnections between the births of Athena, Zeus, and Cronos in the Greek succession myth indicate that the birth of Athena as a pyrrhic aetiology inherits and is reinforced by the motif of hiding and emerging from the preceding phases of the myth. The war goddess is but the last element in the chain of myths that inform the pyrrhic.

The specific connection between vigorous dancing and the motifs of hiding and emerging (*lochos* and epiphany) is prominent in the births of Athena and Zeus. The birth of a divinity, a form of divine epiphany, is a vigorous leaping (i.e., dancelike) activity, and by definition Athena's leaping birth in armor is a weapon dance, as seen in literary and artistic representations. As the divine prototype of choral dance in the *Hymn to Apollo* illustrates, divine epiphany is often expressed by dance. In art the role of dance in bringing about the epiphany of a deity goes back to the Minoan period on the Isopata gem and other examples from glyptic art.[80] Literary analogies to dancelike epiphany in art can be found in several texts in which the verb "to leap" (*thrōiskō*) is used for the birth of a god, notably Athena. Apollonius alludes to Athena's birth in armor by using the verb for leaping (*thore pamphainousa*),[81] and Apollodorus again uses the verb to describe her emergence from Zeus's head with her weapons, *sun hoplois anethoren*.[82] The verb is also used for the birth of Zeus.[83]

The verb to leap (*thrōiskō*) occurs repeatedly in the *Hymn of the Couretes* in a passage celebrating the yearly rebirth of Zeus (which coincides with the spring season) in which the Couretes address Zeus, the "greatest kouros":

> O Greatest Kouros,
> hail, son of Cronos . . .
> We weave it with lyres
> and mix it with pipes
> and sing as we stand
> round your well-walled altar . . .
> For here they took you, child immortal,
> the shield . . .
> took you from Rhea, and [danced . . .]
> Leap (*thore*) in the fleecy flocks
> and leap (*thore*) in the cornfields
> and leap (*thore*) in . . . of fulfillment . . .
> O Greatest Kouros [etc.]
> Spring up (*thore*) in our towns
> and in our seagoing ships,
> spring up (*thore*) in our young citizens,
> spring up (*thore*) in the . . . order
> O Greatest Kouros [etc.][84]

When Zeus is invoked in the refrain he is called not Zeus, but the Greatest Kouros; he is the leader of the *daimones*, the Couretes.

Hymn and dance, accompanied by lyre and flute,[85] are the vehicles for summoning the god whose birth is recounted in a short narrative section. The hymn expresses the wish that he leap into the cattle, sheepflocks, grain, cities, and young citizens—the very adolescents whose prosperity will guarantee the protection of the community. It is a general prayer of rejuvenation expressed through vigorous birth and vegetative imagery. Here the verb *thrōiskō* appears each time with the preposition "toward" (*es*) and in this sense can imply aggressive action, very much like leaping in the pyrrhic, or sudden emergence in an ambush.[86]

Hiding and Emerging in Heroic Narratives

The epiphany of a divine weapon god is paralleled by the sudden appearance of an armed hero. The *aristeia* of Teukros in the eighth book of the *Iliad* is a sort of *lochos*, a furtive form of combat in which the warrior leaps from a hidden place, attacks his opponent, and retreats.[87] In Teukros's *aristeia* (military flourish) eight warriors make up the ambush: Agamemnon, Menelaos, the two Aiantes, Idomeneus and his companion Meriones, and Eurypylus. Teukros, the eighth, carries a bow. Teukros gathers behind the huge shield of Ajax, and at the appropriate moment the mighty warrior lifts his shield to allow his protégé to emerge and attack. "Ajax would lift his shield up over him and the warrior would glance about; and when he had shot his arrow and struck one dead in the throng . . . the archer would return to Ajax as a child seeks shelter from his mother, and he would hide him with his shining shield." The passage then goes on to name the first victim of Teukros, one Orsilochos. The possibility that the text describes, without mentioning it, a *lochos* as a sort of furtive dance to outfox one's opponent, is suggested by the significant name of Teukros's first victim: Orsilochos means "he who rouses the *lochos*."[88] Among the *lochos* group are two Cretan participants, Meriones and Idomeneus. Crete, of course, was famous for its dances and its dancers, such as Meriones. In the sixteenth book of the *Iliad*, Aeneas ironically mentions Meriones' dancing skill that permitted him to elude Aeneas's spear-shot.[89] It was on Crete that the Couretes allegedly invented the war dance.

In the ambush tactics of Teukros we can detect the alternating movements of hiding and emerging seen in theogonic myth. The gynecological character of the ambush is moreover suggested by a simile: the attacking warrior is like a child (*pais*) who returns to his mother—as if Ajax had produced in his *lochos* a leaping warrior to terrify the enemy, much as Gaia did in hiding and setting Cronos against Ouranos with the sickle. The towering shield of Ajax is a portable ambush, an enlarged version of the shield also used as a mobile *lochos* in hoplite warfare from which the soldier emerges to attack when he treads his measures on the battlefield.

To appreciate the ritual context of furtive fighting in a group we may turn from the ambush of Teukros to the hand-to-hand combat of Menelaos and his men with Proteus in the fourth book of the *Odyssey* where the word *lochos* is attested several times.[90] In this episode, which Menelaos presents as a paradigm to Telemachos at the Spartan court, the Spartan king tells how upon his return from Troy he was stranded on the island of Pharos with his companions. In their isolated state they had to forage for food and fish, a most unheroic activity. In order to learn the reason for their detainment it was necessary to wrestle and pin down Proteus, the Old Man of the Sea, who was able to transform himself at will into different animals and natural elements. Luckily Proteus's daughter Eidothea fell for Menelaos and assisted him in his struggle by plotting a *lochos*. She disguised the hero and his three most trusted companions in seal-skins, and digging cavities in the sand covered them over until they could surprise the Old Man when he was asleep. The synonyms used for this *lochos*—"beds" (*eunai*) and a "trick" (*dolos*)—recall the gynecological and furtive senses of the ambush that Gaia plots with Cronos against Ouranos.[91] Eidothea arms them not with a weapon but with secret knowledge that will permit them to master the pernicious arts (*olophōia*) of the slippery Proteus. The method Eidothea prescribes for overcoming Proteus is gymnastic. They must bind him in a special hold and not let go of him.

The gymnastic form of the secret knowledge transmitted by Eidothea to Menelaos and his men recalls that in archaic societies education consists principally in physical and musical training, which the Greeks called *gymnastikē* and *mousikē*. The fluid boundaries between musical and gymnastic activity in the Greek world are clearly indicated by the context in which Plato discusses the pyrrhic in the *Laws*; the discussion of dance follows upon his treatment of the activities of the palaestra, where, as we know from vase painting, the weapon dance was practiced by young males. Cultural information of this type is typically transmitted after a period of separation and isolation during which the young are disguised in animal skins, made to forage for food, and witness transformations enacted by masked dancers—in short, the type of activities undergone by Menelaos and his men on Pharos. Proteus, for his part, is the champion shape-shifter. In his treatise on the dance Lucian said that Proteus was "a dancer, an imitative sort, able to transform himself into anything."[92] His metamorphoses, moreover, suggest masked dancing, and the tale may refer obliquely to trials for initiates at Sparta and elsewhere in the Peloponnese.[93] The discovery of grotesque masks at the sanctuary of Artemis Orthia as well as at Tiryns has led scholars to postulate a ritual struggle between young males and a masked dancer.[94]

The context for the agonistic activity of Menelaos and his men is the *lochos*, from which they emerge to display their arts to the master dancer. Of course Menelaos and his men are not ephebic warriors, but Menelaos tells the story as a paradigm for the benefit of Telemachos, an inexperienced warrior, who has ventured forth to seek information about Odysseus from his native Ithaca, where the suitors are plotting a *lochos* for him.[95]

Let us turn now from the Homeric narrative recited by Menelaos to a young warrior at the Spartan court to Euripides' *Andromache*, where the male protagonist, Neoptolemos, the "Young Warrior" and inventor of the pyrrhic, is married to Menelaos's daughter Hermione, as well as to Andromache by whom he has a child. The words for *lochos* and pyrrhic dancing overlap in a coda to the play describing how Neoptolemos defended himself against an ambush by pyrrhic dancing.[96] The play was performed c. 425 during the Peloponnesian War. Like other plays of the period it adopted as a backdrop aspects of the Trojan legend known from epic poetry while questioning heroic conventions in order to air issues arising from the struggle between Sparta and Athens. Indeed, Athenian military values of the fifth century preserved ideals of Homeric fighting, while emphasizing the need for cooperative fighting in the newer hoplite phalanx. In *Andromache* the tension between fighting surreptitiously in a *lochos* and openly in face-to-face combat (*kat' omm'*) is pointedly aired when Neoptolemos defends himself against an ambush led by Orestes.[97] A *lochos* in the sense of an ambush was a stealthy activity, as we have seen from Teukros's *aristeia*. Although the covert military maneuver implied by ambush was condoned by Homer, epic approval was fundamentally at odds with the later Greek view, which held it to be morally taboo—the type of activity practiced by Spartan youths.[98]

Despite the name of the Trojan princess in the title of *Andromache*, the play has a Spartan accent, and Menelaos has come from Sparta to Peleus's kingdom to slay Andromache and her child. Meanwhile, Orestes and a band of followers (*lochos*) are at Delphi where Neoptolemos has gone to assuage the anger of Apollo. A confrontation takes place at the altar of Apollo between the *lochos* of Delphians and Neoptolemos, who defends himself unsuccessfully. Neoptolemos's last stand is related to Peleus by a messenger. The grandfather insists on knowing if his grandson died by ambush fighting or in face-to-face combat. From the messenger's response it is clear, as we might expect, that the *lochos* fought in a stealthy manner. "But with sword in hand an ambush awaited him in the shadow of the laurel tree. The son of Clytemnestra was the author of the stratagem."[99] The *lochos*, under the leadership of Orestes, fights with stones, arrows, and javelins, and even the instruments of sacrifice. These barbarian weapons situate the group in the context of savage groups like the Cyclopes or the Centaurs who fight with boulders and tree branches.

Neoptolemos, for his part, is without armor at the outset of the fighting (*ateuchēs*), but he seizes a shield from the altar to defend himself. He thus passes, like the Young Warrior he is, from a naked, unarmed state to an armed status; the passage is effected through the intermediary of a dance in arms. For Neoptolemos, confronting the Delphian *lochos*, jumps with both feet and executes terrifying pyrrhic steps (*deinas pyrrhichas*) before going on to make the "Trojan leap" (*Troikon pēdēma pēdēsas*). This last maneuver is an allusion to the legend that Neoptolemos invented the dance that annihilated Troy.[100] Another ancient *aition* of the pyrrhic specifies that Neoptolemos danced it when he was the first to leap from the Trojan Horse, which is called a *lochos* by Homer.[101]

Here we see clearly what has before been suggested, that the pyrrhic is part of a sequence of movement coordinate with the *lochos*. In *Andromache* Neoptolemos's manner of fighting does not differ markedly from that of Orestes' band emerging from the deceitful *lochos*; they are in a sense mirror images of one another. Neoptolemos's mode of attack prompts a comparison with a bird known for its treachery. Neoptolemos is a falcon, while the Delphians are doves. The doves in the simile flee when they eye the raptor behind them. The solitary and stealthy pursuit of this airborne hunter, whose mere aspect terrifies its victims, is full of deceit. The treachery of the falcon responds indirectly to Peleus's original question about whether they fought stealthily or face to face. The hawk habitually pursues its victims from behind, not face to face.

Although Orestes and Neoptolemos are initially distinguished by the category of armed and naked and the outward manner of fighting, the two warriors behave in their own ways like ephebes, which prompts the following question. Does the pyrrhic and its Trojan leap correspond to our ideas of hoplite warfare, or does it represent rather the opposite: a way of surprising, even ambushing an enemy, a sort of fighting reserved for Spartans and barbarians? The epithet attributed to the pyrrhic in the passage is *deinos* (full of treachery). In its offensive mode, at least, the pyrrhic appears to be deceitful, like the *lochos*, and like the hawk to which the poet compares Neoptolemos in the animal simile.

As in the Proteus episode, the coda of *Andromache* has a Spartan background and an ephebic trial centering on the confrontation of the New Warrior and Orestes and his *lochos*.[102] The hawk image situates Neoptolemos in the domain of the hunt. As Vidal-Naquet has shown, a link exists between the hunter and ephebe. The imagery of the hunt and the deceitful manner of combat implied by the pyrrhic in Euripides now lead us to consider the pyrrhic as an ephebic rite executed at Athens, it is proposed, in conjunction with the awarding of armor and the ephebic oath.[103]

The Pyrrhic as a Qualification Rite in Fourth-Century Athens

Among studies of the weapon dance those anthropological approaches that have explored the significance of the weapon dance and aetiologies as a coming-out ceremony in initiation structures are of special interest.[104] Most explicitly we have in the Couretes—the first civilizers, the ones who danced the world into order—a prototype of adolescent initiation groups.[105] The fourth-century historian Ephorus, in a passage on training for boys, recommends that Cretan boys should be raised with armor and that they should be made to practice archery and armed dancing (*enoplioi orchēsei*), which, he said, was first displayed by the Couretes.[106] The only specific dances Plato prescribes for educational purposes for the young are weapon dances. He mentions those of the Couretes on Crete (where the dialogue is taking place) and the weapon dance of the Dioscouroi at Sparta; he then goes on to say that at Athens the patron goddess herself danced in full armor.[107] This is an allusion to the *aition* for Athena as the inventor of the pyrrhic dance at Athens.

What do the historical evidence and the mythological prototypes of the pyrrhic tell us about dancing with weapons in the fourth-century Athenian ephebeia, the institution that provided military training of young men eighteen years old? We know from the mid-fourth-century Panathenaic prize lists that one of the three groups performing the pyrrhic were the "beardless ones." These are presumably ephebes. But was the weapon dance at Athens also a qualification rite for the ephebes, the new warriors? Aristoxenus, the fourth-century musician and author of *On Choruses and On Tragic Dancing*, states that the ancients first practiced the *gymnopaidikē*, then shifted to performing the pyrrhic before they entered the theater.[108] What Aristoxenus alludes to is given a context in Aristotle's *Constitution of the Athenians* in a passage on the qualifications, responsibilities, and privileges of the ephebeia.

Aristotle says that Athenian males who could prove citizenship in both parents were registered in the deme rolls at age eighteen. Three men over forty were then elected as supervisors over the ephebes, with a *cosmētēs* elected as grand marshal. These led the ephebes in a circuit (*periienai*) around the temples and the garrisons marking the boundaries. Trainers and instructors were hired to teach them drills in hoplite armor and how to use the javelin and sling. The ephebes ate in a mess together. These activities took place over a year. In the second year an assembly was held in the theater. The ephebes gave a display of military drill before the people, and they received a shield and a spear from the state. They continued their service patrolling the boundaries of Attica, and when the two years were up, they were admitted as full citizens.[109]

Several ephebic inscriptions contemporary with Aristotle's *Constitution of the Athenians* show that certain ephebes, at least in the second year of service, were designated *lochagoi* (leaders of a *lochos*). From this it can be inferred that internally the ephebeia was divided into *lochoi*. The title *lochagos* is not to be confused with that implied by the subdivision of the ten hoplite units in post-Cleisthenic Athens. Although the status of the ephebic *lochagoi* is disputed, it is probable that the title designated a superior rank among certain ephebes. I would postulate that the *lochagos* may have had special authority over a smaller unit of ephebes when it was on border patrol. This designation suits well the marginal status of the group as reinforced by its remove from Athens. The main military function of the ephebes of guarding the boundaries of Attica is called a *peripolos*, a "going around," and Aristotle uses the verb "to go around" (*periienai*). The circling of the boundaries is the common form of ritual movement known as circumambulation, and has the effect of protecting the area drawn by the boundaries. The practical guard duty of the ephebes, in other words, was reinforced by the ritual movement in a circle. This circular motion, of course, is the basic movement of the chorus, and the protective goal of circular dancing and singing by a group can be clearly inferred from the image of the Couretes performing around the altar of Zeus. In a similar way the ephebes in their circling groups protect the territory of Athena and the citizens within it. The relationship between the *lochagos* and *lochos* is thus similar to that between the *chorēgos* and *choros* in both types of circular movement. Did the *lochos* group perform as a *choros* group in the Panathenaea and on other festival occasions?[110]

Of interest in Aristotle's account of the ephebeia is the proof it provides for the handling of the armor of a hoplite, the spear and shield, as well as the manipulation of the javelin. These are the weapons that figure in Plato's description of the pyrrhic. Although Aristotle does not say that the military drill included any weapon dancing, it is possible to infer from the hiring of the trainer (*paidotribēs*) that various gymnastic rites, including very probably the pyrrhic (which prepared for the deployment of the very weapons mentioned), qualified the ephebes for full military service. Aristoxenus's account reinforces the supposition that the pyrrhic was a qualification rite.

The significance of giving weapons to the ephebes in Aristotle's account can be coordinated with motifs prominent in pyrrhic aetiologies. Aristotle mentions that in the second year the shield and spear are given to the ephebe on the occasion of the military display before the people in the theater. The awarding of arms follows upon a year's training to manipulate them through various paramilitary exercises, including, as earlier postulated, the pyrrhic.[111] The armor awarded the ephebe in Aristotle's account and as seen in visual representations is the armor worn by Athena in depictions of her birth, and on the Panathenaic amphoras, in both of which contexts she is dancing. The motif of giving weapons to gods occurs in theogonic myth, which reinforces the specifically Athenian aetiology for the pyrrhic. The Cyclopes rewarded Zeus with weapons for his first military act; Gaia gave Cronos a sickle for the stealthy mission she conceived for him; and Zeus assured Athena's ability to defend herself by giving birth to her with weapons.

The sacredness of weapons is prominent in the oath that Athenian ephebes were made to swear in the sanctuary of Aglauros where musical contests occurred.[112] It begins, "I will not dishonor the sacred weapons, nor will I abandon my comrade in arms wherever I shall stand in the line of battle." The ephebic candidate then promises to defend the religion of the state, and to obey and protect its laws. He then calls to witness various divinities, beginning with Aglauros, in whose sanctuary the oath is being sworn, continuing with war gods, Zeus and Athena, various fertility divinities, the boundaries of the country, and the crops. The divinities first mentioned in the oath are those most strongly associated with pyrrhic aetiologies. The ancestral oath of the ephebes invokes Athena and Zeus, who themselves received weapons at critical stages in theogonic or artistic portrayals. The three fertility figures called to witness are Thallo (one of the Horai), and two Charites: Auxo, and Hegemone (meaning "leader," as in "leader of the choral dance").[113] The Charites and Horai belong to the class of divinities called societies of gods; their corporate unity is emphasized by their essential activity of dancing. The solidarity expressed by the female personages dancing in a circle on the *choros* is comparable to the ideal solidarity of hoplite soldiers on the battlefield expressed in the first words of the oath; as such it is a restatement in choreographic terms of the ideal of the cooperative hoplite phalanx. The overlapping of choreographic and military imagery in the oath is further suggested by the verb for standing in a line of battle (*stoicheō*), related to the noun *stoichos*, which is attested with the meaning of rows or files of the chorus in plays.[114]

The juxtaposition of warrior gods with fertility figures recalls the two aspects of the pyrrhic aetiologies—the destruction of enemies with weapons and the protection of the young citizens and the community in general. The mention of Athena and Zeus in conjunction with societies of gods known for dancing activity in the ephebic oath recalls the *Hymn of the Couretes* for which we have a probable performative context. The hymn, which is roughly contemporary with the ephebic oath, is closely linked to the oath of the ephebes at Itanos on Crete, supporting the hypothesis that weapon dancing and oath taking coincided at Athens.[115] According to P. J. Perlman's interpretation the hymn was sung at an annual festival of Zeus.[116] The festival in his sanctuary provided the occasion for the newest citizens, the ephebes, to pronounce their oath and thereby celebrate the renewal of the body politic.

In the Athenian ephebic oath the minor goddesses were invoked here in league with Athena, the patroness of the pyrrhic, I would suggest, to witness the fact that an ephebe had completed all requirements, including the gymnastic rite of the pyrrhic; having proven himself, he secured the right to protect and to be protected. The traditional function of the two female fertility figures (Thallo and Auxo) is to shield adolescents in various ways. Hegemone is an epithet of Artemis and like the epithet *Soteira* was used to invoke the goddess as savior in critical situations.[117] There are numerous literary parallels to the appearance of the goddess as helper in a critical situation on the battlefield, as in the fourth book of the *Iliad*, when Athena gracefully swoops down to deflect a spear from Menelaos, as easily as a mother whisks a fly from her sleeping child.[118] A fifth-century parallel can be seen in Orestes' invocation to Athena for aid in the *Eumenides* with a reference to the goddess's defiant leap when she brings assistance to her friends near the stream of Triton in Libya.[119] The widespread allusions to the pyrrhic in the iconography of the birth of Athena would have had an added impact on the pyrrhic as an ephebic rite at Athens, where the birth of Athena was portrayed on the East Pediment of the Parthenon.

The emphasis on hiding and emerging in pyrrhic aetiologies reinforces the supposition that the weapon dance was a suitable rite of passage for the Athenian ephebeia. While the dance outwardly displays the warrior's control of his body and the orderly manipulation of weapons, it conveys images of the stealth and deceit implied by their divine prototypes. Stealth and deceit were positive virtues for male initiates in the Spartan equivalent of the ephebeia, the *krypteia*, which prepared, among other things, for ambush warfare in a *lochos*. The Cretan and Spartan origins of the weapon dance seem to have left traces of their being an initiatory trial of the ability to outfox an opponent, as if from a *lochos*. Plato's description of the crouching and elusive movements of the pyrrhic give some sense of the craftiness necessary to execute the dance properly. The marginal status of the ephebes, their removal from the political center of Athens, and the nature of the pyrrhic as a test conducted in the nude are the structural equivalent of the Spartan *lochos*. But whereas Spartan youths were openly encouraged to perform such deceitful acts in the *krypteia*, the deceitful aspect is latent in myths informing the Athenian pyrrhic.

As a physical contest for the ephebes at Athens the weapon dance was a "coming-out" dance that in part marked the successful transition of the ephebe from adolescence to manhood. The sequence of movement in pyrrhic, that is crouching (hiding) and leaping (emerging), is an analogy of the separation and debut of the ephebic candidate. The potential danger implied by the transition parallels the battlefield situation implied by a *lochos*, which as a covert military activity is eminently suitable as an initiation exercise. Satisfactory performance of the dance implied proof of the soldier's ability to defend himself and his community. Successful completion of the rite would ensure divine approval on the battlefield where a tutelary deity might appear in critical situations in an epiphany. The motif of the awarding of weapons occurring in the myths that lie behind Athena's pyrrhic *aition* suggests that the weapons, the distinguishing feature of the dance, were perhaps awarded along with the magical power inherent in divine weapons to an ephebe who could show that he knew how to manipulate them to the satisfaction of no less a judge than the weapon goddess and founder of the dance, Athena herself.

What possible significance does the weapon dance hold for women dancing in the context of the cult of Artemis? In the same way that the battlefield represents to the male a critical situation from which the soldier hoped to emerge unscathed, so childbirth is a perilous activity that potentially endangers the life of the mother and child. The presence of births in pyrrhic aetiologies is striking. The story that the Couretes danced at the birth of Zeus to ward off Cronos has a doublet in the story of their dancing at the birth of Artemis to ward off the jealous Hera. After a long search for a suitable place to give birth, Leto lands on the island of Delos and gives birth to twins, first Artemis and then Apollo. The birth of so great a god as Apollo required the assistance of Artemis. In cult Artemis had the function of midwife, and one of her epithets was *Lochia*, related to the word "*lochos*" and meaning "of or for childbirth."[120] Although difficult to prove, the weapon dance in the cult of Artemis was plausibly a fertility dance of a very real sort in which the dancer, whether a priestess of the cult, or the would-be mother, performed the steps of the dance to guarantee the growth and future protection of her young, as well as herself. This interpretation is consistent with the analysis of theogonic myths in which weapons double as birth charms. If the pyrrhic had the magical significance of a birth charm, then what the adolescent male characteristically does is not so very different from what the young woman does at the dangerous hour, the most critical moment, be it in the ambush situation (*lochos*) or in the birthing place (*lochos*). The concern of the ephebes is the protection of state, the concern of the women and the female warrior divinity is the perpetuation and protection of the citizens.

Upon closer examination it soon becomes apparent that Plato's opposition between civic dances (of which the pyrrhic is Plato's only example) and Bacchic dances in the *Laws* is too idealizing. The overtly military character of the dance does not always indicate its only, or even its dominant, function. The idea of the weapon dance as a fertility rite, practiced by the Salii at Rome and known from non-Greek cultures, is latent in the Greek weapon dance. Plato's opposition of the pyrrhic to Bacchic dances is clearly too categorical. When Athenaeus described the "Dionysiac" pyrrhic in his day with the dancing maenad carrying a thyrsus for a spear and an animal pelt for a shield, he came closer to appreciating the fundamentally ambivalent nature of the weapon dance.[121] For every shield in the weapon dance we should also look for the plowshare.

Six

Rehearsals for Womanhood: Dance and Ritual Play in Female Transition Rites

In comparative anthropology rites of passage for young girls are relatively rare. As J. S. La Fontaine shows in his book on initiation, the most common status transition for girls is marriage.[1] But in Greece and in certain African societies, among others, rites of passage were held for young girls before marriage. In *Chisungu*, the classic study by Audrey Richards of female initiation rites among the Bemba of Zimbabwe, young girls were segregated and subjected to varied rites and tests prior to marriage.[2] For example, they had to prove themselves in dance contests; they were made to imitate the behavior of animals and certain social types; they were shown models of objects considered sacred by the group, such as a serpent, with the aim of inspiring fear and instructing them about respect and social limits; the arrival of the husband in the guise of a lion was celebrated, and so on. There is more evidence for male rites of passage, characterized by trials and ordeals, ritual wounding, the use of masks, *rhombi* (bull-roarers), and other means for instilling fear and respect. In the Greek world, Spartan initiation rites, with their races, trials, and ritual nudity, are the best understood. A rite for young boys is attested at Sparta from the classical period in the sanctuary of Artemis, and it has been possible to reconstruct antecedents of this rite in the archaic sanctuary. At the sanctuary, terra cotta masks of females, or at least sexually ambiguous figures, with grotesque wrinkles have been found. Michael Jameson suggests that such masks from Sparta and Tiryns were worn by dancers during performances at initiation rites for boys, which represented the struggle of a youthful hero against a female monster.[3] This type of mask display in the context of ritual terrorization is widespread in initiatory structures for young males.[4]

Is it possible that similar rites using masks, dance, and ritual play as mechanisms of social control existed for girls in Greece? This question will be explored in the first part of the chapter by examining the evidence for the participation of young girls in the Attic cult of Artemis Brauronia. In the second part of the chapter we will turn to the evidence from Alcman for ritual play among marriageable girls in archaic Sparta.

In many parts of Greece girls of marriageable age came together to dance in choruses. As the divine prototypes of choral dancing stress, Artemis, the goddess who delights in the hunt, also leads young girls in choral dances that are preludes to marriage and childbearing. Paradoxically, it was a virgin goddess who oversees the development of females, their marriage, and first pregnancy. The display of female solidarity through dance and other collective actions typically occurred at festivals in honor of Artemis, and the dancing often took place at night.[5] In the cults of Artemis girls were sometimes placed in the service of the goddess for longer periods, during which they underwent puberty initiation rites. Once again the rites characteristically involved the formation of dancing groups, as well as foot-races, processions to altars and other sacred objects, and the sacrifice of an animal as a substitute for the human victim demanded by Artemis in myth. Both types of rites can be seen as successive phases in a sequence in which females progressed from being girls (*parthenoi, korai*) to women (*gynaikes*). But the phases may differ in nature. Calame and others have made a distinction between the essentially private character of puberty initiation rites which are marked by physiological transformations (menstruation, growth of breasts) and the public character of tribal initiation ceremonies when adolescents are integrated as adults with the larger community.[6]

The Arkteia

It is not possible to write about ritual dance in ancient Greece without considering the complex of activities associated with the Arkteia, a rite for prepubescent girls called "bears" (*arktoi*) who enacted with dances and other collective activities the mystery of "playing the bear" (*arkteuein*) in the Attic cult of Artemis Brauronia. At the same time the nature of the evidence and the rite itself do not allow the interpreter to isolate dance as a single element. Dancing existed as an activity cognate with foot-races, mimetic aspects of ritual play, masquerade, and metamorphosis. Examining the ritual in its entirety is not a digression from the subject of dance but places in relief the multivalent aspects of *choreia* in Greek religion manifest in *mimēsis*, contests, and, according to an interpretation developed in this chapter, ritual terrorization.

The cults of Artemis in Athens and throughout Attica were widespread and of great antiquity.[7] In Artemis's festivals dancing in many forms was clearly an essential element. The particular role of dance and its relationship to sacrifice in playing out the status transition of young girls in Attica is best known from the literary, archaeological, and ceramic evidence relating to the main Attic sanctuary of Artemis at Brauron, located some twenty-five kilometers to the east of Athens and a few kilometers to the south of the site of the festival of Artemis Tauropolos. The Brauron sanctuary originated as early as the eighth century and dancing very well may have occurred there since its inception; the earliest evidence for dance at Brauron, however, is a fragment of a pyxis or bowl dateable to 560 found in the *heroon* of Iphigeneia on which three females holding hands dance to the tune of an *aulētēs*.[8] A fragment of a late fifth- or early fourth-century red-figure amphora found at Brauron represents two girls performing the so-called basket (*kalathiskos*) dance known from an Apulian vase to have been performed at the Karneia at Tarentum.[9] The use of the sanctuary clearly was not restricted to rites for young Athenian girls. In addition to ritual vessels decorated with dancing and other aspects of a prepubescent rite found at this site, scores of dedications from women, including mirrors, jewelry, and instruments used in the production of textiles, have been discovered. Garments of women who died in childbirth were probably dedicated at Brauron, as at nearby Tauropolos.[10]

The Brauronian festival was penteteric, at least in the late fifth century, although earlier the rites may have taken place annually.[11] Hesychius records that the "bears" sacrificed a goat to the goddess and that the *Iliad* was recited. The Leyden scholion on Aristophanes' *Lysistrata* 645 states that the participants were girls between five and ten years of age.[12] It is not known how many "bears" participated in the rites nor where they stayed while at Brauron; the buildings around the stoa in the sanctuary, formerly thought to have been used as dormitories for young girls during ritual seclusion, are now generally interpreted as dining areas.[13]

What it meant for an Athenian girl to "play the bear" (*arkteuein*) has attracted many interpretations, partly because of the fascination with the bear as a prepubescent symbol for girls, but mainly because of the relatively large sample of black-figure ritual vessels discovered in the excavations at Brauron in the early 1960s on which it is generally agreed that aspects of the rite can be glimpsed.[14] Interest about the meaning of "bearhood" in classical Attica was further sharpened by the publication in 1977 of three related red-figure fragments, on two of which the bear and human figures masked as or transformed into bears can be discerned in the context of Artemis or engaged in ritual play.[15] To complicate matters very young boys are seen in the iconographic material.[16] But although there is disagreement on how iconographic evidence, especially the red-figure fragments, should be interpreted, when all of the literary and archaeological testimony is weighed there is a consensus that the Arkteia was a status transition rite among young girls and that a mystery was acted out.[17] The age of the girls, their ritual activities (including dancing, processions, and racing), their occasional ritual nudity, the symbolism of bears, and the possible use of bear masks all corroborate this impression.

Christiane Sourvinou-Inwood's exhaustive iconographic study distinguishes two age groups: a younger group of girls between five and seven or eight, and an older group of girls about ten years old.[18] This interpretation accords with the scholiast's remark that the "bears" should not be younger than five nor older than ten. Sourvinou-Inwood points out that whereas the younger group is shown clothed, for the most part the older group is depicted naked. A close inspection of the anatomy of the older, unclothed group reveals that they have small, emerging breasts. She interprets this iconographic feature not so much as a depiction of biological reality (although it may have such been for certain girls of that age) as a metaphor for girls on the threshold of menarche. The meaning of the breasts, that is, "not having flat breasts," is to be no longer a child, but a pubescent female.[19] The Arkteia is accordingly interpreted as a rite that represents the end of childhood, and the transition to the beginning of a stage when girls first show signs of being marriageable.

Beyond an understanding of the general outlines of the rite little has been advanced about the nature and ritual dynamics of the Arkteia. Lloyd-Jones's proposal that the significance of the bear in the Arkteia be understood by analogy with the wolf in boys' initiation structures in connection with the Lykaia festival in Arcadia, however, is a useful and suggestive lead. Like the Arkteia, the Lykaia and its *aition* involved identification between a gender-specific group and a wild animal, and tales of human sacrifice. In the foundation myth for the Lykaia in Arcadia the sacrificial victim is Arkas, whose name was often connected with the bear (*arktos*); his mother was Callisto, the attendant of Artemis who was transformed into a bear.[20] The suggestion that we understand the Arkteia in relation to boys' initiations also contains the reminder that the Brauronian festival is not just a rite about little girls; it is about the girl in relation to the bear and what it represents, in short the girl in relation to the divine and social forces that comprise her world. Any interpretation therefore must be pursued in the context of the larger concerns of Artemis, as protector not only of girls but of all young creatures, male and female, human and animal; she should also be seen as destroyer, for the goddess of the hunt also delights in blood sacrifices and hunts the same creatures that she guards.

Rites for the young, male and female, have the ultimate purpose of instilling correct behavior, imparting information, and integrating, often in a gradual way, children into a more mature age group. Typically such rites rely on the children's propensity to play, but they also involve intimidation and various forms of ritual terrorization carried out under darkness by the use of masks, sound effects and ghostly tales, blinding lights, and ritual wounding and death. Such ceremonies characteristically take place at some remove from the everyday civilized world. Frequently the initiates are assigned metaphorical equivalents in the animal world, and sometimes are clothed in skins and made to adopt animal habits. During the period of seclusion their altered status is designated by animal names, such as the metaphorical term "bears" used for the girls in the Arkteia.

To support a reconstruction of the Arkteia as an example of initiation involving playful persuasion on the one hand and ritual terrorization on the other we can take a cue from Plato who comments on the importance of instilling in boys and girls from a very young age pleasurable but appropriate responses to processions, dances, and other ritual play.[21] From early childhood a girl was expected to conduct herself properly in the presence of the goddess, in her dress, her comportment, and in dances. Dances were symbolic of the way that girls presented themselves to their community, especially to the young men, to whom they would one day be betrothed. Young girls in ancient Greece (and women in general) were rarely seen in public. One of the contexts in which they could be viewed, however, was while dancing during the celebration of festivals for Artemis.[22] Moreover, one of the salient features of the Arkteia, ritual nudity, is indirectly commented on by Plato in the *Laws* when he says that boys and girls may be made to dance naked, insofar as appropriate limits and modesty allow.[23] But how were such limits regulated? And what happened if they were transgressed?

We have an indication of the type of response to such a transgression in the *aitia* of the Arkteia and in myths about the abduction of young girls from dancing grounds examined in the next chapter. Myths popular in the art and literature of the classical period emphasize the risk to unmarried girls exposed to view in Artemis's festivals, especially in the vicinity of the dancing floor. The locale was potentially dangerous because dancing made the girl physically alluring. Being the most beautiful carried its risks, as Callisto, whose name means "the most beautiful," learned when she was seduced by Zeus and later turned into a bear by Artemis. The charged atmosphere moreover made them vulnerable to outsiders. Helen, for example, was said to have been abducted by Theseus while dancing in the sanctuary of Artemis Orthia.[24] Herodotus, in fact, tells a legend about the abduction of Athenian women by the Pelasgians while the women were celebrating the festival of Artemis at Brauron.[25]

Evidence for the hypothesis that leads to postulate for the Arkteia a rite of terrorization is found above all in the *aitia* and in certain fragments of the ritual vessels found in the sanctuaries of Artemis Brauronia examined later. In the foundation legend for the Arkteia, the animal sacred to Artemis, a bear, is killed by ephebes after it scratched their young sister during a playful dance in Artemis's sanctuary. This act of symbolic hunting by the girl's brothers lies at the heart of the rite; for the expiation of the murder of the animal was, according to a related legend, in the first instance to be the sacrifice of young girls. The actual rites substituted for expiation through human sacrifice, however, are animal sacrifice and the ritual of "playing the bear" (*arkteuein*). That which replaces the human sacrifice demanded by the divinity in the myth, playing the bear, should have at least a partly violent nature, like the animal sacrifice that accompanies it. But inasmuch as playing the bear involves dance and metamorphosis the rite must also be playful in nature. The two perspectives can be seen in the portrayal of the bear in the *aitia*. The bear is not simply an animal victim. Before being killed, it dances and plays with the young girl, and in an aggressive manner scratches his playmate. In the iconography the bear is also represented as an actor in ritual play. In the analogical language of ritual the scratching suggests a ritual wounding, while the participation of the girl in a game with a bear suggests masquerade and mimetic dance.

Literary Evidence and the Temple Legends for the Arkteia

The only contemporary literary evidence for the Arkteia in classical Attica and thus our principal written source comes from Old Comedy. In an often-quoted passage from Aristophanes' *Lysistrata* the chorus of women occupying the Acropolis gives advice to the citizens of Athens in the *parabasis*. Before beginning they present the credentials that allow them to speak with authority on behalf of the city that reared them.

> Citizens one and all! We are about to begin
> a speech that will be useful for the city;
> it is proper, since the city nourished me splendidly and in comfort.
> At seven years I promptly became Arrhephoros;
> then at ten I ground meal for offering cakes to the Leader;
> and shedding the saffron robe I was a bear at the Brauronian
>   mysteries;
> and when I was a fair young girl I carried the basket wearing a
>   necklace of figs.[26]

It is essential to recognize that our principal literary source for the Arkteia is comedy and cannot be interpreted, as some have done, as a historical document of female age-class distinctions. The four ritual offices mentioned by the chorus should not be seen as progressive stages, as some have thought, but rather as a "pseudo-cycle" invented for comic purposes, perhaps to highlight the incongruity between more graded participation by boys in pre- and paramilitary rites and the less clearly structured involvement of girls in status transition rites.[27] For the entire period between childhood and the moment she was married the young girl was a liminal personage poised on a boundary, vacillating between one state and the other, while the young man passed through progressive initiatory stages.

Because the source is comedy we must ask what assumptions

about the Arkteia the playwright could call upon to make the reference humorous, and how the dramatic conventions of Old Comedy could be exploited to underline the irony of the situation. At this point in the play the chorus, divided into two semichoruses, was dancing, carrying cultlike paraphernalia, and performing other quasi-ritual actions. Dramatically these actions were the equivalent of aspects of the very ritual play they describe in this passage; though exaggerated for comic effect and performed by males enacting female roles, their words and actions were a carnivalesque mirror of serious ritual realities, at least as they were perceived by the mostly male audience.[28] The passage occurs in the *parabasis* when, according to theatrical convention, comic choruses shed items of clothing to allow dancers more freedom of movement.[29] We know from the ritual vessels found at Brauron that ritual nudity was a feature of the transition rite at the Arkteia; Sourvinou-Inwood has argued convincingly that it was the girls in the upper age limit (ten years) who are depicted without clothing because at this point they left behind the bear (childhood) and emerged as young girls—in short, they graduated. The scholia on Lysistrata 645 mention a saffron-dyed garment (*krokoton*) worn by the "bears." Support for the possibility that the girls shed the garment during the ritual is provided by a passage in Aeschylus's *Agamemnon* about the sacrifice of Iphigeneia at Aulis. At the moment of her death the chorus reports that as the servants are dragging Iphigeneia toward the altar she "lets fall on the ground her saffron colored robe."[30] The parallel is pertinent. A scholion on the passage, following the alternate version of the sacrifice of Iphigeneia where an animal is substituted by Artemis, says that what happened to Iphigeneia occurred at Brauron, not at Aulis.[31] "It is believed that Agamemnon sacrificed Iphigeneia at Brauron, not at Aulis, and that a bear, not a deer was substituted."[32] The temple legend, the passage from the *Agamemnon*, and evidence for nudity on the ritual vessels from Brauron have supported a textual emendation at line 645 of the *Lysistrata* adopted by Jeffrey Henderson, the editor of the Oxford Classical Text, and to be translated as "shedding the saffron robe I was a bear at the Brauronian mysteries."[33]

I would suggest that the dramatic convention of removing garments in the *parabasis* indicates why a reference to shedding the *krokoton* is the aspect of the Arkteia to be singled out. Popular knowledge about the nudity of the girls in the Arkteia may have been part of the perception that, in contrast to the other ritual offices mentioned, the Brauronian rite was an unpretentious and moreover egalitarian ritual.[34] Carrying the robe for Athena (Arrhephoros) and the basket (Kanephoros) are examples of luxury persisting in elite cults formerly under the control of the aristocratic families of Athens. The women in the chorus clearly like to think of themselves as privileged. Before enumerating their qualifications, the chorus boasts that they had been raised in a luxurious manner, using a participle (*chlidōsan*) that in its substantive form (*chlidē*) is related to costly ornaments and garments, luxuriant hair, personal charms, and other cosmetic qualities possessed by the Charites in the divine prototype of choral dance in the *Hymn to Apollo*.[35] The related adjective appears in a roughly contemporary Chian inscription in the epitaph of a dancer on a stele representing five dancers.[36] The pretension of the chorus seems to be contrasted with the perceived simplicity of the Arkteia, which to judge from the crude quality of the ritual vessels found in the sanctuary at Brauron was a rather humble affair.

The allusion to the Arkteia in *Lysistrata* 645 stimulated several comments among the ancient scholia. The Leyden scholia state that girls such as those referred to in *Lysistrata* 645 used to play the bear. "Those participating in the Arkteia for the goddess [Artemis] were dressed in a saffron garment and [they] sacrificed to Brauronian Artemis and to Artemis the Mounychian; they were girls (*parthenoi*) chosen when they were between five and ten years of age. The girls performed the sacrifice to appease the goddess, since the Athenians had been visited by a famine for having slain a tame bear sacred to the goddess."[37] Other scholia connect the expiation with the eventual rite of marriage. Artemis, angered by the death of an animal sacred to her, requires that in recompense every girl must play the bear before her marriage. One of the scholia quoted in the Suda records that the Athenians voted not to let any girl marry unless she had "done the bear" for the goddess.[38] The detailed circumstances of the appearance and subsequent death of the bear were explained in various ways. A bear either finds its way to Brauron or is given to the temple of the goddess for safekeeping. While at the temple the bear is tamed. One day when a certain girl (*parthenos*) is playing with the tame bear it becomes angry and scratches her in the face. The brother or brothers of the girl are angered by the violent action and kill the bear. In the *aition* for the Arkteia contained in the Leyden and Ravenna scholia the bear blinds the girl.[39]

As we have seen, a quite different *aition* involving Iphigeneia is told by one of the Leyden scholia, referring to the attempted sacrifice of Iphigeneia at Brauron and the substitution of a bear. The temple legend for the cult of Artemis at Mounychia is similar. A bear was killed, plague followed, and an oracle proclaimed that it would cease only if a girl was sacrificed. One Embaros offered to sacrifice his daughter. But he then hid her, disguised a goat as his daughter, and presented the disguised animal for sacrifice in her place. It is known that a goat was sacrificed at the Brauron festival, and the Mounychian *aition* seems to have been invented to explain the substitution of a goat for a girl in ritual sacrifice.

As Calame has shown, the *aition* for the Arkteia fits into a larger pattern of foundation legends for Artemis's festivals involving a mythical act of piety (the gift or presence of the sacred bear at the sanctuary), transgression of this act (the killing of the bear), divine retribution (famine), and expiation (girls must imitate the bear).[40] It is possible to show that there are likely connections between the *aition* and the Arkteia ritual at Brauron (or elsewhere in Attica) on several points. The first is the type of sacrificial animal. Hesychius states that a goat was sacrificed. In the Embaros version of the *aition*, as we have seen, the substituted animal is the goat. The second is the relationship between substitution in the *aition* and dance as the likely vehicle for transformation in the ritual. The substitution of the goat for the girl in the Embaros version is paralleled in the Mounychian legend where a bear was substituted for Iphigeneia. The substitution of an animal for a human being is a well-known motif in myths about human sacrifice. In ritual, this substitution, I would suggest, took on the form of a transformation through disguise and mimetic dancing. In the story the girl is said to be playing with the bear. The verb used in all three scholia for the particular form the girl's play takes is a form of *paizō*, meaning both to play and to dance. Dance was essentially a mimetic activity, particularly among the young, who learn dances by imitation. A ritual meaning of the compound *prospaizō* found in two of the *aitia* is attested in two passages in Plato, where it is used of singing a hymn of praise in honor of the gods.[41] Such hymns as presented in Plato's *Laws* and in actual practice were performed by a chorus. The language of the *aition* thus may preserve a vestige of the choral medium in which the rite was acted out. Another possible link between the *aition* and the ritual is the bear's hostile activity against the girl. When the girl plays with the bear she herself is scratched by the animal. The mention of the scratch in the *aition* may be related to the fact that during initiation candidates are ritually marked. For example, the famous narrative flashback in *Odyssey* 19 to Odysseus's wound inflicted by a boar on Mt. Parnassus during his first hunt alludes to hunting initiation practices. The wound, which for the girl in the Arkteia possibly symbolizes the advent of menarche, represents the symbolic death of the girl.[42] But it is truly a symbolic and vicarious death, since it is the bear who in fact is killed.

The girl is "transformed into" the various ritually killed animals of the myth and of the sacrificial custom through ritual play, that is, by dancing the role of the pursued or sacrificed animal. As a young, wild creature she herself is a type of animal and expresses her proper relationship to the goddess by allowing herself to be ritually killed. The *aition* thus reveals a straightforward meaning, while it conceals a ritual significance. The verb *paizō* has the straightforward meaning to "play" and a ritual meaning "to dance." The narrative motif of a sacrificial substitute translates into transformation through dance and costume.

The Bear as Model and as Symbol of Otherness

The unique feature of the Arkteia is, of course, the bear, and any reconstruction of the significance of the rite must take into account the ritual implications of this animal in the context of Artemis's cult. Although the bear is attested in classical Greece by Aristotle, beliefs about this creature must go back to the prehistoric period.[43]

The bear's prominence in art and ritual of the Paleolithic era was used extensively by Karl Meuli to support his theory of the origin of sacrifice in attempts of hunters to assuage their guilt for killing victims in various reparation rituals.[44] The physical force of the bear, its craftiness, and its ability to stand and confront its attacker make it a fearsome and respected opponent for the hunter. The bear's unique ability to walk upright on its hind feet also has an uncanny resemblance to human locomotion. This and other traits have led to numerous anthropomorphic portrayals of bears in stories and legends in hunting cultures throughout Eurasia. The urge to place the bear in human situations has also led to successful attempts in many cultures to teach the bear "to dance" on its hind legs. It is unclear when this custom originated, but it may stretch back to the Paleolithic. Though the bear is essentially a wild and frightening creature, it is tameable, as its ability to "dance" suggests.

The two faces of the bear are stressed in the temple legend. Before coming to the temple the bear is wild, but in course of time it becomes tame and plays with the girl. (The scholion quoted by the Suda says that it was brought up with human beings.) The language used to describe their play is *paizō* or a compound (*prospaizō*). Thus the usual interpretation of the symbolism of the bear in the Arkteia is that the girl, like the bear, is a wild creature and must be tamed of her wildness before she can marry and produce children. This attractive reading can be correlated with the emphasis in the Arkteia on dancing, which as a collective activity, has a civilizing effect.[45] But as we shall see, the bear, like the goddess to whom it is sacred, has a more complex range of meanings.

Artemis is closely linked to the bear. Though attempts to relate the name Artemis etymologically to the Greek word for bear (*arktos*) remain unconvincing,[46] the goddess is known from the earliest literary sources as the mistress of animals (*potnia thērōn*), especially animals of the wild, deer, lion, boar—animals that were hunted.[47] Among votive offerings of animals, bears are quite uncommon in Greece, but the handful of known examples were all found in sanctuaries of Artemis.[48] In mythology Callisto was transformed into a bear by Artemis and shot by the goddess because she betrayed her vow of virginity; the name of her son Arkas, the eponymous founder of Arcadia, was frequently construed with the Greek for bear (*arktos*). Iphigeneia, the priestess of Artemis, we may recall from one temple legend, was interchanged with a bear at the moment before she was to be sacrificed at Brauron. When Atalanta was abandoned as an infant she was suckled by a she-bear.[49] The tame but wild, human but animal, natures of the bear are stressed in the *aitia* for the Arkteia: girls dance with the bear as a tame creature, but when it reverts to its wild nature it is hunted by the girl's brothers. The activities of the bear reflect the concerns of Artemis and her protégées Atalanta, and the nymphs, Muses, and Charites whom she leads now in the chase, now in the dance.[50]

In ancient Greece the bear was principally of interest in relation to the human female. Note that the word for bear in Greek is feminine. Aristotle, after commenting on the bear's omnivorous habits and its striking anthropomorphic ability to ambulate on two feet, concentrates on the bear as mother.[51] She copulates lying down (again like human beings), she gives birth to one or two cubs, but never more than five offspring. She delivers her young during a period of semihibernation; she keeps them and herself in seclusion, for when they are young they are hairless and helpless, much like the girls entrusted to the care of Artemis. The bear can thus be associated with Artemis as *kourotrophos* of all young creatures, human and animal. The bear is a model of desirable maternal behavior: it represents the mother the girl will eventually become.

It would be surprising, however, if the bear in the ritual setting of the Arkteia had only one set of metaphorical (i.e., tame, maternal) associations. Indeed the bear's aggressive nature and predatory habits did not go unnoticed in ancient Greece. Aristotle comments on the ferocity of the pregnant bear and her anger and reprisals against the hunter if her cubs are stolen. The bear, Aristotle says, attacks wild boar, deer, and bulls.[52] Like Artemis the bear is a hunter, but it is also a hunted animal. Artemis transforms Callisto into a bear so that she may shoot her with an arrow. In the folktales of many cultures the aggressive nature of the bear has led to its portrayal in folklore as an abductor of women, and myths about the virgin made to marry the bear are plentiful.[53] The bear typically steals the woman and makes her his wife, keeping her captive in his cave.[54] A variation of this mythological type is found in the story of Arkas, the son of Callisto, who in a later source either hunts or marries his mother.[55]

There is independent evidence to suggest that the bear in the Arkteia was an ambivalent symbol, like Artemis herself, and that the bear in part represented male sexual aggression. The two sides of the bear, the tame and docile, the aggressive and impetuous, are captured in the *aitia* for the Arkteia in which the bear, while playing with the girl, reverts to its wild state and scratches his playmate. The physical attack on the girl by the bear amounts to a sexual violation. But this behavior is not unprovoked. The particular turn the girls' play takes is mocking, expressed by a compound of the verb *paizō*, i.e., *prospaizō*.[56] There is a suggestion that the girl somehow danced inappropriately, to tantalize, and thus provoke the aggression of the bear.[57] She responds to the bear not as the pet sacred to Artemis but as an older girl would toward a potential suitor. The scholion quoted by the Suda is more explicit. The little girl behaved in a lascivious manner (*aselgainousēs tēs paidiskēs*).[58] For her conduct she is scratched and, according to the scholia, blinded by the bear—in short, violated and permanently maimed by the creature.[59] The bear's illicit action leading to its death is tantamount to a sexual assault. The girl, in other words, acts in a manner unfitting to her age. She has not yet come, to use a Greek proverbial saying, into her "time for a husband" (*eis andros hōran hēkousa*).[60]

Plutarch begins the story of the first rape of Helen by Theseus by reporting that according to his source, the fifth-century Atthidographer Hellanicus, Theseus was already fifty years old, while Helen was not of marriageable age (*ou kath' hōran*). This alleged act of cradle robbing reflected so badly on Theseus, Plutarch says, that some authors tried to preserve the hero's reputation, claiming that Theseus did not abduct Helen himself. Plutarch, however, finds more probable the account in which Theseus was the abductor along with Peirithous. The pair seized the young Helen when she was dancing in the sanctuary of Artemis Orthia. The abductors eluded their pursuers (presumably again Helen's brothers) and made their way out of the Peloponnese to Attica. Later the pursuers were either punished or killed when Theseus, to return the favor, tried to help Peirithous abduct Persephone. But when Hades learned their motive Peirithous was killed by the hell-hound Cerberus and Theseus imprisoned. In other versions of the story, the Dioscouroi, unable to find Theseus, lay waste to Attica.[61]

The story of the first abduction of Helen, which may have been known to Herodotus, belongs to a type of myth popular in the archaic and classical periods (treated in greater detail in the next chapter, on dance in courtship and marriage).[62] It tells of a god or hero who abducts a girl from a dancing ground sacred to Artemis and, in certain versions, has a child by her. In its outlines the myth of the abduction from the dancing ground is similar to the widespread folktales of bears who abduct females, keep them in caves, have children by them, and so on. In another respect the tales are similar: the male relatives of the abducted girl, relying on their hunting skills, seek to retrieve her.

A comparison between the story of Helen's first abduction and the temple legend points up several similarities. In both legends a young girl is engaged in playful activity at a sanctuary of Artemis. Hellanicus mentions that Helen was seven, while later authors in slightly different versions of the story fix her age between nine and twelve years. In the temple legend the bear violates the girl; in the rape of Helen, Theseus (with Peirithous) is the abductor. In both legends the offense against the girl causes the brothers to come to their sister's defense. The brothers of the maimed girl shoot the bear, while Hades dispatches Peirithous by unleashing the hound Cerberus. The Dioscouroi mount an expedition to hunt down Theseus. Although the Dioscouroi are not successful in finding the offending male, the consequence of their anger, that is, the ravaging of Athens, is the same as the result of the anger of Artemis, who sends a plague or famine against Attica.

Certain details of the abduction stories are relevant to the Arkteia. Like the bear (and by inference Helen as a young girl), the girls who participated in the Arkteia were sacred to Artemis. The age of the girls, which we know from literary and archaeological evidence was between five and ten, corresponds with the age of Helen in the literary sources. This was not, as Hellanicus stresses, marriageable age. Hellanicus meant that no male should do what

Theseus did; the temple legend in condensed form says both that suitors should wait for a girl to come of age and that a girl should not prematurely behave as if she were of marriageable age.

The temple legend for the Arkteia is thus similar to the story of a bear abducting a girl, and to the myth of the hero carrying away a girl from the dancing ground. Without claiming any causal relationship between the *aition* and the story of the first rape of Helen, I would suggest that the urgent concerns about appropriate behavior by and toward girls who were not yet of a marriageable age were expressed in such myths and legends, and that we have in the Arkteia *aition* a vestige of such a story or perhaps even a fable version intended for the young participants as a warning of their increased vulnerability and of the need to observe proper limits. By chance we have in Herodotus a legend about the abduction of Athenian women by the Pelasgians while the women were celebrating the festival of Artemis at Brauron.[63] Because of its seclusion and their knowledge that no Athenian men would be at Brauron to defend the women, the Pelasgians—in reprisal for an earlier wrong —sailed from Lemnos to carry away the women and make them their concubines. This story has been interpreted as a reminiscence of primitive customs of marriage by abduction and exogamy; but a simpler explanation may be offered.[64] Herodotus's report is another indication of the type of minatory tale told to and about females, including, in some form, prepubescent initiates at Brauron.

The bear in the Arkteia is thus a positive model of eventual motherhood, but also a negative model of unwanted, premature male attention and the need to avoid it. The message contained in tales such as the disfigurement of the girl by the bear may have been conveyed by other means. A statue (of which only the head survives) found at Brauron shows a beautiful young girl wearing a diadem; she is blind. It may well represent the blind girl of Brauron and may have been displayed as a kind of example for the participants.[65] From the Acropolis, perhaps the shrine of Artemis Brauroneion, comes a bear sitting on its haunches and lifting up its front paws. Was it originally part of a group showing the blinding of the little girl?[66]

The blinding of the girl, the ritual nudity of the participants in the Arkteia, and Plato's recommendation to dance naked (provided proper limits are observed) all revolve around the theme of seeing and being seen, and its advantages and dangers. The part of the body attacked by the bear in one version, the eyes, recalls the myth of Artemis's victim Actaeon, who is punished for looking at the goddess at her bath by being transformed into an animal pursued by his own hounds. A similar punishment is visited upon those whose behavior is the obverse, who exhibit themselves while in the service of Artemis. Callisto, who showed herself to be "the most beautiful," attracted the unwanted sexual attention of Zeus and betrayed her vow of virginity to Artemis; she became pregnant and a child Arkas was born. For this betrayal to the goddess she was transformed into a bear and hunted down by Artemis's arrow. The transformation of Callisto into a bear and the rescue of her son Arkas by Hermes was portrayed by Apulian vase painters in graphic detail.[67] We see the moment when the maiden, her head inclined in grief, trades her human beauty for the features of a bear: the ears grow pointed, the fingers of the hand turn into claws, tufts of hair crop up on the skin once delicate. A similarly ambiguous figure is seen in the ceramic evidence to which we now turn.

Ceramic Evidence

The meaning of "playing the bear" in the cult of Artemis Brauron can be recovered with the help of ceramic evidence, although, as Richard Hamilton has stressed, there is a dissonance between literary and visual evidence, the latter emphasizing typical features of the rite, the former the distinctive.[68] The type of ritual vessel on which aspects of the ritual are depicted has been called krateriskos by Lilly Kahil, who first published fragments of this characteristic shape in 1963. They are small cups mounted on a tall, flared stem and resembling a chalice.[69] They have been found in some abundance at Brauron and other Attic sanctuaries of Artemis, including the Brauroneion on the Acropolis.[70] The krateriskoi date from the sixth and fifth centuries. Analysis of the clay indicates that they were made from local wares, from which it can be inferred that they were probably made separately for each sanctuary. Except for three much larger red-figure krateriskoi fragments, the decoration is black figure and done in a somewhat crude style. The fact that they were found only in the sanctuaries of Artemis suggests not only ritual use but that the rites were to be kept secret.[71] The vast majority were found at Brauron during the excavations of the sanctuary by J. Papadimitriou.[72] Of the hundreds and hundreds of krateriskoi found at that site only a small sample has been published; but taken together with krateriskoi found at other sites connected with Artemis, a pattern of three repeated scenes emerges.[73] Young girls are seen dancing, engaged in foot-races, and in procession toward an altar or tree. Analysis of the iconography reveals that the participants in the rites are portrayed in a manner not inconsistent with the literary evidence.[74] The central figures are prepubescent girls shown both naked and clothed in chitons of varying length. Older female figures also appear: one would not expect the activities of the very young to go unsupervised by female relatives or the priestesses of the cult.

Among the relatively small sampling of published krateriskoi a dozen or so are generally thought to depict dancing.[75] In several cases the impression of dance movement or dancers can be corroborated by the presence of *krotala* held in the hand or by the iconographic convention of linked hands.[76] In discussions of the evidence for dancing on the krateriskoi scholars most often characterize the movement of the dancers as "stately." The puffed-out dress of some dancers and the outstretched arms and high-stepping feet of others, however, suggests fast, whirling, and generally animated movement.[77] The presence of *krotala*, which appear in ecstatic contexts, also indicates that not all of the dancing was stately and solemn. Pindar mentions the percussive sounds produced by the clappers along with the thundering tympanum (*rhomboi tympanōn*) used in the worship of the Mother.[78] The rhombos and other noise-makers are anthropologically attested in ritual terrorization ceremonies; they are under the control of the initiators. The *krotala* on one krateriskos from Mounychia is held by an older woman.[79] Unfortunately the sampling of fragments with dancing and other musical phenomena is too small to draw any specific conclusions, except that we do not see in the dancing scenes any indication that the girls are mimetically reproducing the behavior or characteristics of the bear.[80]

We do glimpse the bear on two of three related red-figure krateriskoi fragments dating from the third quarter of the fifth century.[81] Their exact provenance is unknown, and certain scholars have doubted their relevance to Brauronian religion, particularly the fragment depicting Artemis and two theriomorphic figures. Any interpretation of these fragments must be regarded as provisional, and certainly not as pivotal to understanding the Arkteia. Nevertheless, Kahil has shown close links between representations on these krateriskoi and the smaller krateriskoi found in the Attic sanctuaries of Artemis and suggests that the red-figure fragments were perhaps made for the sanctuary of Artemis Brauronia on the Acropolis. The three krateriskoi fragments are iconographically interrelated and may in fact have belonged to the same vessel.[82] Two of the fragments presumably represent the *aition* of the foot-race of the girls, which is seen elsewhere on the smaller krateriskoi, while it has been argued by Kahil that the third depicts the mystery of Brauron, the so-called sacred hunt (*to hieron kunēgesion*).[83] The first of the two race fragments (Fig. 22 *top*) is divided into two scenes. On one side women and girls in alternating positions make preparations for the race. The women, holding ritual objects, inspect the chitons of the girls. On the other side the race is under way. In the second of the two race fragments (Fig. 22 *middle*) the participants are shown naked. They appear to be girls of the older group and run with wreaths in their hands. Over the handle of the vase a palm tree, an object sacred to Artemis, is depicted. In front of the palm is an animal, the sacred bear. The bear probably situates the race as part of the Brauronia. Does it also indicate that the foot-race is the ritual reaction to the bear as a symbol of terror? The girls run in opposite directions away from the bear, the one nearest the bear apparently turning around to look at the creature as she flees.[84] In the foreground of the scene hounds pursue a hare. If this hunting frieze is to be taken as an analogy for the main scene, the girls flee because they are being pursued or "hunted" by the bear.

On the third fragment (Fig. 22 *bottom*) Leto, Apollo, and Artemis are represented to the left of the handle of the vase. Artemis

Figure 22. *Top*: Preparation for girls' foot-race. *Middle*: Girls carrying garlands in a foot-race running in opposite directions from bear and palm tree. *Bottom*: Artemis (*left*) firing an arrow; a male and a female figure masked as or transformed into bears.

fires an arrow at a fawn who is leaping above the handle of the krateriskos. To the right of the handle the body of a young male is shown naked; he appears to have the head of a bear and looks to the left toward the bounding fawn. To his right stands a female figure clad in a chiton and himation. She is shown with the face frontal, and like the male, has the same pointed ears and features of the bear. She holds her arms upward. To the right another fawn frames the scene, thus linking it to the other side.[85] Like the grotesque masks found at the sanctuary of the goddess Orthia the figure portrayed here is androgynous, an essential feature of many figures of fright.[86]

Although the red-figure fragments contain features that are unique, they share elements in common with smaller black-figure krateriskoi. The motif of flight and dancing can be related to fragments of two black-figure krateriskoi from Athens on which deer are seen in the context of music and dance. In the first fragment a woman plays the *aulos*.[87] To her right a partially preserved figure either runs or dances; to the left of the *aulētēs* is a bounding deer. The likelihood that the partially preserved figure is dancing and not running is enhanced by the presence of a musical instrument in the scene and by a similar scene on the second krateriskos fragment. In this fragment (Fig. 23) two girls with hands linked in the characteristic gesture of choral formation appear to be dancing; to their left are preserved the legs of a leaping deer.[88] It should be recalled that in the red-figure krateriskos representing Artemis, a deer, not a bear, is the target of the goddess's arrow.[89] In the red-figure krateriskos representing an excerpt of a hunt, a hare is the object of the hounds' pursuit. This hunting frieze should be read as an analogy for the main scene which shows the girls running from the bear. In the world of the epic animal simile, the deer and hare are symbols of flight before the more powerful predator or the hunter; Artemis's epithet in the *Iliad* is deer-slayer (*elaphēbolos*).[90] If we think of the dynamics between the single predator and multiple prey in choral terms, we have an inversion of the *chorēgos/choreutai* relationship. Instead of encircling the *chorēgos*, the chorus members move away from the hunter (*kunēgos*).

One message conveyed by the red-figure krateriskoi is flight. Girls flee the bear; the deer flee from Artemis's arrow; hares flee before the hounds. It is natural to suppose that the girls flee from the bear because they are being ritually hunted, just as Artemis hunts Callisto as a bear, or as she hunts deer on the third krateriskos. I suggest that the foot-race is the agonistic version of a

Figure 23. Two girls forming a ring dance by joining hands.

ritual hunt. The frightened reaction of the girls may be a reference to ritual terrorization of initiates by masks and other means, as has been postulated for the grotesque masks found at the sanctuary of Artemis Orthia near Sparta. Although it is unlikely that we are seeing a phase of any actual ritual on the red-figure krateriskoi, I would suggest that at a climactic phase in the Arkteia ritual a priestess wearing a bear mask and other grotesque features, or a specially chosen girl corresponding to the blind girl portrayed in the Brauron statue, was presented to the girls made impressionable by ecstatic dancing. The type of terror such a revelation inspired in them is perhaps conveyed in the second red-figure krateriskos.

If it is correct to infer from the bear masquerade on the third red-figure krateriskos the ritual terrorization of initiates, the ecstatic dancing seen on the smaller krateriskoi would have occurred just prior to the mystery. The delirious, out-of-control state so induced would make the girls impressionable and enhance the frightening effect. As a sequence of events I would suggest a procession to altars, sacrifice, ecstatic dancing by girls and the revelation of the bear-goddess, racing, and performing in choruses.[91] The ecstatic dancing and running, both images of fear and flight, may have been followed by orderly dancing to express self-control and solidarity. The mastery of fear and the ability to dance in a group proved that the participant is not wild but on her way to becoming socialized. The rhythms of the dance regulated that passage from a wild to a tame state.

In postulating the performance by maskers at the Arkteia I do not wish to suggest that the ceramic evidence, any more than the temple legends, captures in exact terms the ritual. That is irretrievable, like the steps of the dance. What they do suggest is the ideology, rationale, and dynamics that informed the ritual. This interpretation accords with the traditional view that the Arkteia was a mystery, where sacred objects (in this case the visage of the bear through masks, among other images) were revealed. At the same time that the bear was revealed the young girl began to reveal herself no longer as a wild creature but as an *agalma* eventually to be exchanged for dowry upon marriage.

Although we will never know what precisely it meant to be a "bear" nor the content of the rite, which was, after all, a *mystērion*, we can go a step beyond calling it a transition rite and reconstruct from the evidence the aim and character of the Arkteia. The goal of the rite, we can assume, was to define and establish appropriate boundaries of behavior for young girls in anticipation of marriage and motherhood. The literary and archaeological evidence suggests that the process of defining these limits revolved around the dynamics of proper and improper display, licit and illicit viewing, and the revealing of frightening objects. The rite took on the character of a spiritual transformation of the young girl from a wild, disorderly creature (reminiscent of Plato's leaping and wailing young) to a tame and nubile being. The highly complex and ambivalent symbol of this transformation was the bear. The likelihood that the rite concentrated on a transformation along these lines is suggested by the earliest literary evidence concerning the bear and Callisto, the youthful devotee of Artemis. In the *Astronomia* Hesiod reports that Callisto chose to lead a disciplined pattern of life (*agōgē*) together with Artemis.[92] This way of life changed when she was seduced by Zeus, for when Artemis saw her pregnant one day when she was bathing, the goddess became enraged and transformed her into a bear. Later she gave birth to a son called Arkas. In this tale we can see the inverse of the Arkteia rite reconstructed from the literary evidence. In the Callisto myth the young girl goes from being a pregnant woman to being a bear. In the course of the Arkteia the young girl goes from being a bear (*arktos*) to becoming a marriageable girl and an eventual mother. Even if the contested red-figure krateriskos represents the transformation of Callisto, the relevance of her legend to an interpretation of the ritual suggests that it and the related two red-figure fragments have a direct bearing on the cult of Artemis Brauronia.

The mechanics for achieving the transformation of the bears into marriageable girls at Brauron were no doubt far more complex than the fragmentary evidence will allow us to perceive; an idea of just how rich and varied the imagery, language, and gestures of initiation can only be documented by modern anthropological studies such as the pioneering work of Richards on the Chisungu. Unfortunately we are unable to recreate the Arkteia in all its richness, even as we cannot rechoreograph dances.

Hieros Gamos: *Alcman's First* Partheneion

Before assessing the role of dance in weddings in the next chapter we should realize that the event is anticipated by preliminary rehearsals acted out in status transition rites, and that within the context of marriage it is not only the union of the young girl and the successful suitor that is of moment. Weddings are occasions that involve the entire community, from the old to the very young, and the renewal of solidarity symbolized by marital union is acted out in formal processions and informal dancing. In the second stasimon of *Iphigeneia in Tauris* the chorus of women, speaking collectively as a mature woman, reminisces about its participation in the wedding dance:

> I wish . . . that I could stand in the dance-choruses at noble weddings, as, when I was a girl, I whirled near my mother's feet in the joyful bands of my young friends, entering the contests [*hamillai*] of the Graces [Charites], the rivalry of our rich, soft hair, and shadowing my face with scarves, intricately adorned, and with my flowing locks.[93]

In this flashback to girlhood the speaker evokes the pleasure of participating among the group of female celebrants, which spans three generations, her mother's, that of the bride, and her age-mates. Coiffure, costume, and adornment, comprising the cosmetic elements of dancing, can be manipulated to draw the attention of the spectators. Alongside the urge to blend harmoniously with the chorus exists the desire to distinguish oneself, to stand out in the contests (*hamillai*) of the Charites. Among the women too there is an *agōn*, a competition for attention. Rivalries such as those hinted at in Euripides were formalized in ritual dances for girls. In dances and contests they vied with one another to be most like the earthly *chorēgos*, who was chosen as leader by virtue of age, maturity, beauty, and stature to embody her divine prototype, Artemis, and in some locales, Aphrodite.[94]

Evidence for the role of dance in such female status transition rites comes principally from the so-called maiden songs (*partheneia*), a genre of choral lyric attested in fragments of poems by Pindar, Alcman, and others. In contrast to the solo poems of Sappho, Alcaeus, and Anacreon that were performed by the poets accompanying themselves on the lyre, choral lyric is a more complex musical form that involves not only words and music but dance as well. The choral poet was responsible not only for inventing the words and composing the music but also for devising steps and gestures for a group of approximately twelve performers. A choral poet lived in close proximity with members of his chorus. He had a chance to observe their personalities and idiosyncrasies and incorporate these details in performance as he taught them the words and choreography of his composition. Such a relationship between a male poet-musician (*chorēgos*) and a female *choros* has been seen in the *Homeric Hymn to Apollo* in Apollo and the Muses and the blind bard from Chios and the Delian Maidens.

The first substantial remains of choral lyric to survive come from Alcman, who lived in Sparta toward the end of the seventh century. In antiquity, as today, the national origin of Alcman was debated: he was said to be from Sardis or Sparta. An ancient commentary of the first or second century C.E. on the life of Alcman favoring his Lydian origin did not register surprise that the Spartans entrusted him with teaching the choruses (*choroi*) of their daughters and young men, since even in Hellenistic times the Spartans still used foreigners to train their choruses.[95] Whatever his birthplace, the poet resided at Sparta in the early seventh century and composed his work for groups and occasions at Sparta, where he was honored after his death.

The choreographic element in Alcman's poetry can be directly inferred from several passages, especially the fragmentary opening of the recently published second maiden song in which the chorus, speaking collectively in the first person, refers to its costume, carriage, and gestures.

> Olympian Muses, fill my heart with longing for a new song: I am eager to hear the maiden voice of girls singing a beautiful melody. . . . It will scatter sweet sleep from my eyes and leads me to go to the assembly (*agōn*) . . . where I shall rapidly shake my yellow hair and [dance with my] soft feet. . . . But Astymeloisa makes no answer to me; no, holding the garland, like a bright star of the shining heavens or a golden branch or soft down . . . she passed through with her long feet . . . giving beauty to her tresses, the moist charm of Cinyras sits on the maiden's hair. . . . If only she came nearer and took my soft hand, immediately I would become her suppliant.[96]

We hear of the chorus being led to the assembly (*agōn*); the place for their ludic activity is well named, because their actions are playfully agonistic in character.[97] In the epic, which shared phraseology with choral lyric, the word *agōn* is a synonym for *choros* in its local sense;[98] it is here that the Phaeaceans display their competitive dancing during the games staged for Odysseus.[99] Once at the dancing ground the girls sing and also execute gestures, to which they call attention in their own language. The self-referential practice amounts to a ritual repetition: they act, and as they act they solemnize their action in words. For example, they toss their heads so as to make their hair undulate. Then, in what is presumably a reference to choreographic movement with the lower part of the body (there is a lacuna in the papyrus text at this point), the "soft feet" of the girls somehow move in response. We hear of the garland held by Astymeloisa, the most important member of the chorus, and of the movement of her feet outstretched, it seems, as she moves in and out among the choral dancers. The structure of the chorus with its leader and members is evident in this and in explicit references elsewhere in Alcman to the *chorēgos*, who is so designated or called by a name with the *ag-* stem for leading, such as Agido, Hagesidamos, or Hagesi-chora, whose name represents a reversal of the linguistic elements constituting the word *chor-ēgos*.[100]

The so-called Louvre maiden song is the only poem of Alcman of any length (just over 100 verses) to survive the fate that consigned the majority of his poetry to oblivion.[101] The difficulties of how to interpret this opaque text have not been resolved by the many book-length studies and articles that have attempted to place the actions of the chorus in an intelligible context.[102] Among the suggested readings, however, there has been fairly general agreement that we are in the presence of some kind of ritual play preliminary to marriage. The first maiden song has indeed been called an epithalamium, a genre for which Alcman in fact was known in antiquity, and at least two of his fragments may be from wedding songs.[103] Some have seen the alliances described in the poem as homoerotic liaisons characteristic of initiation structures,[104] while another scholar has recently interpreted the ritual as an enactment of a sacred marriage (*hieros gamos*).[105] Whereas consensus probably will never be reached about the exact nature of the ritual, the mention of a divine wedding to Aphrodite in the moral of the poem and the exclusively female choral medium of performance make it likely that the ritual served as a preliminary paradigm for eventual marriage.

Alcman's poem was composed for performance by a chorus of ten young girls (all designated by name) under the guidance of the female *chorēgos* (Hagesichora) at a Spartan festival. They offer their performance to a goddess named Aotis. The poem falls into three main sections: a (lost) invocation, a mythical interlude, and the chorus's description of its ritual play. An agonistic element is suggested throughout the third section of the poem by the playful banter in which the chorus engages and by contests, including a dramatized version of a horse race. We may assume that the locus of the choir's performance, as in the second maiden song cited earlier, is the *agōn*. The time at which the competitive activity takes place is at the first dawn, when the first rays of the sun, to which Hagesichora's putative rival, Agido, is compared, appear. In the poem, Aotis, whose name should mean "Dawn," is invoked.[106] An all-night revel with informal dancing, the *pannychis*, was a regular preliminary stage of festivals in honor of divinities, especially female deities. At the Panathenaea, for instance, a nocturnal festival was held in anticipation of the events which commenced at dawn with a torch race.[107] In a similar way the competitive play of the chorus begins at the first dawn, a time of reordering and renewal.

A translation of the most relevant portions of the poem is presented here, beginning with the moral to a fragmentary myth that contains a warning against trespassing mortal limits: "Let no man fly to heaven or attempt to marry Aphrodite, the Cyprian queen . . . nor a daughter of Porcus. It is the Graces [Charites] with love in their eyes who frequent the house of Zeus."[108]

A second myth, in an even more fragmentary state, follows. When the poem shifts from the mythical narration to the choral ritual, the time changes from the distant past to the immediate present as the members of the chorus particularize themselves and their actions.

And so I sing of the brightness of Agido: I see her like the sun, which Agido summons to shine on us as our witness; but our illustrious choir-leader [Hagesichora] by no means allows me either to praise or to fault her; for she herself seems pre-eminent, just as if one were to put a horse among grazing herds, a sturdy, thunderous-hoofed prize-winner, one of those seen in winged dreams. Why, don't you see? The race-horse is Venetic; but the hair of my cousin Hagesichora has the bloom of undefiled gold, and her silver face—why do I tell you openly? This is

197

Hagesichora here; and the second in beauty after Agido will run like a Colaxaean horse against an Ibenian; for the Pleiads [doves], as we carry a robe to Orthria, rise through the ambrosial night like the star Sirius and fight against us. . . .

Choir-leader—if I may speak—I am myself only a girl screeching pointlessly, an owl from a rafter; but even so I long to please Aotis most of all, for she proved the healer of our sufferings; but it was thanks to Hagesichora that girls trod the path of lovely peace.

For like the trace-horse . . . , and in a ship too one must obey the helmsman most of all; and she is of course not more melodious than the Sirens, for they are goddesses; but this our choir of ten sings as well as eleven girls; why, its song is like that of a swan on the waters of the Xanthus.[109]

The myth to which the moral is appended concerns the actions of Hippocoon, a mythical king of Sparta who had exiled his brother Tyndareus, the father of Helen. This act of hybris was punished by the destruction of Hippocoon's sons, whose names are tallied in the fragmentary beginning of the papyrus.[110] The political myth justifies the triumph of moral order with the help of two archaic divinities, Destiny (Aisa) and Resource (Poros). The moral against attempting to fly to heaven, or to wed a goddess or a figure cryptically called the "child of Porcus," is the sort of reminder of mortal limits frequently found in myths in the archaic period. The manner in which it is expressed here, though, suggests that the myth somehow concerned a wedding theme, perhaps the oath of the Tyndarids to defend Helen, or perhaps a presumptuous suit of the Hippocoontids for the daughters of the Tyndarids.[111] The moral of the myth and its probable interweaving with a wedding theme are important for the interpretation of the remainder of the poem. The bellicose band of Hippocoon's sons are structurally equivalent and yet opposed to the *choros* of dancers: as the pyrrhic dance stresses, the military phalanx is cognate with choral formations. Notably, among the many actions to which the chorus alludes in the veiled language of poetic imagery are a rising skyward and a mock wedding with the quasi-divine *chorēgos*, a sort of *hieros gamos*. Whereas the sons of Hippocoon are morally censured, the band of dancers is privileged. They act out in the "as if" language of ritual a new order. In the allusive medium of poetic imagery they all but fly to the heavens and mingle with a goddess.

The privileged status of the chorus in contrast to the damnation of the sons of Hippocoon can be inferred from the verse following the moral, "It is the Charites with love in their eyes who frequent the house of Zeus." In the divine prototype of choral dancing in the *Hymn to Apollo* Artemis as *chorēgos* directs Aphrodite and Charites, among other divinities. Elsewhere Aphrodite (who alternates with Artemis in cult as a divinity presiding over female transitions) and the Charites form an independent choir.[112] In Alcman's poem the supereminent *chorēgos* of the earthly choir is Hagesichora. She is a quasi-divine figure like Hagesidamos, the *chorēgos* mentioned in Alcman fragment 10a, whose epithet is "loved by the gods" (*siophilēs*). Hagesichora is thus an impersonation or substitute of the divine *chorēgos*, Aotis, a local goddess of the Aphrodite type like Spartan Helen, who was worshipped as a goddess of fertility and marriage. The chorus enjoys union with Aphrodite/Aotis by emulating her divine chorus of Charites. The Charites are a society of goddesses who have access to the divine realms. The Olympian gods, moreover, are dependent on them, Pindar says, for their dances and festivals.[113] Alcman's epithet for the Charites, "with love in their eyes" (*eroglepharoi*), is compounded with the noun *erōs*, and emphasizes their connection with the erotic aspects of the choral dance embodied by Aphrodite in the Olympian chorus and played out among the members of the earthly chorus.[114] The Charites gravitate toward Aphrodite, and as members of her divine chorus are models to human worshippers such as the maidens in Alcman's poem. Unlike those who are admonished not to attempt to marry Aphrodite, the girls have special access to Aphrodite through the Charites. Despite the earthly setting of their performance the chorus executes its activity against the backdrop of an imaginary, quasi-divine festival. They adopt as their model venue festivals such as the Charites frequent, and in so doing perhaps reverse the interdiction contained in the moral of the myth not to strive for divine intercourse.

The two principal characters in the choral dramatization,

Hagesichora, called "the illustrious choir-leader," and Agido, her assistant, are paragons of beauty, speed, and musical talent. These two are playfully compared and contrasted with one another in beauty and personal adornment and at the same time distinguished from the other, lesser members of the chorus in two extended animal metaphors, one relating to horses, the other, to birds. The use of animal metaphors and horse and bird imagery in particular can be related to the choral medium of the performance and the initiatory structure of the group. Animal identities are often assigned to differentiate stages of initiations within a group. The initiates do not necessarily dress up and take on point for point the attributes and behavior of a species, but rather stand in relation to one another as species of animals do to one another. It is a matter of animal analogy rather than masquerade. The animal identity of the initiate can be translated into symbols worn as part of the costume or incorporated into mimetic dances reproducing qualities of animal behavior such as submission that have an equivalent meaning in the context of the initiation structure.

In the first maiden song an analogy is made between the choral dynamic implied by a leader and followers and the relationship between horses and cattle. In the divine prototype of choral dancing in the *Hymn to Apollo* we have seen that Artemis, as *chorēgos*, is the one who stands out among the chorus members by virtue of her greater stature and beauty.[115] This essential idea of supereminence translates readily into an animal idiom. "But our illustrious choir-leader (Hagesichora) by no means allows me either to praise or to fault her; for she herself seems pre-eminent, just as if one were to put a horse among grazing herds, a sturdy, thunderous-hoofed prize-winner, one of those seen in winged dreams."[116] Hagesichora is compared to a prize-winning thoroughbred with thunderous hooves that should naturally stand out (*ekprepēs*) when placed in the pasture with cattle (*bota*). The image has a close parallel in a Homeric simile appearing as the culmination of a chain of similes to magnify the stature of Agamemnon, who as commander in chief of the allied forces stands out among his troops (*ekprepe'*), as a bull does among the herd (*agelēphi*).[117] The herd metaphor has a special meaning in a male Spartan initiatory context on which female education was based.[118] As a synonym for *bota*, the word *agelē* designated the band of Spartan boys subjected to training. Pindar and Euripides use *agelē* to designate groups of women—young women (*parthenoi*) and maenads—who in a ritual context perform choral dances. In a fragment of a hyporcheme by Pindar a "herd" of Laconian women is mentioned.[119] There is an analogy between the chorus and the privileged chorus leader, on the one hand, and between the placid herd animals and horses who are free to run wild, on the other. The horse race metaphor, which has homoerotic connotations, as elsewhere in choral lyric,[120] suggests that whereas the chorus members "walk," the lead pair "runs" (*dramētai*). We simply do not know enough about the extent of correspondence between the text and performance to specify how such a distinction was acted out—by spirited dancing on the part of the "horses," punctuated by the percussive imitation of the horses "with thunderous hooves" with *krotala*, while the "herds" conveyed more docile behavior? But even if the poetic analogy for the choral dynamic is not a detailed script for dramatic performance, the passage at least hints at one of the many ways of playing out variations on the basic hierarchical relationship between *chorēgos* and *choreutai* in order to reinforce differences in the age, maturity, beauty, costume, and musical and choreographic proficiency of the initiates.

A similar contrast is made, through avian imagery, between two varieties of birds, the owl and the swan; these are further contrasted with the winged Sirens, who are divine. The chorus, addressing Hagesichora, self-deprecatingly begs permission to speak: "Choirleader, if I may speak—I am myself only a girl screeching pointlessly, an owl from a rafter." Later they compare Hagesichora to the winged Sirens: "She is of course not more melodious than the Sirens, for they are goddesses." Then they liken their song under Hagesichora's tutelage to that of "a swan on the waters of the Xanthus." Whereas the equestrian imagery corresponds to choral movement, the ornithological metaphor is to be correlated with song. Together the two types of imagery emphasize the rhythmic and vocal elements of choral performance that Plato said constituted *choreia*. Here the animal imagery stresses a difference in the levels of vocal proficiency. Because they are still girls (*parsenos*), the chorus, when they speak alone, cry in vain, like an owl. The screeching quality of their untrained and unassisted voice vividly evoked by the image is later contrasted with the tuneful song of the swan. Under Hagesichora's musical guidance the choir sings like a swan. Her own singing, however, is said to be not *more* tuneful than that of the Sirens: it would be blasphemous to say that she excelled these goddesses. In the Sirens and bird imagery there is a hierarchy, beginning with the divine Sirens—the prototype to which Hagesichora aspires but naturally falls short of attaining, since the Sirens are goddesses. Next comes the swan, to whom Hagesichora as *chorēgos* is comparable, and to whom the chorus aspires. The owls, on the other hand, represent the less trained voices of the other chorus members.[121]

Since the quadruped and avian imagery concerns the gulf between *chorēgos* and *choreutai*, it is best to take the remaining animal image as referring to Hagesichora and Agido, as the scholiast interprets this most difficult crux of the poem. "For the Pleiads (doves), as we carry a robe to Orthria, rise through the ambrosial night like the star Sirius and fight against us." The ritual action which the "doves" are said to fight (*machontai*) against is perhaps the delivering of the peplos to the cult statue by the chorus.[122] Some have thought the *agōn* is to be imagined in the form of two rival choruses,[123] while others have supposed a race to complete the ritual task before the star-cluster known as the Pleiades, after an absence, appears in the sky just before the rising sun.[124] In either case the mock battle suggested by the military metaphor conforms to the notion that the competition among female initiates distantly mirrors the male military organization on which the female structure is based, and for which dance provides a natural medium for reproducing military hierarchy and maneuvers. In the description of the "doves" rising upward like Sirius we seem to have an allusion to the superior movement of the *chorēgos* and her assistant that reverts to the moral: they alone are able to reach heavenward, without, of course, attaining the Olympian height.[125] Through the indirect language of the dance they emulate divine movement but stop short of committing a hybristic act such as that of the sons of Hippocoon at the beginning of the poem, or that of Bellerophon, who in an ode of Pindar was said to be thrown by Pegasus as he vied to attain Olympus.[126] The metaphor of doves, which are sacred to Aphrodite, may be quite specifically connected with the second part of the moral, which cautions against wedding this goddess.

The Poet as Choreographer of Social Order

The swan imagery also serves to draw the chorus close to its temporal source of musical inspiration, the poet who provides the music, choreography, and script for their dramatization. An epigram in the *Palatine Anthology* refers to Alcman as "the swan who sang wedding hymns."[127] The mutual bond between chorus members and the poet who devises the music, words, and steps is reflected in the divine prototype where the Muses are independent yet depend on Apollo for musical impetus. Alcman's script, however, implies much more than a musical performance. Responding to social exigencies Alcman imposes a temporary order on the girls out of which more permanent, lasting order will emerge. The temporary order replaces the old order embodied by the sons of Hippocoon which has been destroyed by Aisa and Poros. Under the leadership of Hagesichora the chorus dances the new world order into being like the Muses at the beginning of the *Theogony*.

What is the order implied by the poem? The imagery indicates that two processes are at work. First, the girls under the leadership and protection of Hagesichora emulate their chorus leader, who embodies the divine qualities of the Charites and the Sirens. There is a hierarchy, expressed in equestrian and avian imagery, running from cattle to horses, on the one hand, and owls to swans and Sirens on the other. It can be inferred that because Agido has proved herself to be most like the chorus leader in personal beauty, ability to dance and sing, and emotional maturity, she becomes the favored of Hagesichora. She is paired with the *chorēgos*. As such she enjoys certain privileges and freedom, while the others are constrained to display more submissive behavior. This pose of submission may be alluded to in an erotic metaphor by the phrase spoken collectively by the chorus: Hagesichora "wears me out" (in love: *teirei*).[128]

Second, the ritual conduces to domestic order. In archaic Greece the dancing ground was a place that helped to create a sense of intimacy in a group that was neither the family nor yet the larger community to which the girl would eventually belong. In this locus for dance and song, dramatizations of initiations preparatory to marriage helped to tame the fear and wildness of the young girls, to submit to the will of the father and the husband who arrange the marriage, and to make them more amenable to domesticated life. The order inherent in rhythm and harmony, joined with the pleasure taken in executing songs and dances, conspired to persuade girls to overcome anxieties and internal doubts experienced prior to marriage. The efforts required to achieve this state of equilibrium and equipoise are embodied in the figure of Agido, who, by achieving harmony with Hagesichora in a mock marriage, serves as model. In the dense imagery of the poem we can only half sense the extent of the girls' internal struggle acted out in symbolic contests and rivalries under the protection of Aotis, who prepares the way for the resolution of their internal conflicts. That is why the chorus is eager to please Aotis: she proved to be a healer of their cares and anxieties (*ponoi*). But it is the chorus leader Hagesichora, whom they call, perhaps with cultic significance, "my cousin," to whom they owe the greatest thanks since she set them on the path to peace (*irēnas*).

In the context of performance this peace refers to the joy and serenity that comes from song and dance. The language in which the chorus thanks Hagesichora for making it possible for them to "tread the path of lovely peace" (*neanides/irēnas eratas epeban*) suggests a reference to the choral medium in which they achieved serenity. The expression of gratitude to a divinity for release from suffering, physical or mental, is appropriate through dance. As noted in chapter 1, Plato in the *Laws* classifies such dances of thanksgiving as peaceful (*eirēnikē*) dances. This designation may well be an example of one of the traditional categories which Plato says he is·following in giving his classification.[129] The model of order and inner peace provided by Alcman and enacted by

Hagesichora and Agido presents another instance of choral dance as a prefigurement of communal peace and stability, seen in chapter 1 in the communal dances of the Couretes and nymphs. Ritual marriage involving dance prefigures social marriage, which is celebrated with songs, dances, and processions.

Seven

Dance in Courtship and Marriage

Boys and girls must be made to dance together at an age when
suitable pretexts can be found for their doing so, and they should
be made to view one another and to be viewed.
—Plato, *Laws* 771e–772a

In a well-known passage in the *Odyssey* that follows on the hero's
shipwreck off the island of Phaeacea, Odysseus is described as
sleeping off the effects of his ordeal near a stream emptying
out into the sea. That morning Nausicaa, at the prompting of
Athena, begged her father King Alcinous to lend her the mule
cart to take the palace laundry to the very stream near which Odysseus lies fast asleep. Athena, speaking to Nausicaa in a dream in the
guise of a mortal companion, had chided her for leaving her clothes
lying uncared for. At her wedding, Athena reminds her, she must
provide shining raiments for herself and her attendants. Her marriage is not far off, she suggests: the best men of Phaeacea are already courting her. Nausicaa, however, suppresses any mention of
her own needs and dutifully reminds Alcinous that three of her five
brothers are flourishing bachelors and are forever wanting clean
clothing when they go to the "dancing place" (*choros*) to show off
their good looks and athletic prowess.[1] Nausicaa and her attendants, for their part, are about to make their own informal dancing
ground by the river where they dance, sing, and play a ball game.

As the activities of Nausicaa and her eligible brothers suggest,
dance, music, and play have a salient function in bringing together

groups within the community in anticipation and celebration of marriage. Although a wedding is a rite of passage for the nuptial pair, marriage and its ritual events involve the entire community. The ability of dance to unite the community and couples alike is most obvious in the case of group marriages, hinted at in the Homeric epics, and for which there is evidence in Crete.[2] The idea of a communal union is anticipated, as we have seen in the last chapter, in status transition rites where young girls were admitted to groups that prepared them for marriage through choral activity. As the chapter epigraph from the *Laws* indicates, groups of marriageable young men and women come together under the spell of the dance at time of courtship, to select partners under the scrutiny of the community. The success of dance in effecting unions of all sorts is related to its role in provoking divine epiphanies, but here it is Eros and Aphrodite, instead of Apollo and the Muses, who conspire as "partners in the dance" (*synchoreutai*), while Dionysus and Ariadne, among others, serve as divine prototypes in the ritually enacted sacred marriage (*hieros gamos*).

In the rituals leading up to marriage and in the ceremonies surrounding the wedding itself, dance, in conjunction with music and processions, helped to bring about and mark the changes in the social order. Contests were held among suitors, and the girls themselves vied to be most like Artemis in beauty, grace, and stature. Winning the more permanent social order implied by marriage was predicated on coaxing order from a preexisting, embryonic order from among the male and female adolescent groups by allowing temporary conflict and disorder to arise from natural oppositions between the sexes and among those competing for the bride. The dancing ground could be a place for working out both harmony and disruption. The well-known story of Hippocleides and the theme of the abduction of the young girl from the dancing ground (taken up later) illustrate the desire to transgress, or at least bypass, the normal order imposed by society at the time of marital union.

Let us begin by analyzing the informal play of Nausicaa and her companions in order to understand certain social assumptions underlying courtship and marriage in antiquity. Once the young girls have washed the laundry and hung it out to dry, they bathe and enjoy a feast in the open air. Then Nausicaa and her attendants throw off their veils. Led by the princess, they play a game that involves singing, dancing, and throwing a ball. One of them misses, and the stray ball awakens Odysseus. A simile compares their activity to the sport of Artemis and her nymphs.

> When she and her attendants had had their fill in eating, they threw off their veils and played (*paizon*) with a ball, and among them it was Nausicaa of the white arms who led in the dancing (*archeto molpēs*); and as Artemis, the archer, roams on the mountains, either along Taygetos or on lofty Erymanthos, delighting in boars and swift deer, and in attendance the nymphs, daughters of Zeus of the aegis, range in the wilds and play (*paizousi*), and Leto is gladdened in her heart, for the head and the brows of Artemis rise above all the others, and she is easily distinguished from them, though all are lovely, so she stood out among her attendants, a young girl unwedded.[3]

The game of Nausicaa and her companions has a musical and choreographic element allowed for by the use of the verb meaning to play and dance (*paizō*). As princess and the next to wed, Nausicaa has the right to lead off the song and dance (*archeto molpēs*) that circumscribe their play. Through the simile there is an overlap of the choral dance of the Phaeaceans under the supervision of Nausicaa and the group play of the nymphs under Artemis whose delight in hunting is also expressed by the verb *paizō*. In using the same verb in both contexts, the poet closely links mortal and divine behavior.

The princess is compared to the goddess not only because of her activity but also for her physical resemblance. At the conclusion of the simile it is established that Nausicaa is preeminent among her companions. In the same way Artemis dominates her nymphs by her stature. The same criteria for physical beauty and superiority is found in the description of Artemis as the leader of the choral dance on Olympus in the *Homeric Hymn to Apollo*.[4] She is taller by a head, better to look at, more enticingly graceful. The comparison of an exceedingly beautiful young girl to Artemis was a literary commonplace that was to persist for several centuries, as shown in a passage from a second century C.E. Ephesian tale of Xenophon of

Ephesus cited later. In the present passage when Odysseus encounters Nausicaa, he compares her to the goddess. "I am at your knees, O queen. But are you mortal or goddess? If indeed you are one of the gods who hold wide heaven, then I must find in you the nearest likeness to Artemis the daughter of great Zeus, for beauty, figure, and stature."[5]

The other possibility that Odysseus presents—that Nausicaa is really a mortal—also contains a reference to the godlike grace imparted by the dance. Odysseus imagines aloud the pleasure that the princess must bring her family who are warmed in their hearts as they see "such a slip of beauty taking her place in the chorus of dancers." What he goes on to say confirms the hypothesis that in the game of Nausicaa we are to see an allusion to the dancing ground as a locus for courtship, for Odysseus concludes his flattering words with the suggestion that the most blessed of all is that one "who, after presenting a dowry, leads Nausicaa home as his bride."[6]

The comparison between Nausicaa and Artemis can be compared with a well-known passage from the Ephesian tale.[7] It is of interest because it concerns a festival of Artemis, the Ephesia, during which brides and grooms were chosen.

> The girls in the procession were all decked out as if to meet lovers. Of the band of maidens the leader was Anthia . . . a prodigy of loveliness who far surpassed the other maidens. Her age was fourteen, and she had bloomed into mature shapeliness. . . . Her eyes were lively, shining sometimes like a girl's and sometimes severe as of a chaste goddess. Her dress was a frock of purple. . . . Her wrap was a fawn skin, and a quiver hung down from her shoulder. She carried bow and javelins and dogs followed at her heels. Time and again when the Ephesians saw her in the sacred procession they bowed down as to Artemis. And now too when Anthia came into view the entire multitude cried out in astonishment; some of the spectators asserted that she was the very goddess, others declared she was a replica fashioned by the goddess. But all did obeisance to her and bowed down and called her parents blessed.[8]

In this passage the true identity of Anthia does not stupefy those who watch the procession, any more than Odysseus is truly mystified by Nausicaa's status. The resemblance of her clothes and accoutrements to those with which Artemis was represented does not confound the Ephesians. They know very well that the girl is human, while recognizing her divine beauty. On this occasion the actors and spectators enter into a drama and share, in an act of collusion, a social script.

Choral dances of young girls accounted for another occasion during which mortals assumed divine roles and, in certain cases, purveyed that fiction to the onlookers. Under the favorable eye of Artemis the dances and games of young girls helped to make them more "divine," that is to say more desirable in the eyes of their suitors. And it was precisely the one who was the tallest, the most beautiful, the most graceful who won the privilege of being the *chorēgos*. This one had the right to lead off the dance and the song, *archeto molpēs*. The audience of our passage from the *Odyssey* would have recognized this social model in the quasi-divine portrait of the princess. Endowed with this cultural knowledge, the audience participated all the more in the delicious ambiguity of the encounter of Odysseus and Nausicaa, who thinks about her future marriage.

Models and Divine Prototypes of Courtship and Wedding Ritual in Literature and Art

Although in practice no single way of courting and marrying in Greece existed, a model for marriage is found in literature.[9] In Plato's *Laws*, the Athenian legislator says that boys and girls must come together for dancing games. The context for these dances are gatherings, *synodoi*. These gatherings have two goals: first, to give thanks to the gods and second, to provide a venue for fellowship, an opportunity to get to know one another, and to enjoy contact of all sorts.

> In anticipation of the partnership and intercourse of marriage it is necessary to remove ignorance about which woman a man marries . . . and to whom a father gives his daughter, doing this above all because it is especially important not to be tripped up insofar as possible in such matters. In view of achieving this serious purpose boys and girls must be made to dance together at an age when suitable pretexts can be found

for their doing so, and they should be made to view one another and to be viewed, and they should dance naked, on condition that modesty (*aidōs*) and restraint are observed by all.[10]

As these cautionary words suggest, there is a danger in revealing and looking upon the body in an indecent manner, without respecting the limits of *aidōs*. It is unlikely that outside of the Platonic city girls danced in the nude; nevertheless, the loose and diaphanous garments that they wore when dancing revealed their bodies as they danced. This increased degree of visibility had great social significance, for an erotic current underlies every dance.

A festival occasion of the type which the Athenian legislator enjoins for the polis is artistically created by the demiurge in book 18 of the *Iliad*. The last vignette that Hephaestus fashions on the great round Shield of Achilles features a courtship dance of *parthenoi* and ephebes, an interpretation confirmed by the epithet for the young women—"fetching many oxen" (*alphesiboiai*)—referring to the eventual rewards a girl will earn her family in the form of a cattle dowry. Perhaps we are to visualize the dominant movement of these young boys and girls with hands linked as a ring dance, for the final scene on the shield is immediately followed by a description of its outer rim consisting of the streams of Ocean, the boundary encircling the whole world in the Homeric cosmogony. This cosmic ring in turn mirrors a crowd of admiring spectators who form a circle around the dancers as they scrutinize their swift movements, costumes, and dazzling accoutrements.

> The illustrious lame god next decorated it with a dancing-ground, like the one that Daedalus designed in broad Cnossos for beautiful-haired Ariadne. In it young men and marriageable maidens were dancing, holding one another's hands by the wrist. The girls wore light linen, the men well-woven tunics faintly glossy with olive oil: the girls had beautiful garlands, and the men had golden daggers hanging from silver belts. At one time they would run round swiftly on skilful feet, just as when a potter sits and spins his wheel with his hands to try it out, to see if it runs smoothly. At another time they would run in lines towards one another. A great crowd stood round the lovely dance in delight; and two tumblers, leaders of the dance, whirled in the midst of them.[11]

As is fitting for the polished surface on which the dance is imagined to be taking place, the description singles out the brilliant adornments of the dancers and traces the patterns of their movements. Like a *chorēgos* outfitting his choir, Hephaestus clothes the women in light robes and crowns their heads with fair diadems that shine;[12] he dresses the men in chitons glistening with oil and hangs from their silver baldrics knives of gold. Next, in order to parade their finery to the best advantage and to make them attractive to one another, he sets them in motion: now they run lightly on their feet in circular formation, now they advance and retreat in opposing rows. Finally, he interjects two acrobats, who lead but also shake up the corps of dancers; their leaps and spins titillate the participants and onlookers alike by playfully promoting the erotic undercurrents of the mixed dance.

A historically attested analogy for the dance on the Shield of Achilles is the *hormos*, a courtship dance described by Lucian in which males and females alternated in a chain.[13] A young man led, displaying his knowledge of the postures that would later be useful to him in war, while a young woman followed, demonstrating that she knew how to move with grace and feminine decorum. After describing the *hormos* Lucian goes on to mention the Homeric simile of Ariadne's dancing floor. But assuming that his reader knows the Homeric passage, he passes over it. The context in which he mentions the passage, however, is telling. Before describing the *hormos* Lucian touches on contemporary dances in Sparta. Spartan men, he says, practice dancing as much as warfare, and they perform not only war dances but choral dances, including those sacred to Aphrodite. While they dance they sing an invocation to Aphrodite and the Erotes, that the gods may join in their dances. The Spartan dances, like the *hormos* and courtship dance on the shield, blend the martial and the amorous, a mixture reflecting an *agōn* on the battlefield as well as in the arena of love: a tension and opposition between natural enemies and between the sexes.

The courtship dance is the last vignette on the Shield of Achilles. The first vignette in the so-called City at Peace is a wedding procession made up of brides in what must be a group marriage; in their train follow young men performing acrobatic dances. Since the series of scenes described on the shield is a self-contained ecphrasis composed according to the principles of ring composition, it is possible to see the two vignettes as a pair, or rather as a sequence in reverse, with the courtship dance naturally leading up to the wedding festivities.

> They were leading the brides from their houses through the town with blazing torches, and a loud wedding song rose up. Young men whirled in the dance, while among them *auloi* and *phorminges* gave out their cry; and the women stood in their doorways admiring the sight.[14]

A more detailed description of a wedding procession intermingled with dances is found in the pseudo-Hesiodic Shield of Heracles, which was modeled on the Homeric ecphrasis.

> Nearby was a city of men with fine towers, and seven golden gates fitted to lintels surrounded it. The men were taking delight in festivities and dances. Some were leading a bride to her husband in a cart with good wheels, while the wedding song rose up; from afar the radiance of burning torches in the hands of the maidservants whirled around. These maidens led the procession, while dancing choruses played behind them. The men sent forth a song from their tender mouths to the accompaniment of shrill syrinxes, and the sound broke around them. The women led the lovely choral dance accompanied by phorminxes. On both sides young men were revelling (*kōmazon*) to the sound of the *aulos*, some playing (*paizontes*) with dance and song, and others going forward laughing, each to the sound of an *aulētēs*. Festivity, dances, and merriment filled and surrounded the city.[15]

While the bridal procession advances, choruses "play" in its train (*tēsin de choroi paizontes heponto*). Young men sing to the syrinx while girls are engaged in a choral dance accompanied by the lyre. Young men revel, some playing at dancing, others laughing. The tension between the orderly procession and the formal choral dances of the girls, on the one hand, and the exuberant play of the young men in the wedding party, on the other, is implied in the verb "to revel" (*kōmazō*). As in the normal festival sequence, the procession is often accompanied or followed by an informal rout, or *kōmos*. Although a civic festival, the divinity is strongly present in the blazing torches, musical instruments, and Hymen's song.

The Hymenaeus song was synonymous with the god, as the paean was with Apollo, and the dithyramb with Dionysus. At weddings the procession was headed by women who raised the cry "Hymen, Hymenai o" in what was understood at least from the time of Pindar to be an invocation of the divinity said to be the son of Apollo and one of the Muses.[16]

The poet contrasts the solemn progress of the *parthenoi* in the nuptial procession with the playful dances of the young men in the groom's party. The disruptive play among the members of the groom's party presents a challenge to the symmetry and solidarity of the all-female procession and is a reminder that the old order must yield to the new, as the bride was removed bodily from her house and transplanted to the *oikos* of the groom's family.

In Greek art the bodily domination of the bride by the groom was expressed by a metaphor of leading. As the groom led her to his house he would forcibly take his bride by the wrist, not by the hand. Whereas the latter gesture implies equality, the former suggests control. The gesture of domination is found as early as the Geometric period. On a lebes, a vessel used in wedding ritual, a male is seen leading a female by the wrist toward a ship.[17] On a cup by Euphronios, Peleus, who was destined to marry Thetis, holds the reluctant goddess by the wrist and leads her to the chariot used in the marriage procession.[18] The gesture of placing the hand on the wrist is clearly attested in a wedding ritual on a white-ground pyxis by the Splanchnopt Painter in the British Museum (Fig. 24).[19] In a procession scene on the pyxis the groom, advancing behind an *aulētēs* toward the altar, turns back to grasp his veiled bride by the wrist. The same gesture of placing the hand on the wrist (*cheir epi karpōi*) is found in the iconography of choral dancing. The equivalent epic formula, "holding one another by the wrists" (*allēlōn epi karpōi cheiras echontes*), describes the linkage of hands among the boys and girls in the courtship dance on the Shield of Achilles as the couples rehearse for the eventual transition to a matrimonial state.[20] Already the measure of control and dominance of the man over the woman is latent in the courtship dance.

The translation of the bride from her familiar domestic space to a foreign environment can be seen on the body of a shoulder lekythos

Figure 24. Bride being led by groom *cheir epi karpōi* (hand on wrist) toward an altar.

by the Amasis Painter. In a wedding procession the bride, holding a wreath in her hand, and groom approach the groom's house in a chariot.[21] On the shoulder of the vase are nine females dancing (Fig. 25). Identification of the main subject of the vase permits the inference that the performers depicted on the circular frieze are somehow dancing in connection with the rite of passage for bride and groom. The round format of the vase, like the courtship dance circumscribed by the streams of Ocean on the Shield of Achilles, again suggests a ring dance. There are nine young female dancers in all, and two musicians, one playing the lyre, the other the *aulos*. Subtle differences in the gait and gestures of the dancers suggest that we are viewing not a single, continuous dance, but two or three phases of dances in conjunction with the wedding. The pairs of feet of each of the three dancers to the right of the lyre player are placed much further apart than the feet of the other six dancers. The wider

Figure 25. Wedding dances; musicians playing an *aulos* and a stringed instrument.

interval of the feet makes the skirts flare open. They are clearly moving at a faster pace than the others. Although the gait of the remaining six dancers appears the same, the gestures for linking the dancers in the two groups differ. Those to the left of the lyre player place the hand over the wrist, *cheir epi karpōi*, of the next dancer in the row, whereas those to the left of the *aulētēs* (like those to the right of the lyre player) hold each other's hands to form the row. The technique of linking arms by placing the hand over the wrist used by the trio of dancers framed by the two musicians suggests leading in a file,[22] whereas the more equal method of clasping hands among the remaining dancers suggests a circular formation; these are the two configurations described in the courtship dances on the Shield of Achilles. If this interpretation is correct, the hand-on-wrist gesture seen among the trio echoes the basic idea of "leading" in the scene on the body of the vase and repeats the gesture enacted by the groom on the wedding day seen on the pyxis by the Splanchnopt Painter. Perhaps we are to see in the central figure of the trio bracketed by musicians the bride who is about to be married.

The wedding lekythos by Amasis was found together with another of the same shape, size, and an identical scheme of decoration disposed between shoulder and body.[23] The two vases moreover are linked by dance subjects on the shoulder. On the body of the lekythos we see women engaged in several stages of wool working: weighing, spinning, weaving on a loom, and finally folding the end product. Like their counterparts on the wedding vase the women all wear peploi and have fillets in their hair. On the shoulder of the lekythos a female figure in a peplos seated in a throne and holding a wreath is approached by two groups of four dancing girls with hands linked. The leader of each group looks back to her companions. As in the wedding vase one group has its feet widely spaced, the other moves with feet close together. The groups are preceded by two youths, one of whom looks back at the dancing girls. The dancing scene on the wool-working vase has been interpreted as a dance in celebration of the weaving of the Panathenaic peplos for Athena;[24] but since the equivalent dance event on the wedding vase is obviously connected with the wedding and not a religious festival, it is more likely that these dances too are more closely related to the domestic scene at hand.[25] The seated figure on the shoulder of the wool-working vase whom the males approach resembles the bride in the chariot on the wedding vase in two respects: she is veiled, and she carries a wreath. Is this figure the bride-to-be receiving a garment? If so, the dances should be seen as a celebration of the presentation of the wedding dress to the bride as she is about to leave her old status (represented by the band of maidens making wool) and undergo the transition to married life depicted on the companion vase.

Flouting the Norm: Hippocleides' Paradoxical Dance

Although marriage represents a rite of passage for young girls more so than it does for young men, the suitors must submit to physical and moral tests organized by the father-in-law. As Plato suggests in the *Laws*, determining suitable partners begins with the scrutiny of the candidates in courtship dances. Eligibility was formally decided in athletic and musical contests arranged by the fathers of marriageable girls. In *Pythian* 9 Pindar recalls the ingenious method employed by Danaus when faced with the daunting task of marrying off his forty-eight daughters. He positioned them at the finish line of a race course and determined that a foot-race would decide which daughter each of the suitors would wed. The term Pindar uses for the group of girls to be married off is *choros* as a collective noun, meaning the band of dancers.

The most famous example of contests for a bride took place at Sicyon. Herodotus's well-known story of the competitions staged by Cleisthenes among the suitors for the hand of Agariste stresses the role of physical, moral, and musical trials in the courtship process under the charge of the bride's father. The father's jurisdiction in matters of moral comportment corresponds to Plato's view in the *Laws* that elders should be the arbiter of dances and melodies and judge the propriety with which they are performed by the younger generation. What Plato does not discuss is the natural resentment on the part of the youthful suitors to the control imposed by the elders, and the potential use of dance by the younger generation as a means to express anger and defiance.

The story of Agariste's courtship takes as its paradigm the myth of Hippodameia and Pelops, who figure prominently in the aetiology of the games of Zeus and of Hera at Olympia. Hippodameia, whom Pelops won by defeating her father Oenomaus in a chariot race, was the legendary founder of the girls' games at Olympia. Pausanias reports that the bride gave thanks to Hera for her marriage to Pelops by gathering together sixteen women and celebrating with them the first games in her honor. In Pausanias's time sixteen women were chosen from the nearby town of Elis to take charge of Hera's games and to arrange dances in two choruses.[26] One chorus performed for Hera, but the other sang and danced for Physkoa, the lover of Dionysus.

It was at Olympia, perhaps in 572, that Cleisthenes of Sicyon, after winning the chariot race, took the opportunity to make public the announcement of his intent to marry his daughter to the most suitable man in Greece. He invited all qualified applicants to present themselves at his palace for a year-long series of trials of physical stamina and character. In a sense he transformed Sicyon into a pan-Hellenic *agōn* and himself into an *agonothetēs* (master of the games).[27] He built a race track and a palaestra and appointed himself, in tyrannical fashion, as Olympian arbiter. Cleisthenes inquired in detail about the fatherland and family of each suitor, and to separate the men from the boys he would take the younger ones into the palaestra. But Cleisthenes' proving-ground for the suitors also imported elements of the Pythian games at Delphi, for there were musical contests as well.

The suitors assembled from all parts of the Peloponnesus, except Laconia, and from northern Greece, from Epidamnus on the Ionian gulf, and from southern Italy. From Athens there were two suitors, Megacles of the powerful Alcmaeonid family, and Hippocleides, the son of Tisander from the Philaids, the wealthiest and best looking of all the contestants. During their year-long stay the suitors were tested for manliness, temper, education (*paideusis*), and manners. But paramount was proper comportment in public. The context for this social interaction is the symposium, which provides the setting for Plato's discussion of *choreia* (in conjunction with the moderate consumption of wine) in the *Laws* as a form of paideia and test of manly behavior.[28]

Toward the end of the year Hippocleides emerged as the most successful candidate. To announce his choice Cleisthenes arranged a banquet followed by a symposium at which he had the suitors compete in a group (*es to meson*) in music and public speaking. What transpired at the gathering is the climax of the story which culminates in the famous saying ascribed to Hippocleides, son of Tisander:

> When they had finished dinner, the suitors competed before the company in music and in speaking. As the drinking went on, Hippocleides, who was proving much superior to the others, told the *aulētēs* to play an *emmeleia*, and when the *aulētēs* complied, he danced to it. As far as he was concerned, his dancing was delightful, but Cleisthenes, who was watching, began to have misgivings about the whole affair. After a pause, Hippocleides called for a table to be brought in: when it was brought he first danced some Laconian figures (*schēmatia*) on it and then some Attic ones, and thirdly he stood on his head on the table and waved his legs about. While he was doing the first and second dances, Cleisthenes, though by now he detested the thought of having Hippocleides as his son-in-law, because of his dancing and shameless behavior, nevertheless restrained himself, wanting to avoid an outburst against him: but when he saw him waving his legs about he could no longer hold himself back. "Son of Tisander," he said, "you have danced away your marriage." "Hippocleides doesn't care," responded Hippocleides.[29]

Hippocleides makes several crucial mistakes or miscalculations.[30] In ordering the *aulētēs* to play and asking for a table (suitable for acrobatic displays) on which to dance, Hippocleides usurps the role of Cleisthenes as organizer of the contest. In effect, he flouts the agonistic element established by Cleisthenes and transforms the contest into a spectacular exhibition. He loses a sense of the collective context of the gathering as he shifts to perform narcissistic solo dances which are to his own liking, but totally inappropriate for a banquet. The melody that Hippocleides orders the *aulētēs* to play is the solemn *emmeleia*, which Plato in the *Laws* classifies among pacific dances, appropriate for a tragic chorus or for civic rites performed in combination with the proper musical accompaniments at sacrificial feasts and other religious holidays. The first set of dances he executes is suspect on two grounds. It is Laconian and apparently trivial, corresponding to the Platonic category of *to phaulon*. To emphasize their triviality Herodotus uses *schēmatia*, the diminutive of the word for a dance-figure (*schēma*), with pejorative force. But the last dance is by far the most outrageous.[31] "Dancing with the hands" (*cheironomia*) apparently was not inappropriate for a symposium, to judge from its mention by a guest in Xenophon's *Symposium*.[32] Hippocleides, however, utterly violates and inverts the convention by using his legs, requiring him to perform on his head in the manner of an acrobatic entertainer. By dancing upside down, Hippocleides made what should have been a decorous dance a lewd display of the type that the Helots were forced to perform when made drunk for Spartan youths in their dining clubs as a warning against excessive consumption of alcohol. It certainly lacked the modesty and restraint which Plato said should be exercised at gatherings in anticipation of arranging suitable marriages.[33] Hippocleides threw all caution and restraint to the winds. In short, he transgressed the boundaries implied by the Platonic categories of appropriate and inappropriate, civic and religious.

A person's carriage, gait, and style of dancing reflect the moral qualities of the soul. Cleisthenes' pronouncement that Hippocleides danced away his wedding was a witty way of saying that his dancing had unmasked a tendency toward shameless behavior. Athenaeus explains Cleisthenes' remark to Hippocleides by reference to a theory attributed to Damon's followers and articulated in Plato's *Laws* that beautiful souls produce pleasing songs and dances, whereas morally base souls produce the opposite.

> It is well said by the school of Damon the Athenian that songs and dances are the inevitable result of a certain kind of motion in the soul: those souls that are beautiful and characteristic of free men create songs and dances of the same kind, while the opposite sort create the opposite. This also explains the remark of Cleisthenes, tyrant of Sicyon, a witty one, giving evidence of his educated intelligence. They say that he saw one of his daughter's suitors (it was Hippocleides the Athenian) dancing in a vulgar manner, and said that he had "danced away his marriage," presumably believing that the man's soul was of the same sort too. For in both dancing and walking, elegance and orderliness are beautiful, while disorder and vulgarity are ugly.[34]

From Hippocleides' point of view the inappropriate dances, including the Laconian schematia and the topsy-turvy gesture dance, are an effective means of expressing youthful resentment against Cleisthenes, who as father of the bride exercised ultimate control over his daughter's fate.[35] The iron-fisted control of Cleisthenes over his future son-in-law was typical of the power structure of the family in ancient Greece, and not simply a result of his position as tyrant.

Trespassing the Norm: The Abduction of the Young Girl from the Dancing Ground

Although the insouciant attitude toward courtship ritual conveyed by Hippocleides' provocative dance was an isolated historical incident, his bold transgression of social norms struck a chord with the Greek audience and found its way into the proverbial expression "Hippocleides couldn't care less."

A similar challenge to the institution and social conventions surrounding marriage is encoded in the motif of abduction of the young girl from the dancing ground. The theft occurs while she is engaged in playful dancing with her companions, or while performing cult dances in honor of Artemis or a similar goddess protective of young females.[36] The idea of violating the woman while she is dancing is played out with variation in the realm of Dionysiac myth in artistic representations of the satyr's pursuit of the dancing maenad.

Although the context for the majority of the abductions is the dancing ground of Artemis, the act can take place in the uncultivated fields beyond town and temple; but Artemis's presence is still felt. In the *Hymn to Demeter* the rape of Core/Persephone by Hades took place while the young girl danced and gathered flowers with her companions in a meadow. Once reunited with her mother Persephone recounts her adventure. She begins: "We were all in a charming meadow. We were playing and dancing [the verb is *paizō*] and gathering flowers in our hands."[37] Then she enumerates her companions, ending with none other than Artemis.

As the meaning of Core's name "Girl/Daughter" emphasizes, myths of this type were widely applicable to the social concerns surrounding young females of a marriageable age. In the archaic period the male aggressor is a god or a hero like Theseus, who attempted to abduct Helen from Artemis's dancing ground. In a quasi-historical context Pausanias reports that the hero Aristo-menes and his band abducted girls performing dances for Artemis Caryae at Sparta.[38] The abduction of a girl from a festival dance by a nonheroic mortal became a theme in New Comedy. In Men-ander's *Samia*, Moschion carries away Plangon while she is cele-brating the Adonia and impregnates her.[39]

The broader theme of the abduction of women was widespread in ancient Greece. Hesiod, for example, attributed the perdition of the race of heroes to the fighting that broke out over the cattle of Oedipus and over the theft of Helen, and bride-theft became a fa-vorite epic theme.[40] Herodotus's *History* opens with a series of sto-ries about the theft of women, first by the Phoenicians, and then in retaliation by the Greeks, who considered abduction an unlawful act. The variation on the theme that localizes the place of abduction at a dancing ground focuses on an especially alluring young girl seized by an older male: Theseus was said to have been fifty when he attempted to abduct Helen, then only seven years of age. Latent in the myth is a prurient element. As Plato's prescription for court-ship dances for boys and girls recalls, dancing provides an oppor-tunity to see and be seen naked, on condition that modesty and restraint are observed by all. The myth, however, transforms the theme of seeing and being seen into a voyeurism from the male vantage point, and from the female perspective, into what we would call exhibitionism. Although actual cases of abduction and rape from festival dances occurred, an explanation for the preva-lence of the motif is not to be found in social reality.[41] Its popularity lay in the fact that such a transgression of the normal pattern lead-ing to marriage expressed natural oppositions between the sexes, and aired the conflict between the groom and the family of the bride, who suffer loss at time of marriage.

In myths of the abduction from a dancing ground the victim is a liminal figure, poised on the boundary between adolescence and married life. The ambiguous status of the young girl is expressed through choral dancing and ritual collective activities which char-acteristically engage her, and with the locale (*choros*) where these acts transpire. Typically the dancing takes place in a precinct under the protection of Artemis, at a marginal area between the city and the fields, or in the case of Core, the boundary between the upper and lower worlds. The dancing ground is a social metaphor for the temporary state in which the young girl is suspended. It is a stopping-off place, so to speak, between the *oikos* of the girl's family and the *oikos* of the groom. In the exclusively female group implied by Artemis's *choros* the girl is protected and at the same time vulnerable to illicit abduction by males who wish to break in on the circle. The cosmetic and erotic components of dancing join forces to make the young female irresistible. She is shown to be at her most beautiful, ready to be plucked like the flowers she gathers. The dancing ground of the unmarried young females is at once a protected and a dangerous place.

The normal pattern for the role of dance in facilitating courtship among boys and girls is sketched out by Plato and represented on the Shield of Achilles. The mythological corollary, however, stresses something quite different: the trespassing of the boundaries of the girls' dancing ground, furtive abduction and violation, and the coupling of opposites—mortals and gods, young girls and mature heroes. The myth dramatizes the normal tension between the sexes and the mistrust between the would-be suitor and the father of the marriageable daughter, who represents the honor (*timē*) of the father. She is a sign of his power and a source of his wealth because of the dowry (*hedna*) she commands in compensation for the eventual loss to her family. In the epic the appropriate form of dowry was cattle. This particular type of dowry exchange explains why in such myths there is frequently an overlap between the theft of girls and the plundering of cattle. The successful pursuit and capture of a bride and the cattle raid are both popular epic themes; in the context of the abduction myth the activities are presented as ephebic tests cognate with the formal contests organized by the father to test the suitors. But there is an important difference: whereas in the normal pattern the fathers control the contests, in the myth of abduction the control falls into the hands of the abductor.

The earliest attested example of the theme of abduction of a young girl from a dancing ground appears in the catalogue of Myrmidon warriors in *Iliad* 16, which juxtaposes the normal pattern of mortal marriage through cattle dowry with the transgression of the norm by a god. In a short digression the poet recounts the biography of one of the Myrmidon leaders, Eudoros. Like Achilles, Eudoros was semidivine: his father was Hermes and his mortal mother Polymele. As a young female Polymele was so ravishing when she danced that Hermes fell in love with her, abducted her, and had a child by her.

> The next contingent was led by warlike Eudoros, a maiden's child, to whom one lovely in the dance, Polymele, daughter of Phylas, gave birth. Strong Hermes Argeiphontes fell in love with her, as he watched her with his eyes among the girls dancing in the choir for resounding Artemis with golden arrows. Presently Hermes the healer went up to her chamber and lay with her in secret, and she gave him a son, splendid Eudoros, a preeminent runner and a man swift in battle.

The biography then passes from Eudoros's divine parentage to his adoption by the father of Echekles, a mortal who wooed Polymele with cattle dowry. "But once Eileithyia giving birth to pains had brought forth the child into the light, and he looked at the rays of the sun, Aktor's son Echekles great in his power led her to his house, after he had given countless gifts, and the old man Phylas nursed the child and brought him up, loving him as if he had been his own son."[42] According to the normal pattern of courtship and marriage ritual in the epic, Echekles earned the right to lead Polymele to his house because he had given to her father Phylas substantial cattle dowry. An inversion of the mortal pattern is expressed in three ways in Polymele's prior union with Hermes: the motif of seeing, the dynamics of leading, and the dynamics of giving. Both the Platonic and epic models for courtship dances emphasize the powerful significance of seeing and being seen. A crowd surrounds the courtship dance on the Shield of Achilles, and in the *Laws* Plato recommends arranging dances of boys and girls so that husbands can evaluate potential brides and that fathers can judge future sons-in-law for their daughters. The display and scrutiny inherent in courtship dances have the specific social purpose of arranging suitable, and thus permanent, marital unions. When Hermes "looks with his eyes" (*ophthalmoisin idōn*) at the dancing ground of Artemis, on the other hand, he is looking with a view to a fleeting sexual union. The gaze of the god toward the dancing ground is prurient.

Although not stated, Hermes' eye is drawn to Polymele in particular because she is the most beautiful. In the female choral dance, as we have seen, the one who is most conspicuous is the leader of the dance, the *chorēgos*. Artemis herself fills this role in the prototype of choral dance in the *Hymn to Apollo*, as does Hagesichora in the first maiden song of Alcman. In the Homeric passage this leading figure is Polymele. The idea of Polymele leading a group of girls in the choral dance has a structural opposition in the function of her son Eudoros, who is a leader (cf. *hēgemoneue*) of one of the Myrmidon contingents; the word *hēgemōn* is attested in later Greek as "leader of the dance."[43] The act of leading also symbolizes the domination of the bride by the groom. When Echekles wed Polymele he led (*ēgageto*) her to his home. The gesture of the groom placing his hand on the wrist of the bride, *cheir epi karpōi*, as he leads her is, as we have seen, clearly attested in Greek art from the Geometric period onward.[44]

Echekles earned the right to lead Polymele to his *oikos* by offering many presents of cattle to Phylas, the father of Polymele, in fulfillment of the wish contained by her name. "Polymele" means "worth many sheep." As a god Hermes does not need to offer anything in exchange; in fact it is Polymele, who, in bearing him a son, gives him something in return. Far from being a provider of cattle, Hermes is traditionally the cattle thief. As an infant Hermes distinguishes himself by stealing the cattle of Apollo.[45] Instead of leading away Polymele he snatches her up in a fit of passion from the dancing floor, much as a predator plunders the sheepfold and takes away one of the flock. Like many Homeric biographies, the story of Eudoros is a paradigm for mortal behavior.

A second example of Hermes' abduction of a young girl from a dancing ground sacred to Artemis is found in the *Homeric Hymn to Aphrodite*.[46] In revenge for making Zeus and other gods fall in love involuntarily, Zeus has compelled Aphrodite to fall in love with a mortal. But the goddess fears that she will frighten away her mortal lover, Anchises, unless she can persuade him that she is not really a goddess (as Anchises suspects). Aphrodite fabricates a lying tale in which she portrays herself as a mortal abducted from the dancing place by Hermes.

> Now [once] Argeiphontes (Hermes) of the golden staff rose up and snatched me from the dancing ground of Artemis of the rushing golden arrows. Many young girls and virgins who fetch many cattle (*alphesiboiai*) were dancing, and an innumerable crowd surrounded them. From that place Argeiphontes of the golden staff seized me and led me over the numerous fields of mortal men and also over untilled and unalloted land where flesh-eating wild beasts roam through shady haunts, and I thought I would never touch the life-giving earth with my feet again![47]

In this passage the marriageability of the girls is emphasized by the epithet meaning "bringing in cattle" (*alphesiboiai*), which also characterizes the girls in the courtship dance in the Shield of Achilles. The predatory aspect of abduction by the god is emphasized by the verb for seizing ([an-]*harpazō*), used twice to describe the act of lifting the girl from the dancing ground. Elsewhere in early Greek hexameter poetry the verb is used of lions and other predators plundering the flocks.[48]

As Aphrodite tells the story, Hermes led (*ēgagen*) her from the dancing ground so long and so far that she feared she would literally lose touch with reality: "I thought I would never touch the life-giving earth with my feet again!" The gesture of leading, which is normally a metaphor of domination and domestication, here leads to something wild, a "walk on the wild side." The romantic escapade over the fields and forests is a sort of ecstatic dance. It is the very antithesis of orderly dancing, which implies contact with the earth. The wild flight is an inversion of the procession of the bride and groom to his *oikos*. The dancing ground, which normally represents a passage between the *oikos* of the young girl and the *oikos* of her eventual husband, here serves as a springboard for progressively remote places, from the cultivated land to the untilled fields inhabited by wild animals. Dancing, of course, is by nature an erotic activity; but in the context of an Artemis cult or courtship ritual the erotic currents, while aired among the participants, are also formally kept under control by the rhythms and regularity of

227

the dance. As an organ of social control dancing in courtship ritual has the purpose of bringing suitable partners together in permanent conjugal harmony. The goddess's story, however, reveals, this time from the female perspective, the attraction of abandoning oneself to a passionate impulse, of yielding to the force of a powerful, godlike lover. In Aphrodite's tale the young woman's concern about losing contact with the earth expresses a sort of sexual allegory for losing one's virginity and suggests that the transition from dancing place to marriage chamber is fraught with danger and exhilaration.

We may now return for the last time to Nausicaa's game, which can be seen as an example of an abduction manqué. The collective play of the girls, which has been orchestrated by Athena, is preparatory to the encounter between Odysseus and the princess; but while the expectation of marriage is aroused in Nausicaa, their meeting does not lead to any permanent union. Unlike Hermes, Odysseus, though himself stark naked and looking on Nausicaa and her handmaidens engaged in informal play, does not in fact abscond with Nausicaa. Yet the episode is clearly modeled on the type of myth in which a young man attempts to abduct a maiden from a sanctuary of Artemis where she is engaged in cultic dances; the expectation of an alliance between Odysseus and Nausicaa, however, is played with but kept at arm's length. The theme of the marriageable young girl as cattle to be plundered is dormant but aired in a lion simile.[49] Odysseus experiences a natural urge to "mix" (*mixesthai*) with the vulnerable young women; his physical attraction is compared to the hunger that impels a lion to leap into a sheepstead to plunder the flocks. As the simile makes clear, Odysseus's desire to "mix" is a metaphor of sexual violation. The same verb, incidentally, is found in the Platonic passage on courtship meaning "intercourse."[50] Of course, Odysseus refrains from taking advantage of the young women; but, as the simile suggests, the natural urge tempts the hero. The lion's penetration of the enclosure around the sheep flocks in the animal world is made analogous to the male who breaks in on the circle formed by the young women's choral activity. But unlike the male in the mythical prototype, Odysseus resists the urge to intrude on the vulnerable group at play. Because the structure of the myth of the abduction of the young female from the dancing place was deeply ingrained in the epic the poet is effectively able to reverse the motif of abduction in order to signal the hero's need to avoid romantic involvement on Phaeacea, in accordance with the plot of the *Odyssey*, all the while airing the sexual tension between the hero and the princess.

The juxtaposition of cattle raid and the theft and violation of girls from a dancing ground is reported in a quasi-historical context in a passage in Pausanias about Aristomenes, a hero in the second Messenian war.[51] After defending the Messenian stronghold, Aristomenes went with a hand-picked troop to Pharae, a city in Laconia, where he killed those who resisted and drove off their cattle toward Messene. On the way back he was attacked and wounded by Spartan troops but did not lose his booty. After the wound healed, Aristomenes made an attack on Sparta but was deterred by an epiphany of Helen and the Dioscouroi. He did, however, lie in wait for the young girls who were performing dances in honor of Artemis at Caryae and abducted the best of them. Leading (*agagōn*) these to a village in Messenia he put them under the protection of the young men in his band. The youths, however, became drunk and attempted to violate the girls. When Aristomenes tried to stop them they disregarded his commands, and he was forced to kill the most unruly. Aristomenes then released the women, still virgins as they were when captured, for a large ransom.[52]

A structural opposition exists between the exclusively female group in which the dancing girl is situated, and the band of male aggressors as seen in the tale of Aristomenes. The hand-picked male ephebic group that attacks the girls dancing in Artemis's sanctuary shortly after the group steals cattle is called a *lochos*, meaning an ambush group. The *lochos* stands in direct opposition to the *choros*, the girls specially chosen to dance for Artemis. Like the word *choros*, which means at once the dancers, their choreographic activity, and the dancing ground, a *lochos* represents the group, the activity, and the ambush place. A *lochos*, moreover, has a leader, a *lochagos*, just as a *choros* has its leader, a *chorēgos*. The juxtaposition of the *lochos* and the *choros* is implicit in the Nausicaa episode. Odysseus, spying on the *choros* in the brush, is comparable to a lion who comes forth from a sort of *lochos*-lair.[53]

The tension between male and female groups ultimately is expressed in the myth by the divine prototypes of the leaders of each group. Artemis is the *chorēgos* of the divine choral dance, and Hermes, who appears as abductor is, in a sense, the leader of the groups such as the *lochos* whose activities, like cattle raiding, are typically covert. Hermes' leading function as shepherd and psychopomp is well known. He is shown in Greek art leading the horses of the groom's chariot or those of Hades in the marriage of Core to Lord of the Underworld.[54]

The abduction of young girls as condoned by Hermes also represents an assault on Artemis, the virgin goddess who protects them. In a final variation on the abduction myth in which Artemis herself is the object of desire, the goddess protects herself from a male aggressor by disguising herself indistinguishably from her nymphs.[55] Pausanias reports the story that the river-god Alpheus had fallen in love with Artemis. Knowing that the virgin goddess would never agree to marry him, he planned to violate her at a night-time festival at Letrinoi which the goddess was holding with the nymphs who danced with her (*paizousa*). When the goddess suspected what Alpheus was plotting, she covered her face and the faces of all the nymphs with mud so that when the god came he could not distinguish between the goddess and the nymphs. He went away disappointed of desire.

We may now situate the concept of leading and abduction of cattle and women in the context of initiatory structures and metaphors for domestication. Another metaphor for groups of adolescents, both male and female, is the Greek word for herd, *agelē*. This metaphor of domestication underlying the taking of the female can be related to dancing in rows by the shared essential activity of leading. The word for herd, *agelē*, from the verb *agō* "to lead," is so called because it implies a group of animals led by a herdsman.[56] In a similar way, the essential action of a *choros* is that of being led, as the frequent use of the verb *agō* with *choros* (the band of dancers), as well as the etymology of *chorēgos*, demonstrates. The word *agelē* may itself have a dance significance. Athenaeus cites a fragment of a hyporcheme by Pindar in which the word for herd (*agelē*) is used metaphorically for a group of unmarried Spartan females (*Lakainōn men parthenōn agelē*).[57] In this context the metaphor for the collective group may be a synonym for *choros*. In Pindar's dithyramb for the Thebans, Artemis is said to arrange dances for Dionysus, who delights in the dancing herds (*choreusaisi . . . agalais*).[58] This phrase describes precisely Polymele's status transition group. In a male context at Sparta the term *agelē* belongs to the vocabulary of male initiation to designate a band of boys who were trained for, among other things, warfare. The coming of military age in Sparta was accompanied by a highly structured transition rite and was regarded as a new phase of life, much as marriage represented a new and significant stage of life for females. Male and female groups near the boundary of marriage are very close to being the "other," and dancing assists in blurring, even trespassing the limits.

We may now summarize and look at an example from comparative ethnography. The epic themes of cattle raid and bride theft are shaped in the myth of abduction from a dancing ground to reflect a tension between ephebes and *parthenoi*. The pursuit and capture of the girl, like that of cattle, is an ephebic test. But the myth also has a particular significance for the girl. Young girls, for their part, are ambivalent about leaving the familiar order and capitulating to the domination implied by marriage. By modeling themselves on the goddess in exclusively female *choroi*, they transfer their allegiance to the goddess. There is a competition between the girls in the *choros* who strive to show their loyalty to the divinity by being most like the goddess. In the myth the ambiguous social status of the young, unmarried female who stands poised between adolescence and adulthood is complemented by ambiguities about her "ontological" status, that is, whether she is a mortal or a goddess. As we have seen, during Nausicaa's encounter with Odysseus the princess is twice compared to Artemis, once in a simile and once by Odysseus. In the *Hymn to Aphrodite* passage the ambiguity moves in the opposite direction. The goddess, wishing to disguise her divinity yet present herself as an alluring female for reasons that suit the internal logic of the narrative, casts herself as a nubile young woman for whom Hermes lusted in the dancing place—precisely the type of female represented by Polymele in the Homeric biography. In her lying tale Aphrodite makes herself out to be the closest thing to an immortal without allowing that she is in fact a goddess.

Being like the goddess means becoming the first dancer. This role is ambivalent, since it distinguishes the girl, but also invites increased scrutiny from the onlookers. In the myth there is an implicit danger that it may lead to the violation by a powerful male or hero. The pressures of being the first dancer have been documented by an ethnographic study in modern Greece.[59] In the town of Sohos in northern Greece when a female dancer takes the lead position in the circle dance the spectators closely watch how she presents herself with her body and judge her bodily movements against an ideal. "Ideally," the people of Sohos say, "the young unmarried dancer—whom they expect to dance most vivaciously because she has a legitimate interest in attracting young men—should be 'tall,' 'slim,' 'well-appearing,' and 'well-dressed.' In her movements she should be 'open,' 'buoyant,' and 'confident.' She should execute improvisations with originality and with spirit and confidence. She should 'differentiate' herself in these ways if she wants a man to notice her." As she dances she is expected to display her beauty, skill, energy, sensuality, and sexuality. But because the Sohoians have ambivalent attitudes about female sexuality, regarding it as pleasurable and threatening, aesthetic expressions of female sexuality are viewed with suspicion. A cold, unsensual performance, on the other hand, is looked upon with criticism and disdain.[60] The limits of acceptable behavior for a female as revealed through dancing are perilously narrow.

In the ancient Greek paradigm the narrow limits of acceptable behavior are expressed by the paradox of what it means to follow the divine model. The unmarried young female in the myth of the abduction of the young girl from the dancing ground, as we have seen, combines the traits of mortal and immortals. The very act of dancing with her age-mates defines her status as one available for marriage, but in so doing she impersonates a goddess and so imitates a pleasing activity that also characterizes divine behavior. Being too much like the goddess also has undesirable consequences, since the deity is a virgin and remains always off bounds to males, as emphasized by the tale of the attempted abduction of the goddess by Alpheus at a festival at Letrinoi. There is a danger that a girl will overimitate the virgin prototype and remain suspended in the *choros* of the goddess forever.

An anonymous votive epigram in the *Greek Anthology* tells us that at the moment of marriage one Timareta consecrated to Artemis Limnatis, among other things, her hand-drum used in the dance, the ball that she loved, and her dolls.[61] The hand-held dance drums and the ball perhaps will recall for us the game of Nausicaa. Among the things of youth which the young girl had gracefully to yield is the pleasure of playing with the other *parthenoi*, of circling in the dance (*paizein*). When a girl entered into the house of her husband under the sway of the mother-in-law she normally did not dance any more: her ritual contribution was rather that of lamenting the corpse.

Eight

The Dance of Death:
Privileges of the Dead

For everything there is a season, and a time for every matter under
heaven . . . a time to mourn and a time to dance.
—Ecclesiastes

Scholars have commented on basic similarities between wedding and funerary ritual revolving
around the abduction of the bride or the snatching
of the body and responses to loss by the family of
the loved one. In art and poetry of the classical
period the tragic wedding, exemplified by the Core myth, became a
topos.[1] In this chapter we begin with the ritual lamentation of the
corpse, investigating its choral nature and its affinities not only
with aspects of marriage ritual but with other forms of choral expression. From this richly documented area we move to the speculative as we go backward chronologically to consider the fragmentary evidence for the role of dance in commemorating heroes.

We are relatively well informed about the funerary customs of
the Greeks through the material remains and also from law codes,
such as those from Delphi, Iulis on Ceos, and other places.[2] Funerary legislation was in the main restrictive in nature, limiting the
costs and period of mourning, imposing bans on wailing out of
doors or subsequent to the actual funeral ceremony, but still ac-
knowledging the need to carry out ritual procedures, including
sacrifice and purification of the deceased's house. The restrictive

nature of the codes concurs with legislation in the Platonic city, generally thought to mirror contemporary Athenian practice.³ Plato's view is of special interest because, while banning dirges and lamentations, he prescribes a limited use of choral rites; in this respect he echoes practices from archaic Athens that still were in use in fourth-century burials of Cypriot kings.

In Plato's polis, funeral observances for the ordinary citizen should be unostentatious and discreet affairs. Death is essentially a private, family concern. Mourning and lamentation should be displayed only within the confines of the house during the wake. When the corpse is taken out for burial it must not be paraded openly in the streets. The removal of the corpse from the house to the burial place outside the city, moreover, should take place before daybreak. Plato makes, however, an exception to the rule in the case of public examiners whose obsequies should include choral hymns and full military regalia. These auditors of the accounts and examiners of the public conduct, called *euthynoi* (a word literally meaning "straighteners"), are priests of Apollo and Helios. The idea that the high priests will "rectify" by careful scrutiny the crooked actions of public officials echoes the notion contained in Plato's account of the origins of civic dance that Apollo and the Muses were given to all mortals as companions in the feast so that people, when they grow slack in their discipline, might be set right (*epanorthōntai*).⁴ It is appropriate that at death the priests of Apollo should be paid respect by the choral arts associated with that divinity. Plato describes in detail the choral hymns and procession honoring these upholders of moral rectitude:

> There shall be no dirges (*thrēnoi*) and lamentations, and a chorus of fifteen girls and one of fifteen boys shall encircle the bier and shall sing antiphonally a song of praise in the form of a hymn (*hymnos*) for the deceased official, celebrating his glory throughout the day in hymn singing. At dawn the bier shall be escorted to the tomb by 100 young men who frequent the gymnasia . . . and in front shall go the unmarried young men outfitted with proper military accoutrements—cavalry with their horses, hoplites with their armor, and the rest in the same way. Round about the bier the boys (of the chorus) shall be toward the front singing traditional songs, with the girls singing in their train.⁵

235

This piece of legislation concerning public funerals bans the use of dirges (*thrēnoi*) and instead endorses antiphonally sung hymns. The former is appropriate, the passage implies, for private mourning within the house, while choral hymns are suitable for public display. But the two forms are patterned on the same basic choral configuration, and the elaborated choral hymn may indeed owe much to the group lament over the corpse known from prehistoric times onward. Plato is reflecting the Greek perception that funerary expression with voice and body is inherently different from other musical and choreographic activity. But are they fundamentally to be distinguished? A closer examination of music and dance in mourning ritual would suggest that formally the funeral lament with its leader (*exarchos*) and band of antiphonally placed mourners in many respects does not differ from other choral forms.[6] While the desire to disassociate the mournful from the joyful is natural, it should not deter us from asking in what ways the ritual response to death contributed to musical and dance forms. How did the physical revulsion at the corpse and the need to contain its abominal powers in ritually prescribed ways influence and interact with other forms of ritual play?

The interaction of mourning and other types of expression is indicated by ritual laments for quasi-human figures known in myths about young men like Linus or Lityerses, who die in the prime of youthful beauty. After death they are invoked and ritually lamented in dirges. The circumstances of their deaths vary, yet the beliefs that occasion the explanations are the same. In Greece the invocation and lament for the dying crop or its personification became the basis of folk songs, such as the Linus song which was intoned at the time of the harvest. According to Herodotus the Linus song was of a type common in Cyprus, Phoenicia, and Egypt. He explains that the Egyptian version of the Linus song was called Maneros, after the only son of the first Egyptian king. His untimely death caused a dirge to be invented in his honor, and this was the first and at that time the only melody in existence.[7] The dirge in Egypt, Herodotus suggests, was a primeval and primitive type of song.

In Homer, the Linus song is more a lively dance than a dirge. It appears, appropriately, in the agricultural vignettes on the Shield of Achilles. The grape harvest is in progress: "Girls and cheerful boys were carrying the honey-sweet fruit in woven baskets, and in the midst of them a boy (*pais*) played lovely music on his clear-sounding *phorminx*, and sang the beautiful Linus song in a piping voice. The others followed him, stamping in unison, skipping on their feet with singing and joyful shouts."[8] This is a clear instance of choral song and dance. The chorus leader in the midst of the joyful activity is the boy, playing the *phorminx* as he sings. The chorus is made up of girls and boys of the same age as those in the courtship dance in the final shield vignette, as the similarity in the phrasing for the group of youthful male and female performers indicates.[9] Linus was a legendary musician whose name is found in the refrain of the lament, *ailinon*, meaning "alas! for Linus." Although the stories told about this figure differ, in all versions he met an early death. According to a fragment of Hesiod, Linus was the son of Ourania and was killed by Apollo for claiming to be as good a singer as the god. Singers and kitharists customarily lament his death, says Hesiod, at musical performances. They invoke the god as they begin and as they end, paying tribute to him as a patron since he is "skilled in all types of wisdom." The occasions on which they intone his name are not themselves necessarily sad, but rather festivals (*eilapinais*) and dances (*chorois*).[10] Significantly, the one who impersonates Linus in the grape-harvesting vignette on the Shield of Achilles is the boy *chorēgos* whose song, like the tune for Linus, provides the accompaniment and impetus for the choral rite of the boys and girls. Like the dirge in Egypt the Linus song seems to have been regarded as a prototypical inspiration for festive musical expression of all kinds.

It is not surprising that the dirge should find an explanation of its origins in the lament for a fair youth. But that the same type of explanation is given for the wedding song as well is striking yet consistent with the structural similarities between wedding and funerary rites in general, which anthropologists and ancient authors have commented upon. In a fragment from a formal lament (*thrēnos*) Pindar mentions the various classifications of genres of choral lyric, including the dirge for "clear-voiced" Linus and the hymn for Hymenaeus, both said to be sons of Apollo and the Muses cut down early in life.[11] Hymenaeus's tragic end is reflected in the portrayals of the god in art, where he is shown with a sorrowful expression; he is capable of transforming wedding celebration into funerary lamentation.[12] In the same vein, the structure and laments for the dead in modern Greece closely resemble those sung by the bride when she leaves the house of her father.[13] Conversely, the Linus song can express happiness as well as lamentation. Aristophanes of Byzantium, the third-century Alexandrian editor, said that the Linus song and the *ailinos* are sung not only on occasions of mourning but also in the "happy dance," as in Euripides. The reference is to a passage in Euripides' *Heracles* in which the chorus intends to use as their model Phoebus Apollo as he accompanies himself on the lyre and joins the *ailinos* to the dance of prosperity (*eutuchei molpāi*). So they will sing a hymn of praise for the labors of the dead Heracles, combining eulogy with lamentation.[14] In the grape-harvesting vignette on the Shield of Achilles a joyful mood prevails among the celebrants around about the boy who sings the Linus song.

As Louis Gernet has shown in a comparative study on terms for lamentation, a wide range of emotions is expressed by the cultic cry of women, *ololygē*.[15] This versatile cry is an expression of sorrow upon death,[16] an exclamation of joy,[17] a battle cry,[18] an utterance of astonishment at the birth of a god,[19] and as Gernet suggests, a chant sung at the nuptial rites.[20]

The Greek personification of the dying fertility god of the ancient Near East as a youthful musician seems to be a singularly Greek contribution and contains an insight into the perceived origins of choral forms from traditional laments. Orderly musical forms developed from a primitive lament are predicated on death, a state that causes temporary disorder. They thus share, in common with myths of origin for the musical instruments that accompany choral forms (the *aulos* and lyre), the belief that a permanent order for the communal expression of ephemeral human emotions—joy as well as sorrow—is founded on the destruction of a potent natural force. In Pindar the *aulos* and its mournful tune (*thrēnos, goos*) represented a transformation of the hissing of serpents, while in the *Homeric Hymn to Hermes* the lyre was born from the tortoise slain by the god.[21] This force is then appropriated by human *technē* through the creation of a musical instrument or refrain that is the basis or impetus for a more artfully developed form of collective expression.

The accent in the myths of lament for the fair youth thus lies on the *human* origins for festivity. Mortality is the state or condition that fundamentally separates people from gods, and the response to death in ritual lamentation is also a distinctly human form of emotional expression. Stories about the primeval expression of human grief for a dying youth are attempts to account for the origins of primitive music in quasi-human, heroic, rather than divine prototypes. In this most mortal manifestation of ritual movement we find a profound case of lasting order evolving from destruction and temporary disorder. The *aitia* for the Linus song and the wedding song from the lament of a youthful figure should not, however, be interpreted as a historical development of these musical forms from the ritual lament of the corpse, but rather as a reminder of the powerful and constant mutual influence of funerary ritual and choral genres in festival hymns and dances. Psychologically, the fluidity between the funeral lamentation and the wedding underlines the fact that both for the young man and the young girl, as well as for the bride's family, the separation from one's age-mates, and, in the case of the bride, the removal from the family, arouse emotions that are not dissimilar from those experienced upon the death of a loved one.

The convergence of joy and sorrow, intense grief and release, is found in the rhythm of cultic worship and in festival sequences. The lament for the dying god has a natural opposite in the joy expressed at the return of the divinity. In Boeotia the arrival of the goddess, represented by a roughly carved wooden image, is followed by her precipitate departure when the images are burned in a nocturnal festival called the Daidala.[22] There is joy and celebration when the cult statues of the goddess arrive, followed by a feeling of loss upon their extinction. The polarities of separation and reunion were expressed in the mood of the two Ariadne festivals taking place on Naxos, where the sacred marriage with Dionysus occurred.[23] One reproduced the joyful spirit of the *kōmos*, the other the lamentation appropriate to separations and death. At the annual Laconian festival to Apollo and Hyacinthus, the beloved of Apollo who was accidentally killed by the god, lamentation yielded to jubilation. The festival took place over three days and had two distinct parts, according to Athenaeus.[24] The first was devoted to mourning Hyacinthus. Beginning on the second day, however, the festivities for Apollo marked a distinct shift in mood. Boys played the lyre and sang praises to the god to the accompaniment of the *aulos*. Some rode into the theater on horseback, and others sang in choirs while among them dancers performed figures in the traditional style. The entire city turned out to participate in music, dancing, contests, and feasting. The transition from grief and lamentation to feasting and contests is perhaps best known from the twenty-third book of the *Iliad* when the mourning for Patroclus gives way to eating followed by formal games and contests that engender joy and excitement, a transition also seen in the following example from comparative anthropology.

The contests in *Iliad* 23 are staged to honor Patroclus, but in an important sense the competitive feats are for the benefit of Achilles, who as chief mourner previously led the Myrmidons in the ritual lament for Patroclus. While staging the games he alone abstains from actively participating in them. A similar division between mourning and celebration and the groups who are responsible for each can be seen in the death dances of the Lugbara of Uganda.[25] After a death among the Lugbara there are two types of dances performed by two distinct groups of people. The first type are the wailing dances (*ongo*), the second the playing dances (*abi*). The first are performed by the lineage kin of the deceased as soon as possible after the death, sometimes even before the burial has occurred. The second type of dances are performed by the relatives by marriage. The playful dances properly occur a year after the death at the home of the deceased. The lineage kin converge at this time as well to dance and to wail. The relatives by marriage, on the other hand come to "play" and to generate joy. The word for joy in the language of the Lugbara refers in this and other situations specifically to the satisfaction that comes when lineage ties disrupted by recent death have been reaffirmed and solidified. The second occasion for dancing is thus a time to mourn, but also to dance in celebration of the fact that the rupture in the family structure caused by death has been healed. In the Homeric world the healing of the rupture in the cosmos and the community of warriors caused by Patroclus's death is effected by *agōnes* more formal than those implied by the playful dances of the Lugbara. But the dynamic between the deceased and the closest mourners (who are in a sense the audience) and the performers who restore festivity is similar.

Temporary Rupture in the Body Politic

Death, being a biological transition, means a temporary rupture in the cosmic and social order. Like birth, death irrupts on the scene. It cannot be planned and controlled like weddings. The event spells a disjunction between living and dead; the pollution emanating from the corpse widens the gulf between mortals and gods. At funerals there is a tendency towards license and social disorder, necessitating legislation at various periods to restrict and prescribe the expression of grief, especially among women who tended the corpse. A funeral is a highly volatile occasion. Funerary rituals tend to ignite conflicts among the community at large by offering a pretext to rival kinship groups to establish a claim or further their interests. Yet the expression of grief at the wake and during the procession and burial is not a spontaneous outbreak of emotion. Carefully controlled and ritually prescribed behavior at every stage of the lament is indicated for the relatives and sometimes professional mourners. In Plato's fourth-century Athens Carian women could be hired as mourners.[26]

A perceived breakdown in the continuum between singing and dancing, the verbal and nonverbal components of expression in Platonic *choreia* and *orchēsis*, occurs during the ritual lament. Instead of engaging the entire body in rhythmic movement (Plato's definition of *orchēsis* in book 7 of the *Laws*) motion is concentrated on the upper body, and attention is drawn to the breast and the head by the hands, a form of expression more closely approximating *cheironomia* than actual dance.[27] The breakdown of order implied by death is especially pronounced in women, whose expression of mourning is compared to the frenzy of the dancing maenad. Thus

Andromache, upon learning of the death of her husband, is said to rave like a maenad.[28] In black-figure representations of the *prothesis* or wake, the women display frenzied gestures of mourning that are iconographically close to the attitudes of maenads engaged in such violent activities as rending animals. At time of death or during the ecstatic state leading to ritual *sparagmos* of an animal it is the women in particular who come into contact with their liminal selves, taking responsibility for the body and the risk of coming into contact with the pollution entailed by the blood.

Tragedy contains several passages describing the female gestures of disfigurement to the upper body, often thought by the Greeks to be a manner of mourning coming from the east. The chorus in Aeschylus's *Suppliant Women*, bewailing its fate, compares itself to the wife of Procne transformed into a nightingale, the better to mourn the child she unwittingly killed: "So I, continually lamenting in the Ionian way, lacerate my tender sun-browned cheek and my heart, unused to tears."[29] In Aeschylus's *Choephoroi* the chorus of slave women sent to convey libations at the tomb of Agamemnon emphatically describes its passionate manifestations of mourning: "I have come, struck by sharp blows with my hand; my cheek shows itself crimson as I tear it with my nails cutting fresh furrows. . . . Ruining the linen, the rending of my robes that enshroud my bosom resounds loud in my grief."[30] Later the choir compares their mode of lamentation to customs in regions of Persia: "I struck with strokes like an Arian, in the style of a Cissian mourning-woman. There were unceasing blows to see, much scattered blood, the stretching of hands one following another, upwards and downwards, and my wretched stricken head rang with the hammer-sound."[31]

The upper torso is emphasized because the organs of emotion were thought in the archaic and classical periods to reside in the region of the diaphragm and chest; the lungs in concert with the voice become the instrument of lamentation, and the gesture of striking the breast accentuates the effect. But there is another reason. The laceration of the cheeks, the pulling of the hair, the pummeling of the breast all imply the undoing of the parts of the body that are otherwise adorned and emphasized in the choral dance in order to bring pleasure to Aphrodite, Artemis, or other presiding divinity. This is the very reversal of the cosmetic component of the dance personified by the "fair-haired" and "fair-cheeked" Charites and Harmony in the divine prototype. Instead of crowning their hair with flowers the women tear at it; where the cheeks were before fair they now stream with blood; the linen garments so lovingly spun, dyed, and scented are now rent. The women are no longer followers of Artemis or Aphrodite. Hades is their lord. In Euripides' *Suppliants* the chorus claims to "moan in the strain of the dance Hades loves," while in his *Hercules*, the chorus, upon learning of the hero's infanticides ironically asks "what dance shall I do for Hades?"[32] Paradoxically the self-directed disfiguration of the mourner erases certain boundaries between the living and the deceased, as it renders the mourner symbolically as a corpse. At the same time the women disfigure themselves they minister to the corpse, washing and anointing the body, dressing it, and placing the head of the deceased on a pillow. Whereas the women come in close contact with the miasma of the corpse, mirroring it and at the same time containing it in prescribed ritual actions, the men, on the other hand, remain at arm's length from the source of grief and pollution during the *prothesis*, approaching the body only during the procession from the house to the place of burial.

Several passages in Greek tragedy indicate that the Greeks made a sharp division between funerary laments and music, the latter conceived as joyful and pleasurable. That perception, however, is belied by the formal similarities between ritual lamentation and other musical expression. In Euripides' *Troades*, Hecabe, who leads the chorus in lament in the wake of the Trojan disaster, is first portrayed at the outset of the play alone, slumped in grief. As she cries out she expresses a wish to move her body: "Oh, my head, my forehead, my ribs! How I long to twist (*heilixai*) and rock my back, my spine, like a boat, to either side in turn, to elegies of continual, miserable tears. Music, ever the same, sounds dance-less (*achoreutous*) dooms for the unfortunate."[33] In this passage Hecabe longs to move her body in coordination with her elegiac wailing. Moreover she seems to wish to move in the manner of a Bacchant. The verb to twist (*heilixai*) is used in Euripides' *Bacchae* of the movement of the maenads led in the dance by Dionysus.[34] The normal conjunction of music and dance, the verbal and the nonverbal, however, becomes disjointed at time of grief. The music of lament implies "dance-less" (*achoreutos*) woes.

A moment later in Hecabe's monologue, just before the chorus enters, the Trojan queen contrasts her present task of leading the song of lamentation with dances for the gods in happier days. "Like the mother of fledgling birds I shall lead [*exarxō*] the cry, the song, not the same as that which I used to lead [*exērchon*], leaning on Priam's sceptre, with the loud-sounding beats of the foot that rules that dance [*archēchorou*], in honor of the Phrygian gods."[35] The contrast between Hecabe's presiding role in lamentation and the dance is, formally speaking, less pronounced than she perceives it to be on an emotional level. In this passage Euripides uses the technical vocabulary for leading the ritual lament and the choral dance. The same verbal stem (*arch-*) is used for both. This usage reflects the fact that both are ritual forms of expression involving a group, and in this case a group of women under the leadership of a dominant person such as the Trojan queen.

Despite the perceived gulf between funerary and other types of choral expression we must again ask to what extent there really is a gap, and to what degree there is a basic structural resemblance between choral dancing and ritual lamentation. A leader, called the *exarchos* and corresponding to the *chorēgos*, begins the lament by uttering a phrase or verse of a more extended plaintive song. The group of mourners then answers with cries or articulated words of grief. In the Trojans' lament for Hector the ritual mourning is carried out in several stages beginning with the professional male singers (*aoidoi*) who lead off with a dirge (*exarchous threnōn*) known as the *thrēnos*; to this the women answered antiphonally. Next Andromache, now acting as *exarchos* of the women, leads an extended lament, and the mourning women wail in answer. Then Hecabe takes her turn as *exarchos*, and finally Helen. The lament over the corpse is accompanied by ritual movement and gestures. In the lament of the Nereids in *Iliad* 18, which some scholars have explained as a survival from an earlier version of the poem in which Achilles actually dies and is mourned like Hector in our version, the sea-nymphs, the followers of Thetis, gathered around (*ampha-geronto*) and beat their breasts while Thetis began the lament.[36]

Much of our exact knowledge of the gestures of funerary behavior in fact comes from funerary art, for the earthen tumulus of the deceased was surmounted by a large painted vase or sculpted stele. The procession (*ekphora*) and especially the wake (*prothesis*) were among the most persistent themes in Athenian vase painting from the Geometric period through the end of the fifth century.[37] In surviving examples of the theme the body laid out on the bier is usually male, although *prothesis* scenes for women are known.[38] A *prothesis* scene on a black-figure cup from the Kerameikos cemetery in Athens (Fig. 26), though in a fragmentary state, contains many of the typical elements of the Greek wake. It is of special interest because of the attention given to the antithetical chorus of male mourners. At the *prothesis* both sexes are present, and the participants span the generations.[39] A small nude child, a common element in *prothesis* scenes, stands directly beneath the head of the deceased, a bearded, and therefore mature male. The corpse is dressed and elevated on a bier. After the deceased, the most important figure is the chief mourner standing at the head of the funeral bed. In this female figure we see clearly the tension between the orderly care of the corpse and disorderly aggression in gestures directed against her own body. The painter has condensed several actions into one pose. In her function as attendant to the dead, the chief mourner lowers the head onto a pillow with one hand. The other hand is raised to the head as she pulls a lock of hair, much like the woman to the far right. The painter has in addition suggested the ritual action of lacerating the cheeks with the nails in a most literal way by depicting five rivulets of blood streaming down from the face, each one made by one of the five fingers of the hand.

Males in the *prothesis* scene typically assume antithetical formations, standing in pairs with their right arm upraised before the face in a gesture of salutation to the deceased. On the other side of the Kerameikos cup (Fig. 26 *bottom*) at least fourteen men are so arrayed. The figure on the right is distinguished from the rest by having a shaven head and beard, a sign of mourning; perhaps he is a slave.[40] The males thus arranged form two antiphonal choruses.

245

Figure 26. *Top:* Females tending the corpse. *Bottom:* Antithetic rows of male mourners with upraised arms.

The artist has suggested that they are singing a dirge or lament of some kind by showing the mouths of those in the far row parted at the lips, while the mouths of those in the near row are closed: they await their turn. In the literary sources this antiphonal form of lament is best known for women, but it is also attested for men: Achilles leads the Myrmidons in a *goos*, and Xerxes leads a chorus of old men in a processional lament in Aeschylus's *Persae*.

In general the contrast between male and female mourners is striking. The women turn the aggression arising at death against themselves by delivering blows with their own hands to the head and breast. The male mourners uniformly direct the hand away from the head, a gesture performed in an orderly ensemble. The neat antithetical arrangement of the male mourners anticipates the *ekphora* or procession when the body is lifted by the men and carried from the house to the place of burial. There is a striking antithesis between the chaotic, disfiguring, individual movements of the female mourners and the serene, uniform, and measured movement of the males. Remarkably, this is a reversal of the pattern that emerges in the stately female bridal procession with lively male dancing in the wake when the body of the bride is in transit, like that of the deceased, from the *oikos* to less familiar ground.

Mourning gestures can continue well into the procession. The Antikenmuseum in Berlin has in its possession 16 fragments of ceramic plaques from the painted frieze of a grave monument. They are attributed to Exekias and are dated between 540 and 530. They were thought to have decorated either the eaves or walls of a mud-brick-built tomb. About 530 single plaques replace friezes composed of multiple plaques, perhaps in response to a law passed at Athens to limit the expenditure on grave monuments. Before the antisumptuary law, funerary legislation attributed to Solon had been introduced to limit the size and potential disorder of the burial ceremony at aristocratic funerals. Among the restrictions "no one was permitted to lacerate flesh as a sign of grief and to sing dirges."[41] To compensate for limitations on the display of grief, aristocrats built costly monuments of built-tombs and decorated them with series of plaques that portrayed in detail what they may have been forbidden from enacting in public during the procession. In the plaques by Exekias the body is carried in a horse-drawn cart, accompanied by mourners who continue the gestures of mourning as they walk along. On a fragment of one plaque (Fig. 27) a young woman raises her left hand to cover her head while she pulls at her hair with the left; a bearded man caps his head with his right hand in a gesture of grief.

Figure 27. Ritual mourning gestures.

Dances for the Heroic Dead

In Plato's legislation concerning public funerals for the high priests we may note that the ceremony with choral hymns and military parades is to have sequels in yearly festivals of musical contests, gymnastic events, and horse racing.[42] The ceremonies Plato envisions are not without parallel in the Greek world. The Platonic funerary celebration itself finds its literary prototype in the funeral observances for Patroclus in *Iliad* 23, whereas the commemorative festival has a nearly contemporary historical counterpart in the lavish festival arranged by Nicocles, son and successor of Evagoras, the king of Salaminian Cyprus, who died in 374 or 373. Isocrates, who wrote an encomium for the occasion, says that Evagoras was honored by choruses (*chorois*).[43] By the fourth century, however, the type of commemoration for Evagoras was anomalous in the Greek world. Indeed, already in the late eighth century, with the rise of hero cult, the lavish funerary games of aristocrats had begun to give way to institutionalized contests in the pan-Hellenic sanctuaries founded by heroes.[44]

It is now generally believed that the peculiarly Greek institution of hero cults was not a continuous development from the Mycenaean cult of the dead but rather an institution directly influenced by the thriving tradition of epic poetry in the early archaic period.[45] Although the epic cannot be used to reconstruct life in Iron Age Greece, its rife interest in the minutiae of funerary practices and ritual laments for heroes, as already seen for Patroclus and Hector, indicates that descriptions of such practices, while glamorized, drew on contemporary customs and in turn directly influenced procedures in hero cult carried out by families and cities looking for genealogical connections with epic heroes. At the local level Pindar and other epinician poets provided such links in celebrations of the exploits and lineage of athletic victors.

The epic paints two types of ritual observances for the deceased hero, one involving the lamentation of the lifeless body, the other the commemoration of the living exploits of the hero in an agonistic context. As seen earlier in the case of Hector, singers (*aoidoi*) as well as the female kin lead the antiphonal wailing around the corpse. The basic pattern of a group of mourners gathering around a central figure is played out in honoring Patroclus's corpse in *Iliad* 23. In a ritual reminiscent in its ceremonial aspects of the funeral procession for the judges in Plato's polis, Achilles orders the Myrmidons to circumambulate the corpse of the slain leader,[46] and Achilles himself, after beginning the lament, lays his hands on the breast of his fallen companion.[47] Achilles specifically orders them not to unyoke their horses from the war chariots but to approach close by with horses and chariots and encircle the corpse of Patroclus three times, a number with a magical significance linked to a belief in the power of circumambulation ritual to purify. As they move around the corpse in a circle they groan in unison, with Achilles taking the lead:

"Myrmidons of the swift-running horses, my trusted companions, we must not yet release our single-foot horses from the chariots, but with these very horses and chariots draw near Patroclus and bewail him, since such is the due of the dead." . . . So he spoke. All assembled groaned, and Achilles led them. Mourning, they drove their horses with flowing manes about the body three times, and among them Thetis aroused the desire for weeping.[48]

The circumabulation of the corpse appears to be an attenuated choral form in two ways. First, the circular movement of a group around (*peri*) any significant object is the characteristic configuration of the choral band, who in linking bodies establish boundaries. It is vital that the circle be tightly drawn around the corpse so as to contain its noxious effects and protect it from pollution from without. The insistence on not unyoking the horses from the chariots stems from a magical belief in completing the circle and thereby strengthening the solidarity of Achilles and his companions. Second, the circular movement of the group is combined with vocal utterance. The lamentation is led by Achilles, who in his leading function (*ērchē*) acts as a *chorēgos*.

Once the immediate duty of respecting the corpse of Patroclus has taken place, the hero is commemorated through games. The context for honoring Patroclus is competitive play with strictly prescribed rules under the supervision of the chief mourner. The games among the survivors are a *mimēsis* of the accomplishments of the deceased in his military milieu. In the funerary games for Patroclus the athletic activity of each participant in some way replicates the martial activity appropriate to his own heroic activity. The athletic analogues in association with the *agōn* have a life-renewing power. The funeral games for Patroclus bring prestige to the deceased but they also help to heal the loss and rupture by having the participants submit to rules that reassert the agonistic tradition of the warrior group. Once again the breach of order brought on by death can be made whole by regulated activity.

The specific use of dance in an agonistic context to honor the hero can be inferred from the Phaeacean interlude in the *Odyssey* where the Phaeaceans entertain their guest with recitations, and games, including competitive dancing. These are the same festival components that made up the funeral games of the hero Amphidamas in Euboea, where Hesiod boasts of having won a tripod in the contest for hymn singing.[49] The hero so honored is, of course, a living man. But Odysseus is no ordinary guest, and Odysseus's heroic wanderings have recently included his descent and return from the Underworld, a journey he is about to narrate to his hosts.

The Phaeaceans for their part are well equipped to honor and move the hero in a variety of ways. While Demodocus's song about Odysseus at Troy aggrieves the hero, the Phaeaceans' games and dances console him. The Phaeaceans, as Alcinous reminds Odysseus, excel in their races and dances.[50] The latter talent is reflected in the epithet of the region *euruchoros*, "having broad dancing grounds." Before the bardic recitation of the song of Ares and Aphrodite (which may have been accompanied by gestures),[51] Alcinous orders the elite dancers, the Betarmones, to commence playful dancing (*paisate* from *paizō*).[52] Although their dance has a playful character, it is situated in an agonistic context. The place where they dance is called the *agōn*.[53] Similarly, in a catalogue of the young Phaeacean males (*neoi*) and their gymnastic exploits, Alcinous announces that Amphialos is best in jumping (*halmati*).[54] The root of the word *halma*—*hal/sal*—is found in the Latin word for dancing, *saltatio*. It also appears in the name of Halios, one of the sons of Alcinous; along with his brother Laodamas, they are the best of the Betarmones, without rivals.[55]

At the conclusion of the song of Ares and Aphrodite, Alcinous orders these two sons to execute a duo. They dance, throwing a ball between them as they leap. Each one must catch the ball before touching the earth.[56] The foot-races, as well as the swift and acrobatic dances of the Phaeaceans, do not merely please the hero, they are appropriate for his own exploits as warrior and former athletic contestant. At the funeral games of Patroclus, Odysseus is the much applauded winner of the running contest.[57]

Although there is no dancing described at Patroclus's funerary games in the *Iliad*, Aristotle is reported to have said that the pyrrhic, in fact, originated from Achilles' dancing in arms around Patroclus's "pyre" (*pyr*). The aetiology sees the dance as a circumambulation rite, like the rounds of Myrmidons in their chariots.[58]

The pyrrhic was known in various parts of the Greek world outside of Athens as an appropriate means of honoring the dead: its appropriateness can be explained by its being a choreographic reenactment of the quintessential military activity of the deceased.[59] The scholia on *Iliad* 23.130, commenting on the circumambulation ritual of Patroclus, report that at royal Cypriot funerals, the army that led the procession of the deceased king danced the pyrrhic.

The funerary weapon dance is perhaps best known from two Attic vases (dated about 500) on which armed warriors wearing short chitons engage in rapid movement to the accompaniment of an *aulētēs*.[60] A context for their movement clearly emerges on a circular frieze on a kantharos in the Cabinet des Médailles that may have been made for an Etruscan client (Fig. 28).[61] Four warriors wearing Corinthian helmets proceed to the right with a spirited step toward a tomb decorated by a snake, which is often a manifestation of a hero. Before the tomb stands an *aulētēs* and a female figure gesturing with upraised arms in an expression of ritual lament as the procession transporting the deceased on the bier approaches from the opposite direction. The tomb is the unifying element. It is the goal of the linear procession, the locus for ritual lamentation, and the focal point for the choral weapon dance. The purpose of the armed warriors' dancing is to energize and purify the space around the tomb. According to the dynamics of circumambulation, the purifying aim is best effected by repeated circuits (as in the funeral of Patroclus), and sometimes by the speed of the circumambulators. The speed of the warriors is shown by their running stride, while the circular movement may be suggested by the circular frieze around the kantharos.

In the same way that athletic activity at funerary games is an appropriate representation of heroic exploits, so choral singing and especially gestures can convey a *mimēsis* of the hero's adventures; in some hero cults such commemorations took place alongside annual lamentation offered as part of the respect due a hero.[62] We hear of tragic choruses reenacting through mimetic representations the heroic actions and sufferings (*pathea*) of the local hero Adrastus of Sicyon. These would have included Adrastus's expulsion from Argos by Amphiareus and his fate in the two expeditions against

Figure 28. Pyrrhic dancers accompanying funeral procession to tomb.

Thebes, stories of valor mixed with suffering that provided pretexts for ritual mourning by the chorus representing the citizens of Sicyon. They were represented not only by song but dance as well.[63]

Herodotus, who is our source for the tragic choruses in honor of Adrastus at Sicyon, says that Cleisthenes, the tyrant of Sicyon, transferred for political reasons the celebration of choruses from Adrastus to Dionysus. He comments that the Sicyonian practice of dedicating tragic choruses to heroes before this reform was unusual because they were normally dedicated to Dionysus.[64] "The people of Sicyon honored Adrastus through the performance of tragic choruses, or songs and dances about his life and sufferings (*pathea*), instead of Dionysus. But Cleisthenes transferred the choral worship to Dionysus and granted the rest of the festival (*thusia*) to Melanippus."[65]

This much-discussed passage in which the word "tragic" is first attested has been the subject of enormous controversy, especially among those seeking an origin for Dionysiac tragedy at Athens.[66] It was the basis of William Ridgeway's theory on the origin of tragedy in dances honoring deceased heroes before their tombs.[67] Cleisthenes' motivation for redirecting the choral worship from the Argive hero to a god indicates the degree to which hero worship is a localized phenomenon. The ruler's apparent ease in reassigning the choruses of Adrastus to Dionysus also reveals that in respect to choral worship hero and divinity are interchangeable. This was allowed by the fact that heroes were half-gods: the Greek word for hero (*hērōs*) is not always clearly distinguished from the word for god (*theos*).[68] Throughout the Greek world the veneration of hero and god overlapped in certain respects, as the situation at Sicyon indicates. Herodotus commends those Greek cities that maintain two cults for Heracles, one in which they venerate him as a god, in the other as a demigod.[69] Pausanias comments that even in his day at Heracles' festival the Sicyonians mix heroic and divine sacrificial procedure.[70] While the boundaries separating god and mortal in Greek belief are impenetrable, Dionysus and certain heroes such as Heracles are exceptions, and the fluid lines between god and hero are reflected in overlapping ritual observances.

In matters musical Sicyon was not only representative but influenced practices elsewhere in Greece. The traditional importance of dancing and musical and literary activity in general at Sicyon is known from various fragmentary works, including the so-called *Sikyonische Anagraphe* collected by Athenaeus.[71] Its Homeric epithet, *euruchoros* ("with broad dancing ground"), implies that Sicyon was already renowned in the early archaic period as a polis with a permanent locus for dancing.[72] Rhapsodic and other musical contests are known to have occurred there and, as already seen, when Cleisthenes wished to wed his daughter Agariste to the best suitor in Greece he arranged musical contests that culminated in the inappropriately uninhibited dancing of Hippocleides.[73] Herodotus himself says that Cleisthenes of Athens, the grandson of the tyrant, was following the model of his namesake in altering the identity and composition of the tribes at Athens.[74] Along with the expansion of Athenian tribes from four to ten Cleisthenes encouraged dithyrambic competitions in honor of Dionysus. We may infer that this move, along with the substitution of names of Athenian heroes for Ionic heroes, politically distanced the Athenians from their Ionic background, just as the grandfather's decision alienated the Sicyonian tribes from their Argive connections. Artistically the transfer of choruses to Dionysus, like the encouragement of the Dionysian dithyramb, may have been prompted by the move toward pan-Hellenization. And yet the urge to celebrate the local hero with hymns and dances persisted at Sicyon and elsewhere. In the third century the Sicyonians received permission from Delphi to bury the body of the hero Aratus within Sicyon's city walls. Wearing garlands and white robes they escorted the body into the city and celebrated with paeans and dances, and established a shrine for Aratus as savior and founder of Sicyon.[75]

The experiences of heroes who encounter death in many forms are perceptible in Greek art and literature. The appropriate response to counteract death is vigorous physical activity, whether it be gymnastic, athletic, or choreographic. Theseus, the heroic prototype of the *chorēgos*, leads the youths and maidens, who themselves were destined for ritual killing, into the labyrinth where the hero removes the threat by annihilating the Minotaur.[76] After this period of separation and encounter with the powerful forces they emerge from Daedalus's artifice, whereupon Theseus teaches them to dance the *geranos*. These and other sufferings (*pathea*) of heroes were in turn sung and acted out by communities, especially for the young. Hero cult is encouraged among adolescents, who are prompted to follow the model of heroes.

Whether or not one accepts the choral hypothesis for the performance of epinicians, one of the probable contexts for performance of the ode was the precinct of a hero. Four of the eleven Aeginetan odes of Pindar mention the Aiakeion, the hero shrine of Aeacus located in the agora. According to W. Mullen, this, the place where the hero lives, and the locus where the chorus celebrates the victor, are one and the same.[77] One of the odes contains a command to venerate the athlete's grandfather, and it has been argued that the statue of the dead man who himself was once a victor was erected in front of the Aiakeion. A choral context is strongly hinted at in the closing lines that mention bringing to the shrine of Aeacus floral sacrifices "in the company of the fair-haired Charites."[78] Another of the Aeginetan odes juxtaposes the celebration of a victor with lamentation for his father who had once gained the prize in the same event; the narrator refers to himself as a suppliant "stretching his hands to the revered knees of Aeacus."[79] The likelihood for a choral performance at the hero's shrine that encodes the words and gestures of hero worship in such an ode is also suggestively strong here.

The possibility of commemorating heroes in choral performances is also suggested in artistic representations. Gloria Ferrari has cogently argued that the Doric form of the name of Menelaos (Menelās) next to a male figure on a Proto-Attic stand depicting a chorus of men carrying spears is not a label of the hero, but rather the title or key lyric of a choral poem performed in a festival with horse races and other contests such as the Panathenaea.[80] The appropriateness of a group of young warriors honoring the former Spartan king in a choral medium is seen by recalling the gymnastic *agōn* of the hero and his selected companions with Proteus in the *Odyssey* in relation to pyrrhic aetiologies.

The hero, who demands gifts and other forms of respect, including ritual lamentation, exerts a special power over the living from the tomb. There are hints that a choral mode for venerating the hero at the tomb may have been used as a model for ritual lamentation in tragedy. The *kommos* scene of Aeschylus's *Choephoroi* describes how Orestes and Electra as relatives of Agamemnon take turns raising up lamentations to make the ghost of the hero appear before the tomb.[81] There is an interaction in word and gesture between worshipper and hero, who in a sense is the *chorēgos*, the choreographer from beyond the tomb. When Xerxes in the *Persae* appears more dead than alive at the tomb before which the ghost of his father Darius has spoken, the commander's words give an idea of the dynamic between the leader and the chorus, and an indication of the choreography during the antiphonal lament beginning with a command to "come homewards," to begin the procession.

Xerxes. Drench suffering with tears: come homewards.
Chorus. I groan and am drenched with tears.
Xerxes. Beat, beat and groan for me.
Chorus. Aiai, aiai! Sorrow, sorrow!
Xerxes. Beat your breasts and raise aloud the Mysian cry.
Chorus. Grievous, grievous!
Xerxes. Tear from your chin the white hairs . . .
Chorus. Clutching tightly, groaning.
Xerxes. Rip with your fingers your flowing robes.
Chorus. Grievous, grievous.
Xerxes. Pluck your hair to lament the army . . .
Chorus. Clutching tightly, groaning . . .
Xerxes. Mourn, go on soft feet.
Chorus. Io, io! The Persian land is hard to tread.[82]

Although Xerxes is still alive, he orders the chorus to lament him and the army in traditional ways, raising their voices, beating their breasts, rending garments, tearing at their hair. The motif of singing and dancing before a tomb so as to call forth the ghost of a hero is found in vase painting, for example on the well-known column krater in Basel.[83]

In Aristophanes' *Heroes*, the heroes appear as a chorus. They return to the upper world to distribute good and evil, according to what is deserved.[84] They come to inspect things to ensure that everything is in order, and that they are receiving their due. The mortal display of order and respect for the hero are intertwined in the ritual lament for the hero that confirms, like the choral dances to which it is inextricably related, order in the polis.

Conclusions

Dance implies motion, order, joy, expressed through the body, the whole body. The very antithesis of dance is found in the still, lifeless, polluting corpse. Paradoxically, dance is in a sense born of a revulsion to the stillness of death. Death means a temporary rupture in the cosmic and social order, a disjunction between living and dead, and an even greater gulf between gods and mortals. Expression of grief, however, is not a spontaneous outbreak of emotion but is carefully controlled and ritually prescribed at every phase, and thus contains and controls the participants. In heroic funerary cult commemoration of the dead is enacted through the typical elements of a festival with sacrifices: choral circumambulation and lament around the corpse, *pompē*, *agōn*. The events associated with the struggle have a life-renewing power. As Walter Burkert has remarked, "*agōn* . . . [is a] transition from an aspect of death to an aspect of life."[85]

As early as the Early Minoan period archaeological evidence can be found for funerary dances in the paved dancing grounds adjacent to the vaulted tombs of the Mesara.[86] The *prothesis*, or wake, is already represented in Late Mycenaean sarcophagi on which female mourners are shown with hands upraised in gestures of grief. Emphasis on the care of the women for the corpse as they ritually disfigure their own hair, cheeks, and breasts continues on the Geometric grave vessels, and persists in classical vase painting. The lamentation of the women involved wailing and singing, and was sometimes accompanied by instrumental music. The simple and uniform gesture of the males raising their right arms in salutation to the deceased contrasts sharply with the variety and ecstatic nature of female gestures of lament. The overall effect of the ensemble, however, was not so very different from other choral rites. Margaret Alexiou, who has studied the ritual lament in ancient, Byzantine, and modern Greece has written, "Since each movement was determined by a pattern of ritual, frequently accompanied by the shrill music of the *aulos* . . . , the scene must have resembled a dance, sometimes slow and solemn, sometimes wild and ecstatic."[87] If gestures and antiphonal lament at the wake followed by contests are not the ritual origin of choral dancing and singing, they are at least very old and provide continuity in ritual gesture between the prehistoric and historical periods, and, as Alexiou and others have convincingly shown, the modern period.

At time of death and at commemorations a great man is honored with hymns and choruses like a god. Although mortals mourn the passing of certain gods in their rituals, the divine prototype of dance does not provide a model for ritual behavior at the time of death, the final biological status transition. The immortal gods, whose blessed existence is typified by continual dancing, experience no need to mourn one another, and none of the gods, except Hermes, Hypnos, and Thanatos in limited ways, trouble themselves with the deaths of mortals, unless they are objects of special love, such as Hyacinthus for Apollo. Among the Greeks the illusion existed that dancing not only had a rejuvenating effect, but that by partnering the gods one became like them. But this fiction was unmasked at time of death. To dance was to become once again like a child,[88] but not an immortal. After the death of a loved one, the survivors alone were left behind to dance near the tomb, both to venerate the dead and to reaffirm their will to live.

Lamentation is not restricted to grieving human loss. The disappearance of a god, sacrificial victims, the harvesting of the crops and the vine, all provoke grief. In the biological cycle the intermediate transitions between birth and death imply a loss that is to be both lamented and celebrated. When the Athenian girl sheds her childhood at Brauron the bear within her is symbolically killed. When the young man marries, Hymenaeus is mourned in the wedding song, and the bride's family feels the loss of Demeter for Core. At the level of meaning, the ideas of death and separation are close, especially in status transitions and other rituals where distancing of all kinds is expressed by symbolic forms of death. For now, we may recall how the symbolism of death is present in sacrificial ritual, in the Arkteia, in the rape of Core by Hades, and how pyrrhic aetiologies suggest that childbirth for the young mother is equivalent to risking life on the battlefield for the young man. The shadowy boundaries between death ritual and other forms of social and religious observance recall that separation and the ambivalent responses to it are not restricted to the final biological transition. And yet an embryonic form of ritual play seems to have originated from the expression of horror and anxiety at the corpse, and this anxious response, blended with a desire to venerate and commemorate, left its mark on the other aspects of divine adoration and human festivity. In the ritual lament we have perhaps the most profound case of lasting order emerging from temporary disorder.

Nine

Change: Pan and Private Worship

lthough Pan is one of the lesser gods in the Greek pantheon, his cult from the fifth century onward was widespread in the Greek world, and frequent written and artistic references to the musical properties of the "dance-loving" (*philochoros*) goat-god whom Sophocles called the teacher of the gods' dances provide striking insights into the religious dynamics of dance in private worship in the fifth and fourth centuries and beyond.[1] Unlike Dionysus who hails from distant places, Pan has a fixed origin in a familiar geographical locale. Pan is situated in Arcadia, a mountainous, isolated region, sparsely populated except by shepherds and their flocks, whose well-being Pan, as the son of Hermes, safeguarded. His entry into Attica was reported by Herodotus as a historical event occurring immediately after the Battle of Marathon in 490 B.C.E.[2] Pan's positive intervention in the first Persian war led the Athenians to consecrate a shrine to him on the slope of the Acropolis and to propitiate the god with annual goat sacrifices and a race. About this time his cult spread to other parts of Greece as well. Pan was worshipped in caves where he was supposed to have lived, and in them sacrificial banquets in his honor took place.

Musical Attributes of Pan in Literature and Art

Pan's unmistakable appearance betrays his dual nature. He is both anthropomorphic god and beast. In artistic representations Pan often has the body of an athletic man, but the pointed ears, horns, and cloven hooves of a goat. Judged by human standards, Pan is deformed in the lower part of the body, like Hephaestus. But Pan is an agile creature, like the goat whose body he shares. The connection between the goat-god and dancing is not far to seek. The goat is an animal that leaps and bounds, sometimes in a playful, sometimes in an ornery way, making percussive noises with its hooves and horns. An Attic fifth-century vase inscription labels Pan *skirtōn*, "the leaper."[3] The word for goat in the plural, *aiges*, also means waves, and both meanings were related to the verb *aissō*, used of rapid, darting motion. A Greek traveling in the countryside might see a goat leaping excitedly over a waterfall, an image elaborated in the *Homeric Hymn to Pan*.[4]

Pan often surrounds himself with the graceful nymphs "accustomed to choral dancing"[5] for whom he serves as *chorēgos*, much as Apollo does for the Muses.[6] The nymphs, whose dancing grounds and assemblies in Homer prefigure human civic institutions and collective activities, complement the rural god of Arcadia.[7] The *Homeric Hymn to Pan*, which has been dated to the first half of the fifth century, highlights the musical aspects of the god and his nymphs.[8] In the invocation attention is immediately drawn to Pan's peculiar mode of locomotion and to his musical sensibilities by two epithets. Pan is the one "with goat feet" and "lover of rattling noise" (*philokrotos*).[9] The second adjective evokes the sounds made during human dances, either by stamping the feet[10] or by clapping the hands or castanets (*krotala*). The reference to percussive sounds situates Pan's dance in the realm of animal mimicry, a frequent component of initiation rites. Indeed, Plato in the *Laws* classified dances in imitation of Pan's along with other Bacchic dances as initiatory and purificatory rites,[11] and Pindar calls Pan the "most complete dancer" (*choreutan teleōtaton*).[12]

Next in Pan's *Hymn* follows a detailed description of the god's agile movements as he tours his natural domain, from the meadows to the highest peak where the god can survey the flock.

> He claims every snowy peak and mountain top and rocky headland. He goes here and there among the close underbrush, now drawn by the gentle streams, now he wanders among the sun-swept peaks, climbing to the highest peak that overlooks the flocks. Often he runs through the white lofty mountains, and often he, the keen-eyed god, speeds along the shoulders of the mountain slaying beasts.[13]

Like the goat, who, as Aristotle points out in the *Historia Animalium*, rambles, Pan is constantly on the move (*eukinētos*).[14] The preponderance of action verbs, including *steibō*, which is used for choral dancing,[15] as well as the sequential reiteration of local and temporal adverbs in these verses from Pan's *Hymn*, correspond to the spatial and rhythmic dimension of ritual movement.[16] The restless god's tour is more' than idle ambling: in circumambulating fields, streams, and mountains the god stakes out his sacred territory. These are places where only Pan and the nymphs may enter. Pan is "guardian of untrodden places [in Arcadia]."[17] His act of boundary display culminates in hunting followed by dancing revels:

> Then at evening he lifts his voice alone, as he comes back from the hunt, gently playing sweet music on his reeds. . . . With him then go the clear-singing mountain nymphs, singing and dancing with swift feet by a dark-water spring. Echo sounds loud about the mountain top; and the god, gliding here and there among the dancers, and then into the middle, leads the dance with swift feet. On his back he has a spotted lynx-skin; and he rejoices in the clear-toned singing.[18]

Musical revelry with the nymphs comes as a relaxation after the hunt, as for Artemis in her *Homeric Hymn*.[19] Both hunting and dancing are collective activities that exercise power over natural forces: the acquisitive goal of hunting animals is analogous to establishing control over territory by dancing. The effect Pan has on the natural world when he takes up his syrinx and plays and dances is similar to the reaction of the Olympians and other divinities when Apollo in his *Hymn* appears with his lyre on Olympus. But Pan is

more versatile than Apollo in musical performance and not averse
to taking a subordinate role. He both leads the dancers as musical
chorēgos and joins in as dancer, weaving in and out of their choral
formations. In Pan's dance, god and participants indistinguishably
merge. This can be seen in a red-figure Attic cup in the Brommer
Collection.[20] In the scene on the inside of the cup a silen and a goat
at his side perform a dance-step. The left front leg of the silen is
lifted in a spirited movement that is mirrored by the goat; but it is
not certain who is imitating whom in this synchronized duet.

In literary representations the accent on the swiftness and agility
of Pan's dance and the sprightly movements his music inspires are
transferable to the battlefield and to the race course, but to different
ends. From a distant lookout Pan surveys the progress of the battlefield and inspires rout, or "panic." It is not by pure accident that
the first Greek whom Pan encounters outside Arcadia prior to the
battle of Marathon is Pheidippides, a professional long-distance
runner. Like his father Hermes, Pan was the patron of runners, and
at Athens a torch race (*lampadēdromia*) was run in his honor.[21] A
similar genetic likeness between dancers and runners has been observed in Pan's half-brother Eudoros. The Myrmidon leader in the
Iliad who was exceptionally swift in running was born to Polymele,
a maiden skilled in the dance whom Hermes abducted from a
dancing place.[22]

The remainder of the *Hymn* narrates Pan's birth to Hermes and
the daughter of Dryops. Although the infant's mortal nurse runs
away in fright when she looks upon the monstrous visage of the
"goat-legged, two-horned, noise-loving, and sweetly laughing"
child, Pan is accorded a warm reception by the immortals, especially Dionysus, when first introduced into Olympus by his divine
father. They called the child Pan, the poet says, punning on the
adjective for "all" in the neuter (*pan*), because he delighted (*eterpse*)
"all" the immortals in their hearts.[23] The verb *terpō* for the gods'
delight in Pan is, as we have frequently seen, specifically used of
pleasure derived from music and song. Unlike the mortal nurse
who sees in Pan only a disgusting sight, the immortals can foresee
the pleasure the child will bring to all through his musical gifts.

Numerous representations of the goat-god in Attic fifth-century art corroborate the literary evidence for Pan as *chorēgos* and dancer. Sometimes Pan is shown dancing alone, as on the inside of a red-figure Attic cup in Leipzig.[24] More often the dancing god is represented along with other divine figures, including the nymphs or other goat-gods. A terra cotta ring model of a circle dance from the Corycic Cave on Mt. Parnassus near Delphi (dated to the second quarter of the fifth century) represents Pan as the musical *chorēgos* playing his syrinx in the midst of eleven or twelve nymphs.[25] In representations of dancing Pan or Pans the head is shown with horns and pointed ears, and the body of the dancer is depicted with a tail. But apart from these distinctly caprine characteristics, the rest of the body is recognizably human. There are often no hooves, no hirsute bodies. Whether the pronounced animal characteristics of the god are underplayed because of artistic conventions or because a vase painter in certain cases has given his version of the dramatic embodiment of the goat-god (i.e., a human player wearing a costume) in proto-dramas and satyr-plays is not ascertainable from the evidence.[26]

On approximately ten Attic red-figure vases of the second half of the fifth century, Pan or a number of Pans are represented in a highly excited state, leaping and gesturing with one hand outstretched, the other curved at the level of the head, while next to them a female figure emerges from the earth. Is the exuberant dancing of the goat-figures meant to represent a reaction to the prodigious appearance, or does it in fact urge on the epiphany? The powerful force of hilarity is manifest in a passage in the *Hymn to Demeter* in which the serving woman Iambe succeeds in softening Demeter's obdurate mood by telling jokes that make her smile and laugh.[27] This in turn prompts Demeter, who has until this point been fasting, to drink a restorative potion and forget her grief momentarily; eventually Demeter releases the world from crippling famine. In the abduction of Core from the meadow leading to the goddess's grief, a *choros* activated by the dancing of the maiden and her companions, the Oceanids, weakens the boundaries and creates in effect a passageway between the upper and lower worlds. The manner in which Demeter's mood is mollified or in which Core's meadow is transformed into a *choros* may be related to a folkloric belief in the ability of music, dancing, percussive noises, laughter, and merriment—in short the components of a festival— to soften up the earth in order to make it yield that which it hides or constrains, much as wine has an uninhibiting effect on the human body and spirit.

It is in this way that the dancing of the Pan figures on the so-called *anodos* vases can be understood. From epigraphic or iconographic indications it is possible to identify the emerging figure as Core (Persephone) or Aphrodite in four cases;[28] in the remaining examples the epiphany figure may be Core, Aphrodite, or Pandora.[29] On a kalyx krater in Dresden which clearly identifies the emerging female figure as Pherephatta (a distinctively Attic variant on Persephone's name), the girl's escape from the Underworld is portrayed as a rebirth from the earth.[30] Also present in the scene are Hermes and three prancing Pans. On a red-figure skyphos in Boston (Fig. 29) the identity of the emerging figure is not discernible. But on the analogy of the Core scene the general background and meaning of the epiphany are clear. The appearance of the female figure is occasioned by the dancing Pans. The excited activity of the caprines transforms the space into a *choros*. Like the humor of Iambe, the ludicrous leaps of the goat-men create a favorable mood and soften the boundary that withheld the female divinity and the favors she symbolizes. The dancing of the Pans reverses, as it were, the fatal choral play of Core and the Oceanids. In representations of dancing in the context of the emerging female figures the Athenian artist seems to suggest that leaping movement has the direct effect of summoning the female figure, who had been constrained in a cavity. The general meaning of the dancing Pans can thus be construed with the belief in the role of music and dance to charm the gods, as the concluding scene of Pan's *Homeric Hymn* suggests.[31]

A fifth-century inscription from Epidaurus addresses Demeter and describes her anger and the exchange necessary to placate the goddess. Elsewhere on the same stele appears a hymn to "all the gods" followed by a hymn to Pan:

Pan, leader of the naiad nymphs, I sing, glory of the golden choruses, lord of babbling music; from his far-sounding syrinx he pours enraptur-

Figure 29. Two leaping Pans and an emerging female figure.

ing musical charm; to the melody he steps lightly, leaping through the well-shaded caves, plying and displaying his protean body, graceful dancer, fair in face, resplendent with blond beard. Your panic echo reaches as far as starry Olympus, pervading the gathering of the Olympian gods with an immortal Muse. All of earth and sea compound your grace; you are the mainstay of all, O Pan, Pan![32]

Pan's beautiful form (in the eye of the beholder) and seductive musical talents pervade the earth, sea, and Olympus. The description of the widespread effects of Pan's grace on the natural and supernatural realms suggests that of all the gods the goat-god counteracts and reverses the disastrous consequences of Demeter's anger best. His light steps and leaps, his cheerful music and propensity to laughter are outward manifestations of the god's counteractive forces of hilarity. These life-preserving powers could be summoned in his civic cult by staging songs and dances with exaggerated movement such as the Pans exhibit in order to delight the gods and provoke human laughter. For laughter is a divine quality but one, like dance, that can be shared between gods and mortals. A fourth-century inscription from Pan's cave at Pharsalia in Thessaly indicates that two gifts, laughter and mirth (*gelos, euphrosynē*), are especially appropriate to Pan.[33] An Attic drinking song addressed to Pan "the dancer" and the companion of the nymphs implores the god to laugh (*gelaseias*) at the high spirits (*emais euphrosynais*) and take pleasure in these songs.[34]

Pan in Private Worship

From the end of the fifth century and extending through the third, Pan is worshipped in private cults. This example of private devotion comes at a time when mystery religions were springing up in the wake of the Peloponnesian War. Pan's worship in Attica and elsewhere is shared with that of the nymphs, whose caves and sanctuaries and forms of address he shared. Typical invocations saluted Pan and the nymphs as "dear Pan, dear nymphs," where the adjective for "dear" (*philos*) recalls the special regard and favors the devotees hoped would come their way through sacrifice, dancing, drinking ceremonies, and other forms of intercourse with these divinities.[35] The nymphs, who are closely associated with the land and water, and various topographical features, such as caves and mountain peaks, promote the fertility of the crops, the flocks, and are guardians of the young of humans. In general they are beneficent, and in antiquity as in parts of modern Greece, people turn to them in times of distress.[36] They were thought to have curative powers and were worshipped in sanctuaries of Asclepius. To express gratitude to Pan and the nymphs, a devotee of some means might organize a revel for friends and relatives in their honor and also dedicate reliefs or figures representing Pan and the nymphs, along with other votive offerings, such as golden cicadas which have been found in caves sacred to them.

Two sources for the private worship of Pan and the nymphs are especially illuminating, the *Dyscolus* of Menander and sculpted reliefs of the nymphs. The worship of Pan in Attica comes very much alive in Menander's *Dyscolus* (*The Misanthrope*), which won first prize at Athens in 317/16. We hear about the proper way to salute Pan, the crowning of the statues of the nymphs, sacrifices to the god, and dances and drinking ceremonies in his cave. The mother of one of the characters, a zealous worshipper of the god, offers a sacrifice to Pan merely because she has dreamed of him. Pan himself appears as a character to deliver the prologue; and although the dramatic convention of the chorus had no place in Middle Comedy, a chorus of the god's devotees (*Panistai*) may have performed the choral interludes in the play. The action of the drama is set in and about the god's shrine which is located between the farm of Cnemon, the misanthrope, and that of Cnemon's stepson Gorgias who supports his mother and sister on an adjoining piece of property.

At Phyle in Attica, the geographical setting of the play, an important cave sanctuary of Pan was known to have actually existed; there votive inscriptions and reliefs dedicated to Pan and the nymphs have been discovered in great numbers.[37] On the opposite side of Athens, near the modern village of Vari, was another cave of Pan and the nymphs. Toward the end of the fifth century a certain Archedamos came from Thera and retired to the cave which he embellished with a garden and, according to one possible reading of a surviving inscription, a dancing ground (*choros*) where the nymphs could come and dance.[38]

Briefly, the *Dyscolus* concerns Pan's indirect influence on Cnemon's daughter, a pious worshipper of Pan and the nymphs, to make a profitable marriage with a well-to-do youth from the city. Cnemon takes no interest in the fortunes of his daughter and shuns social and religious intercourse, including Pan's cult. As the play progresses he becomes more and more isolated from society. His total remove from humanity is symbolized by falling down a well midway through the play. Although Cnemon's stepson Gorgias rescues him, the old man is badly bruised and injured in the legs. He has had a close scrape with death and retreats within his house to recover.

In the meantime preparations for not one, but two, weddings accompanied by dancing are taking place. The women are to hold a *pannychis*, and the men and women together will hold a prenuptial *symposion* in the cave of Pan and the nymphs. Members of the bridal party wish to have Cnemon participate in the banquet, but the son despairs of being able to win him over. That challenge is taken up by the slave and cook, Getas and Sicon. The comic pair decide that they will have some fun. They dump the invalid man before his house while he is sleeping and then pound at the door to ask for various household objects, including tripods, tables, a bronze wine bowl, and other provisions for the banquet in the cave. All the while Cnemon is lying helplessly by, repeatedly beseeching his tormentors to set him upright (*tis an me stēseien orthon?*).[39] At first Sicon takes advantage of the curmudgeon's helpless situation to provide his captive with enticing news of the banquet in the cave, including a description of the mixing and distribution of wine followed by dancing. But eventually Sicon and Getas respond to Cnemon's request by helping him up on his feet, followed by the charade of trying to get the surly old man to dance. When he recoils at the notion of dancing with one of his tormentors, Getas then presents him with the alternative of going into the cave. To Cnemon's question "What shall I do?" Getas replies, "Dance, of course." When confronted with the awful decision of having to dance with one of these low-lifes or being carried into the cave of revels, Cnemon chooses the latter. He relents and orders them to take him in.

The influence of Pan and the nymphs in bringing about the marriage of Cnemon's daughter includes the indirect effect they have on the sour father. Although Cnemon shuns any interaction with society he cannot escape the divine attraction of Pan and the nymphs. An early sign of the influence of the nymphs on Cnemon comes when the old man falls down his well. Greek myth and epigraphic evidence attest to the belief that the nymphs sometimes abducted mortal victims by pulling them into wells. Thus when Hylas came looking for water he encountered a chorus of nymphs who dragged him into the waters.[40] Funerary inscriptions from the Hellenistic period indicate that children who accidentally fell into wells were said to have been singled out by the nymphs.[41] When Cnemon tumbles down the well, the cook Sicon remarks that the nymphs have justly gained revenge on him.[42] By a comic reversal the nymph's victim is not a young and beautiful creature such as Hylas but a surly old man. Nevertheless Cnemon is shown to be susceptible to the nymphs, and by falling victim to their forces he begins to experience the closest thing (for him) to a mystical union. The injury to his legs has, ironically, made him deformed in the lower half of the body like the goat-god Pan; in the course of the therapy administered by Getas and Sicon he acquires, as it were, a new pair of legs. The very name Cnemon, perhaps derived from the Greek word for "shank" (_knēmē_), may draw attention to the lower part of the body with which the dancer comes into contact with earth. It is his fall and recovery that lead Cnemon, albeit reluctantly, to enter the cave of Pan where we are left with the possibility that he will actually engage in the dances.

Before entering the cave three ritual dances are alluded to, including the sympotic dances in the cave reported by Sicon. When Getas and Sicon get ready to pound on Cnemon's door Getas announces that he will "lead off first" (_proaxō prōteros_) and instructs Sicon to follow "in measure."[43] The verb for leading (_proagō_) is used elsewhere of leading a revel.[44] The ostensible purpose of their banging on the door is to beg for implements for the banquet in the cave. The ritual of going from door to door begging for food while performing songs and dances was practiced by young boys, as the concluding verse of a popular song, the so-called Swallow song from Rhodes, insists: "We are not old men, but young boys (_paidia_)."[45] As Getas knocks he repeats (punning on the verb for knocking, _paiō_) "lovely boys, oh boy, little boy, boy, boys." Literally he is calling out to the slaves within to answer the door, but like the imaginary slaves within, Getas and Sicon are themselves linguistically ambiguous boys/slaves. They conceive of their charade as a sequence of begging attempts. Sicon asks at one point, "Shall we try another door?"

Begging rituals such as the Rhodian Swallow song imply a mutual exchange. By performing a song and a dance the begging boys earn the right to something to eat. But if the owner of the house shows no sign of reciprocity, the beggars threaten to persist and inflict some sort of punishment. In the case of Cnemon the old man has already effectively been humiliated by being dumped before his house. The charade of Getas and Sicon, with the ambiguous status of slaves/boys knocking at Cnemon's door, has all of the elements of a komastic begging ritual, including their caper, their demands for implements for the banquet, and the victimization of Cnemon. Despite Cnemon's reluctance to cooperate, Sicon and Getas nevertheless manage to involve the misanthrope in a ritual that has a built-in provision for such antisocial behavior. This is the first step in triumphing over Cnemon's refusal to participate in ritual customs.

The second dance we hear about through the words of Sicon, whose ornately poetic description of the banquet in the cave may be a pastiche of contemporary dithyramb. Sicon is speaking:

> Now one man with his hands put to rest hoary old man Dionysus in a hollow urn, and mixed in the spring water of the nymphs, and then went round in a circle [offering each a cup with the right hand] to make a toast, and another man got the ladies to toast. . . . One of the girls with the bloom of her fair young face shaded, and growing tipsy, embraced the dance rhythm, but modestly, both hesitant and trembling. Another girl joined hands with her and danced.[46]

Despite its flowery language Sicon's description provides an extremely realistic picture of the ritual inside the cave: how the wine was mixed, how solidarity was achieved among the celebrants by encircling the wine vessel while raising the right hand in a sign of affirmation, and by informal dancing.

When Sicon and Getas finally succeed in getting Cnemon to agree to enter into the cave, they proclaim "O Kallinikos." With this proclamation, which similarly marks the resolution of an *agōn* in the finale of Aristophanes' *Acharnians* and the *Birds*, the play effectively comes to an end as Cnemon is carried into the cave.[47] *Kallinikos* is the name for a joyous victory song and dance. It is also a cult title of Heracles, and in a passage in Euripides' *Hercules Furens* the nymphs join the chorus of old men of Thebes in singing the *kallinikos agōn* of Heracles.[48] In cult dances in honor of Heracles the *kallinikos* celebrated the hero's various triumphs over monsters, particularly Cerberus who guarded the entrance to the Underworld.[49] The irrepressible shout is appropriate for the triumph of the life-affirming power of the dance over the gloomy Cnemon.[50]

Another illuminating source for the private worship of Pan are sculpted reliefs. These votive offerings to the goat-god and the nymphs point to the mystical dimension of Pan's musical presence. The reliefs from Vari and elsewhere typically represent a group of three nymphs, led by Hermes. Pan often appears behind the scenes, peering in from behind a rock. He is looking intently, but does not allow himself to be seen. The dedicant is sometimes included among the divine figures. The setting is usually the cave sacred to the nymphs, but it may also be a sanctuary, as in an example from Cos (Fig. 30).[51] This remarkably fine relief, which shows influence from Attic art, was discovered, along with another relief of the Charites from the Hellenistic period, by accident on the site of Mesaria on Cos.[52] On the relief the three nymphs are substituted by the Charites, in whose sanctuary the offering was found. The work can be dated to the end of the fifth century. The inscription reads: "Peithanor, son of Charmis dedicated this to the Charites of the beautiful locks and erected it in their precinct."[53] The Cos relief is a good example of the need for caution in identifying mythological figures from iconographical indications alone. The near parallels to the numerous ex-votos of Pan and the nymphs from Attica would encourage an identification of the female figures as nymphs, when in fact, as the inscription states, they are Charites.[54]

Like the nymphs, the Charites were gentle goddesses, helpful to worshippers in time of need and distress. The divinities are shown on the relief holding hands at the wrist in the manner of ring dancers, and they circle the altar. Pan is visible in the upper left-hand corner. He is easily recognizable by his horns and pointed ears. Of his body only the right hand can be seen. With it he supports himself as he strains to get a closer look. As Pan's *Hymn* recalls, the divine herdsman is known for his penetrating gaze.[55] The spatial relationship between the goat-god and the dedicant is important for the interpretation. Usually when the dedicant is present, he, as well as Pan, are shown by an iconographic convention to be of a smaller stature than the female divinities. The smaller scale of Pan and the dedicant indicates a personal bond between the mortal and the goat-god, whose vicarious participation in the dance mediates the experience of the worshipper. On the Cos relief only the worshipper is shown to be on a smaller scale, but the same intimate relationship between him and Pan is suggested by placing

Figure 30. Charites dancing around an altar, while Pan and dedicant look on.

the head of the god directly above the dedicant. The right arm of the worshipper is raised in a gesture of greeting and piety. He is invisible to the Charites, as is Pan. The lusty gaze of Pan contrasts with the pious reverence of Peithanor the dedicant.

Pan's keen interest in the activity of the Charites in their sanctuary recalls the mythological theme of the abduction of the dancing girl from the sanctuary. But there is no sense of imminent danger in the scene. Pan, separated by a natural boundary, maintains, along with the dedicant, a respectful distance. Surprisingly, the Charites who are referred to in the inscription as possessing "beautiful locks" have their hair tightly bound upon their heads. The bound hair and the fully developed breasts indicate that the sculptor conceived of his Charites as mature women, not pubescent girls. The theme of the mortal desire to share in the dances of the gods is expressed in this relief as a wish for a mystical union, to be, as Socrates says in the *Phaedrus*, "seized by nymphs" (*nympholēptos*).[56]

The mystical experience of abandoning oneself to the dancing Charites that lies behind this and related dedicatory reliefs can be seen as an inversion of the theme of the abduction of the dancing girl from the sanctuary. In a variation on the theme of the divine observer, as known from this mythical motif and from the *Hymn to Apollo*, the worshipper becomes an ideal observer of the dance by identifying and merging identities with Pan.

Whereas the dedicant on the relief ardently desires to participate, if only mystically, in the dances of the Charites and affirms his desire by commissioning and dedicating a costly relief in their sanctuary, Cnemon willfully excludes himself from the cave of Pan where the sympotic dances are taking place. He is like the surly character defined by Theophrastus who refuses to sing, recite, or dance.[57] But try as he may, supernatural and social forces conspire to bring Cnemon into contact with the power of Pan and the nymphs. The turning point occurs when Cnemon falls into the well and becomes, as it were, an involuntary nympholept. It is Getas and Sicon, the comic pair representing the low life, who triumph over the resistance of Cnemon. Ultimately it is the charade of the dance that prompts Cnemon to enter into Pan's grotto. We see again that dance, like laughter, food, and other things which bring pleasure, has a socializing, even life-affirming force that can triumph over the most obdurate curmudgeon. We must all one day face the music!

List of Abbreviations

Abbreviations of journal titles are from *L'Année philologique*.

ABV	J. D. Beazley. *Attic Black-figure Vase Painters*. Oxford, 1956.
ARV	J. D. Beazley. *Attic Red-figure Vase Painters*, 2d ed. Oxford, 1963.
Barker	A. Barker, ed. *Greek Musical Writings*. Vol. 1, *The Musician and His Art*. Cambridge, 1984.
Beazley Addenda	*Beazley Addenda*, 2d ed., comp. T. H. Carpenter. Oxford, 1989.
Calame	C. Calame. *Les Chœurs de jeunes filles en Grèce archaïque*, 2 vols. *Filologia e critica* 20 and 21. Rome, 1977.
Chantraine	P. Chantraine. *Dictionnaire étymologique de la langue grecque*. Paris, 1968–80.
CIL	*Corpus Inscriptionum Latinarum*.
CorVP	D. Amyx. *Corinthian Vase-Painting of the Archaic Period*. Berkeley, 1988.
CVA	*Corpus Vasorum Antiquorum*.
Deubner	L. Deubner. *Attische Feste*. Berlin, 1932.
DFA	A. Pickard-Cambridge. *The Dramatic Festivals of Athens*, 2d ed., rev. J. Gould and D. M. Lewis. London, 1968.
DTC	A. Pickard-Cambridge. *Dithyramb, Tragedy and Comedy*. Oxford, 1927; 2d ed., rev. T. B. L. Webster, 1962.
FGrHist	F. Jacoby. *Die Fragmente der griechischen Historiker*. Berlin, 1923–58.

Frisk	H. Frisk. *Griechisches etymologisches Wörterbuch*. Heidelberg, 1954–72.
GF	Martin P. Nilsson. *Griechische Feste*. Leipzig, 1906.
GGR	Martin P. Nilsson. *Geschichte der griechischen Religion*, 3d ed., vol. 1. Munich, 1967.
GR	W. Burkert. *Greek Religion*, trans. J. Raffan. Cambridge, Mass., 1985.
HN	W. Burkert. *Homo Necans*, trans. P. Bing. Berkeley, 1983.
IC	*Inscriptiones Creticae.*
IG	*Inscriptiones Graecae.*
LIMC	*Lexicon Iconographicum Mythologiae Classicae.* Zurich, 1981–.
Spencer	Paul Spencer, ed. *Society and the Dance.* Cambridge, 1985.
PM	A. Evans. *The Palace of Minos*, 4 vols. London, 1921–35.
PMG	*Poetae melici Graeci*, ed. D. L. Page. Oxford, 1962/1975.
RAC	*Reallexikon für Antike und Christentum.*
RE	*Paulys Realencyclopädie der classischen Altertumswissenschaft.*
SEG	*Supplementum epigraphicum Graecum.*
SIG	*Sylloge Inscriptionum Graecarum*, ed. W. Dittenberger, 3d ed., vols. 1–4. Leipzig, 1915–23.

Notes

Preface

1. The relevant chapters in Kurt Latte's 1913 reliable monograph in Latin, *De saltationibus Graecorum, RVV* 13 (Giessen, 1913), discuss ritual aspects of dance, especially in the Hellenistic period, from a historical perspective.
2. L. B. Lawler, *The Dance in Ancient Greece* (Middletown, Conn., 1964). Many of Lawler's individual articles on dance in ancient Greece published in *TAPA* and other journals between 1927 and 1965 are extremely useful; cf. *AJA* 70 (1966): 79. Among specialist studies drawing on archaeological, philological, metrical, and other types of evidence, T. B. L. Webster, *The Greek Chorus* (London, 1970), should be singled out for its collocation of literary and archaeological sources that provides a sound basis for further study of the chorus as a social and religious institution. For further studies on dance, see the bibliography.
3. For a good discussion of recent advances in understanding the *Laws*, especially in correlating it with the *Republic*, see A. Laks, "Legislation and Demiurgy: On the Relationship Between Plato's *Republic* and *Laws*," *CA* 9 (1990): 209–29, esp. 210 and n. 4.
4. *GR*, 333.
5. Pl., *Laws* 660c.
6. Dramatic choruses are treated in English in a neglected but reliable monograph by L. B. Lawler, *The Dance of the Ancient Greek Theatre* (Iowa City, 1964).

Introduction: *Problems and Sources*

1. L. H. Jeffery, *The Local Scripts of Archaic Greece*, 2d ed. (Oxford, 1990), 68.
2. Corinth C-54-1; *CorVP* 165, 560–61; cf. M. C. and C. A. Roebuck, "A Prize Aryballos," *Hesperia* 24 (1955): 158–63; plates 63, 64; see A. Boegehold, "An Archaic Corinthian Inscription," *AJA* 69 (1965): 259–62 for an emendation of the inscription.
3. Pl., *Ti.* 40cd.
4. Cf. J. Cowan, *Dance and the Body Politic* (Princeton, 1990), 182.
5. For the most recent statement of the opposing views, see M. Heath and M. Lefkowitz, "Epinician Performance," *CPh* 86 (1991): 173–91, and C. Carey, "The Victory Ode in Performance: The Case for the Chorus," *CPh* 86 (1991): 192–200; cf. A. P. Burnett, "Performing Pindar's Odes," *CPh* 84 (1989): 283–93. The solo hypothesis relies mainly on the mutually exclusive use of *kōmos* (informal band of revelers) and *choros* (formal performance).
6. W. Mullen, *Choreia: Pindar and Dance* (Princeton, 1982).
7. A. P. Burnett, "Jocasta in the West: The Lille Stesichorus," *CA* 7 (1988): 107–54.
8. *PMG* 212.1.
9. *PMG* 1.
10. *PMG* 3.9–10.
11. *PMG* 3.64–76.
12. *PMG* 26.
13. Much insight into (and confusion about) the nature of choruses has been offered by works interested in the origins, development, and performance context of Greek poetry and drama. See, for example, H. Herter, *Vom dionysischen Tanz zum komischen Spiel* (Iserlohn, 1947); H. Schreckenberg, *Drama: Vom Werden der griechischen Tragödie aus dem Tanz* (Würzburg, 1960); F. R. Adrados, *Fiesta, comedia y tragedia* (Barcelona, 1972); A. P. Burnett, *The Art of Bacchylides* (Cambridge, Mass., 1985); J. Herington, *Poetry into Drama* (Berkeley, 1985); G. Nagy, *Pindar's Homer* (Baltimore, 1990).
14. Nagy, *Pindar's Homer*, 378.
15. J. M. Bremer, "Greek Hymns," in *Faith, Hope, and Worship*, ed. H. S. Versnel (Leiden, 1981), 213.
16. Pl., *Laws* 815bc.
17. Pl., *Laws* 672b, cf. 790d–791a; *Phdr.* 244, 265b; *Euthd.* 277de.
18. For a recent discussion of the poles of interpretation of the female pyrrhic in vase painting, see R. Osborne, *Arion* 3d series 1 (1991): 261.
19. R. Tölle, *Frühgriechische Reigentänze* (Waldsassen Bayern, 1964).
20. E.g., Hom., *Il.* 18.594.

21. Lekythos, Brussels A 1311; *ABV* 488, 3; F. Frontisi-Ducroux, *Le Dieu-masque* (Paris, 1991), 124 and fig. 63.

22. The exploitation of the circular format of a vase can also be seen in chapter 7 in the series of three wedding dances on the shoulder of a lekythos by the Amasis Painter (Fig. 25). We can assume, incidentally, that these are wedding dances, since the wedding procession is depicted on the main scene of the vase. Black-figure lekythos (shoulder type), New York 56.11.1; *Beazley Addenda* 45; D. von Bothmer, *The Amasis Painter and His World* (Malibu, Calif., 1985), p. 183, cat. no. 47.

23. Occasionally the religious nature of a dance representation is known from its archaeological context, for example the lead cut-outs of dancers (among other types) found in votive deposits at the shrine of Helen and Menelaos at Therapne near Sparta; see W. G. Cavanagh and R. R. Laxton, "Lead Figurines from the Menelaion and Seriation," *ASBA* 79 (1984): 22–36. But since the provenance of objects is often unknown we must rely on recognizing shapes or types which are typically cultic, as well as on internal iconographic criteria which at best indicate the context in a shorthand way.

24. Dinos, Louvre E 876, *ABV* 90,1; C. Bérard, *La Cité des images* (Paris, 1984), fig. 187b.

25. Pyxis, Berlin Inv. 4856, *CorVP* 449, 655. For a recent interpretation of the social role of fat-belly dancers and bibliographic references see B. Fehr, "Entertainers at the *Symposion*: The *Akleitoi* in the Archaic Period," in *The Greek City from Homer to Alexander*, ed. O. Murray and S. Price (Oxford, 1990), 185–95.

26. Skyphos, Louvre CA 3004; *CorVP* 190, 561; pl. 73:2.

27. Cf. *CorVP*, 655.

28. Plu., *Lyc.* 28.4.

29. P. Schmitt-Pantel, "Collective Activities and the Political in the Greek City," in *The Greek City from Homer to Alexander*, ed. Murray and Price, 199–213.

30. Ibid., 207.

31. Xen., *Hell.* 2.4.20.

32. H. Jeanmaire, *Couroi et Courètes* (Lille, 1939), ch. 3, "Rites d'éphébie et classes d'âge dans l'Afrique contemporaine," 147–227, while not claiming historical causation, argued for vestigial remains of classical and preclassical age-systems and corresponding rituals in parts of traditional Africa.

33. P. Spencer, ed., *Society and the Dance* (Cambridge, 1985). T. C. Ranger, *Dance and Society in East Africa 1890–1970* (London, 1975) is an example of an earlier study that successfully analyzed dance in a meaningful historical context. The application of anthropological theory to dance in general is a relatively recent development. In the early 1970s the

Conference on Research in Dance held a series of colloquia in response to the pioneering work of Gertrude Kurath, a specialist on ethnic dance who had made an appeal a decade earlier to move away from the descriptive approach in dance ethnology and to consider dance as a branch of anthropology. In 1977 A. P. Royce published the first scholarly work on the subject, *The Anthropology of Dance* (Bloomington, Ind.).

34. Spencer, 3.

Chapter One. Dance and Play in Plato's Laws:
Anticipating an Anthropological Paradigm

1. Pl., *Laws* 803de.
2. Pl., *Laws* 799e–800a, cf. 700b, 722d.
3. Hom., *Il.* 18.591–92.
4. P. Bourdieu, *Outline of a Theory of Practice*, trans. R. Nice (Cambridge, 1977), passim.
5. Pl., *Rep.* 401de.
6. Pl., *Laws* 700d–701a.
7. Pl., *Laws* 654ab.
8. Pl., *Laws* 653e–654a.
9. Pl., *Laws* 664cd.
10. Pl., *Laws* 657d.
11. Pl., *Laws* 667b–668b.
12. Pl., *Laws* 814e.
13. Pl., *Laws* 815e.
14. Eur., *El.* 859–65, 874–78.
15. Pl., *Laws* 816bc.
16. Athen. 631d.
17. Pl., *Laws* 700b.
18. Hom. *Hymn to Apollo* 158–61.
19. H. Jeanmaire, "Le Satyre et la ménade: Remarques sur quelques textes relatifs aux danses 'orgiaques,'" *Mélanges d'archéologie et d'histoire offerts à Charles Picard* (Paris, 1949), 463–73, interprets the dances referred to in this and related passages not as theatrical but as possession dances.
20. Pl., *Laws* 816e.
21. Plu., *Lyc.* 28.4.
22. Pl., *Laws* 804de.
23. Pl., *Laws* 806b.
24. Pl., *Laws* 796b.

25. J.-C. Poursat, "Les Représentations de danse armée dans la céramique attique," *BCH* 92 (1968): 586–604.
26. Mixed choruses in Greek art and literature are attested. There are a handful of examples from Attic art of the eighth to the sixth centuries, some of them, like the Analatos hydria, ambiguous since the women and men are segregated into two groups, not alternating (*anamix*) in a single circle or row. R. Crowhurst, *Representations of Performances of Choral Lyric on the Greek Monuments, 800–350, B.C.* (Ph.D. Diss., Univ. London, 1963), 219–21, lists six examples, including the scene of Theseus on the François vase. K. F. Johansen, *Thésée et la danse à Délos* (Copenhagen, 1945), 13–20, figs. 3–8, discusses the relevant examples.
27. Pl., *Laws* 813b. This division can be explained in part because girls and boys in the ideal city-state are to be separated from one another at age six.
28. Pl., *Laws* 802de.
29. Pl., *Laws* 669bc; trans. Barker, 154.
30. Pl., *Laws* 771d–772a; cf. Lucian, *On the Dance* 12–13.
31. Pl., *Laws* 672e.
32. Plato's explanation appears to be a modification of the *logos* on the natural origins of dance mentioned at *Laws* 653e–654a and discussed later in chapter 2.
33. Pl., *Laws* 816a.
34. Lucian, *On the Dance* 63.
35. Hdt. 6.129; Xen., *Sym.* 2.19.
36. Hom., *Od.* 4.278–79; Lucian, *On the Dance* 19; Hom. *Hymn to Apollo* 162–63.
37. Pl., *Laws* 655d.
38. Pl., *Laws* 653cd.
39. Pl., *Laws* 653d.
40. Pl., *Laws* 656b.
41. Hom. *Hymn to Apollo* 163.
42. H. Koller, *Die Mimēsis in der Antike* (Bern, 1954).
43. Pl., *Laws* 803c.
44. Pl., *Laws* 803e.
45. Pl., *Laws* 673a, 803e. Linguistic support for considering dance within the anthropological concept of play is also provided by *hepsiaasthai*, implying a group movement involving song and dance (Hom., *Od.* 21.429, cf. 1.152), and related to the word *hepsia*, meaning "amusement, toy." Similarly the verb *athurō*, with meanings ranging from the play of children to musical activity including dancing (Pl., *Laws* 796b), is related to the word *athurma*, also meaning a plaything. Hesychius

records a dance called *strobilos* (spinning top); cf. Ar., *Pax* 864, Athen. 630a.

46. Plato makes one of his frequent word-plays on *paideia* and *paidia* at *Laws* 656c.

47. Pyxis, New York 09.221.40; *ARV* 1328, 99; cf. pyxis, London, British Museum E 775, *ARV* 1328,92, *LIMC* II.2, pl. 120, (Aphrodite 1196); lekythos, Baltimore, Walters Art Gallery 48.205, *ARV* 1330, 8, *CJ* 42 (1947), figs. 7–8; cup, Würzburg 492, *ARV* 1512, 18, E. Langlotz, *Griechische Vasen in Würzburg* (Munich, 1932), plates 162–63.

48. Pl., *Laws* 794a.

49. Pl., *Laws* 797a.

'50. Pl., *Laws* 799e–800a; cf. *Rep.* 424c; 424e–425a.

51. Pl., *Laws* 673cd.

52. E.g., G. Bateson, "A Theory of Play and Fantasy," in *Steps to an Ecology of Mind* (San Francisco, 1972), 178.

53. J. Huizinga, *Homo Ludens* (1944; reprinted Boston, 1955), 31–33.

54. The riotous side of playful behavior is then expressed by the verb *kōmazō*, memorably used in a substantive form to describe Alcibiades' interruption in the *Symposium* (Pl., *Symp.* 212c).

55. Hom., *Od.* 8.259–60.

56. *Hom. Hymn to Apollo* 149–50. Other terms for festive gatherings for play and contests including dance are *heortē* for a religious festival, *synodos* for a national assembly.

57. Cf. Pl., *Laws* 771d–772a.

58. K. Groos, *Die Spiele der Thiere*, 1896; K. Groos, *Die Spiele des Menschen*, 1899.

59. R. Thom, *Structural Stability and Morphogenesis: An Outline of a General Theory of Models*, trans. D. H. Fowler (Reading, Mass., 1975), 323, 317.

60. T. Arbeau, *Orchesography*, trans. C. W. Beaumont (London, 1925).

61. J. Blacking, "Movement, Dance, Music, and the Venda Girls' Initiation Cycle," in Spencer, 64–91.

62. Spencer, 11.

63. At *Laws* 813b Plato says that boys and girls will be assigned dancing masters and mistresses.

64. Plu., *Lyc.* 21.

65. Pl., *Laws* 657d.

66. Spencer, 156.

67. Pl., *Laws* 831b; 796c.

68. A. Gell, "Style and Meaning in Umeda Dance," in Spencer, 183–205.

69. Ibid., 190–91.

Chapter Two. *Origins and Divine Prototypes:*
Dance as an Ordering Force

1. Pl., *Ti.* 40c; cf. *Epin.* 982e. On the cosmic dance in general see James Miller, *Measures of Wisdom: The Cosmic Dance in Classical and Christian Antiquity* (Toronto, 1986); L. B. Lawler, "Cosmic Dance and Dithyramb," in *Studies in Honor of Ullman*, ed. L. B. Lawler et al. (St. Louis, 1960), 12–16.
2. A. Laks, "Legislation and Demiurgy: On the Relationship Between Plato's *Republic* and *Laws*," *CA* 9 (1990): 226–29.
3. Pl., *Ti.* 48a.
4. Pl., *Laws* 664e–665a.
5. Pl., *Laws* 653cd.
6. Pl., *Laws* 653e–654a. Plato makes a playful but untranslatable etymology on *chara* ("joy") and *choros* ("dance").
7. Arist., *Pol.* 1340b5–18, 1341b27–1342b34. The most likely candidate for authorship of the *logos* of Plato's day is Damon, the musical theorist and advisor to Pericles, whose own theoretical positions on music would have been incomplete without reference to dancing. At *Rep.* 400b Plato associates Damon's theory of musical ethos with *baseis* (steps) and *rhythmoi*. In what may be a reference to the kernel of such a theory, Athen. 628c reports that Damon's followers thought that songs and dances were the result of the soul being in motion. C. Lord, *Education and Culture in the Political Thought of Aristotle* (Ithaca, N.Y., 1982), 215, thinks that the concluding passage from the *Politics* (1341b17–34) is an interpolation by someone of the Damonian school.
8. Pi., fr. 31SM.
9. *Titanomachy* fr. 5 Allen, *apud* Athen. 22c.
10. Bacch. 17.103–8.
11. *Hom. Hymn to Aphrodite* 259–61.
12. Pi., *P.* 10. 38–44.
13. Hom., *Od.* 8.250–65.
14. Diod. 5.65 mentions the Couretes; Lucian, *On the Dance* 7, mentions the Corybantes and the Couretes.
15. Lucian, *On the Dance* 7; cf. Hes., *Th.* 120–22.
16. In Eur., *Bacchae* 121–34, the dancing of the Couretes at Zeus's birth on Crete and the related invention by the Corybantes of the drum is sung in the first choral ode. The persistent myth for the genesis of human dancing not only ties the event to the birth of Zeus but localizes it on Crete where the Greeks believed that many of their dance rituals originated. Indeed the appearance of the Couretes in Cretan cult is attested in a fourth (?) century B.C.E. hymn (*IC* III.2.2) discovered at Palaikastro in eastern Crete, which invokes Zeus, the greatest of the Cou-

retes. The cult of the Couretes is known elsewhere, e.g. Messenia (Paus. 4.31.9).

17. Hes., fr. 10a.19MW.
18. Call. 4.300–301.
19. The performance of the *Hymn* as a unified whole for Polykrates' *Pythia kai Delia* of 522 B.C.E. was independently proposed by W. Burkert, "Kynaithos, Polycrates, and the Homeric Hymn to Apollo," in *Arktouros. Hellenic Studies Presented to Bernard M. W. Knox*, ed. G. W. Bowersock, W. Burkert, and M. C. J. Putnam (Berlin, 1979), 54–58, and by R. Janko, *Homer, Hesiod and the Hymns* (Cambridge, 1982), 109–14.
20. A. N. Athanassakis, *The Homeric Hymns* (Baltimore, 1976), xii.
21. A partial list of references to the topos of divine festivity and related matters follows: Alc., fr. 349 LP (Return of Hephaestus); Bacch. 17.100–108 (Nereids); Eur., fr. 752N (Dionysus dances with the maidens at Delphi); Eur., *Ba.* 133–34 (dances in which Dionysus delights); Hes., *Th.* 1–21, 36–52 (Muses); Hes., *Th.* 50–52 (Muses sing for Zeus); Hes., *Th.* 60–73 (Muses' dancing places and hymns); Hes., *Aspis*, 201–6 (divine *choros*); Hes., fr. 123 (dance-loving Couretes, satyrs, nymphs); Hom., *Il.* 1.597–604 (Hephaestus restores festivity to Olympus); Hom., *Od.* 9.250–65 (Phaeaceans); *Hom. Hymn to Apollo* 182–206 (*homēguris* of Zeus); *Hom. Hymn to Aphrodite* 259–61 (Muses' dancing places); *Hom. Hymn to Artemis* 13–20 (Artemis leads the chorus of nymphs); *Hom. Hymn to Hermes* 480–82 (presentation of lyre and instructions for festival use); *Hom. Hymn to Pan* 1–5 (Pan leads nymphs); *Hom. Hymn to Pan* 44–46 (reception of Pan on Olympus); Pi., fr. 31SM (demiurgic powers of divine music); Pi., fr. 156SM (silens); Pi., *I.* 8.63–69 (*thrēnos* of Heliconian *parthenoi* for Achilles); Pi., *N.* 5.22–25 (Muses); Pi., *P.* 1.1–6 (Apollo and Muses); Pi., *P.* 10.31–39 (Hyperboreans); Pl., *Ti.* 40c (cosmic dance); Soph., *Aj.* 693–705 (Pan as *chorēgos* of gods); Soph., *Ant.* 1146–52 (Dionysus as leader of cosmic dance); *Titanomachy*, fr. 5 Allen, *apud* Athen. 22c (Zeus as *chorēgos*).
22. *Hom. Hymn to Apollo* 182–206.
23. Hes., *Th.* 901–9.
24. Hom., *Il.* 18.604–6; *Od.* 4.18–19.
25. Black-figure olpe, Wilson College, Pennsylvania; *Aspects of Ancient Greece*, ed. G. F. Pinney and B. S. Ridgway (Allentown, Penn., 1979), 56, no. 25. The same high-stepping gait can be seen in a procession of musicians carrying stringed instruments, e.g. on a black-figure amphora, Paris E 861, *Beazley Addenda* 24, M. Maas and J. Snyder, *Stringed Instruments of Ancient Greece* (New Haven, Conn., 1989), 51, no. 15c.
26. Pi., *P.* 1.1–4.

27. Hom. *Hymn to Hermes* 31.
28. Hom. *Hymn to Hermes* 480–82.
29. Pl., *Laws* 796b.
30. Hes., *Th.* 2–8. Nearby in Thespiai there was a well-known cult of Muses with musical contests: *GGR* 1:254.
31. Hes., *Th.* 62–63.
32. Hes., *Th.* 68–71.
33. Hes., *Th.* 1–8.
34. *LIMC* III.2, 151, Charites no. 8.
35. Hom. *Hymn to Hermes* 450–52.
36. Hes., *Th.* 918–20.
37. Hom. *Hymn to Artemis* 11–15.
38. Hom. *Hymn to Apollo* 164.
39. Eur., *Or.* 233, Soph., *OC* 199L–JW.
40. Pl., *Phd.* 86b.
41. *Cypria*, fr. 6 Allen, fr. 5.4 Allen, *apud* Ath. 682df.
42. Hom., *Il.* 18.382, etc.
43. Hom., *Od.* 18.194.
44. Hes., *Th.* 907–11. In the Orphic hymns they are born to Eunomia: M. L. West, *Orphic Poems* (Oxford, 1983), 221 and n. 141.
45. Hes., *Th.* 64–65.
46. Pi., *O.* 14.8–12.
47. Hes., *Th.* 901–3.
48. Hes., *Op.* 75; Pi., *O.* 13.17.
49. Pi., *O.* 14.1–5.; Paus. 9.38.1; *GF*, 413.
50. Cf. M. Blech, *Studien zum Kranz bei den Griechen* (Berlin, 1982), 330–38.
51. Hom. *Hymn to Gaia* 30.14–15.
52. Hom. *Hymn to Apollo* 204.
53. Pl., *Laws* 657d.
54. Hom., *Il.* 1.601–4.
55. Hom., *Od.* 22.330.
56. Hes., *Th.* 78.
57. Hom. *Hymn to Apollo* 146–73.
58. Reading *krembaliastun* at 162.
59. Lebes gamikos, Mykonos Museum 12; *ARV* 261, where Beazley identifies the figures as "Apollo, and Muses (or Delian Maidens) dancing."
60. Thuc. 3.104.
61. Cf. the *prosōdion* of Eumelus, *PMG* 696.
62. Thuc. 3.104.
63. *Ath. Pol.* 56.3.
64. C. J. Herington, *Poetry into Drama* (Berkeley, 1985), 6.
65. The linguistic echoes are set out by A. Miller, *From Delos to Delphi: A Literary Study of the Homeric Hymn to Apollo* (Leiden, 1986), 68–69.

66. Hom. *Hymn to Apollo* 196.
67. Eur., *Hec.* 463–65.
68. Linguistically the idea of gathering is present in *ēgerethontai* (147) from the *ag-* stem, cf. *an/agō* used with the noun *choros*, notably at Thuc. 3.104.3 in describing the Delian festival; cf., e.g., Ps.-Hes., *Aspis* 280, Eur., *Tr.* 326.
69. Hom. *Hymn to Apollo* 146, 153–54, 204.
70. Hom. *Hymn to Apollo* 156.
71. Hom., *Od.* 6.100–106.
72. Hom., *Il.* 24.719–76.
73. Hom. *Hymn to Apollo* 200.
74. Hom. *Hymn to Apollo* 201.
75. Cf. Hom. *Hymn to Hermes* 450–52.
76. Hom. *Hymn to Apollo* 153.
77. Hom. *Hymn to Apollo* 168.
78. Hom. *Hymn to Apollo* 161; on so-called Stesichorean performance, see W. Burkert, "The Making of Homer in the Sixth Century B.C.: Rhapsodes Versus Stesichoros," in *Papers on the Amasis Painter and His World* (Malibu, Calif., 1987), 54.
79. On the correspondence between the Deliades and the Muses, see G. Nagy, *Greek Mythology and Poetics* (Ithaca, N.Y., 1990), 55–56.
80. See J. S. Clay, *The Politics of Olympus* (Princeton, 1989), 52.
81. Eumelus, *PMG* 696.
82. Calame, 1:174–209.
83. Hom. *Hymn to Apollo* 148.
84. Hom. *Hymn to Apollo* 206.
85. Pl., *Laws* 657d.
86. Hom. *Hymn to Apollo* 146, 150, 153, 170, 204.
87. Pl., *Phd.* 58ac; Townleian scholiast; H. Erbse, *Scholia Graeca in Homeri Iliadem* (Berlin, 1975) 4:565–66.
88. Hdt. 4.35; cf. Call. 4.283–95.
89. Eur., *Hipp.* 1425–29.
90. Pi., *P.* 10.31–39.
91. Hom., *Od.* 6.157.
92. Bacch. 17.124–32; G. Ieranò, "Il Ditirambo XVII di Bacchilide e le feste apollinee di Delo," *QS* 15 (1989): 157–83.
93. Singer: *theios aoidos*; Hom., *Od.* 4.17, 8.87, etc.; Hom. *Hymn to Apollo* 151.
94. Their congruence strongly argues for the much-debated unity of the Hom. *Hymn to Apollo.*
95. Hom. *Hymn to Apollo* 514–19. The influence of the young as subjects and performers in choral genres is evident in the titles of tragedies named for their adolescent choruses, such as Aeschylus's *Neaniskoi.*
96. Alc., fr. 307LP.

Chapter Three. Further Divine Prototypes: Dance as a Disruptive Force

1. Pl., *Laws* 815cd.
2. Eur., *Cyc.* 3.
3. Pl., *Laws* 672b.
4. The punitive interpretation of wine is consistent with an agrarian myth of origin in which Dionysus leaves the vine-plant and instructions how to make the potion with a resident of Attica named Icarius. The first vintner, however, was hurled down a well by his neighbors who had been invited to taste the liquid. The drunken stupor it induced led them to suspect Icarius of willfully poisoning them with intent to murder: Hyginus, *Astronomica* 2.4 Bunte.
5. Pl., *Rep.* 399d; Arist., *Pol.* 1341a. Aristotle believed the *aulos* should be occasionally used to effect *katharsis*.
6. Eur., *Ba.* 130–34.
7. Apollod. 2.2.2.
8. Pl., *Laws* 790de, trans. Saunders.
9. Pl., *Laws* 791ab.
10. In the *Phaedrus* (244, 265b) Plato recognizes the telestic madness that comes with ecstatic and frenzied dancing accompanied by wine as a divine gift that has curative powers against emotional disorders. See I. M. Linforth, "The Corybantic Rites in Plato," *University of California Publications in Classical Philology* 13 (1946): 121–62.
11. Arist., *Pol.* 1342a; cf. *Poet.* 6.
12. Pl., *Laws* 649de, 672d, 790d–791a.
13. Cf. E. Belfiore, "Wine and *Catharsis* of the Emotions in Plato's *Laws*," *CQ* 36 (1986): 421–37, who situates the two views of catharsis in the larger perspective of philosophical and medical writings.
14. Hom., *Od.* 14.463–66; wine makes an old man dance even if he does not want to: Athen. 428a.
15. Belfiore, "Wine," 433.
16. Ibid., 434–35.
17. Soph., *Ant.* 1146–52; in the first choral ode Dionysus is portrayed leading (*archoi*, 154) the all-night dances at the temple.
18. Eur., fr. 752N.
19. Pelike, London, British Museum E 362, *LIMC* III.1, p. 464, no. 472; cf. the *sparagmos* scene on a stamnos in the British Museum, London E 439; *LIMC* III.2, pl. 312, no. 151. In two surviving examples the god dances while holding flaming torches: *LIMC* III.1., p. 440, nos. 149–50.
20. Amphora, Würzburg, Inv. L 265 and L 282; cf. *LIMC* III.1, p. 451, no. 292; pp. 463–64, nos. 467–73.
21. T. S. Eliot, *Four Quartets*: "At the still point, there the dance is . . .

Except for the point, the still point, There would be no dance, and there is only the dance."

22. Pl., *Laws* 653e–654a.

23. The views of M. Gluckman, C. Geertz, M. Douglas, V. Turner, B. Babcock, M. Bakhtin, E. Le Roy Ladurie, J. Carrière, and others as they apply to Greek notions of carnival are summarized by S. Goldhill in *The Poet's Voice* (Cambridge, 1991), 176–88.

24. Hom., *Il.* 1.591–93.

25. Alc. fr. 349LP. U. von Wilamowitz, "Hephaistos," *Kleine Schriften* V.2 (Berlin, 1937), 5–35, believed that the literary and artistic representations of the story could be traced to a (lost) Homeric Hymn to Hephaestus.

26. F. Brommer, "Die Rückführung des Hephaistos," *JDAI* 52 (1937): 198–219; A. Seeberg, "Hephaistos Rides Again," *JHS* 85 (1965): 102–9.

27. Amphoriskos, Athens 664; *CorVP* 497, 621–22; *LIMC* IV.2, Hephaestus no. 129. M. Detienne and J.-P. Vernant, "Les Pieds d'Héphaistos," in *Les Ruses de l'intelligence* (Paris, 1974), 253, connect the crab with the Kabeiroi on Lemnos.

28. Hes., *Op.* 59–64.

29. Cf. Gen. 4:22. On the traditional association between metallurgists and mummery and dance, cf. M. Eliade, *Shamanism: Archaic Techniques of Ecstasy*, trans. W. Trask (New York, 1964), 473, n. 36; W. Burkert, "Jason, Hypsipyle, and New Fire on Lemnos," *CQ* 20 (1970): 9; on the Kabeiroi, B. Hemberg, *Die Kabeiroi* (Uppsala, 1950), 268 and passim.

30. Cf. Detienne and Vernant, "Les Pieds d' Héphaistos," 242–60.

31. The formula is *choleuōn hypo de knēmai rōonto araiai*: Hom., *Il.* 18.411 = 20.37.

32. Acheloös: Hom., *Il.* 24. 615–16 (Niobe paradigm); cf. Hes., *Th.* 8, of the Muses, and the *Hom. Hymn to Aphrodite* 261, with *choron* as direct object. The verb is used in the second Nekyia (Hom., *Od.* 24.69) of the mourners moving around Achilles' pyre in what has sometimes been taken as evidence for a funerary dance (Leaf, *Commentary*, ad loc.).

33. Hom., *Il.* 18.382–83.

34. Hom., *Il.* 18.491–96, 567–72, 590–606.

35. M. Delcourt, *Héphaistos* (Paris, 1957), 157–62; F. Frontisi-Ducroux, *Dédale* (Paris, 1975), 21.

36. Hom., *Il.* 1.571–600.

37. In mimetic performances Hephaestus becomes the laughable hero of the padded dancers. Delcourt, *Héphaistos*, 121–23, draws attention to the connection between padded dancers and Hephaestus.

38. On a ceramic astragalos by the Sotades Painter (cf. Fig. 1a), a male figure is seen shepherding three female figures into a cave. E. Simon, *Die Götter der Griechen* (Munich, 1969), 225, figs. 211–12; cf.

G. Neumann, *Gesten und Gebärden in der griechischen Kunst* (Berlin, 1965), fig. 9, who has identified the male figure as Hephaestus. If the identification is correct, Hephaestus is shown as a *chorēgos*.

39. *GR*, 134.

40. The Return of Hephaestus belongs to a large class of vase-painting scenes placing gods in human situations (eating, drinking, fighting, attending weddings, and so on), hardly surprising in a society with an anthropomorphic pantheon and a vivid literary tradition of humanizing gods. The tendency is so strong that even the paradoxical situation of Olympian gods pouring libations or sacrificing animals to other divinities occasionally arises. Among the possible interpretations for the paradox is that the divine activity serves as a paradigm for human worship; cf. Kimberly C. Patton, "Gods Who Sacrifice: A Paradox of Attic Iconography," *AJA* 94 (1990): 326.

41. The *symposion* grew out of the Homeric feast. Instead of funerary games, private entertainments were held. See O. Murray, "The Symposion as Social Organization," in *The Greek Renaissance in the Eighth Century, B.C.* (Stockholm, 1983), 95–99.

42. Chalcidean amphora, Beaulieu-sur-Mer, Villa Kerlyos, *LIMC* IV.1, p. 639, Hephaestus no. 135. In later red-figure representations of the Return the contrast between mobility and lameness becomes less pronounced, and occasionally Hephaestus is shown on foot beside his mount or proceeding entirely on his own steam. Beside mount: *LIMC* IV.1, p. 644, no. 168; on foot, no quadruped in scene: *LIMC* IV.1, pp. 644–45, nos. 169b–72c.

43. Hom., *Il.* 18.382–83, cf. Pl., *Laws* 653c.

44. In addition to Paros, Naxos and Thebes were early centers for dithyrambic celebrations. Schol. on Pi., *O.* 13; *DTC*, 11–12.

45. Archil., fr. 120 W. The dithyramb attained its fully developed form in the festivals of Dionysus at Athens, first under the tyrants, and then in festivals under the democracy when it regularly became a choral competition among the ten tribes in Attica.

46. Epich., fr. 132 Kaibel.

47. Pl., *Laws* 672b.

48. Copenhagen, Thorvaldsen Museum 97; *DTC* (2d ed.), 5, fig. 1.

49. C. Fränkel, *Satyr- u. Bakchennamen auf Vasenbildern* (Halle, 1912), 69, 94.

50. Poll. 4.104–10.

51. Pi., fr. 70b.1SM.

52. Athenaeus 617c, who quotes the passage, calls it a *hyporchēma*, but it has also been interpreted as a dithyramb and as a satyr-play; cf. D. Sutton, *The Greek Satyr Play* (Meisenheim am Glan, 1980): 7–12.

53. H. Lloyd-Jones, "Problems of Early Greek Tragedy: Pratinas, Phrynichus, the Gyges Fragment," in *Estudios sobre la tragedia griega,*

Cuadernos de la Fundación Pastor 13 (Madrid, 1966), 15–18, argues that the "Pratinas" fragment was wrongly attributed and belongs to the late fifth century. Evidence for the performance of dithyramb by satyric choruses is unattested before the fifth century.

54. R. Seaford, *Maia* 29–30 (1977–78): 81–94, argues that the poem is almost certainly satyric.

55. *PMG* 708, trans. Barker, 273–74.

56. R. Seaford, *Maia* 29–30 (1977–78): 83–84, believes that the satyrs in the poem attack the innovations in the dithyramb by Lasus of Hermione (who is associated with the institution of dithyrambic contests at the City Dionysia) that altered the rhythms of the genre and adjusted it to the polyphony of the *auloi* (Ps.-Plu., *De Mus.* 1141c).

57. For a complete list of dithyrambic titles, see D. F. Sutton, *Dithyrambographi Graeci* (Hildesheim, 1989), 121–22.

58. D. Mendelsohn, "*Synkeraunoō:* Dithyrambic Language and Dionysiac Cult," *CJ* 87 (1992): 105–24.

59. Pi., *O.* 13.19.

60. Simon., fr. 79D.

61. Athen. 181c.

62. Pi., *O.* 13.19.

63. W. Pax, "Circumambulation," *RAC* 3, cols. 143–52.

64. Pi., fr. 70b.22–23SM. In Pindar's dithyramb (which provides a fanciful account of a lavish celestial festival on Olympus) Artemis is presented as the animal driver. Her beasts are savage lions, the divinely glamorized version of the bull in the mortal contest.

65. In the myth of the pursuit of the infant Dionysus by the Titans (Nonnus 6.169–205) the child eluded his followers by undergoing several transformations until finally apprehended and torn apart in the shape of a bull. Prior to this violent finale the Titans attempted to entice the infant by showing him a mirror and holding up various toys.

66. The third-century Parian monument appears to quote a short poem, written by Archilochus to honor Dionysus, which may have been a dithyramb. See A. E. Harvey, *CQ* n.s. 5 (1955): 172–74.

67. N. M. Kondoleon, *ArchEph* 1952 [1955], 32.

68. Hdt. 1.24. G. A. Privatera, "Il ditirambo come spettacolo musicale: Il ruolo di Archiloco e di Arione," in *La musica in Grecia,* ed. B. Gentili and R. Pretagostini (Rome, 1988), 123–31.

69. Schol. on Pi., *O.* 13.19 claims that Arion's innovation was to introduce a stationary chorus. But this source has no independent authority, and it is more likely, as suggested by the Pratinas fragment and by Pindar's comment in his dithyramb to the Thebans cited earlier, that as musical tastes shifted, the dance element became more or less pronounced. H. Patzer, *Die Anfänge der griechischen Tragödie* (Wiesbaden, 1962), has suggested that Arion's innovation was to make the heroic lyric mimetic, using the satyr-chorus as a model.

70. J. T. Hooker, "Arion and the Dolphin," *G&R* 36 (1989): 141–46, explains that Herodotus in part included this as well as other marvels to indicate popular credulity.
71. Pi., *O.* 13.19 independently corroborates the invention of the ox-driving dithyramb at Corinth.
72. The musical analogy can be seen most clearly in the case of oared ships for which there was a boatswain, a *keleustēs*, who called out the strokes with the assistance of a *triēraulēs* playing an *aulos*, which was used in choral performance.
73. Hom. *Hymn to Apollo* 399–403, 514–19.
74. Hom. *Hymn to Dionysus* 52; Hdt. 1.24; Eur., *Ba.* 306–7; fr. 752.3N. The verb *pedaō* is used of a dolphin leaping in Longus 1.2.26.25; 1.2.29.3.3.
75. Hdt. 1.24.7.
76. I. Loucas, "Ritual Surprise and Terror in Ancient Greek Possession-Dromena," *Kernos* 2 (1989): 97–104, speaks of the "ecplectic spectacle" and gives as an example the priestesses of Apollo frightened by the Furies at *Eum.* 34–38.
77. Hom. *Hymn to Dionysus* 50.
78. Plot. 3.3.5.8–10.
79. Phalanthos, oikist of Taras: Paus. 10.13.10; Taras, eponymous hero of Taras: Arist., fr. 590R; Ikadios, son of Apollo: Serv. ad *Aen.* 3.332.
80. Archippus wrote a comedy entitled *Ichthyes* in which the chorus was almost certainly dressed as fish.
81. T. B. L. Webster, *The Greek Chorus* (London, 1970), 39, no. 163; J. R. Green, "A Representation of the *Birds* of Aristophanes," in *Greek Vases in the J. Paul Getty Museum* (Malibu, Calif., 1985), nos. 13, 14, 16, 17.
82. Archil., fr. 122W.
83. *PMG* 939.8. C. M. Bowra, "Arion and the Dolphin," *MH* 20 (1963): 121–34, suggests a date toward the end of the fifth century when reforms in dithyrambs gave increased prominence to the musician who sang a solo while the chorus only danced.
84. Eur., *Ba.* 306–7; fr. 752.3N.
85. Pl., *Laws* 673cd.
86. Pi., fr. 70b.22–23SM.
87. Bowra, "Arion."
88. On the dancelike movement of the dolphin in poetry see further M. Mantziou, "A 'Hymn' to the Dolphins: *Fr. Adesp.* 939 *PMG*," *Hellenika* 40 (1989): 229–37, at 233. See also *PMG* 939.5–9.
89. Paus. 3.25.7, cf. 9.30.2.
90. If Bowra's hypothesis ("Arion") for a late fifth-century author is correct, the inscription may well have been added at this time and passed off as Arion's own composition.
91. An autobiographical fragment about Alcman (*PMG* 26) in his old age suggests that the chorus could physically elevate the musician-poet.

92. The satyr has been studied as a figure of the topsy-turvy world primarily in the context of Athenian vase painting by F. Lissarrague, *The Aesthetics of the Greek Banquet*, trans. A. Szegedy-Maszak (Princeton, 1990), 91 and passim.

93. Choros is also attested in vase inscriptions as the name of a Nereid (*LIMC* III.1, p. 274, s.v. Choro I) and as the name of a Muse (*LIMC* III.1, p. 275, s.v. Choro III).

94. Naples Nat. Mus. H 2419; *ARV* 1151, 2; cf. Fränkel, *Satyr- u. Bakchennamen auf Vasenbildern*, 50, 100, letter "theta."

95. Pausanias 2.20.4. mentions at Argos the tomb of Choreia, who was said to have joined Dionysus and other maenads in an attack against the Argives. The attacking force, including the god, were annihilated by Perseus. Most of the followers were given common graves, but Choreia, because of her high rank, was accorded a tomb.

96. A. Henrichs, "Greek Maenadism from Olympias to Messalina," *HSCP* 82 (1978): 152–53.

97. Stamnos, Naples Nat. Mus. H 2419; *ARV* 1151, 2. Other examples listed in *LIMC* III.1., p. 426–27, nos. 34–35, 37–39, 41.

98. A. Frickenhaus, *Lenäenvasen* (Berlin, 1912); Nilsson, *GGR* 582, assigned the vases to the Anthesteria. For a complete discussion of the debate see F. Frontisi-Ducroux, *Le Dieu-masque* (Rome, 1991), 21–63. On a Corinthian alabastron Dionysus appears as a head, danced about by a komast accompanied by two other komasts, one with a stringed instrument and one with an *aulos*: *CorVP* 110; *LIMC* III.1, p. 428, no. 49.

99. Henrichs, "Greek Maenadism," 147, cf. Diod. 4.3.2–3.

100. Amphora, Würzburg, Inv. L 265 and L 282; amphora, Basel Kä 420, *Beazley Addenda* 43; amphora, Berlin 1690, *ABV* 151, 11. D. von Bothmer, *The Amasis Painter and His World* (Malibu, Calif., 1985), 78, fig. 58; amphora, Berlin 3210 *Beazley Addenda* 43, von Bothmer, *Amasis Painter*, 49, fig. 45b; amphora, Paris Louvre F 36, *ABV* 150, 6. D. von Bothmer, *Amasis Painter*, 82, cat. no. 5; cf. two fragments of an amphora from the Heraion of Samos, *MDAI (A)* 46 (1931), pl. 3.

101. Victor Turner, *Dramas, Fields, and Metaphors* (Ithaca, N.Y., 1974), 253.

102. Hes., fr. 123MW *apud* Strabo 10.3.19.

103. Hes., fr. 123MW: *outidanos; amēchanoergos*.

104. Pi., fr. 156SM.

105. R. Seaford, "Dionysiac Drama and the Dionysiac Mysteries," *CQ* 31 (1981): 252–75, at 264.

106. Pl., *Laws* 815c.

Chapter Four. *Divine Prototypes and Their Human Realizations*

1. On the full implications of *heortē*, see J. D. Mikalson, "The *Heortē* of Heortelogy," *GRBS* 23 (1982): 213–21.
2. Arist., *Rh.* 1380b3; *NE* 8.1160a25–30.
3. Ar., *Ra.* 370–71, 390.
4. The cathartic explanation of festivity may have been traditional, cf. Thuc. 2.38: "We have provided all kinds of recreation for our spirits when our work is over. There are various kinds of contests and sacrifices regularly throughout the year."
5. Hdt. 6.138.1; Ar., *Ach.* 1079.
6. See C. Calame, "Morfologia e funzione della festa nell' antichità," *AION* (filol.) 4–5 (1982–83): 7–21, cf. *Kernos* 4 (1991): 196–200.
7. Dem., *Meid.* 21.51.
8. Dem., *Meid.* 21.52.
9. Dem., *Meid.* 21.53.
10. F. Sokolowski, *Lois sacrées des cités grecques*, Suppl. (Paris, 1962), no. 46.
11. For a discussion of *orchēsis*, *molpē*, and other terms for dance see M. Wegner, *Musik und Tanz* (= *Arch. Hom.* III U) (Göttingen, 1968), 40–44.
12. Divine context for *choros*: Pi., *O.* 14.9, *P.* 1.1–6, *P.* 10.38, *N.* 5.22–23; cf. M. Heath, "Receiving the Kōmos: The Context and Performance of Epinician," *AJA* 109 (1988): 183–84.
13. Ar., *Ra.* 335–36; Cassandra calls the *choros hosios*, Eur., *Tr.* 328.
14. In antiquity, Plato, *Laws* 654a, said that the gods invented the word *choros* because of the *chara* (joy) implanted in the blissful activity. Etymologically the two words are unrelated; the attempt to connect them reveals Plato's fondness for word-play.
15. The *Etymologicum Magnum* (EM) repeats Plato's etymology and in addition derives *choros* from the noun for "space" (*choros* with long initial *o*, cf. *chōra*).
16. *Choros* has most plausibly been construed with the word *chortos*, "an enclosed space" (cf. Latin *hortus*, "garden"), cognate with Lithuanian *zaras* ("row, arrangement") through a verbal root (*gher-) meaning "to contain/hold"; Frisk, s.v. with bibliography. Others have linked the meaning of the root "to hold" to the action of dancers joining hands: *EM*; cf. W. Porzig, *Die Namen für Satzinhalte* (Berlin, 1942), 276, 307. That the essential gesture of the members of the chorus was to grasp one another by the hand and so unite themselves into one body is suggested by the existence of an epic formula for choral dancers "holding hands at the wrist" (*epi karpōi cheiras echontes*). This epic formula has a counterpart in the shorthand artistic convention of depicting

rows of dancers with hands conjoined: R. Tölle, *Frühgriechische Reigentänze* (Waldsassen Bayern, 1964), 56–57. By linking bodies the members form a human cordon and define a space. The etymology of *choros*
from *gher- "to grasp/contain" may thus relate its essential social purpose of creating solidarity among the participants to the territorial
function of dance as an act of boundary display. On the history of
choros as a troupe of dancers, see F. Perpillou-Thomas, "P. Sorb. inv.
2381, *gryllos, kalamaulēs, choros,*" *ZPE* 78 (1989): 153–54. As for the
shape of the dancing arena, it is circular. Under the definition for
choros Hesychius gives *kyklos*, meaning a circle, and *stephanos*,
"crown."

17. Hom., *Od.* 8.260.
18. Hes., *Th.* 2–8, 63.
19. Hom., *Od.* 12.318.
20. Hom., *Od.* 12.4.
21. Pl., *Laws* 653d.
22. Hom., *Il.* 18.183.
23. Hom., *Il.* 18.592.
24. Signet ring, Knossos, Herakleion Museum, J. T. Hooker, *Mycenaean
    Greece* (London, 1977), 198, cf. A. Evans, *PM* 1: 159–60 and fig. 115;
    the Isopata gem was published by A. Evans, *Archaeologia* 65 (1913): 10,
    fig. 16.
25. P. Warren, "Circular Platforms at Minoan Knossos," *ABSA* 79 (1984):
    319–23.
26. D. Levi, *ASSA* 23–24 (1961–62), fig. 174a; *PM* 3, fig. 41.
27. A. Evans, *PM* 3: 28, thought that the *choros* was a paved area located
    northwest of the palace.
28. Hom., *Il.* 18.590–91. The exact meaning of the word *choros* in this
    passage has been debated since antiquity, when it was variously un-
    derstood to be some type of sculpted work (a relief or statues of the
    dancers themselves) or else an actual dance; Paus., 1.22.3, 9.40.2, cf.
    8.16.3, mentions in his catalogue of Daedalus's surviving works a
    white marble relief at Knossos of Ariadne's dancing floor; it was con-
    sidered a dance by the scholiast in Venetus A; H. Erbse, *Scholia Graeca
    in Homeri Iliadem* (Berlin, 1975) 4: 564–66. The various interpreta-
    tions are all allowable by the range of meanings for *choros*; however,
    the local meaning of *choros* as the dancing place is intended here; the
    verb *ēskēsen* (fashion), used elsewhere of a chariot and gifts made by
    Hephaestus, implies something crafted. Hom., *Il.* 18.592, cf. chariot
    of Rhesus (10.438), horn (4.110), clothing (14.178), gifts made by
    Hephaestus (14.240), etc. The local meaning is the generally accepted
    interpretation. See K. Fittschen, *ArchHom* II N (Göttingen, 1973), 15,
    nn. 70 and 71; contra: E. Kunze, *Kretische Bronzereliefs* (Stuttgart,
    1931), 213 and n. 45, believes the word designates the band of dancers

portrayed on the shield; N. Himmelmann, *Über bildende Kunst in der homerischen Gesellschaft* (Wiesbaden, 1969), 27, n. 1, thinks it is a relief.

29. Hom., *Il.* 18.591.

30. Sometimes translated in a more general sense as "spacious," but cf. S. Scully, *Homer and the Sacred City* (Ithaca, N.Y., 1990), 132.

31. Boeotian Mykalessos mentioned at the beginning of the Catalogue of Ships in the *Iliad* has a wide dancing place, as do Ithaca, Thebes, Sparta, and Sicyon: Hom., *Il.* 2.498; *Od.* 24.468; 11.265; 13.414, cf. 15.1; *Il.* 23.299. The vital role of dance in Spartan culture is well known from Herodotus, Plato, and other authors, and Sicyon was the home of tragic choruses in honor of the hero Adrastus (Hdt. 5.67), as well as of the musical contests for Hippocleides and the other suitors invited by Cleisthenes to compete for the hand of Agariste: Hdt. 6.126–32.

32. Hom., *Od.* 6.4, 8.246–49.

33. Paus. 10.4.2.

34. Hom., *Od.* 6.266.

35. Hom., *Il.* 18.504.

36. Ar., *Ra.* 445. As Hesychius suggests, the circle is the characteristic configuration of the dancing ground, and by extension, the principal pattern for choral dancing; Simonides 148.9 [Bergk] can use the word *kyklos* alone to mean *kyklios choros* (circular dance).

37. Paus. 3.11.9.

38. Pl., *Ap.* 26e. The use of the word *orchēstra* for the area before the *skēnē* in Dionysus's theater is first attested in [Arist.], *Pr.* 901b30.

39. Pi., fr. 74a.1–5SM.

40. J. Boardman, *Greek Sculpture. The Archaic Period* (London, 1978), fig. 201.

41. Cf. F. Robert, *Thymelē* (Paris, 1939), 424–25.

42. Bacch. 5.104–6: *kallichoros*.

43. A. D. Ure, "Threshing-floor and Vineyard," *CQ* 49 (1955): 225–30.

44. Cf. Hom., *Od.* 8.260.

45. Thuc. 3.104.

46. *Archēchoros*: Eur., *Tr.* 151; *IG* XIV.1618.

47. A linguistically close parallel for *choros* is the military *lochos*. Like *choros*, *lochos* is a versatile word which designates at once an ambush, the place of lying-in-wait, and the band of men who carry out the covert activity under the guidance of a *lochagos*.

48. Xen., *Mem.* 3.4.3–6.

49. On this issue, see R. Hamilton, *Choes and Anthesteria* (Ann Arbor, Mich., 1992), 83, who distinguishes between the large *choes* (with minimal connection with the Anthesteria) and the miniature *choes* with a consistently repeated tableau of elements that loosely connects

them with the Anthesteria. Although situating the *choes* in the Anthesteria helps explain certain features, the interpretation of the iconography is not entirely dependent on the festival.

50. Thuc. 2.15.3–4.
51. E. Simon, *Festivals of Attica* (Madison, Wisc., 1983), 92.
52. *GF*, 267–71; Deubner, 93–122; *DFA*, 1–25; H. W. Parke, *Festivals of the Athenians* (London, 1977), 107–24; *HN*, 213–43; Simon, *Festivals of Attica*, 92–99.
53. Scholia on Ar., *Ach.* 1002. The contest was conducted by the *archon basileus* in the *thesmothetion*.
54. For a critique of approaches to ancient sacrificial ritual allegedly made against the backdrop of the Christian sacrament, see J. Z. Smith, *Drudgery Divine: On the Comparison of Early Christianities and the Religions of Late Antiquity* (Chicago, 1990).
55. Ar., *Ach.* 1085–93.
56. Phot., s.v. *Thyraze Kares*.
57. *P. Oxy.* 853, col. x.7–18.
58. Call., fr. 305Pf.
59. Cf. R. Seaford, *Euripides Cyclops* (Oxford, 1984), 14.
60. Bell-krater, Copenhagen, NM 13817, *ARV* 1145, 35. K. Friis-Johansen, *Eine Dithyrambos-Aufführung* (Copenhagen, 1959), 39–41. A. Pickard-Cambridge, *DFA*, 16–17, and fig. 15, remains cautious about the interpretation, whereas Simon, *Festivals of Attica*, 98–99, believes the performance to be part of the Dionysia.
61. *FGrHist* 325 F 12 = Athen. 465a.
62. K. Reckford, *Aristophanes' Old-and-New Comedy* (Chapel Hill, N.C., 1987), 456.
63. Hyg., *Astron.* 2.4, accounts for the dance on the goatskin as follows. Icarius killed and flayed the goat that nibbled on the most tender leaves in the vineyard. From the skin he made a wineskin bag, filled it, and ordered his companions to dance on it, whence the saying attributed to Eratosthenes that the Icarians were the first to dance around the goat.
64. Ar., *Ra.* 209–19, trans. K. Reckford.
65. Ar., *Ra.* 324–459; cf. C. Segal, "The Character and Cults of Dionysus and the Unity of the *Frogs*," *HSCP* 65 (1961): 207–42, at 224–25, on the prevalence of *choroi* in the *Frogs*.
66. Ar., *Ra.* 207.
67. Athen. 629f; further references in Barker, 113, n. 56.
68. Anthesteria (Deubner, Nilsson, Simon); first day (Simon); third day (Deubner); Great Dionysia (Burkert).
69. *GF*, 269.
70. Phot., s.v. *ta ek tōn hamaxōn*.
71. Cf. M. Detienne, "Le phoque, le crabe et le forgeron," in *Hommages à*

Marie Delcourt (Brussels, 1971), 219–23, on seals as ambiguous dwellers on land and sea.

72. Cf. Eur., *Ion* 161–66.

73. *IG* II/III² 1368.130.

74. Ar., *Lys.* 757; Schol. Pl., *Tht.* 160e.

75. Philostr., *Her.* 187.9 de Lannoy.

76. Oinochoe (fragmentary), Baltimore; *CVA* Robinson Coll. 3 (Cambridge, Mass., 1938), p. 21, pl. 12, 3.

77. J. R. Green, "Choes of the Later Fifth Century," *ABSA* 66 (1971): 189–228, thinks *choes* of this period were intended for burial. E. M. Stern, "Kinder-Kännchen zum Choenfest," *Castrum Peregrini* 132–33 (1978): 27–37, questions the interpretation that the juglets were made principally for child burials.

78. Dancing is represented on seven *choes* among Van Hoorn's examples: G. Van Hoorn, *Choes and Anthesteria* (Leiden, 1951), nos. 19, 20, 89, 500, 536, 637, 821.

79. S. Karouzou, "Choes," *AJA* 50 (1946): 139, connects the symposia of the *Laws* with the Anthesteria.

80. Oinochoe, Paris, Louvre CA 8; G. Van Hoorn, no. 821, fig. 180; Deubner, pl. 17.2.

81. Athens, NM 1222; G. Van Hoorn, no. 19, cf. Deubner, pl. 31.3.

82. Oinochoe, Berlin 2658, *ARV* 1318; H. Immerwahr, "Choes and Chytroi," *TAPA* 76 (1946): 250, asserts that this and other names for parts of the festival were also given for good luck.

83. Athens NM 14527; Van Hoorn, no. 101, cf. Deubner, pl. 31.2.

84. Oinochoe, Athens NM; cf. Deubner, pl. 33.3.

85. Oinochoe, Copenhagen, National Museum inv. 5377; *Beazley Addenda* 357; Van Hoorn 475; *CVA* Copenhagen, 4, pl. 157, fig. 6a–b.

86. Oinochoe, Athens 1218; *ARV* 1212; Van Hoorn, no. 15; Deubner, pl. 8.3.

87. M. P. Nilsson, "Die Anthesterien und die Aiora," *Eranos* 15 (1915): 181–200, argues that the Aiora was celebrated at Icaria, not Athens; contra: Deubner, p. 119, n. 2; Maria S. Funghi, "Il Mito escatologico del *Fedone* e la forza rituale dell' aiora," *PP* 35 (1980): 176–201.

88. Hyg., *Astron.* 2.4; Apollod. 3.14.7, cf. *Analecta Eratosthenes*, Maass, 70–75.

89. *Analecta Eratosthenes*, Maass, 132–36.

90. Deubner, p. 121.

91. *Analecta Eratosthenes*, Maass, 76–77.

92. *Hom. Hymn to Demeter* 98–99.

93. Plu., *de Is. et Osir.* 357a.

94. *HN*, 242–43.

95. Athen. 618e–619a.

96. Hdt. 2.79.

97. Isa. 24:7–12.
98. Isa. 5:1–17; 1 Sam. 2:1–19; Judg. 21:16–24.
99. Hom., *Il.* 18.567–72.
100. On the metaphorical interpretation of swinging, see Funghi, "Il Mito escatologico del *Fedone* e la forza rituale dell'aiora," 176–201.
101. Skyphos, Berlin 2589; *ARV* 1301, 7; Deubner, pl. 17.1.
102. Oinochoe, Athens, Vlasto Collection; *ARV* 1249, 14; *DFA*, pl. 9.
103. This interpretation was first proposed by J. D. Beazley, cf. *DFA*, p. 11.

Chapter Five. Preparations for Manhood: Zeus, Athena, and the Weapon Dance

1. Studies of the pyrrhic include W. E. D. Downes, "The Offensive Weapon in the Pyrrhic," *CR* 18 (1904): 101–6; K. Latte, *De Saltationibus Graecorum*, *RVV* 13 (Giessen, 1913), 27–63; W. K. Pritchett, *The Greek State at War* (Berkeley, 1974), 2:216; J. E. Harrison, *Themis*, 2d ed. (Cambridge, 1927); J. J. Winkler, "The Ephebes' Song: *Tragôidia and Polis*," *Representations* 1 (1985): 26–62, rev. in *Nothing to Do with Dionysos?* ed. J. Winkler and F. Zeitlin (Princeton, 1990), 20–62; J.-C. Poursat, "Les Représentations de danse armée dans la céramique attique," *BCH* 92 (1968): 550–615; P. Scarpi, "La Pyrriche o le armi della persuasione," *DArch* n.s. 1 (1979): 78–97; G. F. Pinney, "Pallas and Panathenaea," in *Proceedings of the Third Annual Symposium on Ancient Greek and Related Pottery*, ed. J. Christiansen and T. Melander (Copenhagen, 1988), 465–77; E. K. Borthwick, "Trojan Leap and Pyrrhic Dance in Euripides' *Andromache* 1129–41," *JHS* 87 (1967): 18–23; E. K. Borthwick, "P. Oxy. 2738: Athena and the Pyrrhic Dance," *Hermes* 98 (1970): 318–31.
2. The imitative nature of the dance is emphasized by the repetition of the idea in Plato's description (*Laws* 815a): *mimoumenēn, mimēmata, mimeisthai.*
3. Hom., *Il.* 7.237–41.
4. Tyrt., fr. 11W.
5. W. R. Connor, "Early Greek Land Warfare as Symbolic Expression," *P&P* 119 (1988): 3–29.
6. Athen. 628f.
7. Hom., *Il.* 11.379.
8. P. Vidal-Naquet analyzed the origins of the Athenian ephebeia against the background of the Spartan *krypteia* in "Le Chasseur noir et l'origine de l'ephébie athénienne," *Annales* (ESC) 23 (1968): 947–64, the first article in classical studies to apply the structuralist principles of Lévi-Strauss; cf. the revised English version in his *The Black Hunter*, trans. A. Szegedy-Maszak (Baltimore, 1986), 106–28.

9. An oinochoe in Boston, for example, shows two figures, one a dancer with sword in hand, the other an acrobat also carrying a sword. Oinochoe, Boston 25.43, cf. R. Tölle, *Frühgriechische Reigentänze* (Waldsassen Bayern, 1964), 15, no. 11, cf. p. 77; A. Fairbanks, *Museum of Fine Arts, Boston. Catalogue of Greek and Etruscan Vases* (Boston, 1928), no. 269c, pl. 18.
10. Athen. 629c; *prylis* is mentioned by Call. 1.51, 3.240.
11. Schol., Pi., *P.* 2.127.
12. Athen. 631a.
13. Eur., *Andr.* 1114.
14. Eur., *Andr.* 1135; Borthwick, "Trojan Leap," 18–23.
15. The use of the plural at Ar., *Nu.* 988–89 indicates that already by 423, the date of the play, the pyrrhic was a choral competition. On nudity, see K. J. Dover, *Aristophanes' Clouds* (Oxford, 1968), 218, who suggests that we are meant to infer at *Nu.* 988 that lowering the shield before the haunch (989) "deprives [Right] of his favourite sight."
16. The shield is mentioned at Eur., *Andr.* 1131, and Ar., *Nu.* 989; the spear, which is seen in artistic representations, cf. Poursat, "Représentations," 578, may be inferred from *Andr.* 1130.
17. Pl., *Crat.* 406e.
18. Xen., *An.* 6.1.1–13.
19. The fact that the Mysian carries a shield in both hands proves that the dancer did not always carry an offensive weapon. W. E. D. Downes, "The Offensive Weapon in the Pyrrhic," *CR* 18 (1904): 104, uses this example in support of his conclusion that the weapon dance is not primarily an offensive, but rather a defensive maneuver. I would argue that the two-shield variation of the dance indicates how it was possible to emphasize at will the defensive or offensive aspects which were characteristic of the general type.
20. This is probably a reference to the *enoplion*, a choreographic movement suitable for the metrical scheme of the same name. As T. B. L. Webster, *The Greek Chorus* (London, 1970), 193, cf. 62, points out, this passage is the best surviving evidence for the combination of armed dancing and singing.
21. *IG* II² 2311 = *SIG*³ 1055, 72–74. The Panathenaic pyrrhic, however, is much older than the inscription: Aristophanes' allusion to pyrrhic choruses competing at the Great Panathenaea in the *Clouds* can be dated to 423. But the presence of pyrrhic choruses in the Lesser Panathenaea as well allows the possibility that pyrrhic competitions predate the institution of the Great Panathenaea in 566/5; Latte, *De Saltationibus Graecorum*, 32.
22. *SIG*³ 1055, 72–74; W. Wyse, *The Speeches of Isaeus* (Cambridge, 1904), 456.
23. Lys. 21.1, where it is stated that a tragic chorus costs 3,000 drachmas.

24. Lys. 21.4.
25. *IG* II² 3025; Athens, Acropolis Museum 1338.
26. J.-C. Poursat, "Une Base signée du Musée National d'Athènes: Pyrrhicistes victorieux," *BCH* 91 (1967): 109–10, believes that the exuberant action is a variation on the more common practice of winners taking a victory lap around the stadium; he observes that this triumphant gesture is unparalleled in Greek art.
27. Small Akr. Mus. 432; *IGII*² 3026. O. Walter, *Beschreibung der Reliefs im kleinen Akropolismuseum in Athen* (Vienna, 1923), 198–99, nos. 402 and 402a.
28. A. A. Papagiannopoulos, *Polemon* 1 (1929): 227–32.
29. Cf. Xen., *An.* 1.6.12.
30. Poursat, "Représentations," 586–609, nos. 30–54. Sometimes the solo female pyrrhicist wears a dancer's belt and a strap to restrain the breasts.
31. Arist., fr. 519R. Two kantharoi, Paris, Cabinet des Médailles 353, 355; *ABV* 346,7 and 346, 8; Poursat, "Représentations," figs. 6–9; cf. H. A. Shapiro, "The Iconography of Mourning in Athenian Art," *AJA* 95 (1991): 633, n. 28.
32. Cup, Vatican 506, *ARV* 73, 27.
33. Poursat, "Représentations," 578–79, considers these to be representations of the pyrrhic proper, the popular dance in the Panathenaic games. There is a short revival of pyrrhic training dances in black-figure lekythoi around 470–60. Representations of feminine pyrrhicists start appearing c. 440, only after representations of males apparently go out of fashion (c. 460), possibly because the pyrrhic increasingly became known as a choral competition among men. When male pyrrhicists finally reappear in Greek art, they are shown in choruses on dedicatory reliefs of the second half of the fourth century.
34. On a black-figure lekythos in Baltimore the musician, also dressed as a soldier, plays the *salpinx*; Walters 48.226, *ABV* 523, L. B. Lawler, *The Dance in Ancient Greece* (Middletown, Conn., 1964), 109, fig. 41.
35. Poursat, "Représentations," 568–74, nos. 13–15, 23.
36. Pyxis, Naples H 3010, cf. Poursat, "Représentations," 601, no. 51, figs. 54, 55.
37. Downes, "Offensive Weapon," 101–6; L. Ziehen, *Bursian* 172 (1915): 51–54. Poursat, "Représentations," 578, points out that the tendency to confuse pyrrhicists with hoplites participating in the *hoplitodromos* can be avoided by observing that the runners do not carry a spear, only a shield; cf. E. Wheeler, "Hoplomachia and Greek Dances in Arms," *GRBS* 23 (1982): 223–33.
38. Xen., *An.* 6.1.5; cf. Downes, "Offensive Weapon," 101–6.
39. Dancer's spear merely suggested by her gesture: Poursat, "Représentations," 590, no. 37, cf. Downes, "Offensive Weapon," 103–4.

40. Cf. Borthwick, "Trojan Leap," 21; a black-figure example (c. 530) can be seen on a lekythos, cf. J. R. Green, *Antiquities: A Description of the Classics Department Museum in the Australian National University, Canberra* (Canberra, 1981), 31.

41. The corroboration of literary and pictorial evidence indicates that the two patterns depicted in vase painting do not result simply from pictorial conventions or limitations of space and medium. Other postures in vase painting can be seen in Poursat, "Représentations": kneeling position nos. 30 and 46; defensive position in nos. 43, 44.

42. Borthwick, "Athena and the Pyrrhic Dance," 319, believes that ephebes executed the back-turned head movement either in imitation of an exploit of Athena (the aversion of her gaze in slaying the Gorgon, according to some versions of the myth) or in imitation of a "defensive" head movement.

43. R. Osborne, *Arion* 3d ser. 1 (1991): 261, arguing against C. Bérard, *La Cité des images* (Paris, 1984), 87–88.

44. Downes, "Offensive Weapon," 101. The suffix *-ichos* in *pyrrhichos* is "Doric" but found in Attica and Euboea, cf. Latte, *De Saltationibus Graecorum*, 28, who calls *pyrrhichos* a diminutive of *pyrrhos*; so Friske, II 32, s.v. *pyrros* (flame-colored, red). Chantraine, II 959, calls the suffix "expressif." He derives *pyrrhichos* from its putative inventor, one Pyrrhichos, *apud* Aristox. (= Athen. 631c) and Strabo 10.3.8. Others explain the significance of the color by reference to a red uniform; but the dance in the classical period is almost always performed in the nude.

45. Arist., fr. 519R.

46. Lucian, *On the Dance* 9.

47. The Dioscouroi dance on behalf of Athena (Aristid., *Or.* 2, 14). Elsewhere Athena is associated with groups of divine pyrrhicists. The scholiast on Pi., *P.* 2.127 records the legend that Athena was the leader of the Couretes. Another legend has it that Athena first played the *enoplios* on the *aulos* for the Dioscouroi (Epich., fr. 75 and Schol., sc. Thaletas).

48. Pinney, "Pallas and Panathenaea," 471.

49. Pl., *Crat.* 406d–407a.

50. Pl., *Crat.* 406e, cf. *Laws* 796bc.

51. In commenting on the origin of the pyrrhic in cults of Artemis at Ephesos, Strabo (14.1.20) said that the Couretes first danced the pyrrhic around Leto while she was bringing to birth Artemis, so that she would escape the attention and jealousy of Hera.

52. Cf. Pinney, "Pallas and Panathenaea," 468.

53. Archil., fr. 304W; Proclus, *Chrest.* 320–21; Lucian, *On the Dance* 9.

54. Hesychius, s.v. *Pyrros*, recounts the tradition that the pyrrhic foot and the pyrrhic dance were named after Neoptolemos/Pyrrhos because he was the first to leap from the Trojan Horse, *apud* scholia (B) to He-

phaestion 299.1 Consbruch. The famous passage from Aeschylus's *Ag.* 824–26 refers to the Argives' leap from the Trojan Horse, where the epithet *aspidēstrophos* (825; Page emends to *aspidēphoros*) for the Argives may allude to the manipulation of the shield in the pyrrhic dance. Borthwick, "Trojan Leap," 18–23, argues that Neoptolemos's famous Trojan leap to escape the ambush of the Delphians carried a traditional association to the Trojan Horse incident. His argument is strengthened by mention a few lines earlier of Neoptolemos enacting the pyrrhic and its typical movements. P. T. Stevens, *Euripides Andromache* (Oxford, 1971), 231–32, thinks it unlikely that Euripides could have made a connection between Pyrrhos and Neoptolemos. He discounts Pausanias's testimony (10.26.4) that Neoptolemos was called Pyrrhos in the *Cypria*, arguing that the name Pyrrhos is not attested until Theoc. 15.140.

55. In artistic representations of weapon dancers, pyrrhicists rarely confront one another, but a duel between pyrrhicists or two leaders, each representing his team, is depicted on a hydria, New York 21.88.2, *ARV* 34, 14; G. Richter and L. Hall, *Red-figured Athenian Vases in the Metropolitan Museum of Art* (New Haven, Conn., 1936), pl. 11 and pl. 172, 11; Poursat, "Représentations," fig. 16.

56. The former meaning is attested in Aen. Tact. 31.8 and Plb. 1.54.2.

57. On epiphanies in general see L. Pfister, *RE* Suppl. 4 (1924), 277–323, and *KlP* 5 (1975) Nachträge, 1598–1601; on military epiphanies see W. K. Pritchett, *The Greek State at War* (Berkeley, 1979), 3: 11–46, with further bibliography, p. 11.

58. *Lochos* as childbirth: A., *Ag.* 136, *Supp.* 677, cf. *locheos*, Hes., *Th.* 178; see also Chantraine, s.v. *lechetai*; cf. N. Loraux, "Le Lit, la guerre," *L'Homme* 21 (1981): 37–67. The ambiguous meanings can be seen in the case of Zeus's head, the place for hiding (*lochos* as ambush), as well as the womblike area from which he gives birth to Athena (*lochos* as childbirth), who appears in all her glory (epiphany). The Trojan Horse is called a *lochos* in Homer, and Aeschylus calls the crew inside the horse's brood (*hippou neossos*): Hom., *Od.* 4.277; A., *Ag.* 824–26.

59. Hes., *Th.* 471.

60. Hes., *Th.* 482–88.

61. Eur., *Ba.* 120–29.

62. E.g., Call. 1.51–53.

63. Translation (with minor modifications) by T. Drew-Bear and W. D. Lebek, "An Oracle of Apollo at Miletus," *GRBS* 14 (1973): 71.

64. Lucian, *D. Deor.* 13.13–19.

65. P. Rehak, "New Observations on the Mycenaean Warrior Goddess," *AA* (1984): 535–45.

66. E. Kunze, *Kretische Bronzereliefs* (Stuttgart, 1931), pl. 31, cf. K. Schefold, *Frühgriechische Sagenbilder* (Munich, 1964), 67, fig. 21.

67. J. D. Beazley, *The Development of Attic Black-figure*, rev. D. von Bothmer and M. B. Moore (Berkeley, 1986), 22, and pl. 20, 2.

68. Amphora, Basel BS 496; *LIMC* II.1, p. 987, no. 353.

69. Pelike, London, British Museum E 410; *ARV* 494; A. B. Cook, *Zeus*, vol. 3 (Cambridge, 1940), pl. 56.

70. Poursat, "Représentations," 576, no. 26.

71. Apollo and lyre: *LIMC* II.2, s.v. Athena, nos. 350, 367, 368; also on a black-figure amphora attributed to Group E in the Yale University Art Gallery (1983.22); Yale 1983.22; *Beazley Addenda* 36; *Bulletin of the Yale University Art Gallery* 37 (1984): 10, figs. 4–5.

72. Black-figure amphora, Louvre E 861; *Beazley Addenda* 24; The suggestion that Athena's birth was the subject of a hyporcheme was made by P. Ghiron-Bistangue, *Recherches sur les acteurs dans la Grèce antique* (Paris, 1976), 296, cf. 295, figs. 152–53.

73. Hes., *Th.* 174.

74. Hes., *Th.* 175.

75. Hes., *Th.* 174–87.

76. Hes., *Th.* 505.

77. Eur., *Ba.* 89.

78. Eur., *Ba.* 94–95.

79. C. Leclerc, "Le Mythe hésiodique: Entre le silence et les mots," *RHR* 3 (1978): 19, argues for a similarly ambiguous meaning of *lochos* in the word *alochos* used for Metis, the only wife of Zeus to be so designated in the Hesiodic account.

80. A. Evans, *PM* 1:159–60 and fig. 115. For a discussion of dance in Minoan and classical Crete, see P. Warren, "Circular Platforms at Minoan Knossos," *ABSA* 79 (1984): 319–23, cf. R. Hägg, "Die göttliche Epiphanie im minoischen Ritual," *MDAI (A)* 101 (1986): 41–62.

81. A. R. 4.1310.

82. Apollod. 1.3.6.

83. The verb also appears in Apollo's birth narratives: Hom. *Hymn to Apollo* 119; Call. 4.255–57.

84. *Hymn of the Couretes* (*IC* III.2.2.24–30); R. C. Bosanquet, *ABSA* 15 (1908–9): 339–48; cf. M. L. West, "The Dictaean Hymn to the Kouros," *JHS* 85 (1965): 149–51.

85. This can be inferred from the word *molpāi* in verse 36.

86. Transitively *thrōiskō* means to impregnate; the cognate substantives *thoros* and *thorē* mean semen. In many cultures the vigorous movements of dance, as well as of sexual intercourse, have a positive effect on plant growth, and in ancient Greece the idea is expressed by a literary metaphor for the leaping birth of a divinity.

87. Hom., *Il.* 8.261–334.

88. *Orsitēs* is one of the names of the weapon dance on Crete, according to Athen. 629c.

89. Hom., *Il.* 16.617–18; cf. R. Janko, *The Iliad: A Commentary,* vol. 4 (Cambridge, 1992), 389–90.
90. See S. H. Lonsdale, "Protean Forms and Disguise in *Odyssey* 4," *Lexis* 2 (1988): 165–78.
91. Hom., *Od.* 4.395, 408, 437–38 (cf. 441), 449, cf. Hes., *Th.* 174–86.
92. Lucian, *On the Dance* 19.
93. M. Nagler, "Entretiens avec Tirésias," *CW* 74 (1980): 89–109, sees in the episode a myth "concerned with the initiation of the hero into the cult service of the god" at 101.
94. M. H. Jameson, "Perseus, the Hero of Mykenai," in *Celebrations of Death and Divinity in the Bronze Age Argolid,* ed. R. Hägg and G. Nordquist (Stockholm, 1990), 213–23.
95. Hom., *Od.* 4.670, 847.
96. Eur., *Andr.* 1114, 1135.
97. Eur., *Andr.* 1064.
98. Pritchett, *The Greek State at War,* 2:177–79.
99. Eur., *Andr.* 1113–16.
100. Lucian, *On the Dance* 9.
101. Scholia (B) to Heph. 299.1 Consbruch; Hom., *Od.* 4.277.
102. Cf. the name of Orestes (from *oros,* "mountain"), mountainous areas being one of the locales to which ephebic candidates are sequestered.
103. P. Vidal-Naquet, "The Black Hunter Revisited," *PCPS* 32 (1986): 126–44, at 136, wrote without developing the suggestion that "the pyrrhic could be described as the equivalent, in dance, of the oath of the ephebes."
104. Cf. J. W. Fitton, "Greek Dance," *CQ* n.s. 23 (1973): 256, "In neither of its two functions—initiation or the securing of fertility—is there any intrinsic connection with the war-dance." J. E. Harrison, *Themis, A Study of the Social Origins of Greek Religion,* 2d ed. (1927), 24, observed that initiation dances taught to boys are frequently armed dances. Latte, *De Saltationibus Graecorum,* 54, rejected Harrison's initiatory interpretation of the dance of the Couretes. Winkler, "The Ephebes' Song: *Tragôidia and Polis,*" 20–62, has suggested in connection with his radical theory on the origin of Greek tragedy that the precision, stamina, and sense of ensemble required of ephebes engaged in military dances uniquely qualified them to perform the virtuoso dancing of Greek tragedy. Although ephebes performed the pyrrhic, Winkler's theory is complicated by trying to make the ephebes the personnel for the dramatic choruses. Winkler's main source, the Pronomos vase, is problematic since it represents the cast of a satyr-play from about 400.
105. The initiatory aspects of the *Hymn* and related material form the basis of *Themis,* Jane Ellen Harrison's landmark study of the social origins of Greek religion that appeared first in 1912 and later in a revised edition in 1927. Harrison interpreted references to armed dancing in

the hymn as evidence for an initiatory rite. Harrison returned to the Hymn of the Couretes in *Epilegomena to the Study of Greek Religion*. In that work she saw the initiatory dance not as an "entering in" but as a "completion or fulfillment" (sc. *teletē*, cf. *teleios* "grown up") that culminated in the mystic marriage of the initiate with the Great Mother. Harrison, *Epilegomena*, xxxii.

106. Ephorus, *apud* Strabo 10.4.16.
107. Pl., *Laws* 796bc.
108. *FGrHist* 2.284.
109. Arist., *Ath. Pol.* 42.
110. For the ephebic inscriptions see C. Pélékidis, *Histoire de l'éphébie attique* (Paris, 1962), 109–10. As for the question of whether the *lochos* group performed as a *choros* group on other festival occasions, by "other festival occasions" I do not include, as does Winkler ("The Ephebes' Song"), performances in dramatic choruses.
111. Although the ephebeia is not attested before the fourth century, the black-ground lekythoi with representations of individual pyrrhicists were perhaps presented to cadets upon completing the dance that would at some point qualify the recipient to receive or bear arms.
112. G. Daux, "Le Serment des éphèbes athéniens," *REG* 84 (1971): 370–83; M. N. Tod, *A Selection of Greek Historical Inscriptions* (Oxford, 1948), II, no. 204, pp. 303–307; cf. R. Merkelbach, "Aglauros," *ZPE* 9 (1972): 277–83. The date of the Ephebic Oath is c. 350, although the antiquity of the formal ephebic system is disputed. P. Siewert, "The Ephebic Oath in Fifth-Century Athens," *JHS* 97 (1977): 102–11, and others see archaic antecedents to the oath.
113. Poll. 4.106, cf. Hagesichora in Alcman, fr. 3 *PMG*. Paus. 9.35.1 mentions Hegemone and Auxo as names of the age-old cult of Charites at Athens.
114. Poll. 4.108–9.
115. The date of the hymn is probably fourth century; cf. West, "Dictaean Hymn," 151; U. v. Wilamowitz, *Griech. Verskunst* (Berlin, 1921), 502, dated it to the fifth century.
116. P. J. Perlman, "Word into Deed: Oath and Myth in Ancient Crete," paper, *American Philological Association* meeting, San Francisco, 1990.
117. Cf. J.-P. Vernant, *La Mort dans les yeux* (Paris, 1985), 23. In Sparta, Artemis Hegemone had a sanctuary at the same place as Apollo Karneios, near the *dromos*, the race course for *neoi* (Paus. 3.14.6); the Karneia was a festival that concerned young soldiers.
118. Hom., *Il.* 4.130–33.
119. A., *Eum.* 293–95; noted by E. K. Borthwick, "Two Notes on Athena as Protectress," *Hermes* 97 (1969): 385.
120. Eur., *IT* 1097, *Suppl.* 958, *SIG*³ 1219.33.
121. Athen. 631a.

Chapter Six. *Rehearsals for Womanhood:*
Dance and Ritual Play in Female Transition Rites

1. J. S. La Fontaine, *Initiation* (Manchester, 1985), 163.
2. A. I. Richards, *Chisungu* (London, 1956). See also B. Lincoln, *Emerging from the Chrysalis: Studies in Rituals of Women's Initiation* (Cambridge, Mass., 1980); K. Dowden, *Death and the Maiden: Girls' Initiation Rites in Greek Mythology* (London, 1989).
3. M. H. Jameson, "Perseus, the Hero of Mykenai," in *Celebrations of Death and Divinity in the Bronze Age Argolid*, ed. R. Hägg and G. Nordquist (Stockholm, 1990), 213–23.
4. Cf. S. H. Lonsdale, *Animals and the Origins of Dance* (London, 1981), 39–40.
5. E.g., Charisios in Menander's *Epit.* 451 abducted his future wife Pamphile during the Tauropolia, an all-night festival of Artemis celebrated at Halai Araphenides along the eastern coast of Attica.
6. Calame, 1:34–35.
7. The sanctuary of Artemis Epipyrgidia on the Acropolis may have been in existence in the Bronze Age. E. Simon, *Festivals of Attica* (Madison, Wisc., 1983), 83.
8. Pyxis, Brauron A3; L. Kahil, "Quelques vases du sanctuaire d'Artémis à Brauron," *AK* Beih. 1 (1963): pl. I, 4.
9. Fragment of a red-figure amphora, Brauron Mus. 526; L. Kahil, "Mythological Repertoire at Brauron," in *Ancient Greek Art and Iconography*, ed. W. Moon (Madison, Wisc., 1983), 239, fig. 15.11.
10. Eur., *IT* 1456–67.
11. Cf. Ar., *Pax* 872–76; H. Lloyd-Jones, "Artemis and Iphigeneia," *JHS* 103 (1983): 92, argues that by analogy with other rites the Arkteia originally occurred on an annual basis.
12. Cf. Suda, s.v. *arktos.*
13. Pierre Brulé, *La Fille d'Athènes* (Paris, 1987), 244–49.
14. For a dissenting view, see R. Hamilton, "Alkman and the Athenian Arkteia," *Hesperia* 58 (1989): 449–72.
15. L. Kahil, "L'Artémis de Brauron: Rites et mystère," *AK* 20 (1977): 86–98.
16. I. Kontis, "Artemis Brauronia," *Deltion* 22A (1967): 156–206; M. B. B. Hollinshead, *Legend, Cult, and Architecture at Three Sanctuaries of Artemis* (Ph.D. diss., Bryn Mawr, 1979); L. Kahil, "La Déesse Artémis: Mythologie et iconographie," in *Greece and Italy in the Classical World* (London, 1979), 80.
17. Kahil, "Mythological Repertoire of Brauron," 238, believes that the *mystērion* is represented on the so-called red-figure krateriskos III.
18. C. Sourvinou-Inwood, *Studies in Girls' Transitions* (Athens, 1988), 15–20. P. Perlman, "Plato *Laws* 883c–884d and the Bears of Brauron,"

GRBS 24 (1983): 115–30, based on Plato's division of girls into two groups (seven to twelve, thirteen to twenty) also divides them into two groups, but believes that the "bears" are between ages ten to fifteen.

19. Sourvinou-Inwood, *Studies*, 60–61.
20. Lloyd-Jones, "Artemis and Iphigeneia," 87–102.
21. Pl., *Laws* 796cd.
22. Plu., *Mulier. Virt.* 254a (Miletos). On the freedom and seclusion of Athenian women, see R. Just, *Women in Athenian Law and Life* (London, 1989), 105–25.
23. Pl., *Laws* 771d–772a.
24. Hellanicus of Lesbos, *apud* Plu., *Thes.* 31.
25. Hdt. 6.138.
26. Ar., *Lys.* 638–47; following the Oxford Classical Text reading *kai cheousa* at 644/5 adopted by Jeffrey Henderson, *Aristophanes' Lysistrata* (Oxford, 1987) *ad loc.*
27. A. Brelich, *Paides e parthenoi* (Rome, 1969), 237–41, views the rituals as reflecting an age-grade system at Athens. P. Vidal-Naquet, in *Myth, Religion, and Society*, ed. R. L. Gordon (Cambridge, 1981), 179, calls the stages a "pseudo-cycle."
28. The chorus dance, e.g., at Ar., *Lys.* 319–40, 541–42. For a recent discussion of the evidence for females attending the theater see Just, *Women in Athenian Law and Life*, 109–11.
29. The reading was proposed by T. Stinton, *CQ* 69 (1976): 11–13. For the dramatic convention see Ar., *Ach.* 626–27; *Ve.* 408–9; *Th.* 656, *Pax* 730, cf. G. M. Sifakis, *Parabasis and Animal Choruses* (London, 1971), 103–6.
30. A., *Ag.* 239.
31. The story of the intervention of Artemis is told in the *Cypria*, and was followed by Euripides in *IT* 28–30.
32. Phanod., *FGrHist* 325 F 14.
33. *Aristophanes' Lysistrata*, ed. J. Henderson (Oxford, 1987), 156–57.
34. Unlike the Arkteia, which may have been intended for any Athenian girl, the privileges of carrying the robe for Athena (Arrhephoros) and the basket (Kanephoros) were restricted to a few girls specially chosen from among the high-born (*eugeneis*). (About the office of "meal-grinder" we know nothing beyond the present passage.)
35. Ar., *Lys.* 640; cf. Eur., *Ion*, 26, *Rh.* 960; A., *Supp.* 1003; Soph., *El.* 52.
36. Dated 400 by Contoléon; P. A. Hansen, *Carmina Epigraphica Graeca* (Berlin, 1983), vol. 1, no. 168.
37. This and the other Aristophanic scholia, as well as other ancient commentaries on the Arkteia, are conveniently collected by W. Sale, "The Temple-Legends of the Arkteia," *RhM* 118 (1975): 265–84.
38. The question whether all Athenian girls or only selected maidens participated in playing the bear at Brauron remains unresolved. Schol.

Leid. Lys. 645 mentions selected maidens (*epilegomenai arktoi*) at Brauron and Mounychia; other scholia say all.

39. L2 and R1 in Sale, *"Temple-Legends,"* 266–67.
40. Calame, 1:189–90.
41. Pl., *Phdr.* 265c; *Epin.* 980b.
42. On the symbolism of ritual wounding, see B. Bettelheim, *Symbolic Wounds* (London, 1955).
43. In the Arkteia the sacrificial animal is normally a goat, not a bear. Brulé, *La Fille d'Athènes*, 195, observes "la substitution d'une chèvre à l'ours s'impose pour des raisons d'ordre pratique: on n'encourt pas le risque de capturer, d'amener et d'immoler un ours véritable."
44. K. Meuli, "Griechische Opferbräuche," in *Phyllobolia für P. von de Mühl* (Basel, 1946), 185–288, at 244–58 (= *Gesammelte Schriften* [Basel, 1975], 2: 907–1021.
45. J. P. Vernant and P. Vidal-Naquet, *Mythe et tragédie en Grèce ancienne* (Paris, 1986), 2:34–36.
46. Cf. L. Bodson, *Hiera Zoia* (Brussels, 1975), 142.
47. Hom., *Il.* 21.470.
48. E. Bevan, "The Goddess Artemis, and the Dedications of Bears in Sanctuaries," *ABSA* 82 (1987): 17–33.
49. Apollod. 3.9.2.
50. Hom., *Od.* 6.102–6, cf. *Hom. Hymn to Artemis* 13–18.
51. J. J. Bachofen, *Der Bär in den Religionen des Altertums* (Basel, 1863), 4–5.
52. Aristot., *HA* 579a18–30; elsewhere bears are discussed at 594b5–16, 600a31–b13, 611b32.
53. S. Thompson, *Motif-Index of Folk-Literature*, 6 vols. (Bloomington, 1966), marriage of woman to a bear: B601.1, cf. 611.1, 631, 635.1.
54. Ibid., B601.1.1; R45.3.1.
55. Eratosth, *Cat.*, 52–53 Robert.
56. Here the meaning of the compound verb has much in common with the English word "to kid."
57. Indeed the verb *prospaizō* is found in Ael., *NA* 4.45, with the word *arktos* meaning "to tantalize the bear."
58. In Jul., *Caes.* 315, the word is used in the sense of lewd sexual acts. J.-P. Vernant, *Mortals and Immortals*, ed. F. Zeitlin (Princeton, 1991), 218, notes that the verb *aselgainō* appears in a passage in the *Republic* (424d–e) on the play of children: "It is under cover of play, or amusement, that a disdain for the law creeps in, which is reinforced little by little, so that finally, with the last insolence [*aselgeia*] there is nothing left. Thus from the beginning, children's games must be subjected to a rigorous discipline."
59. Recorded in the *aition* for the Arkteia in the Leyden and Ravenna scholia: (L2 and R1) in Sale, *"Temple-Legends,"* 266–67.

60. Pl., *Criti.* 113d.
61. On the story and its distribution in antiquity see L. Ghali-Kahil, *Les Enlèvements et le retour d'Hélène* (Paris, 1955), 305–13.
62. Hdt. 9.73.2, cf. ibid., 307.
63. Hdt. 6.138.
64. W. W. How and J. A. Wells, *Commentary on Herodotus* (Oxford, 1928), *ad loc.*
65. S. Papaspyride-Karouzou, "*Hē typhlē arktos*," *ArchEph* (1957): 68–83, plates 18–21, interprets the statues as representing an *arktos* who happens to be blind. Several unpublished statues from Brauron represent blind *arktoi*, perhaps intended as dedications to commemorate the legend.
66. Athens, Acropolis Museum 3737, cf. Kahil, "L'Artémis," 94, pl. 21, 6–7.
67. A. D. Trendall, "Callisto in Apulian Vase-Painting," *AK* 20 (1977): 99–101, pl. 22.
68. R. Hamilton, *Choes and Anthesteria* (Ann Arbor, Mich., 1992), 127.
69. Kahil, "Quelques vases," 5–29; Kahil, "Autour de l'Artémis Attique," *AK* 8 (1965): 20–33; Kahil, "L'Artémis de Brauron," 86–98; Kahil, "Le 'Cratérisque' d'Artémis et le Brauronion de l'Acropole," *Hesperia* 50 (1981): 253–63; Kahil, "Mythological Repertoire of Brauron," 231–44.
70. As Kahil, "Mythological Repertoire of Brauron," 237, points out, krateriskoi have also been found at Halai, Mounychia in the Piraeus, Artemis Aristoboule near the Agora, as well as at the shrine of Pan and the Nymphs in the agora near Eleusis.
71. H. A. Shapiro, *Art and Cult under the Tyrants in Athens* (Mainz, 1989), 65.
72. J. Papadimitriou, *PAAH* 1955 [1960]: 118–20; 1956 [1961]: 73–87; 1957 [1962]: 42–47; 1959 [1965]: 18–20; *AK* 3 (1960): 95.
73. A large number of vases from Mounychia has more recently been published by L. Palaiokrassa, *To hiero tēs Artemidos Mounichias* (Ph.D. Diss., University of Thessaloniki, 1983).
74. Sourvinou-Inwood, *Studies*, 21–30.
75. Hamilton, "Alkman and the Athenian Arkteia," 449–72, in a catalogue of thirty-two fragments identifies (sometimes following the interpretation of Palaiokrassa) numbers 8, 10, 11, 12, 16, 21, 22, 25, 26, 27, and 30 as dancing.
76. *Krotala* in ibid., nos. 18, 25; linked hands in 30.
77. Dress puffed out: ibid., nos. 4, 21; outstretched hands: no. 12; high step: nos. 12, 16.
78. Pi., fr. 70b.9–10SM; Hesychius defines *rhombos* as a noise of one thing striking against another (*psophos*).
79. Hamilton, "Alkman," no. 18. The other example (no. 25) is too fragmentary to ascertain the status of the holder.
80. Analysis of fragments on which dance is depicted indicates that older

"supervising" women, on the one hand, and the younger clothed group both dance.

81. Simon, *Festivals of Attica*, 87–88, sees in this fragment a representation of Callisto and Arkas; cf. Hamilton, "Alkman," 462–63, who accepts Simon's interpretation. Hamilton believes that the distinct iconography, size, fabric, and quality of this krateriskos fragment should be grounds to exclude it from a discussion of the Brauron ritual. His objection that "there is no testimony that anyone was transformed at the Brauronia" reveals too literal an interpretation of "transformation."

82. Fragments of a red-figure krateriskos, Basel, Private Coll. Kahil, "Quelques vases," 5–29; Kahil, "Autour de l'Artémis Attique," 20–33; Kahil, "L'Artémis de Brauron," 86–98; figs. A–C, 3–8, plates 18–20.

83. *Hypothesis* to Dem. 25. G. F. Pinney, in a forthcoming work (Chicago, 1994), questions that the mystery itself would be revealed, even on vases intended for Artemis's sanctuary and suggests that the fragments represent some aspect of the foundation legend.

84. Hamilton, "Alkman," 463, believes that she is looking back at the other contestants.

85. The female figure wearing the bear mask has been identified by Kahil, "Mythological Repertoire of Brauron," 238, as the priestess of Artemis at Brauron impersonating Iphigeneia. She tentatively identifies the male figure as a young priest.

86. Cf. D. A. Napier, *Masks, Transformations, and Paradox* (Berkeley, 1986), 89–90.

87. Black-figure krateriskos, Acr. 621a; Kahil, "Le 'Cratérisque,'" pl. 62.1.

88. Black-figure krateriskos, Agora P 27342.

89. Perhaps we are meant to see in the deer a metaphorical equivalent for the younger age group discerned by Sourvinou-Inwood, *Studies*.

90. Hom., *Il.* 18.319. On deer and other animals as figures of flight in the epic simile see S. H. Lonsdale, *Creatures of Speech: Lion, Herding, and Hunting Similes in the Iliad* (Stuttgart, 1990), 36–38.

91. Cf. Hamilton, "Alkman," p. 471.

92. Hes., fr. 163MW.

93. Eur., *IT* 1142–51; translation by Barker, 79.

94. The overlap between Artemis and Aphrodite is reflected in the divine prototype of choral dancing in Apollo's *Hymn* in which Artemis is the *chorēgos* for the choir made up of various female divinities, including Aphrodite: Hom. *Hymn to Apollo* 195–99.

95. P. Oxy. 2506, fr. 1, col. ii = *PMG* 10a.

96. Alcman, fr. 3 *PMG* 3, trans. (with modifications) D. A. Campbell, *Greek Lyric* (Cambridge, 1988), 2:378–81.

97. The actual location of the performance alluded to in the poem is impossible to ascertain, though the most likely place is the Sanctuary of Orthia at Sparta, where ceramic votive masks (perhaps used in conjunc-

tion with male status transitions and related dance rituals) have been found; cf. Jane B. Carter, "Masks and Poetry in Early Sparta," in *Early Greek Cult Practice*, ed. R. Hägg et al. (Stockholm, 1988), 89–98.

98. Hom., *Od.* 8.260 (*agōn* = *choros*); cf. Jacqueline Duchemin, *L'Agōn dans la tragédie grecque* (Paris, 1945), 12.

99. Hom., *Od.* 8.250–53.

100. Alcman, fr. 1 *PMG passim*; cf. Hagesidamos, who is explicitly equated with the *chorēgos* in *PMG* 10a.30–37.

101. Alcman, fr. 1 *PMG*.

102. A. P. Burnett, "The Race with the Pleiades," *CP* 59 (1964): 30–34; D. L. Page, *Alcman, the Partheneion* (Oxford, 1951); C. Segal, "Alcman," in *Cambridge History of Classical Literature*, ed. P. E. Easterling and B. M. W. Knox (Cambridge, 1985), 1:168–77.

103. A. Griffiths, "Alcman's *Partheneion*: The Morning After the Night Before," *QUCC* 14 (1972): 7–30.

104. B. Gentili, "Il *Partenio* di Alcmane e l'amore omoerotico femminile nei tiasi spartani," *QUCC* 22 (1976): 59–67; Calame, 2:86–97.

105. Carter, "Masks and Poetry in Early Sparta," 89–98.

106. Page, *Alcman, the Partheneion*, 74.

107. Schol. Soph. *OC* 701.

108. Alcman, fr. 1.16–21 *PMG*; trans. (modified) Campbell, *Greek Lyric*, 2:363.

109. Alcman, fr. 1.16–19 *PMG*; 40–101 *PMG*. Trans. (modified) Campbell, *Greek Lyric*, 2:365–69.

110. In other versions of the local myth about the descendants of Hippocoon, Heracles plays an influential role in restoring the throne to the exiled Tyndareus. Apollod. 2.7.3; Diod. 4.33.5; Paus. 3.15.4.

111. Segal, "Alcman," 171.

112. The Charites as attendants of Aphrodite: *Cypria, apud* Athen. 682de; sharing the choir with Aphrodite: *Od.* 18.194.

113. Pi., *O.* 14.8.

114. *Ianoglepharos*, Alcman, fr. 1.69 *PMG*; *potiglepoi*, 75.

115. *Hom. Hymn to Apollo* 197–99.

116. Alcman, fr. 1.44–49 *PMG*; trans. Campbell, 2:365.

117. Hom., *Il.* 2.483; noted by Calame, 2:68.

118. P. Vidal-Naquet, "Les jeunes . . . ," in *Faire de l'histoire*, ed. J. Le Goff et al. (Paris, 1974), 3:160.

119. Pi., fr. 112SM.

120. Cf. Anacreon 360.4 *PMG*, where the *erastēs* speaking to the *erōmenos* says, "You are the chariot driver of my soul" (*tēs emēs/psychēs hēniocheueis*).

121. Cf. Calame, 2:79.

122. Others, following Sosiphanes, interpret *pharos* as a plough. For a discussion of the astronomical interpretations of Sirius (the strongest

star) and the Pleiades (a faint constellation) see G. Gianotti, *RFIC* 106 (1978): 257–71.

123. The theory of two rival choruses (one designated by *peleiades*) was proposed as early as 1868 by H. Ahrens, *Philol.* 27 (1868): 577–629 (esp. 611–13), and was strongly endorsed by Page.

124. Proposed by Burnett, "The Race with the Pleiades," 30–34.

125. The rising upward conveyed by this image is reinforced by the horse imagery if the reading "winged dreams" at 49 (*hypopetridiōn* versus *hypopetrōn*, "rock-sheltered") is adopted.

126. Pi., *I.* 7.44–47.

127. A.P. 7.19.

128. The metaphor of domestication in preliminary rites of marriage is found in many cultures; it is widespread in fifth-century Athenian drama; see, e.g., R. Seaford, "The Eleventh Ode of Bacchylides," *JHS* 108 (1988): 119, 123.

129. Pl., *Laws* 815d.

Chapter Seven. Dance in Courtship and Marriage

1. Hom., *Od.* 6.1–24, 6.64–65.

2. Hom., *Il.* 18.490–96, 590–604; *Od.* 4.17–19: when Telemachos arrives at the Spartan court the palace is jointly celebrating the weddings of Megapenthes and Hermione with song and dance. Cf. L. Gernet, "Ancient Feasts," in *The Anthropology of Ancient Greece*, trans. J. Hamilton and B. Nagy (Baltimore, 1981), 23.

3. Hom., *Od.* 6.99–109.

4. *Hom. Hymn to Apollo* 197–99.

5. Hom., *Od.* 6.149–52.

6. Hom., *Od.* 6.158–59.

7. Cf. W. R. Connor, "Tribes, Festivals and Processions in Archaic Greece," *JHS* 107 (1987): 43–45.

8. Xen. of Ephesus, 1.2.2–7; trans. M. Hadas.

9. See G. Hoffmann, *La Jeune fille, le pouvoir et la mort* (Paris, 1992). Iconography offers striking analogies to literary portraits. See, for example, C. Reinsberg, *Ehe, Hetärentum und Knabenliebe im antiken Griechenland* (Munich, 1989).

10. Pl., *Laws* 771e–772a.

11. Hom., *Il.* 18.590–606; trans. Barker, 23–24. Nineteenth-century philologists rejected these lines as spurious largely on linguistic grounds (e.g., the unparalleled use of *poikille* [decorated] as a verb), and they are bracketed in the 1908 Teubner edition of Ameis and Hentze.

12. The emphasis on the hair of Ariadne and the crowns of the dancers may be an allusion to the ritual importance of what is on the head of

the dancer; according to Calame, 2:112, loose hair (as opposed to hair bound in a mitre) connotes an unmarried woman. In Minoan art attention is drawn to the hair and headdresses of female dancers, e.g., the flying tresses of the woman in the Queen's Megaron Fresco; see A. Evans, *PM* 3: 70–71 and pl. XXV (bottom).

13. Lucian, *On the Dance* 12–13.
14. Hom., *Il.* 18.492–96; trans. Barker, 22.
15. Ps.-Hes., *Aspis* 270–85; trans. Barker, 36–37.
16. Pi., fr. 128cSM.
17. Lebes, London, British Museum GR 1899.2–19; G. Neumann, *Gesten und Gebärden in der griechischen Kunst* (Berlin, 1965), 19, fig. 6.
18. Cup by Euphronios, Athens, Acr. 176; *ARV* 17, 18; *Art Bull.* 21 (1939): 266, fig. 7.
19. I. Jenkins, "Is There Life after Marriage? A Study of the Abduction Motif in Vase Painting of the Athenian Wedding Ceremony," *BICS* 30 (1983): 139; cf. Neumann, *Gesten und Gebärden,* 59.
20. Hom., *Il.* 18.594.
21. Black-figure lekythos (shoulder type), New York 56.11.1; *Beazley Addenda* 45; D. von Bothmer, *The Amasis Painter and His World* (Malibu, Calif., 1985), 183, cat. no. 47.
22. On the Crowe corselet one female leads another with the hand on the wrist; H. Hoffmann, *Early Cretan Armorers* (Cambridge, Mass., 1972), pl. 25 a–c. I owe this reference to G. F. Pinney and am much indebted to her for discussing the Amasis lekythoi.
23. Black-figure lekythos (shoulder type); New York 31.11.10, *ABV* 154, 57; von Bothmer, *Amasis Painter,* 187, cat. no. 48.
24. S. Karouzou, *The Amasis Painter* (Oxford, 1956), 44.
25. If a goddess is intended in the throne she will not be Athena but Artemis or Hera, both of whom oversee weddings.
26. Paus. 5.16.
27. Van Groningen, in his commentary on Hdt. 6.126, observes that the verb describing Cleisthenes' efforts to find the best suitor (*exeuriskō*) is used of determining the winner of an athletic competition.
28. Pl., *Laws* 652a, 671e.
29. Hdt. 6.129.
30. J. J. Winkler, "Women in Armor; Men in Drag: The Poetics of Manhood in Athenian Drama," *Stanford Humanities Review* 1 (1989): 6–24, at 7, believes that Hippocleides' disastrous performance was not the result of drunkenness but rather a miscalculation of what would best display his manliness "in a forum that was both competitive and festive."
31. A. B. Cook, *CR* 21 (1907): 169, thought this a Theban Dionysiac or Kabeiric dance.
32. Xen., *Sym.* 2.19.
33. Pl., *Laws* 772a.

34. Ath. 628c, trans. Barker, 287.
35. Cf. Pl., *Laws* 774e, where the right of granting betrothal is said to belong first to the father, next to the grandfather, and third to the brothers of the bride.
36. The theme is discussed by Calame, 1:176–77, 189–90. Although the myth is known mainly from literary sources, in Attic vase painting a dance motif may be alluded to in scenes of Peleus's rape of Thetis, according to an interpretation that sees the response of the Nereids accompanying the goddess as dance and not flight, cf. J. Barringer, "Thetis, Nereids, and Dionysos," *AIA Abstracts* 14 (1990): 53. In an iconographic analysis C. Sourvinou-Inwood, "Erotic Pursuits: Images and Meanings," *JHS* 107 (1987): 131–53, at 144–45, interprets the theme of girls abducted from choruses of girls dedicated to Artemis as a metaphor for marriage in which the girl is wrenched from a familiar and protected world.
37. *Hom. Hymn to Demeter* 417–24.
38. Paus. 4.16.9.
39. Cf. Men., *Epit.* 451, where a girl is abducted from the Tauropolia.
40. Hes., *Op.* 163–65.
41. Marriage by abduction was an alternative to a formal marriage in certain parts of the ancient classical world, and "bride theft" survives today in parts of Crete and the Aegean and the Balkans. J. Evans Grubbs, "Abduction Marriage in Antiquity: A Law of Constantine (*CTh* IX.24.1) and Its Social Context," *JRS* 79 (1989): 59–83. For a treatment of a modern example see M. Herzfeld, "Gender Pragmatics: Agency, Speech and Bride-Theft in a Cretan Mountain Village," *Anthropology* 9 (1985): 25–44. P. Cartledge, "Spartan Wives," *CQ* 31 (1981): 100, points out the lack of evidence for this phenomenon in Sparta. Others have seen in the myth a reference to a mock abduction, a ritual occurring before modern weddings in Greece. See C. Sourvinou-Inwood, "The Young Abductor in the Locrian Pinakes," *BICS* 20 (1973): 12–21.
42. Hom., *Il.* 16.179–92.
43. Poll. 4.106.
44. Cf. Jenkins, "A Study of the Abduction Motif," 139, pl. 18a.
45. *Hom. Hymn to Hermes* 69–86.
46. Briefly discussed by K. Reinhardt, *Festschrift B. Snell* (Munich, 1956), 11.
47. *Hom. Hymn to Aphrodite* 117–25.
48. E.g., Hom., *Il.* 17.62.
49. Hom., *Od.* 6.127–36.
50. Pl., *Laws* 771e.
51. Paus. 4.16.9.
52. Although there is no overt reference to wedding in the narrative, there

are echoes of marriage ritual in the motif of leading; also Aristomenes' main interest, to return the girls as virgins for ransom, resembles a father's concern to surrender the daughter in exchange for dowry. It is probable that the prototype of the tale is the motif of the abduction from the dancing ground. Pausanias's source is the fifth-century epic *Messenika* by the Cretan poet Rianos.

53. Hom., *Od.* 6.127–36. The lair of a lion elsewhere in the *Odyssey* (4.335) is called a *xulochos*.

54. The examples are discussed by Sourvinou-Inwood, "Young Abductor," 16.

55. Paus. 6.22.9.

56. P. Chantraine, *Études sur le vocabulaire grec* (Paris, 1956), 31–33, on the verb *agō* and its appearance in compounds (88–92). The verb is used of leading something alive, such as cattle, slaves, soldiers.

57. Pi., fr. 112SM., *apud* Ath. 14.631c.

58. Pi., fr. 70bSM.22–23.

59. Jane K. Cowan, *Dance and the Body Politic in Northern Greece* (Princeton, 1990).

60. Ibid., 194, 190.

61. *A.P.* 6.280.

Chapter Eight. The Dance of Death: Privileges of the Dead

1. M. Alexiou, *The Ritual Lament in Greek Tradition* (Cambridge, 1974); J. Redfield, "Notes on the Greek Wedding," *Arethusa* 15 (1982): 188–89; R. Seaford, "The Tragic Wedding," *JHS* 107 (1987): 106–30; R. Garland, *The Greek Way of Death* (Ithaca, N.Y., 1985), 72–74.

2. Law code from Delphi in F. Sokolowski, *Lois sacrées des cités grecques* (Paris, 1969), no. 77; from Iulis in Sokolowski, no. 97; cf. R. Garland, "The Well-ordered Corpse: An Investigation into the Motives Behind Greek Funerary Legislation," *BICS* 36 (1989): 1–15.

3. Garland, "Well-ordered Corpse," 7.

4. Pl., *Laws* 653d.

5. Pl., *Laws* 947bd.

6. Barker, 20, n. 4, lists passages in epic, lyric, and tragic poetry that demonstrate the similarity in the relation between leader and chorus.

7. Hdt. 2.79.

8. Hom., *Il.* 18.567–72; trans. Barker, 23.

9. *Parthenikai de kai ēitheoi*, cf. *ēitheoi men kai parthenoi*, Hom., *Il.* 18.567, 593; cf. Judges 21:2, perhaps a mating dance associated with the grape harvest.

10. Hes., fr. 305 MW. Linus is the son of Apollo, exposed by Psamathe, an

Argive princess, and devoured by dogs (Paus. 1.43.7–8); another variant casts Linus as Heracles' music teacher whom the hero brained with a *kithara* (Apollod. 2.4.9).

11. Pi., fr. 128c.7–9SM.
12. M. Alexiou and P. Dronke, *Studi Medievali* 12 (1971): 830–37.
13. Alexiou, *The Ritual Lament in Greek Tradition*, 120–22; in a modern Greek context, see S. Auerbach, "From Singing to Lamenting: Women's Musical Role in a Greek Village," in *Women and Music in Cross-cultural Perspective*, ed. E. Koskoff (New York, 1987), 25–44.
14. Eur., *Her.* 348–51. A similar blending of joy and sorrow occurs in the first choral ode of A., *Ag.* 121, where the chorus sings "*ailinon, ailinon* but may the good triumph."
15. L. Gernet, "You-you en marge d'Hérodote," In *Les Grecs sans miracles* (Paris, 1983), 247–57.
16. Soph., *El.* 750 (reading *anōlolyxe*); Eur., *Med.* 1172–75.
17. A., *Ag.* 25, 587, 595; Eur., *Or.* 1137.
18. Thuc. 2.4.2.
19. *Hom. Hymn to Apollo* 119; Paus. 9.11.3.
20. Gernet, *Les Grecs sans miracles*, 252.
21. Pi., *P.* 12.18–22; *Hom. Hymn to Hermes* 24–54.
22. W. Burkert, "Katagógia-Anagógia and the Goddess of Knossos," in *Early Greek Cult Practice*, ed. R. Hägg et al. (Stockholm, 1988), 81–88.
23. *GR*, 164.
24. Athen. 139df.
25. Death dances among the Lugbara are discussed by John Middleton, "The Dance Among the Lugbara of Uganda," in Spencer, 167–70.
26. Pl., *Laws* 800de.
27. Pl., *Laws* 814e.
28. Hom., *Il.* 22.460.
29. A., *Supp.* 69–72; trans. Barker, 63–64.
30. A., *Choe.* 23–30.
31. A., *Choe.* 423–38; trans. Barker, 65.
32. Eur., *HF* 1027, cf. *Supp.* 75.
33. Eur., *Tr.* 115–21; trans. Barker, 70.
34. Eur., *Ba.* 569–70.
35. Eur., *Tr.* 146–52; trans. Barker, 68–69.
36. Hom., *Il.* 18.37; cf. M. Edwards, *The Iliad: A Commentary* (Cambridge, 1991), 5:15–19, 141.
37. H. A. Shapiro, "The Iconography of Mourning in Athenian Art," *AJA* 95 (1991): 629–56.
38. E.g., Athens, N.M. C. C. 1167; W. Zschietzschmann, "Die Darstellungen der Prothesis in der griechischen Kunst," *AM* 53 (1928): pl. XVII.
39. The exact relationship of the mourners to the deceased can be seen on

a pinax in Paris, Louvre MNB 905 [L4], Zschietzschmann no. 37, Beil. XI, in which all of the kin are labeled.

40. D. J. R. Williams, "Close Shaves," in *Ancient Greek and Related Pottery*, ed. H. Brijder (Amsterdam, 1984), 275–81.

41. Plu., *Solon* 21.4.

42. Pl., *Laws* 947e.

43. Isoc., *Evagoras* 9.1.

44. Pl., *Mx.* 249b contains a purported funeral oration for Pericles by Aspasia, in which she mentions the annual public rites on behalf of all war heroes who are individually honored in private ceremonies. To this end the city instituted gymnastic contests, horse racing, and all manner of musical contests such as those celebrated at the Panathenaic Games.

45. *GR*, 204.

46. Hom., *Il.* 23.7–8, 13–14.

47. Hom., *Il.* 23.16–17, cf. 18.316–17.

48. Hom., *Il.* 23.6–14.

49. Hes., *Op.* 651–59.

50. Hom., *Od.* 8.253.

51. I have argued this in "Simile and Ecphrasis in Homer and Virgil," *Vergilius* 36 (1990): 7–30; cf. W. Burkert, "Das Lied von Ares und Aphrodite," *RhM* 103 (1960): 36, n. 15.

52. Hom., *Od.* 8.251–53.

53. Hom., *Od.* 8.260.

54. Hom., *Od.* 8.128.

55. Hom., *Od.* 8.371.

56. The use of the verb to test (*peiraomai*) at Hom., *Od.* 8.377, emphasizes the agonistic element.

57. Hom., *Il.* 23.740–83.

58. Arist., fr. 519R *apud* Schol. Pi., *P*.2.127.

59. K. Meuli, *Der griechische Agon* (Cologne, 1968), 68–72.

60. J.-C. Poursat, "Les Représentations de danse armée dans la céramique attique," *BCH* 92 (1968): 558–64. Pyrrhic dancing in a mortuary context is also attested on the lid of a Clazomenian sarcophagus, London, British Museum 96.6–15.1; *CVA* Great Britain 133, British Museum II.D.q, pl. I.2 (bottom).

61. Paris, Cabinet des Médailles 353; *ABV* 346, 7; Poursat, "Représentations," 559–60, no. 3 and figs. 6 and 7; cf. Shapiro, "Iconography," 633, n. 28.

62. *GGR*, 1:187; E. Reiner, *Die rituelle Totenklage der Griechen* (Berlin, 1938).

63. Hdt. 5.67. See G. Nagy, *Pindar's Homer* (Baltimore, 1990), 43, on the force of *pros* in the expression *pros ta pathea autou*.

64. The background of the transference of tragic choruses to Dionysus

is briefly told in Hdt. 5.67. Because Sicyon was at war with Argos, Cleisthenes forbade rhapsodes in competitions to recite from the Homeric poems because they constantly praised Argos and the Argives. He further wished to abolish the worship of the Argive hero Adrastus, a former king to whom the territory around Sicyon had been bequeathed. He appealed to the oracle at Delphi for the god's permission to expel Adrastus's cult. When the oracle refused to grant it, Cleisthenes devised a stratagem to make Adrastus leave on his own accord. He sent to Thebes for the bones of the Theban hero Melanippus, who, as slayer of Adrastus's brother and son-in-law in the war against Thebes, was a bitter enemy, and whose mere presence would force Adrastus to depart. When the Thebans complied with his request, Cleisthenes built a sanctuary in honor of Melanippus and assigned to him the sacrifices previously belonging to Adrastus, while he dedicated the choruses to Dionysus. Herodotus states that in assigning the choruses to the god instead of a local hero Cleisthenes had his people follow the normal practice of other city-states.

65. Hdt. 5.67.

66. Because of the etymology of "tragic" from "goat," some interpreters have seen in this passage evidence of performances by choruses of men dressed as satyrs or other creatures displaying caprine characteristics. G. Else, *The Origin and Early Form of Greek Tragedy* (Cambridge, Mass., 1965), 17–18; A. Pickard-Cambridge in the first edition of *DTC*, 137, discusses objections to choruses of goat-men in detail; but in the second, revised edition (1962), 103–4, T. B. L. Webster argues that the members of the chorus could have represented "fat men" or satyrs supposed to have appeared in the early dithyramb of Arion at neighboring Corinth. The dances at Sicyon, however, are called "tragic choruses," not because goat-men performed them, but because the prize for the contest was a goat to be sacrificed, as the bull was for the dithyrambic contest; cf. W. Burkert, "Greek Tragedy and Sacrificial Ritual," *GRBS* 7 (1966): 91 and n.7.

67. W. Ridgeway, *The Origin of Tragedy* (Cambridge, 1910).

68. Called *hēmitheos* (demigod) in Hom., *Il.* 12.23.

69. Hdt. 2.44.5.

70. Paus. 2.10.1.

71. A. Griffin, *Sikyon* (Oxford, 1982), 158–64.

72. Hom., *Il.* 23.299.

73. Hdt. 6.129.

74. Hdt. 5.69.

75. Plu., *Arat.* 53.3–4.

76. For a summary of the literary and artistic evidence of Theseus as *chorēgos* see Calame, 1:108–14.

77. W. Mullen, *Choreia: Pindar and the Dance* (Princeton, 1982), 76.
78. Pi., *N.* 5.53–54; cf. Mullen, *Choreia*, 76.
79. Pi., *N.* 8.13–16.
80. Proto-Attic stand, once Berlin A 42; *CVA* Berlin 1 (Germany 2, 1938), pl. 33; G. Ferrari, "Menelās," *JHS* 107 (1987): 180–82, pl. IV.
81. A., *Choe.* 306–478.
82. A., *Pers.* 1038–75; trans. Barker, 66–67.
83. Column krater, Basel BS 415; J. R. Green, "Depicting the Theatre in Classical Athens," *GRBS* 32 (1991): 34–35, pl. 6.
84. Ar., *Heroes*, fr. 58 in *Comicorum fragmenta in papyris repertis*, ed. C. Austin (Berlin, 1973).
85. *GR*, 106.
86. *GR*, 33–34.
87. Alexiou, *The Ritual Lament in Greek Tradition*, 6.
88. Sc. *paizō* from *pais* (child).

Chapter Nine. Change: Pan and Private Worship

1. *Philochoros*: Aesch., *Pers.* 448; Soph., *Aj.* 698.
2. Hdt. 6.105.
3. Red-figure oinochoe, Athens Agora P 21860; *Hesperia* 22 (1953): 66, no. 9, pl. 26.
4. *Hom. Hymn to Pan* 19–26.
5. *Hom. Hymn to Pan* 3.
6. Eur., *Ion* 492–502 stresses Pan's role as musical *chorēgos*.
7. Hom., *Od.* 12.318.
8. R. Janko, *Homer, Hesiod and the Hymns* (Cambridge, 1982), 185.
9. *Hom. Hymn to Pan* 2.
10. Cf. Eur., *Heracl.* 783, *Tr.* 546, *Cyc.* 37.
11. Pl., *Laws* 815c.
12. Pi., fr. 99SM.
13. *Hom. Hymn to Pan* 6–14.
14. Arist., *HA* 574a.
15. *Hom. Hymn to Pan* 4; Eur., *Ion* 495.
16. *Hom. Hymn to Pan* 8–13: *entha kai entha; allote . . . allote; pollaki . . . pollaki.*
17. Pi., fr. 95SM.
18. *Hom Hymn to Pan* 14–26; trans. Barker, 46, with modifications.
19. *Hom. Hymn to Artemis* 6–15.
20. Cup, Brommer Collection; *Kunst und Archäologie, Die Sammlung Brommer* (Berlin, 1989), cat. no. 271; illustrated on cover.
21. P. Borgeaud, *The Cult of Pan in Ancient Greece*, trans. K. Atlass and J.

Redfield (Chicago, 1988), 134–35, on the torch race (*lampadēdromia*) in honor of Pan and its mythic model.

22. Hom., *Il.* 16.179–92.
23. Cf. Pl., *Crat.* 408cd; see E. L. Brown, "The Divine Name 'Pan,'" *TAPA* 107 (1977): 57–67.
24. Cup, Leipzig, Antikenmuseum der Karl-Marx-Universität, T 658; H. Walter, *Pans Wiederkehr: Der Gott der griechischen Wildnis* (Munich, 1980), 40, fig. 48.
25. Terra cotta ring model, Delphi; Walter, *Pans Wiederkehr,* 40, fig. 28.
26. E. Reisch, "Zur Vorgeschichte der attischen Tragödie," in *Festschrift Theodor Gomperz* (Vienna, 1902, reprinted 1979), 451–73.
27. Hom. *Hymn to Demeter* 202–4.
28. Persephone: krater, Dresden 350, *ARV* 1056, 95, C. Bérard, *Anodoi* (Rome, 1974), pl. 16, fig. 53. Aphrodite: pelike, Rhodes 12.454, *ARV* 1218, Bérard, *Anodoi,* pl. 18, fig. 63; hydria, Syracuse 23912; *ARV* 1041, 11, Bérard, *Anodoi,* pl. 18, fig. 62; krater, Berlin F 2646, *ARV* 1443, 6, Bérard, *Anodoi,* pl. 10, figs. 35a, b.
29. *Anodoi* are fully treated by Bérard, *Anodoi.*
30. Krater, Dresden 350, *ARV* 1056, 95, Bérard, *Anodoi,* pl. 16, fig. 53.
31. Hom. *Hymn to Pan* 42–47.
32. *IG* IV 1² 130 = *PMG* 936.
33. *SEG* 1.248.17.
34. *PMG* 887.
35. E. Benvéniste, *Indo-European Language and Society,* trans. E. Palmer (London, 1973), 279.
36. J. C. Lawson, *Modern Greek Folklore and Ancient Greek Religion* (Cambridge, 1910), 30–32.
37. H. Herter, *RE* XVII, 1560, with references.
38. W. R. Connor, "Seized by the Nymphs: Nympholepsy and Symbolic Expression in Classical Greece," *CA* 7 (1988), 171–72, and n.54, discusses this and other readings.
39. Men., *Dys.* 915, 929.
40. Theoc. 13; Ap. Rhod. 1.1207.
41. *IG* XIV 2067; *CIL* VI 29295.
42. Men., *Dys.* 644.
43. Men., *Dys.* 910.
44. Pl., *Phd.* 228b.
45. *Carm. Pop.* 848.19 *PMG.*
46. Men., *Dys.* 946–53.
47. Men., *Dys.* 956–58; Ar., *Ach.* 1230, 1232; *Av.* 1764.
48. Eur., *HF* 785–89.
49. Hesych., s.v., defines *kallinikos* as a dance commemorating the bringing back of Cerberus.
50. There is a certain resemblance between Cnemon and Demeter in the

Core/Persephone myth. In different ways both Demeter and Cnemon are opposed to blessing the union of their children, but their mood is not irreversible. Sicon and Getas's therapeutic handling of the misanthrope leading to his entrance into the cave is analogous to the cheering up of Demeter and the raising up of Persephone. The literal meaning of the title of the play, *Dyscolos*, is "discontent with food." We may recall Demeter's refusal to have any food or drink until cheered up by Iambe. In Menander's play, it is Sicon, the cook, who helps to bring Cnemon around. What is done to Demeter in the cosmic myth is done to Cnemon in the context of social satire, but both actions have the same effect. Food, laughter, dance, and music prove to have the power to remove obstacles to reunion.

51. Marble relief, Cos Museum. On stylistic grounds J. Frel, "The Krito Sculptor," *AAA* 3 (1970): 368–71, has identified the sculptor of the relief as the artist who carved the stele of Krito and Timarista in Rhodes.

52. F. T. van Straten, "Daikrates' Dream: A Votive Relief from Kos, and Some Other *kat' onar* Dedications," *BABesch* 51 (1976): 1–38.

53. The inscription was published by G. Konstantinopoulos, *AD: Chronika* 23 (1968): 449, pl. 416a.

54. In Greek literature Pan and the Charites are rarely associated. Pi., fr. 95SM, seems to join the worship of Pan and the Charites. In Eur., *IT* 1123–51, Pan and the society of gods are mentioned in the same choral passage, but the Charites are spoken of in the context of wedding dances, whereas Pan is evoked in his capacity of playing the syrinx to help rowers keep time.

55. *Hom. Hymn to Pan* 14.

56. Pl., *Phdr.* 238c, 241e. On nympholepsy and related phenomena see N. Himmelmann-Wildschütz, *Theolēptos* (Marburg-Lahn, 1957), and Connor, "Seized by the Nymphs," 155–89.

57. Theophr., *Char.* 15.10.

Select Bibliography

Bibliographic Index

Marouzeau, P., ed. *L'Année philologique* for 1924–. Paris, 1926–. S.v. "Chant, musique, choréographie."

General Studies on Festivals and Other Aspects of Greek Religion Related to Dance and Ritual Play

Bremer, J. M. "Greek Hymns." In *Faith, Hope, and Worship*, ed. H. S. Versnel. Leiden, 1981. 193–215.

Brumfield, A. C. *The Attic Festivals of Demeter and Their Relation to the Agricultural Year.* New York, 1981.

Burkert, W. *Greek Religion Archaic and Classical*, trans. J. Raffan. Cambridge, Mass., 1985.

———. *Homo Necans*, trans. Peter Bing. Berkeley, 1983.

Connor, W. R. "Tribes, Festivals and Processions in Archaic Greece." *JHS* 107 (1987): 40–50.

Deubner, L. *Attische Feste.* Berlin, 1932.

Farnell, L. *Cults of the Greek States.* Oxford, 1896–1909; reprinted, 1970.

Funghi, M. S. "Il Mito escatologico del *Fedone* e la forza rituale dell'aiora." *PP* 35 (1980): 176–201.

Hamilton, R. *Choes and Anthesteria.* Ann Arbor, Mich., 1992.

Herington, C. J. *Poetry into Drama: Early Tragedy and the Greek Poetic Tradition.* Berkeley, 1985. App. I, "Performances (Especially *Agōnes Mousikoi*) at Religious Festivals," 161–66.

325

Jameson, M. H. "Perseus, the Hero of Mykenai." In *Celebrations of Death and Divinity in the Bronze Age Argolid*, ed. R. Hägg and G. Nordquist. Stockholm, 1990. 213–23.

Lawler, L. B. *"Orchēsis Kallinikos."* TAPA 78 (1948): 254–67.

———. "Cosmic Dance and Dithyramb." In *Studies in Honor of Ullman*, ed. L. B. Lawler et al. St. Louis, 1960. 12–16.

MacDowell, D. M. "Athenian Laws about Choruses." *Symposion 1982* (1985): 65–77.

Mikalson, J. D. "The *Heortē* of Heortology." GRBS 23 (1982): 213–21.

Nilsson, M. P. *Geschichte der griechischen Religion*, 3d ed., vol. 1. Munich, 1967. 149–52 ("Tänze und Maskentänze").

———. "Die Anthesterien und die Aiora." *Eranos* 15 (1915): 181–200.

———. *Griechische Feste*. Leipzig, 1906.

Parke, H. W. *Festivals of the Athenians*. London, 1977.

Parker, R. *Miasma*. Oxford, 1983.

Pfühl, E. *De Atheniensium pompis sacris*. Berlin, 1900.

Rouse, W. H. D. *Greek Votive Offerings*. Cambridge, 1902.

Rudhardt, J. *Notions fondamentales de la pensée religieuse et actes constitutifs du culte dans la Grèce classique*. Geneva, 1958.

Schmitt-Pantel, P. "Collective Activities and the Political in the Greek City." In *The Greek City from Homer to Alexander*, ed. O. Murray and S. Price. Oxford, 1990. 199–213.

Simon, E. *Festivals of Attica: An Archaeological Commentary*. Madison, Wisc., 1983.

Winkler, J., and Zeitlin, F., eds. *Nothing to Do with Dionysus?* Princeton, 1990.

General Studies on Music and Dance in Ancient Greece

Barker, A., ed. *Greek Musical Writings*. Vol. 1, *The Musician and His Art*. Cambridge, 1984.

Bélis, A. "L'Organologie des instruments de musique de l'antiquité: Chronique bibliographique." RA (1989): 127–42.

Borthwick, E. K. "Music and Dance." In *Civilization of the Ancient Mediterranean, Greece and Rome*, 3 vols., ed. M. Grant and R. Kitzinger. New York, 1988. 2:1501–14.

Ferri, S. *"Khoros kuklikos."* RIA 3 (1932): 299–330.

Fitton, J. W. "Greek Dance." CQ N.S. 23 (1973): 254–74.

Haldane, J. A. "Musical Instruments in Greek Worship." G&R 13 (1966): 98–107.

Latte, K. *De Saltationibus Graecorum capita quinque*. Giessen, 1913.

Lawler, L. B. *The Dance in Ancient Greece*. Middletown, Conn., 1964.

Michaelides, S. *The Music of Ancient Greece: An Encyclopedia.* London, 1978.

Miller, J. *Measures of Wisdom: The Cosmic Dance in Classical and Christian Antiquity.* Toronto, 1986.

Moutsopoulos, E. *La Musique dans l'œuvre de Platon.* Paris, 1959.

Prudhommeau, G. *La Danse grecque antique,* 2 vols. Paris, 1965 (rev. Brommer, *Erasmus* 23 [1971]: 300–302).

Séchan, L. *La Danse grecque antique.* Paris, 1930.

Sittl, C. *Die Gebärden der Griechen und Römer.* Leipzig, 1890. 224–52.

Warnecke, B. "Tanzkunst." *RE* IVA (Stuttgart, 1932), cols. 2233–47.

Webster, T. B. L. *The Greek Chorus.* London, 1970 (rev. Diggle, *CR* 22 [1972]: 230–31).

Wegner, M. *Das Musikleben der Griechen.* Berlin, 1949.

———. *Musik und Tanz* (= *Arch. Hom.* III U). Göttingen, 1968.

Prehistoric Aspects of Dance and Ritual Movement in the Aegean

Alexiou, S. "Hē minoikē thea meth' hypsomenōn cheirōn," *KChron* (1957): 179–294.

Brandt, E. *Gruss und Gebet. Eine Studie zu Gebärden in der minoisch-mykenischen und frühgriechischen Kunst.* Waldsassen Bayern, 1965.

Evans, A. *The Palace of Minos,* 4 vols. London, 1921–35.

Groenewegen-Frankfort, H. A. *Arrest and Movement: An Essay on Space and Time in the Representational Art of the Ancient Near East.* Reprinted Cambridge, Mass., 1987.

Lawler, L. B. "The Dance in Ancient Crete." *Studies Presented to David M. Robinson,* 2 vols. St. Louis, 1951. 1:23–51.

Matz, F. "Göttererscheinung und Kultbild im minoischen Kreta." *Abh-Mainz* (1958): 383–449.

Nilsson, M. P. *Minoan-Mycenaean Religion,* 2d ed. Lund, 1968.

Warren, P. "Circular Platforms at Minoan Knossos." *ABSA* 79 (1984): 319–23.

Dance and Ritual Play in Dionysiac Religion

Bremmer, J. N. "Greek Maenadism Reconsidered." *ZPE* 55 (1984): 267–86.

Detienne, M. *Dionysos mis à mort.* Paris, 1977.

Dodds, E. R. *The Greeks and the Irrational.* App. I, "Maenadism."

Henrichs, A. "Greek Maenadism from Olympias to Messalina." *HSCP* 82 (1978): 121–60.

Segal, C. *Dionysiac Poetics and Euripides' Bacchae.* Princeton, 1982.

Select Bibliography

Ritual Movement in Mystery Cults

Burkert, W. *Ancient Mystery Cults.* Cambridge, Mass., 1987.
Linforth, I. M. "The Corybantic Rites in Plato." *University of California Publications in Classical Philology* 13 (1946): 121–62.
Mylonas, G. *Eleusis and the Eleusinian Mysteries.* Princeton, 1962.
Richardson, N. J. *The Homeric Hymn to Demeter.* Oxford, 1974; reprinted 1979.
West, M. L. *The Orphic Poems.* Oxford, 1983.

Dance and Ritual Play in Local Cults

Carter, J. B. "The Masks of Ortheia." *AJA* 91 (1987): 355–83.
Dawkins, R. M., and Woodward, A. M. *The Sanctuary of Artemis Orthia at Sparta.* London, 1929.
Graf, F. *Nordionische Kulte.* Rome, 1985.
Kahil, L. "Autour de l'Artémis attique." *AntK* 8 (1965): 20–33.
———. "L'Artémis de Brauron: rites et mystère." *AntK* 20 (1977): 86–98.
———. "Le 'Cratérisque' d'Artémis et le Brauronion de l'Acropole." *Hesperia* 50 (1981): 253–63.
———. "Mythological Repertoire of Brauron." In *Ancient Greek Art and Iconography,* ed. W. Moon. Madison, Wisc., 1983. 231–44.
Parker, R. "Spartan Religion." In *Classical Sparta,* ed. A. Powell. London, 1988. 142–73.
Willetts, R. F. *Cretan Cults and Festivals.* London, 1962.

Studies on Individual Divinities or Societies of Gods

Hemberg, B. *Die Kabiren.* Uppsala, 1950.
Nock, A. D. "A Cabiric Rite." *AJA* 45 (1941): 577–81.
Otto, W. F. *Die Musen.* Darmstadt, 1961.
Vernant, J.-P. *La Mort dans les yeux.* Paris, 1985.

Interpretations Based on Literary Sources
Homer, Hesiod, and the Hymns

Clay, J. S. *The Politics of Olympus.* Princeton, 1989.
Janko, R. *Homer, Hesiod, and the Hymns.* Cambridge, 1982.

Lyric Poetry

Bowra, C. M. *Greek Lyric Poetry*, 2d ed. Oxford, 1961.

Burkert, W. "The Making of Homer in the Sixth Century, B.C.: Rhapsodes Versus Stesichoros." In *Papers on the Amasis Painter and His World*. Malibu, Calif., 1987. 43–62.

Burnett, A. P. "The Race with the Pleiades." *CP* 59 (1964): 30–34.

———. *The Art of Bacchylides*. Cambridge, Mass., 1985.

———. "Jocasta in the West: The Lille Stesichorus." *CA* 7 (1988): 107–54.

Calame, C. *Les Chœurs de jeunes filles en Grèce archaïque, Filologia e critica* 20 and 21. Rome, 1977.

———, ed. *Rito e poesia corale in Grecia*. Rome, 1977.

Contiades-Tsitsoni, E. *Hymenaios und Epithalamion: Das Hochzeitslied in der frühgriechischen Lyrik*. Stuttgart, 1990.

Fitton, J. W. "The *oulos/ioulos* Song. Carm. Pop. 3 (= no. 849) *PMG* Page." *Glotta* 53 (1975): 222–38.

Gentili, B. *Poetry and Its Public in Ancient Greece*, trans. A. T. Cole. Baltimore, 1988.

Heath, M. "Receiving the *kōmos*." *AJP* 109 (1988): 180–95.

Herington, J. *Poetry into Drama*. Berkeley, 1985. App. IV, "Choral Lyric Performance," 181–91.

Lefkowitz, M. "Who Sang Pindar's Victory Odes?" *AJP* 109 (1988): 1–11.

Marco, M. di. "Osservazioni sull' iporchema." *Helikon* 13–14 (1973–74): 326–48.

Mullen, W. *Choreia: Pindar and Dance*. Princeton, 1982 (rev. Burnett, *CP* 79 [1984]: 154–60; Austin, *AJP* 106 [1985]: 379–81).

Nagy, G. *Pindar's Homer: The Lyric Possession of an Epic Past*. Baltimore, 1990.

Privatera, G. A. "Il Ditirambo come spettacolo musicale. Il ruolo di Archiloco e di Arione." In *La musica in Grecia*, ed. by B. Gentili and R. Pretagostini. Rome, 1988. 123–31.

Segal, C. "Archaic Choral Lyric." In *The Cambridge History of Classical Literature*. Vol. I, ed. P. E. Easterling and B. M. W. Knox. Cambridge, 1985. 165–201.

Smyth, H. W. *Greek Melic Poets*. London, 1900; reprinted 1963.

Weiden, M. J. H. van der. *The Dithyrambs of Pindar*. Amsterdam, 1991.

Drama

Adrados, F. R. *Fiesta, comedia y tragedia*. Barcelona, 1972.

Ghiron-Bistangue, P. *Recherches sur les acteurs dans la Grèce antique*. Paris, 1976.

Herington, J. *Poetry into Drama: Early Tragedy and the Greek Poetic Tradition*. Berkeley, 1985.

Select Bibliography

Herter, H. *Vom dionysischen Tanz zum komischen Spiel*. Iserlohn, 1947.
Kranz, W. *Stasimon: Untersuchungen zu Form und Gehalt der griechischen Tragödie*. Berlin, 1933.
Lawler, L. B. *The Dance of the Ancient Greek Theatre*. Iowa City, 1964 (rev. Bieber *AJA* 70 [1966]: 78–80, with "A Rejoinder" by the author, 288).
MacCary, W. T. "Philokleon *Ithyphallos*: Dance, Costume and Character in the *Wasps*." *TAPA* 109 (1979): 137–47.
Pickard-Cambridge, A. *Dithyramb, Tragedy and Comedy*. Oxford, 1926; 2d ed., 1962.
————. *The Dramatic Festivals of Athens*, 2d ed., rev. J. Gould and D. M. Lewis. London, 1968.
Reckford, K. J. *Aristophanes I*. Chapel Hill, N.C., 1987.
Rossi, L. E. "Mimica e danze sulla scena comica greca." *RCCM* 20 (1978): 1149–70.
Schreckenberg, H. *Drama: Vom Werden der griechischen Tragödie aus dem Tanz*. Würzburg, 1960.
Seaford, R. *Euripides* Cyclops. Oxford, 1984.
Sifakis, G. M. *Parabasis and Animal Choruses*. London, 1971.
Stoessl, F. *Die Vorgeschichte des griechischen Theaters*. Darmstadt, 1987.
Taplin, O. *Greek Tragedy in Action*. Berkeley, 1978.
Vaio, J. "Aristophanes' *Wasps*: The Final Scenes." *GRBS* 12 (1971): 335–51.
Winkler, J. J. "The Ephebes' Song: *Tragōidia* and *Polis*." *Representations* 1 (1985): 27–62 (rev. in *Nothing to Do with Dionysos?* ed. J. Winkler and F. Zeitlin [Princeton, 1990], 20–62).

Interpretations Based on Metrical Sources

Dale, A. M. *The Lyric Meters of Greek Drama*. Cambridge, 1968.
————. "Words, Music, Dance." In *Collected Papers*. Cambridge, 1969. 156–69.
Webster, T. B. L. *The Greek Chorus* (in conjunction with archaeological sources). London, 1970.

Interpretations Based on Epigraphic Sources

Bowra, C. M. "A Cretan Hymn." In *On Greek Margins*. Oxford, 1970. 182–98.
Guarducci, M. *Inscriptiones Creticae*, 4 vols. Rome, 1935–50.
Moretti, L. *Iscrizioni agonistiche greche*. Rome, 1953.
Poursat, J. C. "Une Base signée . . . Pyrrhicistes victorieux." *BCH* 91 (1967): 102–10.
Sokolowski, F. *Les Lois sacrées des cités grecques*. Paris, 1969.

———. *Les Lois sacrées des cités grecques.* Suppl. Paris, 1962.

West, M. L. "The Dictaean Hymn to the Kouros." *JHS* 85 (1965): 149–59.

Archaeological and Iconographic Studies

Bérard, C. *Anodoi: Essai sur l'imagerie des passages chthoniens.* Rome, 1974.

Brommer, F. *Satyrspiele.* Berlin, 1959.

———. "Antike Tänze." *AA* (1989): 483–94.

Buschor, E. *Satyrtänze und frühes Drama.* Munich, 1943.

Crowhurst, R. *Representations of Performances of Choral Lyric on the Greek Monuments, 800–350, B.C.* Ph.D. diss., Univ. London, 1963.

Emmanuel, M. *La Danse grecque antique d'après les monuments figurés.* Geneva, 1890; reprinted 1984.

Fränkel, C. *Satyr- und Bakchennamen auf Vasenbildern.* Halle, 1912.

Franzius, G. *Tänzer und Tänze in der archaischen Vasenmalerei.* Ph.D. Diss., Göttingen, 1973.

Frontisi-Ducroux, F. *Le Dieu-masque: Une figure de Dionysos d'Athènes.* Paris, 1991.

Hamilton, R. *Choes and Anthesteria.* Ann Arbor, Mich., 1992.

Johansen, K. F. *Thésée et la danse à Délos.* Copenhagen, 1945.

Jucker, I. "Frauenfest in Korinth." *AK* 6 (1963): 47–61.

Kolb, F. *Agora und Theater: Volks- und Festversammlung.* Berlin, 1981.

Maas, M., and Snyder, J. M. *Stringed Instruments of Ancient Greece.* New Haven, Conn., 1989.

Napier, D. *Masks, Transformations, and Paradox.* Berkeley, 1986.

Neumann, G. *Gesten und Gebärden in der griechischen Kunst.* Berlin, 1965.

Poursat, J.-C. "Les Représentations de danse armée dans la céramique attique." *BCH* 92 (1968): 550–615.

Scarpi, P. "La Pyrriche o le armi della persuasione." *DArch.* (1979): 78–97.

Seeberg, A. "Hephaistos Rides Again." *JHS* 85 (1965): 102–9.

Tölle, R. *Frühgriechische Reigentänze.* Waldsassen Bayern, 1964.

Trendall, A. D., and Webster, T. B. L. *Illustrations of Greek Drama.* London, 1971.

Weege, F. *Der Tanz in der Antike.* Halle, 1926.

Studies on Dance in Education and Status Transitions

Anderson, W. D. *Ethos and Education in Greek Music: The Evidence of Poetry and Philosophy.* Cambridge, Mass., 1966.

Brelich, A. *Paides e Parthenoi.* Rome, 1969 (rev. Sourvinou, *JHS* 91 [1971]: 172–77).

Select Bibliography

Calame, C. Les Chœurs de jeunes filles en Grèce archaïque, Filologia e critica 20. Rome, 1977.

Gennep, Arnold van. The Rites of Passage. 1909; reprinted Chicago, 1960.

Jaeger, W. Paideia, trans. G. Highet. Oxford, 1961.

Jeanmaire, Henri. Couroi et Courètes. Lille, 1939; reprinted New York, 1975.

Sourvinou-Inwood, C. Studies in Girls' Transitions. Athens, 1988.

Choral Competitions and the Relationship of Dance to Agōn

Borthwick, E. K. "P. Oxy. 2738: Athena and the Pyrrhic Dance." Hermes 99 (1970): 318–31.

Gardiner, E. N. Athletics of the Ancient World. 1930; reprinted Chicago, 1978.

Harris, H. A. Sport in Greece and Rome. Ithaca, N.Y., 1972.

———. Greek Athletes and Athletics. London, 1964.

Lonis, R. Guerre et religion en Grèce à l'époque classique. Paris, 1979.

Meuli, K. Der griechische Agon. 1926; reprinted Cologne, 1979.

Pritchett, W. Kendrick. The Greek State at War, vol. 2, Greek Military Training. Berkeley, 1974. 208–31.

Reinmuth, O. W. KlPauly I, s.v. "Agōnes."

Reisch, E. "Chorikoi agōnes." RE III. Stuttgart, 1899. Cols. 2431–38.

Sansone, D. Greek Athletics and the Genesis of Sport. Berkeley, 1988.

Scheliha, R. Vom Wettkampf der Dichter: Der musische Agon bei den Griechen. Amsterdam, 1987.

Wheeler, E. "Hoplomachia and Greek Dances in Arms." GRBS 23 (1982): 223–33.

Anthropological and Social Theory

Cornford, F. M. The Origin of Attic Comedy. Cambridge, 1914; 2d ed. 1934.

Geertz, C. "Religion as a Cultural System." In Anthropological Approaches to the Study of Religion, ed. Michael Banton. London, 1965. 1–46.

Gernet, L. The Anthropology of Ancient Greece, trans. J. Hamilton and B. Nagy. Baltimore and London, 1981.

Huizinga, Johan. Homo Ludens. 1950; reprinted Boston, 1955.

Lonsdale, S. H. Animals and the Origins of Dance. London, 1981.

Royce, A. P. The Anthropology of Dance. Bloomington, Ind., 1977.

Spariosu, M. I. Dionysus Reborn: Play and the Aesthetic Dimension in Modern Philosophical and Scientific Discourse. Ithaca, N.Y., 1989.

Spencer, P., ed. Society and the Dance. Cambridge, 1985.

Turner, V. *Dramas, Fields, and Metaphors*. Ithaca, N.Y. 1974.

―――. *From Ritual to Theatre: The Human Seriousness of Play*. New York, 1982.

―――, ed. *Celebration: Studies in Festivity and Ritual*. Washington, D.C., 1982.

Index of Passages

General Index

Achilles, 148, 149, 240, 244, 246, 249–50, 251, 286 n. 21, 290 n. 32
achoreutos (danceless; ignorant of dance), 25, 243–44
Adrastus, 252–54, 297 n. 31, 319 n. 63
Aeschylus, as dancer and choreographer, 7
agelē (herd), as choral metaphor, 201, 230–31
Aglauros, 164
agōn (contest), 36, 68, 74, 94, 113, 212; contrasted with *paidia*, 36; musical (see *mousikoi agōnes*); as synonym for *choros*, 195, 197, 251. *See also* competition in dances; games, funerary
agricultural pretext for festivity, 113
Aiora (ritual swinging), 122, 132–36; hanging of Erigone as *aition* of, 133, 299 n. 87
aischrologia (invective), 127
Alcman, 5–6, 194–97, 199, 203, 293 n. 91
Amasis Painter, 215–18
amphidromia, 129
animal dances and imagery, in choral lyric, 98, 200–203, 228–30
anodos (ascent), 266

Anthesteria. *See* festivals, individual
anthropological parallels: ceremonial walking among the Umeda of Papua New Guinea, 41–42; dances among unmarried girls in Sohos (northern Greece), 231–32; death dances among the Lugbara of Uganda, 240; female initiation rites among the Bemba of Zimbabwe, 169; initiation cycle among the Venda of South Africa, 38
anthropology, contributions of, to understanding dance, 18–19, 281 n. 33; functionalist approach, 110. *See also* anthropological parallels; sources for dance, anthropological
anxiety, release from, in dance, 204, 260
aoidoi (professional singers), 244, 249
Aphrodite, 13–14, 54, 59, 65, 194, 196, 199, 203, 207, 212, 226–28, 231–32, 266, 312 n. 94, 313 n. 112
Apollo, 25–27, 33, 49, 51–75, 82, 95–96, 98, 114, 128, 129, 152, 166, 167, 188, 235, 238, 240, 263–64, 307 n. 117; and the Muses, 45, 47, 54, 65, 82, 98, 115, 214, 235
Aratus, 255
Archilochus. *See* dithyramb

343

demiurge: as choreographer of body politic, 44–48; Hephaestus as, 86, 151

Demosthenes, as *chorēgos* of dithyrambic chorus, 113–14

Dionysiac rituals, ch. 3 passim, 113. *See also* Bacchic dances; Plato, on Bacchic dancing; wine and dance

Dionysus, 12, 17, 25, 31, 33, 38, 45, ch. 3 passim, 114, 117, 119–20, 121–29, 131–32, 150, 207, 231, 239, 244, 254–55, 264, 286 n. 21, 289 n. 4, 319 n. 64; birth of, 154; Eleuthereus, 119–21; as focal point in dance, 10, 81, 119; Limnaion, 123, 124, 126, 131. *See also* festivals, individual, Anthesteria; maenads; prototypes of dance and play; satyr

Dioscouroi, 148, 162, 184

disorder, as prelude to order, 80, 260. *See also* dance, as a disruptive force

display: of defiance by male suitors, 218, 221–22; of solidarity, 17, 66, 165, 170, 214, 250, 272. *See also* boundaries, display of

dithyramb, 27, 89–99; Archilochus and, 89, 91, 93; *aulos* accompaniment in, 90–91; evidence for dance as a disruptive force in, 89; fifth-century innovations in, 98; represented in vase painting, 125; sacrifice of bull in, 92; transformation of, in sixth century, 90; wine as integral part of, 89. *See also* Arion; Demosthenes; *kyklioi choroi*; Lasus of Hermione; Pindar; Pratinas

dolphin: as choral metaphor, 97–98; as lover of music, 98; as metaphor for divine transformation, 97; playful nature of, 98; as vehicle of salvation, 95

drama and dramatic dances. *See* Athenian drama

drums, and percussive aspects of dance. *See* musical instruments

ecstasy and ecstatic religious phenomena, 19–20, 82, ch. 3 passim, 187, 191–92, 241–42, 259;

in Dionysiac worship, 90

education. *See paideia*

eirēnikē (peaceful dance), 26, 204

ekphora (funeral procession), 245–47

emmeleia (solemn, tragic dance), 27, 220

ephebeia, 162–64, 166–67

ephebes, opposed and paired with *parthenoi*, 231

ephebic oath: Athenian, sacred weapons in, 164–66; on Crete, 165

epinician odes, possible modes of performance of, 4–5

epiphany, 81, 96, 149–50, 155–56, 265–66; in choral worship, 125; of goddess on battlefield, 166; in Minoan ecstatic religion, 115–16; as vigorous leaping, 156

Eretria, civic dances in, 114

Erigone. *See* Aiora

Eros, 207

ethical behavior and dance. *See* Plato, on dance in character formation

exarchō (to lead off)/*exarchos*, 89, 236, 244

Exekias, 247

"fat-belly" or "padded" dancers in art, 12–16; and Hephaestus, 290 n. 37

fertility, role of dance and processions in promoting, 60, 137, 167–68, 268

festivals: as context for play and contest, 36; disruptive and stabilizing effects of, on community, 80; Greek views of, 44, 113, 295 n. 4; human origins of, 239. *See also* prototypes of festivity, dance, and play

—Greek words for: *homēguris*, 52, 65–66; *panēgyris*, 63, 65; *synodos*, 113, 210

—individual: Anthesteria, 121–35; Brauronia, 113; Charitesia, 60; Choes, 122, 123, 128, 130; Chytroi, 123, 126; Daidala, 239; Delia, 286 n. 19; Ephesia, 209; Great Dionysia, 6, 113; Hyakinthia, 240; Karneia, 171; Lykaia, 173; Panathenaea, 36, 111, 140, 142, 143,

ANCIENT SOCIETY AND HISTORY

The series Ancient Society and History offers books, relatively brief in compass, on selected topics in the history of ancient Greece and Rome, broadly conceived, with a special emphasis on comparative and other nontraditional approaches and methods. The series, which includes both works of synthesis and works of original scholarship, is aimed at the widest possible range of specialist and nonspecialist readers.